Here I Am, Lord, Send Me

Here I Am, Lord, Send Me

Ritual and Narrative for a Theology of Presbyteral Ordination in the Reformed Tradition

Neal D. Presa

RESOURCE *Publications* · Eugene, Oregon

HERE I AM, LORD, SEND ME

Ritual and Narrative for a Theology of Presbyteral Ordination in the Reformed Tradition

Resource Publications
An Imprint of Wipf and Stock Publishers
199 W. 8th Ave., Suite 3
Eugene, OR 97401
www.wipfandstock.com

ISBN 13: 978-1-61097-616-9
Manufactured in the U.S.A.

Dedicated to Grace,
God's gift of grace,
my best friend, lover, companion on the Way
It still is a *Midsummer Night's Dream*
Thank you from the top & bottom of my heart

Contents

Preface

This book originated from my Ph.D. dissertation at Drew University. As with that dissertation and the doctoral program, this book is the product from the wise and loving communities to which I belong.

My graittude to Wesley Ariarajah, Heather Murray Elkins, and James Farwell—they provided the tethering flexibility to research, think, pursue tangents, but their regular reminders of "Just write the thing" kept me from going too far afield. Thanks to the three of you for your wise counsel and humor along the way.

To Jonathan Reader, chair of the Institutional Review Board at Drew, for reviewing and refining the survey instruments for the four field sites, and doing so without the usual red-tape bureaucracy.

To the four field sites, the ordinands, your communities of faith, and the governing bodies that authorized my research at these sites – thank you for allowing me to be a part of your ordinations. God bless you in your vocations as you serve Christ and his Church. I would not have been able to make a connection with two of the four field sites were it not for the Presbyterian Church (U.S.A.) Facebook® group, whose members offered generous leads on forthcoming ordinations and connected me to the right people to contact. (As of February 22, 2012, there were 17,975 members on that Facebook® group). Thanks to Robert Cirillo, Inc. for arranging the four transcriptionists to record the focus groups and preparing a verbatim transcript.

To my other colleagues and friends in the Liturgical Studies program at Drew, in particular former Dean Maxine Beach, former Associate Academic Dean Anne Yardley, and Professor Deok Weok Ahn, and Jill Burnett Comings, thank you for your gentle encouragement.

To the Interlibrary Loan staff at the Rose Library at Drew—you are amazing! Thanks to the former head of the ILL, Lois Sechehay, and the present, Kathleen Juliano, for successfully obtaining 99.9% of my requests.

To members of the Re-Forming Ministry Core Cluster initiative of the Office of Theology and Worship, Presbyterian Church (U.S.A.), especially Darrell Guder, Jerry Andrews, Barry Ensign-George, Charles Wiley, and Joseph Small III, for the four years of sustained theological conversation over ecclesiology and the teaching office, and the wonderful friendships that developed.

To the staffs of the Presbyterian News Service, *The Presbyterian Outlook*, *The Layman*, and the Office of Theology Worship and Education (General Assembly Mission Council, Presbyterian Church (U.S.A.), for assisting with archival research.

To Hughes Oliphant Old and his wife, Mary, for their hospitality, encouragement, and wise counsel.

To the secretariat of the former World Alliance of Reformed Churches and the World Communion of Reformed Churches, with whom I was privileged to serve, thank you for the assistance in sending me materials from Geneva.

To the staff of the Office of the General Assembly of the Presbyterian Church (U.S.A.), particularly Robina Winbush, Tom Hay, Bobbie Montgomery, and Loyda Aja for granting me access to historical archives and papers of ecumenical dialogues.

To Iain Torrance and the late Tom Gillespie, present and immediate past president of Princeton Theological Seminary, respectively, for their encouragement and counsel.

To Middlesex Presbyterian Church and the Presbytery of Elizabeth, for giving me the privilege to serve as a Minister of Word and Sacrament/Teaching Elder among/with you.

To the Liturgical Theology seminar of the North American Academy of Liturgy—thank you for hearing an early version of this project, receiving it so graciously, critiquing it with even more grace, and welcoming me among you. A special thanks to Martha Moore-Keish, whose doctoral dissertation on a Reformed Eucharistic theology got me to thinking about the methodology used in this book.

To the Sacraments Work Group of the Presbyterian Church (U.S.A.), who between 2002–2006, we reflected, worshipped, talked, ate, drank, feasted—our work led me to focus on liturgical theology.

To the staff of Wipf and Stock Publishing for taking on this project, most especially Christian Amondson, assistant managing editor, for guiding this book from contract to publication.

The backbone of this entire project has been God's blessing to me through my family and friends.

Special thanks go to my parents in-law, Gene and Sowon Rhie, whose tireless support of my studies financially and with daily early morning prayer, whose own life example of hard work and education, serve as a constant model for perseverance and excellence. Kamsahamnida, nae abuji wha omanim.

Thanks are due to my grandaunts in-law, Myong Won Kahng and Hewon Kahng, both scholars and professors emerita in their own right, who continuously and fervently prayed for a good completion of this program and project.

To my paternal grandparents—Lorenzo Presa and Paciencia Presa, and my late maternal grandmother, Purificacion Dionida— the three of them loved me with a steady hand, and encouraged me to be, "Dr. Presa."

To my parents, Noel and Carol Presa, for their love and encouragement.

To my sister, Crystle, "Kuya is done! It's your turn" and to my sister in-law, Ann Kubera, for her encouragement and frequent query, "So, how's it going?"

To my sister in-law, Julie Rhie, for her time and effort in conducting the statistical analysis of the survey questionnaires from the four case studies, and simplifying it for me.

I am blessed to have a company of friends who serve Jesus Christ in the Church and in the workplace, and who have been a source of strong support, encouragement, genuine love, and who help me to understand and appreciate the multiple identities of child, husband, father, scholar, and pastor during the research and writing of this book. Noteworthy among this community are: Andy Justice, Kwang Sik Chu, Wayne Parinas, Bill Golderer, and Stephen Na.

Lastly, and most importantly, my own family. It's been said that the hearth of the home is the Church in miniature: a place where mistakes are forgiven, where love and joy are freely given and received, where playing, dancing, laughing and learning are the daily currencies of life; that has been so true in our home. I have been blessed beyond my wildest imaginations by my two walking parables of joy, my sons, Daniel and Andrew. Thank you for letting daddy work, read, and write and patiently waiting for me to finish. I love you both.

Gracing our home with her tender love, humility, and compassion is my wife, Grace. "I am my beloved's, and my beloved is mine," so says the Song of Songs. Grace has been God's gift of grace to me from the start. She has heard every permutation of ideas of this project, every detail of my thoughts, patiently listening to my frustrations over a project that didn't seem to have an end in sight, and caring for me and our family when I traveled, researched, and wrote. When others have wondered how I am able to do what and how much I do, my beloved is my secret weapon, my fellow prayer warrior. She kept me disciplined and focused on the prize. With my deepest gratitude and profound love, I dedicate this book to you.

Neal D. Presa
Middlesex, NJ
Lent 2012
Ad majorem Dei gloria

Abbreviations

BEM	*Baptism, Eucharist, and Ministry*
BOC	*The Book of Confessions*
BoO	*The Book of Order*
BOS	*The Book of Occasional Services*
CD	*Church Dogmatics*
EC	Elder Ordination site in central New Jersey
EN	Elder Ordination site in upstate New York
FOG-RGA	Form of Government Task Force Report to the General Assembly
G	Form of Government section of the *Book of Order*
MP	Minister Ordination site in urban, eastern Pennsylvania
MW	Minister Ordination site in suburban, eastern Pennsylvania
NMC	*The Nature and Mission of the Church*
nFOG	New Form of Government
PC(U.S.A.)	Presbyterian Church (U.S.A.)
PUP	Theological Task Force on Peace, Unity, and Purity
W	Directory of Worship section of the *Book of Order*
WARC	World Alliance of Reformed Churches
WCC	World Council of Churches

Introduction

THE SANCTUARY BEGAN FILLING with family and friends. It was a Saturday evening. The choir was getting ready, the large chalices and even larger bread loaves were carefully placed on the Eucharistic table, the baptismal font was positioned in the center of the nave, just below the steps leading to the chancel. The written liturgy was being distributed and I wondered, "Is this a celebration of a calling? Or a ritual to give me special gifts to minister? A sending off from my home church and presbytery-of-care to the congregation I would serve in New Jersey and to my presbytery-of-call? What were we about to do?"

As the ordination service began, the various elements and *ordo* of the single liturgy suggested in *The Book of Occasional Services* unfolded: presentation of the presbytery commission, greetings from the presbytery moderator, call to worship, sentences of Scripture, opening hymn, confession and pardon, passing of the peace, prayer for illumination, Scripture readings, choral anthem, sermon, song, statement on ordination, reaffirmation of the baptismal covenant, propounding of the constitutional questions, prayer of ordination with laying on of hands by other ordained ministers of the Word and Sacrament and elders, concluding prayer by the moderator, welcome by the presbytery commission and others, pastoral charge, presentation of symbols of the office, celebration of the Eucharist, closing songs, benediction by the ordinand, and sending.[1]

1. *Book of Occasional Services*, 45–80

Prior to my ordination nine years ago, I had little understanding of what ordination meant. There was no particular class among the course offerings at seminary that focused on ordination, the rites of ordination or the theology of ordination. When I prepared the liturgy of my ordination service, the only model I had available to me was the liturgy referenced above from the *Book of Occasional Services*. Because the presbytery committee on preparation for ministry required a course in worship and the sacraments, and passage of the ordination exam on that topic, I took a course on Reformed worship, within which a section on baptism was taught. But even then, there was no clear link of baptism to ordination[2]; there was a heavy focus on one's incorporation into the body of Christ, the washing away of one's sins, and the mysterious union that one has with Christ's own baptism.[3]

In seminary, discussions over ordination focused on the present ecclesiastical debates over standards of ordination, particularly over the inclusion of self-affirming, practicing homosexual persons into the ordained ministry. I entered the Reformed family through the United Church of Christ, USA, having been baptized as a Roman Catholic previous to that. Even in the UCC/USA, I did not explore what it meant to be ordained. In fact, when I sensed a call to ministry, I did not enter the ordination process at the time because my own understanding of ordination was that persons who sensed God's call to serve as a local parish pastor were the ones who were to be ordained; at the time, I sensed a call to theological education as a professor of theology or church history.

2. There are only two explicit references to baptism in the Ministry section (Sections 3 and 34) of *Baptism, Eucharist, and Ministry*, 20, 28. (hereafter "BEM") The first mention deals with providing evidence of the Holy Spirit's power and presence upon Jesus Christ, and therefore, the Spirit's continuing activity in and through the Church. The second reference relates to baptism as a distinguishing characteristic of the Church that is in continuity with the apostolic tradition. In recent times the term "baptismal vocation" has been used, such as in paragraph 77 of *The Nature and Mission of the Church*, 45. Hereafter "NMC." A critique of the absence of the baptism-ordination linkage in the BEM and its significance for a theology of presbyteral ordination will be discussed in Chapter 2.

3. See Moore-Keish and Presa, "Finding a Theology." We call the Church to begin at baptism and the theological implications that that would have on our corporate understanding of ordination.

It was not until I entered the Presbyterian Church (U.S.A.)[4] that I began to understand the notion of ordination extending to the offices of deacon, elder, and minister. Being a young Presbyterian, my home congregation was eager for me to be ordained, so in 1996 I was ordained a deacon, and then an elder. As I entered the ordination process, I discerned with the presbytery's committee on preparation for ministry whether my sense of call was to both being a minister and a teacher; the committee had insisted that I had to choose one or the other. My sense of vocation and call was that ordination could encompass both. Neither the committee on preparation for ministry nor seminary enabled me to adequately address what ordination meant.

As the time to schedule and arrange for my own ordination approached, I had pieces and fragments of various sources that spoke about ordination, but none were definitive on the issue. I had John Calvin's theology, I had the Directory for Worship of *The Book of Order*, and I had policy papers from the liberal and conservative affinity groups within the Presbyterian Church (U.S.A.), each offering their theological, biblical, and ecclesiastical perspective on ordination to buttress their arguments for or against the debates of the day.

It was not until I began to prepare for my own ordination and seeing both the baptismal and Eucharistic rites couched within the ordination rite in the *Book of Occasional Services* that I began to see the intricate linkage between baptism, eucharist, and ministry implemented, celebrated, and incarnated within a local, gathered assembly. I noticed how the other sources that spoke about ordination mentioned above, made no reference to *The Book of Occasional Services* or the act of worship. The affinity groups that were waging a theological battle over the ordination standards rested their arguments on biblical interpretation, the confessions, and, to a large degree, the polity and constitutional implications of amending the relevant sections of *The Book of Order*.

When I began serving as a local church pastor in central New Jersey, I began to see "on the ground" what a theology of ordination meant for the people of the congregation I serve. For most, they looked to the pastors and active elders as the "leaders" and "doers." [5] Those

4. Hereafter abbreviated, "PC(U.S.A.)"

5. See Small, "Ordained? To What?" in *Ordination and Authority*, 3–10. Small summarizes the tragic misunderstanding of ordination:

> Today, in far too many congregations, pastors act as managers of an organization,

elders whose terms were completed in the governing body felt that their "tour of duty" had passed and they could return back to the pew while the "leaders" led the congregation. I observed this ecclesiastical fissure liturgically enacted upon my arrival, with the baptismal font tucked away in the corner of the sanctuary gathering dust and monthly observances of the Eucharist. Through my service on both the Sacraments Work Group and the Re-Forming Ministry Initiative of the Presbyterian Church (U.S.A.), the linkage of baptism, eucharist, and ministry was further clarified, and it was in those forums that I saw the theological and liturgical gaps in my own congregation, as well as the discontinuity between the local setting and what was written in the official documents of the Church and the Reformed tradition.

Throughout this time, as I pondered these questions, the Presbyterian Church (U.S.A.) continued its debate over ordination standards. Unfortunately these debates have focused little on the actual liturgical enactment of ordination, nor on seeking to understand how local or regional communities have grappled with the received Reformed tradition as they have come to understand and discern it for their actual contexts.

A theology of ordination can and is expressed by the gathered community for all members of the baptized community are theologians as they and the triune God encounter one another in worship; theology, in other words, is being made and expressed in that divine-human encounter. Because the rite of ordination occurs within the context of a worshipping community, can a proper theological understanding of ordination be discovered apart from the worship event and the community in which ordination occurs?

---

working to rationalize mission, enhance efficiency, and increase market share. Elders act as a board of directors, reviewing and approving management's strategy and programs, and monitoring financial and property assets. (p.7)

ONE

Sources and Methods

ORDINATION DEBATES ARE NOT new to the PC(U.S.A.). Since the founding of American Presbyterianism almost 220 years ago, the Presbyterian Church (U.S.A.) and its predecessor denominations have struggled to understand the nature of ordination that is truly Reformed, catholic, and evangelical.

Reformed/Presbyterian history is familiar with controversy in determining which of the functionally-differentiated officers (minister as "teaching elder," lay elder as "ruling elder") best corresponded with the ancient church title, "presbyter."[1] The two distinct understanding of the office of presbyter was one of either "pastoral-liturgical" —- attending to pastoral care and ministry oversight – and the "jurisdictional" model, which focused more on aspects of governance and representation. The former model was connected with Calvin and eventually to the northern branch of American Presbyterianism; the latter model took root in a second generation of the Reformed tradition, winding its way into the Scottish Church's *Second Book of Discipline* (gaining legal status in 1592), and eventually into the southern branch of American Presbyterianism. The jurisdictional model became an important feature early

1. Here I will summarize the history of this controversy from Calvin to the historic 1983 reunion of the northern and southern branches of the Presbyterian Church in the United States, by the well-documented study of Holper, *Presbyteral office and ordination in American Presbyterianism*, 557–579. A more detailed survey of John Calvin's theology of presbyteral ordination will be discussed in Chapter 4.

on as lay elders were employed in ecclesiastical battles, particularly in Scotland, over the independence of the church vis-à-vis the state.[2]

The two models were joined at the Westminster Assembly's form of church government, and by the time of the first General Assembly of the PCUSA in 1789, the "pastoral-liturgical" model became connected to the local congregation whereas the "jurisidictional" paradigm to higher governing bodies (regional presbyteries and the national General Assembly). With this arrangement, the minister assumed the duties of what a classical bishop would have done — liturgical presidency, pastoral care, and teaching—while the lay elders and deacons were regarded as assistants to the ministers in carrying out their local duties. Because of the integration of the jurisdictional aspect of the office, elders were regarded as the people's representative, advocating for the views of the laity in congregational affairs, and the congregation's representative at the regional presbyteries.[3] In this way, elders were seen as a check-and-balance on the powers of the clergy.

As higher governing bodies began to assume larger and expanding responsibilities for the church's overall mission (e.g. the formation of a denominational mission board), the role and office of presbyter were re-examined. In the 1840s, during the Old School-New School schism, the southern Church shifted the emphasis of the presbyteral office towards institutionalizing the jurisdictional aspect of the office, underscoring the equal status of lay elders and ministers in their governing function, thereby equalizing both officers as presbyters. Practically speaking, then, both elders and ministers would decide who would be ordained, both would participate in the laying on of hands upon ordinands, and, hitherto, both would be regarded as equally important in establishing a quorum of the presbytery.[4]

The northern branch of the American Presbyterian Church maintained the view of the lay elder (ruling elder) as a representative of the laity and the historic view of "minister-as-presbyter." It was not until after the second World War that the northern branch began to abandon its view on the pastoral-liturgical paradigm and assume the jurisdictional pattern of the southern branch. By the time of the 1950s and late 1960s, the jurisdictional model expanded to not only include

2. Ibid., 560–561.

3. Ibid., 562–563.

4. Ibid., 565.

the distinctions of lay-clergy or local governing body-higher governing body, but began to include categories of a representative character, explicitly expressing the advocacy nature of the office (e.g. male-female, youth, racial ethnic representation).[5]

When the *Plan for Union* was being negotiated in the mid-1970s, it became clear that the jurisdictional aspects of the presbyteral office espoused by the southern branch and the political dimensions of the presbyteral office held by the northern branch would find a common marriage by the time of the historic 1983 reunion of both branches into the present Presbyterian Church (U.S.A.). The southern branch had for almost a century held to the notion that lay elders were to share in church government alongside ministers beyond the local congregation (jurisdictional model). The northern branch saw the office of elder as one that was representative in character, viz. representing the lay constituencies of the church. In uniting both views, the jurisdictional-political model that was codified in the *Plan for Reunion* meant several things:

- Governance is the principal and essential function of the office of presbyter and the very purpose of the ordained ministry, rather than as one among many representative functions in the Church;
- A distinctive Reformed polity of two offices – presbyter (minister and elder) and deacons—which seeks to wed the tradition with American democratic ideals of equal rights and representation;
- Access to church governance gave special consideration to categories such as gender, racial ethnicity, age, disabilities, etc., in an effort to represent those constituencies at decision-making forums.

Holper pointed to nine implications of the integration of the jurisdictional and political dimensions of the presbyteral office at the 1983 reunion of the northern and southern branches:[6]

1. The emphasis on governance and representation in distinction to Calvin's emphasis on the pastoral-liturgical function of the presbyteral office meant that the dynamics of structure and polity versus personal relationships would be the primary means in edifying the Church;

5. Ibid. 566.

6. Ibid., 573–579.

2. Local governing bodies have a relatively wider parameter in selecting their representatives to serve in higher governing bodies, thereby, increasing access of the laity to share in the governance of the Church;

3. Ministers are ordained by the presbytery, which represents the Church catholic. Elders are ordained by the local congregation. However, the equalizing of elders and ministers in the presbyteral office can be seen, for instance, in the fact that elders are ordained by the session (local governing body composed of the minister/pastor who serves as moderator, and the ordained/installed elders of the local congregation), not one minister; thus the session acts as the minister. On the presbytery level, the ordination of ministers is no longer conducted by the minimum requirement of "three ministers" but the ordaining commission (and for that matter, installation commission, when the minister is installed at a particular ministry context) is composed of both ministers and elders. Presbyter, then, is no longer a name designation for an individual office-holder (minister), but designates an office with governance functions, of which there are two kinds, minister of Word and sacrament, and elder.

4. The power of order (the so-called *potestas ordinis*) was superseded by the power of jurisdiction (the so-called *potestas jurisdictionis*[7]). Previously, it was understood that ministers exercised the power of order by virtue of their pastoral-liturgical function, which meant they had exclusive responsibility to preach and administer the Sacraments with elders and deacons assisting in that regard. The southern branch challenged that notion and insisted that ordination was about governance. Under the new paradigm, each office exercises the power of order within their own ministries, while sharing collegially in governance.[8]

7. These two distinctions of ecclesiastical authority and power were proposed by the Scot, Andrew Melville, a disciple of Theodore Beza (successor of Calvin in Geneva). According to Melville, the *potestas ordinis* designated ecclesiastical power exercised by individuals, whereas the *potestas jurisdictionis* referred to ecclesiastical power exercised jointly (all who bear office together). He then coupled the tasks of the two aspects of power to what he called the "power of the keys" as depicted metaphorically in Matthew 16. It was Melville's view that prevailed in the Scottish church's *Second Book of Discipline*. See Holper, 88–91 on these points.

8. See Small, "Undivided Plural Ministry," 5–11.

5. The tension of ministerial and magisterial authority remain. Magisterially authority is exercised by all presbyters (Holper calls the presbyteral office the common genus, within which are two species, minister and elder). Ministerial authority, concerned with the traditioning of the apostolic faith through preaching and the administration of the sacraments, is ordinarily designated to ministers, but the ordering of worship in a local congregation is ultimately the responsibility of the session. The act of ordination, once regarded as a purely ministerial function, now includes and applies to both sets of presbyters.
6. Both ministers and elders have personal and collegial functions of ministry.
7. A shift from governance by presbytery to governance by presbyters. The original PCUSA (northern branch) polity favored government by presbyteries – "hierarchically-ordered assemblies comprised of representatives of the universal (minister) and particular (elders) churches."[9] The original PCUS (southern branch) polity favored governance by presbyters – officers called "presbyters" who were empowered to assemble and govern. The 1983 reunion and the present state of the PC(U.S.A.) integrates both features, with the PC(US) model as the one being determinative.
8. The tension of Melvillian Presbyterianisms at the higher governing body levels (i.e. emphasis on the power of jurisdiction) versus the Calvin/Westminster brand of Presbyterianism (i.e. emphasis on the pastoral/liturgical functions or power of order) at the local level. What was clear from the 16th century writings of Melville, which gained sway in Scottish polity and which made its way across the Atlantic into southern Presbyterianism, eventually into the reunited PC(U.S.A.), was the fact that the presbyteral office was the normative genus upon which to view Presbyterian polity.[10]
9. The incorporation of the power of jurisdiction and the power of order leaves the present tension of ministry jointly exercised versus ministry individually exercised.[11] At present, an incoherent,

9. Holper, 577.

10. Ibid., 92–93.

11. See especially Ibid.,276–288 on the classical 19th century debate between the northern Princeton Seminary professor, Charles Hodge, and the southern Columbia

inconsistent understanding of what is meant by presbyteral ordination underscores the confusion of how and what are collegial functions of ministry to be exercised and whether jurisdictional authority is truly the foundation and constitutive character of the presbyteral office.

In 2006, the 217th General Assembly of the Presbyterian Church (U.S.A.) convened to consider a historic report titled, *Final Report of the Theological Task Force on the Peace, Unity, and Purity of the Church*, in which issues of ordination, biblical authority, and the Lordship of Christ were addressed. The task force which drafted the report noted what has been problematic in the Presbyterian Church (U.S.A.), specifically, but, one can extend it, to the worldwide Reformed church family, the following:

> . . . Scripture does not provide a thoroughly developed theology of ordination, and a theology of ordination has not been clearly and consistently articulated in the development of Reformed and Presbyterian doctrine.[12]

One result of the absence of an official Reformed theology of ordination has led to an ecclesial situation of ordination where there are more than 90 different ordainable positions.

Previous attempts to articulate a specifically Reformed theology of ordination have come from an "upper-tier" conciliar level or from professional theologians and creedal statements, dating from the continental Protestant Reformation to the present time. Problematic with this method is that those who are then placed in positions of authority (judicatory officials, seminary faculty) soon discover that the formal tradition and official teachings are inconsistent with the local understanding of that tradition, and, thus, efforts to enact the official

Seminary professor, James Thornwell. Holper summarized each position:

> Whereas Hodge was willing to "concede" a parity in the power of jurisdiction between ministers and elders while insisting upon a primary understanding of ministry as several (among which that of the minister-presbyter was the most normative), Thornwell was willing to "concede" a disparity in the power of order while insisting upon a primary understanding of ministry as joint (within which the ruler-presbyter was seen as normative). (288)

12. *The Final Report of the Theological Task Force on Peace, Unity, and Purity of the Church*, lines 565–567.

teachings over and against local situations devolves into disciplinary and judicial proceedings within the church court system.

Joseph Small identifies two attempts that the church has taken to deal with ecclesiastical debates over ordination: one, is to use a "top-down" approach of ecclesiastical regulation and discipline over higher governing bodies over lower governing bodies; the other is a "bottom-up" approach that seeks obedience through the reconstituting of collegial patterns of ministry.[13] Small rejects both attempts, seeing that regulations and relationships are the church's attempt to establish its own authority instead of the authority that belongs to the gospel. Drawing on Barth's distinction between *ecclesia docens* (teaching church) and *ecclesia audiens* (hearing church), Small enjoins the Church to more faithfully hear and receive the Scriptures and the confessions so as to be more faithful and credible in teaching.[14]

Therein lies the problem. For those within the Church who are not aware of the Scriptural, confessional, and theological heritage of the Reformed tradition on the issue of ordination, then education is necessary. For those within the Church who have received the tradition but find themselves at variance with others who have likewise received the tradition but hold to different interpretations, then continuing dialogue and establishment of relationships are key in maintaining a healthy, constructive tension. In both cases, doubtless, hearing is happening at some level. How is one to determine whether the *ecclesia audiens* has adequately and faithfully listened and is therefore ready, legitimate, and credible enough to be the *ecclesia docens*?

What Martha Moore-Keish sought to do with a Reformed Eucharistic theology[15], I wish to do with respect to a Reformed theology of presbyteral ordination.[16] Moore-Keish's critique of Reformed epistemology with regards to doctrine, generally, and the Eucharist, especial-

13. Small, "Authority in the Church and The Authority of the Church in the World", 16–17.

14. Ibid., 24.

15. Moore-Keish, *Do This In Remembrance of Me: A Ritual Approach to Reformed Eucharistic Theology*

16. This book focuses primarily on presbyteral ordination, not diaconal ordination. The past and present conflicts in the Presbyterian Church (U.S.A.) have dealt with the office of presbyter: teaching elder (commonly called, "Minister of Word and Sacrament") and ruling elder (laypersons ordained and installed to co-govern with the teaching elders).

ly, focused on the privileging of abstracted, written doctrine separated from the actual enactment of the Church's worship.[17]

This is not to disregard doctrinal formulations for they were important for the 16th century Reformers in correcting the perceived abuses of Eucharistic practice, and, therefore, Eucharistic theology, from the medieval church. But as Moore-Keish stated, such an approach is "insufficient" for, at least in the case of the Eucharist, "we trivialize the power of ritual action," and when doctrinal beliefs are privileged over ritual practice then "this understanding of the liturgy as secondary to doctrine can lead to an idolatry of reason."[18] This is also not to disregard the real possibility that professional theologians applied their pastoral experiences to the work they did in crafting theological statements. This book will critique the prevalent method of the Reformed theology that appears to elide actual, lived experiences and the multiplicity of interpretations of the received tradition.

With regards to the present internecine battles over ordination standards and what ordination means, is there an idolatry of reason, power, authority, and polity in the ecclesial life of the Presbyterian Church (U.S.A.)? If it is within the event of worship, through Word and Sacrament, where the people of God primarily and most powerfully encounter the reconciling power of God, then perhaps a shift in the methodology of discovering and articulating a theology of presbyteral ordination must necessarily move from the formulated doctrines of the Reformed tradition and begin to account for the actual, enacted rites of ordination in gathered assemblies.

Underlying Joseph Small's injunction is the long-held privileging in the Reformed tradition of the "upper-tier" sources, so that when there is disagreement and debate over what those "upper-tier" sources are saying, the solution, as Small suggests, is to enjoin the Church to more properly and faithfully hear the Spirit of God by properly and faithfully receiving the Scriptural and confessional tradition.

In the end, we will side with Small in calling for a better hearing on the part of the Church towards the tradition. Where this book differs with Small's recent proposal is in steering away from the abstract notion of the *ecclesia audiens* and locating the "hearing" act of the Church at all levels, in a dynamic relationship of theological giving-and-receiving

17. Moore-Keish, *Do This In Remembrance of Me*, 10.

18. Ibid., 11.

between and within the global, national, regional, and local levels. What is much needed in our present climate is an honest valuation of one another's views as we all genuinely grapple with the received tradition, how we interpret the tradition in the present and future Church, and how the tradition is being refined as local communities participate in the diachronic process of "traditioning." Hearing, therefore, occurs within each level and across all levels, a mutual interaction of the top-down and bottom-up, privileging neither one over the other, but finding a dynamic process of hearing and listening for the Spirit of God's leading in each context.

This volume seeks to bridge the gap between the top-down and bottom-up approaches in two ways: first, by surveying the "upper-tier" theologies expressed in the official, formal tradition of Reformed traditions through examination of conciliar statements, Reformed confessions and creeds, *The Book of Order*, and the writings of a representative sampling of Reformed theologians from the 16th century to the late 20th century.

The bottom-up approach will be lifted as hitherto it has not within the Reformed tradition with respect to ordination. Local assemblies are theologians; they, too, are members of the body of Christ just as those at ecumenical global gatherings, denominational headquarters, and seminary faculties belong to the same Church. This book will privilege the "on-the-ground," grassroots level, so to speak, for the sake of the argument, so that we may discover the areas of continuity between the official tradition and the meaning-making that occurs at the local level. Where there are areas of discontinuity, we will be interested in whether, how and why a local, gathered assembly nuances, critiques, or even rejects parts of the tradition as it seeks to implement and enact the official tradition in their given ministry context.

Just as Moore-Keish employed ritual studies in enriching an understanding of Reformed Eucharistic theology, this project gleans learnings from liturgical theology, ritual studies, narrative theory, and Chauvet's symbolic mediation. In doing so, liturgical theology will be proposed as the umbrella field that enables us to see the event of worship as both expressing theology and forming theology, within ritual studies as the cognate field that enables us to appreciate the cultural and gestural context of the liturgical ecology within a particular assembly gathered for ordination. Louis Marie-Chauvet's recent proposal for viewing the sacraments as a means of symbolic mediation and exchange between God and the Church will assist us in that, while ordination is not formally a sacrament in the Reformed tradition but possesses sacramental characteristics, Chauvet's critique of what Heidegger calls the "onto-theological" epistemology squares with this project's critique of "upper-tier theology" and therefore interests us in how he advances liturgical and sacramental theology towards the notion of a dynamic, divine-human/human-human relationship around the three marks of Scripture, sacrament, and ethics, roughly the same Reformation marks of the church (the *notae ecclesiae*), namely faithful preaching of the Word, administration of the sacraments according to the Lord's institution, and church discipline. Of special interest to this project is Chauvet's emphasis on the human body, for as he conceives it, the body is the existential nexus that weds "the triple body of culture, tradition, and nature" and in the exchange of who we are individually with other human beings and with the Divine, each is, as it were, "a living memory."[19]

Recent Scholarship on Similar Methodologies But Different Topics

In addition to Moore-Keish's work on introducing the locus of the Divine-human/human-human encounter in the assembly of the worshipping community, two recent works, one in sacramental theology and another in homiletics, sought to shift epistemological considerations from abstract, Aristotelian categories of causality by employing postmodern scholarship and liberation theology to value the theological meaning-making capacity of local assemblies.

Siobhán Garrigan's work *Beyond Ritual: Sacramental Theology after Habermas*[20] followed the trail blazed by Karl Rahner and Edward Schillebeeckx in their critique of Catholic sacramental theology's reliance on Thomistic preoccupation with causality that was undergirded by an Aristotelian metaphysical cosmology. The two Catholic critics proposed that the efficacy of the sacraments lay not in the causation of sacerdotal words, gestures and presence (*ex opera operato*), but in

19. Chauvet, *Symbol and Sacrament: A Sacramental Reinterpretation of Christian Existence*, 150ff.

20. Garrigan, *Beyond Ritual: Sacramental Theology after Habermas.*

moments of "encounter" between God and human beings.[21] Garrigan seeks to uncover the "practical meaning of Christian worship" at the Eucharist as ritual is enacted and unfolded, and categories of inclusiveness and justice in terms of language and experience are brought to the center from the margins of the Church.[22] In addition to employing Chauvet's twin emphasis on ritual and corporeality, Heidegger's discussion on Being and Levinas's notion of the Other, Garrigan buttressed her work on Habermas's notion of communicative action, giving careful attention to the linguistic interaction of individuals in a worshipping community in order to see how the assembly understands their performative actions.

In the field of homiletics, Ruthanna Brinton Hooke discussed the constitutive and integral role that the relationship between preacher and congregation has in the revelatory nature of preaching.[23] Using postmodern philosopher Jacque Derrida's notion of "logocentrism," or the Western tendency to flatten difference with sameness, to critique Søren Kierkegaard's notion of indirect communication in religious discourse and Barth's doctrine of preaching as a witnessing means of the Word of God, Hooke contended that both, with the latter influenced in his writings by the former, underscore the divine-human difference. For Kierkegaard, the incommensurable difference of God vis-à-vis humanity is such that faith can only be apprehended by separating oneself from the universal social sphere. Hooke put it thusly: "Any continuity between the religious life and the social sphere or the universal would dissolve the paradox of Christianity into continuity and homogeneity with secular culture."[24] Thus, to preserve the paradox of faith in human existence necessitates a "radical isolation" of the individual. For Barth, preaching becomes a locus of the Word of God mediating divine presence to a congregation. Kierkegaard seeks to collapse the difference into sameness in the person of the individual believer or hearer. Barth, on the other hand, negotiates the divine-human difference by highlighting the sovereignty of God over and against any thoughts, experiences, or contributions of the preacher, let alone the congregation. Hooke

21. Ibid., 4.

22. Ibid., 1.

23. Hooke, *The Preacher's Words and God's Word: The Divine-Human Relationship in Preaching.*

24. Ibid., 242.

employs Emmanuel Levinas's notion of the relational subject and Luce Irigaray's notion of "self-differing subjectivity" to speak of the necessity of maintaining the difference and preaching authentically from that difference. With regards to Irigaray, a preacher does not suppress difference, but presents oneself as originating in difference, embodying one's experiential, cultural, gender, racial ethnic, ontological difference vis-à-vis herself, God, and her hearers.[25] With regards to Levinas, our relational selves require that our journey towards fuller humanity requires our ethical connection to others, which means preaching and the sermon emerge from and are inspired by the other, and that the other's interpretation of the sermon is required for the revelation to be whole.[26]

This book seeks to advance a methodology that takes seriously the divine-human, and human-human encounter within the context of an ordination service. In doing so, it sees great value in examining the interplay of various elements of the ordination service, such as the liturgical texts, ritual gestures, the preacher's posture and use of Scriptural texts, the assembly's responses, and the liturgical space.

Recent scholarly works, such as Garrigan's, Hooke's and Moore-Keish's, offer insight and buttress the main thrust of this book by accounting for the meaning-making that occurs within a worship service. These three works are demonstrative of the need for an examination of the interplay between the theological tradition and the enacted theology as human beings seek to understand what they have been taught and what they have received. Akin to the traditioning process, from the Latin *traditio* ("to hand down"), which necessarily involves human-to-human, relational interaction, this book, like the three representative works referenced above, seeks to analyze how human beings understand the tradition as the tradition unfolds and as they themselves are participants within the tradition.

This Book's Contribution to the Study of Ordination

While Moore-Keish's and Garrigan's work focused on ritual action in the Eucharist and Hooke's work focused on the assembly's role in the preaching event, no such work or methodology exists for a Reformed

25. Ibid., 612.

26. Ibid., 617–618.

theology of ordination, let alone a theology of ordination. In Bard Thompson's authoritative bibliography in the section on ordination in the Reformed churches, seven article entries are listed, all of which used the classical epistemological methods of combing the scriptural, confessional, and theological heritage through Calvinistic lenses.[27] Two authoritative, representative writers listed among those entries are the eminent Reformed theologians, the late Jean Jacques von Allmen and the late Thomas F. Torrance. We will examine Torrance's writing on a theology of presbyteral ordination in greater detail in Chapter 4, but his methodology was akin to Allmen's. Allmen cited his methodology: "I will follow the Second Helvetic Confession, which, together with the Heidelberg Catechism, is without doubt the confessional Reformed document which has received widest approval."[28] For Allmen, like Torrance, and other representative Reformed theologians, the methodology employed did not account for the actual, enacted rite of ordination within a gathered assembly and for the theological understanding present by the gathered people.

Two doctoral dissertations in the last 25 years both written by present ministers in the Presbyterian Church (U.S.A.), likewise, do not attend to the richness of liturgical theology, ritual studies, or any of the cognate fields to discover the meaning of ordination in the Reformed tradition as understood and expressed in actual rites of ordination. Holper's book previously referenced is a magisterial study of the history of the presbyteral office from Calvin to the 1983 reunion of the northern and southern branches of American Presbyterianism. It is a helpful guide in unearthing the various understandings of Reformed thinkers as they influenced the decisions of Presbyterian governing bodies and theological statements. Holper set out his methodology as one that investigated "the history of ordination praxis" as it provides "a lens through which debates over the nature of presbyteral office come into focus."[29] What he termed, a "tradition-historical analysis," Holper sought to analyze changes in constitutional standards or authoritative reinterpretations of those standards, as well as seeing the historical patterns of development related to ordination practice in American Pres-

27. Thompson, *A Bibliography of Christian Worship*, 527–528.

28. von Allmen, "Ministry and Ordination According to Reformed Theology" in *Scottish Journal of Theology*, 75.

29. Holper, *Presbyteral office and ordination*, 15.

byterianism.[30] So that while Holper does examine ordination practice, he does so through historical lenses and not necessarily nor primarily through a theological or ritual hermeneutic.

A second, relatively recent work on a Reformed theology of ordination was a doctoral thesis written by Carlos Wilton.[31] The subtitle of his project is explicit about the chosen method of analysis: history of doctrine. Specifically, Wilton selected a "biblical-theological" paradigm: *diakonia*, or servanthood, and then traces that paradigmatic model in the biblical witness, the early church, to the 16th century Reformation, to American Presbyterianism, all the way to the mid-1990s. By doing so, he lifted up *diakonia* as a "paradigm for ministry." Like Holper's study, Wilton's work was especially helpful in tracing the historical development of a theology of ordination from the Bible to present-day American Presbyterianism. Yet, by pre-selecting a paradigm and seeking to discover traces of it, implicit or explicit, such an *a priori*, deductive method of analysis necessarily undervalued other possible, equally valid, equally controlling images and models such as *marturia* (witness). Also, he privileged published theological writings and confessional statements as the sole loci of doctrinal development that buttressed the model of *diakonia*. Even for argument's sake were we to grant that several sources he cited lifted up *diakonia* as a model, that was not the only model in those sources. As we will see in our study of Calvin and Torrance in Chapter 4, other images and models come into play.

A valuable and particularly helpful source for this book was the four volume *magnum opus* of Fr. James Puglisi, a published doctoral thesis that studies the meaning of ordination and ecclesiastical ordering through a comparative analysis of the writings of various theologians in a given tradition with their liturgical reforms. For our purposes, volume two, a study that includes Reformed rites, will be especially helpful as we look at John Calvin, Martin Bucer and others who influenced them and whom they influenced in turn in Chapter 4.[32] Just as in this

30. Ibid., 25.

31. Wilton, "*As One Who Serves*". I am grateful to the Rev. Dr. Fred Anderson for directing my attention to Wilton's work. George Hunsinger lifts up the terms *marturia* (witness), *leiturgia* (worship) and *diakonia* (service) as orienting the Church to its whole ministry, paralleling Christ's own acts of "self-witness, self-mediation, and self-anticipation" as *totus Christus*. See Hunsinger, *The Eucharist and Ecumenism*, 213.

32. Puglisi, *The Process of Admission to Ordained Ministry*. I am grateful to Geoffrey

project he sought to compare areas of consistency and discontinuity between the theological writings of a selection of 16th century Reformed theologians with their actual liturgical reforms. Even then, the only access Puglisi had at his disposal were the actual texts, not the ordaining community in action; hence, only a one-dimension analysis was allowed in his method. This book enhances Puglisi's findings by extending the comparison to contemporary Reformed theologians and actual worshipping communities that I have observed, participated in, and listened to. Such a method enables us to have a diachronic, comparative analysis of how the Reformed tradition has understood presbyteral ordination.

Stephen V. Sprinkle's work will be a valuable resource for this book.[33] His method was akin to the one employed in this book as he compared the ordination liturgies, manuals, polities, and general theological beliefs of four mainline North American denominations: the Presbyterian Church (U.S.A.), the United Church of Christ, the Christian Church (Disciples of Christ) and the American Baptist Churches-USA. His work takes seriously the theology of the liturgies of the various traditions, as well as the rhythm and flow of the liturgy's rubrics. Because of the book's goal to both compare the theological traditions of the four churches as well as provide practical tips and advice on how to prepare for one's ordination service, the book described the four traditions in general terms without much depth. The sermons from ordinations at the end of the book had none from any PC(U.S.A.) ones: there was one from a Baptist ordination and five from Disciples of Christ ordinations. Thus, the only two places we get an analysis of the PC(U.S.A.)'s tentative theology of ordination was a citation in the first chapter of a committee on preparation for ministry manual[34] from the national offices in Louisville, KY and seven pages of a general description of the ordination liturgy previously cited in the *Book of Occasional Services.*[35]

Wainwright for directing my attention to this work.

33. Sprinkle, *Ordination: Celebrating the Gift of Ministry*. I am grateful to John Thomas, immediate past general minister and president of the United Church of Christ/USA, for directing my attention to Sprinkle's work.

34. Ibid., 14.

35. *Book of Occasional Services*, 45–80

The citation of the preparation for ministry manual that contains a definition of ordination needs a brief mention. As one who served on the General Assembly Council of the PC(U.S.A.), which oversaw the programs of the program unit that developed that manual, I can say that the definition of ordination in that manual has no authoritative standing in the church but was developed by program staff and, therefore, was not the official definition agreed upon by the PC(U.S.A.) for there is none! The General Assembly Council (presently called the "Presbyterian Mission Agency") is the national mission agency of the denomination, responsible to the highest governing body, the General Assembly. The manual's definition itself was deficient, for instance, in its summation of the ordained ministry: "Thus the ministry of the Word and Sacrament is one among many *occupations* through which men and women express their God-given interests and abilities in life and daily work."[36] Ordained ministry, as we will see in Reformed attempts to establish a theology of presbyteral ordination, is not an "occupation" or to be likened to a career choice, but is a gift and calling. While Sprinkle's work is commendable for its comparative analysis, it falls short in fully explicating a Reformed theology of presbyteral ordination, both in its methodology and even the sources of those methods and the depth to which the sources were analyzed and engaged.

What this book proposes instead is a methodology that values both the "official" theology through the source methods employed by others (history of doctrine, liturgical-historical history) in combing the vast treasury of the Reformed tradition in its conciliar statements, creedal and confessional/constitutional documents, and a representative sampling of major theologians in that tradition. At the same time, our methodology will hold in healthy tension the "official" theology with the actual, enacted rite of ordination in a gathered assembly, where "lived" theology is given its proper place at the theological colloquy, and where we begin to see the dynamic dialogue that takes place under the classical Reformed rubric, *ecclesia reformata semper reformanda secundum verbum Dei* (the church reformed always being reformed according to the word of God), expressing the people of God being moved and shaped in their encounter with God in Word and Sacrament, most especially within the event of worship itself.

36. Cited in Sprinkle, *Ordination*, 14. (emphasis is mine)

In summary, our sources will be a comparative analysis of the "official" theology of the Reformed tradition (as found in conciliar statements, confessional and constitutional documents, writings of a representative sampling of major theologians) and the "lived" theology of four case studies. Our methods for examining the "official" theology will be historical analysis, paying close attention to major themes and patterns. For analyzing the "lived" theology of the four case studies, we will employ liturgical theology, ritual studies, and narrative theory. With regards to narrative theory we will use statistical analysis of a survey questionnaire distributed to the gathered assembly, transcript of focus group interviews I conducted, textual analysis of the ordination liturgy, and observation analysis of my own experience as an observer and guest at the four field sites. In this way, narrative theory can be regarded as a secondary liturgical theology for it involves post-worship reflection and observation by participants.

We now direct our attention to our first source of "official" theology of presbyteral ordination in the Reformed tradition: councils of the Church.

TWO

Councils

DECISION-MAKING IN PRESBYTERIAN POLITY centers on a collegial system of groups (councils, committees) tasked to discern the will and mind of God and to make a decision based on that discernment. Such a decision, while not necessarily binding on every communicant member, is important for it expresses the collective will of a representative group of duly elected and commissioned individuals sent from their governing bodies.[1] For the local (session), regional (presbytery and synod), and national (General Assembly) governing bodies, presbyters (ministers and elders) who are elected and commissioned to serve are not delegates who represent the will of the people who elected them; they are commissioners – prayed for and sent by their governing body, entrusted to discern with other presbyters the leading of God for the Church. For the governing bodies above the session (i.e. the presbytery, synod and General Assembly), there is an equal number of minister/elder commissioners.

When it pertains to ecumenical relations of the Presbyterian Church (U.S.A.), only the General Assembly can initiate and recognize formal relations with other churches and councils of churches with which the Assembly has determined is in keeping with the PC(U.S.A.)'s historic commitment to seeking visible unity in the church of Jesus

1. In the recently amended New Form of Government for the Presbyterian Church (U.S.A.), the term "governing bodies" has been replaced with the term "council" to underscore the convening character of presbyters in council rather than the governance responsibilities of those councils.

Christ.[2] Decisions and statements of ecumenical councils in which the PC(U.S.A.) is a member are not binding upon the PC(U.S.A.), but provide an important expression of theological consensus at a broader, representative level of ecclesial relations in the Church catholic, and serve as a significant source "to guide the particular churches and governing bodies of this church as they share in joint action with other ecclesiastical bodies seeking ways to express the unity of the Church and to discover its possible future form."[3]

In this chapter, we will consider statements from the World Alliance of Reformed Churches (WARC), the World Council of Churches (WCC), and the PC(U.S.A.) General Assembly as they pertain to the question of a theology of presbyteral ordination for the PC(U.S.A.).

In looking at WARC statements, we will be interested to see whether there is broad consensus in the Reformed churches as to what is meant by presbyteral ordination.

In looking at the WCC, we will pay particular attention to the historic 1982 document, Baptism, Eucharist, and Ministry (Faith and Order Paper No. 111, also known as "The Lima Document"), and the official responses of the PC(U.S.A.) and other WARC member churches that are also members of the WCC.

In looking at two PC(U.S.A.) General Assembly reports, we seek to determine how the denomination has sought to address this question of presbyteral ordination for itself.

These source statements, while not binding upon the PC(U.S.A.), will enable a comparative analysis between what is presented in ecumenical circles on a global scale with what is being discussed at the national PC(U.S.A.) level, particularly in light of the fact that the PC(U.S.A.) and its predecessor bodies were founding members of both WARC and the WCC, and provide significant personnel and financial leadership in both ecumenical organizations.

We now direct our attention to WARC.

2. *The Constitution of the Presbyterian Church (U.S.A.), Part II, Book of Order, 2011–2013*, G-3.05a.

3. Ibid., G-15.0302a.

The World Alliance of Reformed Churches (WARC)[4]

WARC was a fellowship of 215 member churches in 107 countries representing more than 75 million Presbyterian, Congregational Reformed, United, Uniting, and Waldensian Christians. WARC was established in 1970 in Nairobi, Kenya with the union of the International Congregational Council (which was founded in 1891 in London) and "The Alliance of the Reformed Churches throughout the World holding the Presbyterian System" (sic), which was founded in London in 1875.[5] Up until 1970, the Alliance was called the World Alliance of Reformed Churches, or the World Presbyterian Alliance or the World Reformed Alliance (WRA). It was not until the 1970 union that the parenthetical designation, "Presbyterian and Congregational," was added to the WARC. In 2010, the WARC united with the Reformed Ecumenical Council to form the World Communion of Reformed Churches (WCRC). WCRC's secretariat is based in Geneva, Switzerland.

The World Reformed Alliance (WRA), the predecessor body of the World Alliance of Reformed Churches, requested a study at the 17th General Council in Princeton in 1954 to "restate the characteristic Reformed understanding for the ministry and ministries of the church."[6] The interim report was presented to the WRA's executive committee at São Paulo, Brazil in 1959, referred to the WRA's theology department, and sent to the member churches of the Alliance for comment.

The 17th General Council of WARC (1954, Princeton) appointed a commission "to formulate afresh the Reformed doctrine of ordination, and of the service in the Church of minister, elder, and deacon, with particular reference to the ministry of women, according to the Word of God and in the light both of the ancient tradition of the Church and the human situation today."[7] The Commission was known as the Commission on Ordination and the Ministry; its interim report was is-

4. In 2010, the World Alliance of Reformed Churches and the Reformed Ecumenical Council united to form the World Communion of Reformed Churches (WCRC). This book will refer to the WCRC's predecessor body, WARC, because ordination was studied by WARC and was conspicuously on the agenda of the WARC, its executive committee, and related instrumentalities.

5. http://www.warc.ch/where/history.html (accessed July 23, 2009)

6. http://www.warch.ch/dt/er12/index.html#txt9 (accessed March 2, 2007)

7. World Alliance of Reformed Churches, "Interim Report of Commission on Ordination and the Ministry", 1.

sued in that same year. The Commission examined Scriptures, patristic sources, writings of 16th century Protestant Reformers, historical and authoritative statements of Reformed churches, and the traditions of the Church catholic.[8] The Interim Report highlighted *diakonia* as the overarching term that refers to the action of the Triune God in Christ, and the term that designates the Church's sharing and continuing of God's action by serving Christ in the world.[9] Therefore, the Report sought to link the interrelated, interdependent, but distinct ministry of Christ with that of the ministry of the Church. The former was constitutive and primary; the latter was derivative.[10]

The Report then described the ministry shared by Christ and the Church along the *triplex munus* (three-offices) of the Lord, viz. prophet, priest, and king.[11]

Christ's prophetic work was grounded in his incarnation, whereby through his word and acts, the will and nature of God are revealed. Analogously, the Church's prophetic function is carried out in its proclamation and confession.[12] In speaking of the prophetic office, the Commission lifted up the universal implications: proclamation and confession are the responsibility of the whole Church, and the Church's witness in Christ must be carried out in and to the whole world.[13]

The priestly office of Christ was expressed in both the Lord's incarnation and crucifixion. Analogously, the Church shares in this priestly function by service towards reconciliation in the world, healing and pastoral care.[14] In this section on the priestly function, the Commission discussed the interrelated, interdependent nature of each of the three offices in the *triplex munus*—the proclamation of the word of God (prophetic) speaks of reconciliation and is used by God to reconcile (priestly), just as the assurance of Christ's redemption (priestly) is itself proclamation of the word of God (prophetic).

8. Ibid., 2.

9. Ibid., 3.

10. Ibid., 8.

11. We will see how Trinity scholar, Philip Butin, expands on the *triplex munus* in our discussion on Karl Barth in Chapter 4.

12. "Interim Report," 4.

13. Ibid., 5.

14. Ibid., 6.

The kingly aspect expressed itself in Christ's anointing as the Savior, that by his life, death, and resurrection, the rule and reign of God are revealed. The Commission saw the kingly office working its way through the Church's ministry of oversight and discipline as it seeks to incarnate the life of Christ in the ecclesial community.[15]

The Report distinguished between the Spirit's gifts for the Church, and the Spirit's gift of ministry. The former designates the charisms the Spirit endows to the Church for the exercise of the *triplex munus*. The latter designates the forms of *diakonia* the charisms take shape, such as pastor, teacher, deacon.[16]

The primary minister in the Church is the ministry of the Word. In preaching, teaching, administration of the Sacraments, and discipline, the ministry of the Word is entrusted to the Church. Ordination "must be seen as guaranteeing the continuation of the proclamation of the Word," *ipso facto*, the minister is not a member of the local congregation but represents the Church catholic.[17]

The Report then discussed the doctrine of ordination. It grounded the doctrine and act of ordination in Jesus calling and setting apart the Twelve, designating them apostles, in Luke 6:13, and derivatively, the calling of the Seven in Acts 6:1–6, the commissioning of Paul and Barnabas in Acts 13:1–3, and the commissioning of Timothy by assembled presbyters in 1 Timothy 4:14.[18] The Report was careful to point out that because Jesus Christ is the fulfillment of the Old Testament *triplex munus* and shares that ministry with the Church, then primacy must be given to the Church's ministry acts and not to any specific "orders" of offices; and secondly, ordination is to a function that involves the whole Church and not just the ordained office-bearers.[19] Therefore, ordination and ministry are gifts from Christ to the Church, and the Church possesses the gift of ministry in two ways, according to the Report: Christ already accomplished all redemptive works in his earthly ministry, and secondly, the Church shares in that work through the power of the Holy Spirit.[20] Because God gives the gift of ministry to the Church, individu-

15. Ibid., 8.
16. Ibid., 9.
17. Ibid., 9.
18. Ibid., 10.
19. Ibid., 10.
20. Ibid., 11.

als cannot share in this gift and task in isolation; thus the act of ordination is done within a community.

The Commission summarized what ordination is:

> (a) Ordination is an act of Jesus Christ. . .
> (b) Ordination means ordination in the sphere where we are all consecrated through participation in Christ's self-consecration on our behalf. Christ ordains within His Church, which He founded upon the Apostles, and it is through the Church that He acts.
> (c) Ordination means ordination to the ministry of Word and Sacraments. . . .
> (d) Ordination is the solemn setting apart to the ministry of Word and Sacraments of a man (sic) who has been called by God, sent by Him, to that ministry. It is an act in which the Church concurs. . . .[21]

The Report pointed to the two significant moments in the rite of ordination: the epiclesis and the laying on of hands. The Report described the epiclesis as the Church's corporate response to God's word, a calling upon and a recognition of the Holy Spirit's intent and act to call and send. Within the epiclesis was the act of laying on of hands, in which the Church was offering and presenting the ordinand to God, dedicating and consecrating the ordinand for Christ's service. The Report summarized the imposition of hands this way:

> It is a corporate and public expression of the fact that both the task of ministry and the gift of the Spirit are given by God to His Church as a whole, and that therefore they are never possessed merely individually but always shared.[22]

The Commission was careful to point out that there was nothing particularly magical about the epiclesis or imposition of hands and that, in fact, God's grace "may both precede and follow the actual laying on of hands." Because of the eschatological significance of ordination and the on-going work of God in the world, the Commission stated that the act of ordination is being completed and fulfilled throughout the course of a minister's life of service.[23]

21. Ibid., 13.
22. Ibid., 13–14.
23. Ibid., 14.

With respect to church orders, the Interim Report named the office of minister, elder, and deacon, but did not make those normative offices for Reformed churches. In broad terms, the Commission described the diversity of gifts given by God to the Church to carry out a diversity of functions. The ordering of church offices was not to be hierarchical for everyone shares and participates in the whole ministry of the Church.[24] The Report cited Calvin's fourfold division of church orders—pastor, doctor, elder, and deacon—but pointed to Calvin's desire that these four offices not be regarded as normative "orders" but what was essential to the Church were the functions, not the names. The Commission concluded:

> The Commission yet believes that these offices—when they are properly understood and faithfully carried out—not only constitute a valid response by the Church to her ministerial task but also provide a structure which is full of insights into the nature of ministry which should not be lost.[25]

A unique contribution that Reformed churches have brought to theological discussions over ordination and church orders is the order of doctor. The Report noted that doctors are an order of ministers whose special function is to train men (sic) for the ministry by teaching the content and meaning of the Church's faith and message. The Report urged that doctors of the Church be accorded a recognized position in the courts of the Church so that they would be understood as having "the same doctrinal functions as is reserved in some communions to bishops."[26]

The office of elder, according to the Interim Report, was to be regarded not as a pastoral assistant to the minister, but considered within the diaconal ministry, attending to the "spiritual government and discipline in the Church," serving as counselors to the pastor in matters pertaining to pastoral care and in discipline.[27] That elders were laypeople with employment in the secular world, it would be the function of elders to lead the witness of Christ not only within the Church but on behalf of Christ within the secular world, and bringing the work

24. Ibid., 15.
25. Ibid., 16.
26. Ibid., 17.
27. Ibid., 18.

of God in the world to the attention of the Church for the Church's prayerful intercession.[28]

The Interim Report was one of several watershed documents in recognizing that there were no biblical prohibitions for women to be fully included in the life and leadership of Reformed churches, and that a majority of the Commission was convinced that there were sound theological bases for the full inclusion of women in the Church's ministry.[29]

At the direction of WARC's 18th General Council in 1960, the Interim Report was sent to all member churches and to invited theologians to offer responses. A sampling of the churches that did respond had the following concerns:

- Evangelical Church in Austria: did not want emphasis on the three offices (minister, elder, deacon) as a basis for the Church's ministry; instead the emphasis should be on the service of the Church; the word "ordination" and any sacramental overtones with that term should be avoided; ordination does not confer a *character indelibilis* for the Spirit was already at work in the life of the ordinand/minister[30]
- The Reformed Church in Hungary: the wholeness of mission for the whole should be stressed, not so much the threefold office: "The reason why the eldership so rarely functions as it should is not so much due to confusion about the theological meaning of the office as to the failure of the congregation as a whole to function as a serving fellowship."[31]
- The Evangelical Church of the Czech Brethren: did not understand the relation of ordination and sacrament, finding it "incomprehensible why ordination should be so closely related to the administration of the sacrament," and questioned why in some instances, a Synod or theological faculty ordained when it was this Church's understanding that "only one chosen by the congregation in a particular place could be ordained."[32]

28. Ibid., 18.

29. Ibid., 22.

30. World Alliance of Reformed Churches, "Study on Ordination and the Ministry: Summary of Comments on the Interim Report on Ordination," 2.

31. Ibid, 3.

32. Ibid., 4.

A sampling of the theologians who responded had these concerns:

- Dr. Jonkyr C.M. van Asch van Wijck: the significance of Church order and ordained ministry needed to be clarified to "men and women in the pew;" queried whether the Reformed churches were just as clerical as the Roman Catholic Church
- Principal William Steward queried, "why does ordination matter at all. Are we in danger of encouraging an idea similar to that of the pagan priesthood having what we call a 'pujari' for certain ritual functions?" He went on to say that ordination should be linked not so much to the "dispens[ing] of sacraments" but to the necessity of having trained persons able to preach and teach the word of God. He concluded, "[w]e need to link ordination more closely to training. It then becomes meaningful to confine the administration of the sacraments to the man (sic) who is the minister of the Word."[33]
- Professor Dietrich Ritschl: baptism is ordination; what,then, is the difference between ordination and installation?

The responses to the Interim Report showed a growing frustration with confusion over what exactly was meant by ordination, the necessity of it, and the preoccupation in the Report over the threefold or fourfold offices as opposed to focused attention on the whole Church's mission. The Interim Report was later folded into a wider report on catholicity. The Interim Report, considered during the decade of union negotiations between WARC and the International Congregational Council, served to rekindle reflections on what was meant by Reformed church orders.

Then in 1964, the WRA's 19th General Council in Frankfurt sought to undertake a study on the question of oversight (*episkopé*).[34] The European Theological Commission, which took up this assignment in 1966, decided to present a "draft statement of principles." After receiving comments from 50 theologians, the European Theological Commission drafted 19 theses in 1967 at Torre Pellice on the theme of the episkopé and the episcopacy. The report made a distinction between the episkopé or oversight function of the Church, and the of-

33. Ibid., 6.

34. "Report on the study of episkopé" in *Report of the Committee on Theology to the 20th General Council (Nairobi)*

fice of bishop (episcopacy). For our purposes, the main themes which emerged from the 19 theses were the following:

- Jesus Christ is the primary shepherd who exercises the episkopé / oversight over His church through Word and Spirit;
- The episkopé of Christ is implemented through humans;
- The episkopé can take on different institutional forms: an epikopé /bishop office, a synodical-collegial system as is in the Reformed tradition, and other forms;
- The essence of the episkopé consists in the "proclamation of the gospel rightly taught and pastorally applied";
- Church organization in the New Testament and early church corpus does not necessarily lead to a "monarchical" episcopate;
- Christ's episkopé is placed upon the ordained ministry as well as the local congregation; and
- Apostolic succession "is primarily succession in doctrine, and in the right discharge of Christ's episkopé." The report further notes that apostolic succession as it relates to the consecration of bishops historically linked to St. Peter does not guarantee the legitimacy of succession but can serve as a sign of the church's apostolicity and its unity throughout time and space.

After the presentation of this report and transmittal to the member churches of the WRA, there is no indication that the WRA or its successor body, the World Alliance of Reformed Churches, took up this subject of ordination in a sustained, focused manner.

While General Councils since the 19th General Council (1964) have not fully dealt with a theology of presbyteral ordination, bilateral dialogues with episcopally-ordered churches,[35] such as the Ro-

35. In 1967, the WARC Executive Committee mandated a study on the eldership, to which Robert W. Henderson was commissioned to spearhead the project: Henderson, *Profile of the Eldership*: 1974. Two articles and a brochure were produced. One article: Henderson, "Concerning the Eldership, Part I," 363–372, noted at the time that more research was needed as to the origin and intent of the 16th century Reformed leadership in establishing the office of elder. Henderson asked if the office of elder was intended to be part of the public office of the church's ministry or an assistance to the pastor? Recent Bucerian and Calvin scholarship as noted in Chapter 4 fill in some of the gaps that Henderson queried in 1974. In the second article: Robert W. Henderson, "Concerning the Eldership, Part II," 10–17, one senses Henderson's frustration at the slow pace and little input from WARC member churches to respond to a questionnaire

man Catholic Church and the Anglican Church, have provided the forums in which to explore and articulate a Reformed understanding of presbyteral ordination and its relationship with the historic episcopate and episkopé. In the final report of the first phase (1970–1977) of bilateral dialogues with the Roman Catholic Church, WARC and the Holy See's Secretariat for Promoting Christian Unity agreed that "the whole church is apostolic. To be an apostle means to be sent, to have a particular mission."[36] The Final Report went on to say that within the general apostolic ministry of the Church was the special ministry of Word and Sacrament, gifted by God, for particular services within the context of a community.[37] Ordination occurs within a community, profession of faith is done within a community, and liturgical sharing by the community occurs within ordination. The Report was careful to connect the integral and indivisible link between the one ordained, the act of ordaining, and the community in which ordination occurs because one's ordination was not to receive a conferral of a special power, but received a call from Christ to share in His and the Church's ministry always in reference to a community.

Of special concern to the Reformed-Roman Catholic dialogue in this first phase was the notion of apostolic succession. At minimum, both sides agreed that apostolic succession consisted of continuity of apostolic doctrine, for which ordination by other ministers was critical for the traditioning of the apostolic faith to the collegia of those called to the ministry of Word and Sacrament from age to age.[38]

---

about their practices and understanding regarding the office of eldership. Henderson noted three things: 1. Historical work on the development of Reformed ministry is needed; 2. A mode for common conversation needs to be developed so that church administrators do not presume to speak for their entire church; 3. The Reformed tradition needs to assert that deacons and elders are public officers of the Church's ministry, but that Christ is the chief minister. In addition, there was a 1990 international consultation held on August 26–31, 1990 in Geneva on the various forms of eldership in different contexts. The consultation arose out of several proposals from the 22nd General Council in Seoul in 1989, but the consultation was not officially mandated by the General Council. The report: Vischer, ed., *Eldership in the Reformed Churches Today*, will be discussed in the concluding chapter as the report's four points for ecumenical consideration will be important for next steps in articulating a Reformed theology of presbyteral ordination.

36. "The Presence of Christ in Church and World," paragraph 94; available from http://warc.jalb.de/warcajsp/news_file/31.pdf; Internet; accessed July 23, 2009.

37. Ibid., paragraph 97.

38. Ibid., paragraphs 100 and 101.

With regards to the understanding of the historic episcopacy and episkopé, both sides agreed that the structure of the Church and its ministry were by nature collegial, that being ordained necessarily meant a collegial function of accepting discipline from and serving alongside fellow ministers. The difference lay in the location of the episcopacy. For Reformed churches, the episcopacy is a corporate one, at the synodical level (in the PC(U.S.A.) it is the regional presbyteries composed of an equal number of minister and elder commissioners from the congregations in a given geographic region), whereas in the Roman Catholic Church it is in the person of the bishop, who is a member of the Eucharist college.[39]

In the bilateral dialogue between WARC and the Anglican Communion (1981–1984), the Final Report explored the collegial nature of ministry.[40] In the ministry section of the Final Report, the dialogue explored the early church pattern of threefold offices –bishop, presbyters, and deacons—and whether the ministry of these offices fulfilled the personal, communal, and collegial patterning of ministry in the New Testament church. They observed how the bishop in the early church was a local church pastor, who was surrounded and assisted by presbyters in teaching, preaching and leadership, with deacons giving special attention to the diaconal ministry of the Church. As congregations multiplied in a given area, local bishops soon became charged with caring and overseeing a group of congregations, thus, leaving presbyters to attend to the local congregations.[41] By the time of the 16th century, the Reformers sought to return to what they regarded as an early church pattern and reintroduced this threefold ministry in the local congregation—pastor (akin to the early local bishop), elders and deacons. At the regional level, what the regional bishop exercised in his one person, a representative group of presbyters exercised governance and oversight over a region. For the Reformed churches, then, the personal, communal and collegial dimensions of ministry occur at the local level, to which, their Anglican interlocutors queried whether enough attention and importance was given to the personal dimension

39. Ibid., paragraph 102.

40. "God's reign and our unity"; available from http://warc.jalb.de/warcajsp/news_file/3.pdf ; Internet; accessed July 23, 2009.

41. Ibid., paragraph 93.

at the regional/presbytery level, the locus of the corporate episkopé in Reformed polity.[42]

Thus, what emerges in this survey of WARC's attempt at articulating a theology of presbyteral ordination for Reformed churches is an admixture without cohesion or consistency. There is no official, approved theology common to Reformed churches. To have a common theology or statement would require an official act of a WARC General Council; hitherto, no such action has occurred.

At ecumenical dialogue reports, what is presented as the "Reformed position" are references to the writings of the 16th century Reformers, particularly Calvin, and general patterns, such as the priority and initiating act of the triune God in Christ through the Spirit in calling and ordaining, and the Church's consequent, concurring action to the divine call. The meaning of the term "apostolic" denotes Christ sending the Church in the power of the Holy Spirit, but also designates a reference to the early first century Church. Likewise, the term "apostolic succession" has been emphasized in Reformed ecumenical dialogue reports to designate continuity of apostolic doctrine through the personality of the episcopate, and, in other instances, to denote continuity of the Church with apostolic mission.

With regards to the threefold pattern of ordered ministry—pastor, elder, deacon—our survey of WARC documents showed that what most mattered was not the names of the offices *per se*, but the functions of the Church's ministry that are attached to those offices. The use of the term "bishop" has universally been downplayed in WARC documents, with emphasis being placed upon the corporate episcopé exercised by regional or synodical judicatories.

When speaking about ordination, WARC documents emphasized the role of community, and the communal nature of decision-making and service. The documents surveyed show the emphasis on the inextricable link of ordination to the community because Christ gifted the Church with ministry and shares His ministry with the Church.

These key features and characteristics are common in the documents we have examined, but beyond mere observations of these common denominators, unfortunately, there is no official statement or action from a General Council to definitively state that these

42. Ibid., paragraph 94.

characteristics form the core of a theology of presbyteral ordination in the Reformed tradition.

World Council of Churches (WCC)

The WCC is the largest global fellowship of churches, bringing together 349 member churches in more than 110 countries and territories around the world representing 560 million Christians.[43] It was formally inaugurated in Amsterdam in 1948, with historic roots to the 19th century student and lay movements, the 1910 Edinburgh mission conference, and a 1920 encyclical from the Orthodox Synod of Constantinople calling for a "fellowship of churches" akin to the League of Nations. The First Assembly in Amsterdam in 1948 incorporated previous world conferences on faith and order, life and work, the International Missionary Council, as well as the World Council on Christian Education.[44]

The most wide-reaching document produced by the WCC was the historic study, *Baptism, Eucharist, and Ministry* (BEM), also known as the "Lima Document," for it was unanimously agreed to be transmitted to member churches by the Faith and Order Plenary Commission at its meeting in Lima, Peru in 1982, carrying out a mandate issued by the Fifth Assembly in Nairobi (1957) and reaffirmed by the WCC Central Committee in Dresden in 1981. It is disputed whether the start of the BEM process began at the Lausanne world conference of Faith and Order in 1927 (with succeeding intervening actions by Faith and Order in 1974 in Accra and in 1978 in Bangalore), as stated in the official preface of the BEM document,[45] or whether the beginnings can be traced to the 1964 meeting of the Faith and Order Plenary Commission meeting in Aarhus, the position of the late eminent ecumenist, Lukas Vischer.[46]

In any event, the BEM's reception by member churches was unprecedented and overwhelming. The "Lima Liturgy" developed by Fr. Max Thurian of the Taizé community, which embodied the theological themes from the Eucharist section in the Lima document, assisted in the reception of BEM to member churches. Three factors are identified

43. http://www.oikoumene.org/en/who-are-we.html (accessed July 24, 2009)

44 http://www.oikoumene.org/en/who-are-we/background/history.html (accessed July 25, 2009)

45. *Baptism, Eucharist and Ministry*, viii.

46. Vischer, "The Convergence Texts on *Baptism, Eucharist, and Ministry*," 432.

by recent Faith and Order staff members for BEM's successful reception more than 25 years ago. First, it changed the ecumenical discourse from being less about how the text represented one's tradition, to more about how the text reflected the faith of the Church catholic "through the ages." Second, the BEM asked churches to consider the specific implications for their relationship with other churches. And third, the language of BEM appealed to many people from all contexts.[47]

When the BEM was transmitted to member churches, they were requested to submit responses back to the Faith and Order staff at the WCC headquarters in Geneva for compilation, in relation to how each member church saw:

> • "the extent to which your church can recognize in this text the faith of the Church through the ages;
>
> • the consequences your church can draw from this text for its relations and dialogues with other churches, particularly with those churches which also recognize the text as an expression of the apostolic faith;
>
> • the guidance your church can take from this text for its worship, educational, ethical, and spiritual life and witness;
>
> • the suggestions your church can make for the ongoing work of Faith and Order as it relates the material of this text on *Baptism, Eucharist and Ministry* to its long-range research project "Towards the Common Expression of the Apostolic Faith Today."[48]

In this section, we will analyze the responses of the Reformed churches and compare those with the official response of the PC(U.S.A.) to the Ministry section of BEM. Because member churches were requested to receive and respond to the BEM text "at the highest appropriate level of authority, whether it be a council, synod, conference, assembly or other body," the published official responses from these churches will come from the governing body of the respective churches that has the widest representative views of that particular church, with broadest representative participation.

47. Best and Grdzelidze, Preface to *BEM* at 25, 7.

48. Lazareth and Nissiotis, Preface to *Baptism, Eucharist and Ministry*, x. (hereafter "BEM" in the footnotes)

Reformed Churches' responses to the Ministry section of the BEM

Of the 217 member churches of the WARC, 116 are not members of the WCC; 13 are members of the WCC, and are characterized as "younger churches"[49]; 66 are also WCC members considered "first world churches" but which did not respond to BEM; and 25 are also WCC members considered "first world churches" and which did respond to BEM. It is the responses of these 25 WARC/WCC member "first world churches" plus the 13 "younger churches" that responded that will be the focus of this section. The 38 "first world churches" and "younger churches" which have dual membership in WARC and WCC and which responded to BEM as recorded by the six-volume compilation edited by Max Thurian are the following:[50] in volume one, the Church of Scotland, the United Reformed Church in the UK, and the Presbyterian Church in Cameroon (a "younger church); in volume two, the Presbyterian Church in Canada, the United Church of Canada, the Church of South India (a "younger church")[51], the Church of North India (a "younger

49. Ahn, *Ecumenism, Inculturation and Postcolonialism in Liturgy*, 7–8. Ahn listed the 26 "younger churches" of the WCC that responded to the BEM, 13 of which are also members of the WARC. Ahn identified four criteria that designate a church as a "younger church":

- churches, usually in the Global South or belonging to so-called Third World countries, that "do not share the same liturgical history with the established churches in the world." These are primarily churches that have some sort of colonial experience (5)
- culturally colonized churches that do not necessarily have a colonial experience (5)
- churches in Third World countries that have long histories but which "demonstrate a new and distinctive view on the Lima document compared to the First World churches." (5)
- churches in third world countries are excluded from the designation "younger church" if they have a shape of liturgy and worship similar to first world Christians and not geographically/culturally distinct (e.g. Malankara Orthodox Syrian churches in India, the Methodist Church of Southern Africa, the Methodist Church-Jamaica District) (6)

50. Thurian, *Churches Respond to BEM.*

51. The Church of South India is not wholly Reformed. It came about as a union of the South India United Church (itself a union of Congregational, Presbyterian and Reformed traditions) and the Anglican Church of India, Pakistan, Burma, and Ceylon, with the Methodist Church of South India. Nevertheless, the CSI is a member church of WARC.

church")[52], Remonstrant Brotherhood, Presbyterian Church of Aotearoa New Zealnd, The Mission Covenant, Church of Sweden, Presbyterian Church of Wales, Reformed Church in America, the United Church of Christ (USA), Presbyterian Church of Korea (a "younger church") and United Church of Christ in Japan (a "younger church); in volume three, United Protestant Church of Belgium, Reformed Church of France, Reformed Church of Alsace and Lorraine, Union of Welsh Independents, the Presbyterian Church in Ireland, Presbyterian Church (U.S.A.), Cumberland Presbyterian Church, Presbyterian Church of Rwanda (a "younger church"), and Church of Jesus Christ in Madagascar; in volume four, Uniting Church in Australia, Evangelical Reformed Church, joint response of Nederlandse Hervormde Kerk (the Protestant Church in the Netherlands) and the Gereformeerde Kerken Nederland (the Reformed Church in the Netherlands), Waldensian Evangelical Church of the River Plate in Uruguay (a "younger church"); in volume five, Reformed Church in Hungary, Evangelical Church of the Congo (a "younger church"), Church of Christ in Thailand (a "younger church"), Evangelical Church of the River Plate in Argentina (a "younger church"); and in volume six, Church of Lippe, Federation of Swiss Protestant Churches, Evangelical Presbyterian Church in Ghana (a "younger church"), and the Presbyterian Church in Sabah in Malaysia (a "younger church").

I will survey the responses of these 38 churches to the Ministry section (hereafter designated "M"), specifically attending to the five divisional subsections of the BEM text pertinent for our study: The Calling of the Whole People of God (M1–6), The Church and the Ordained Ministry (M7–18), The Forms of the Ordained Ministry (M19–33), Succession in the Apostolic Tradition (M34–38), Ordination (M39–50). It must be noted that the churches' responses do not follow the linear sequencing of the Ministry section, but freely incorporate thoughts and gleanings from various sub-sections, but every effort will be made to order them in some analyzable format.

The first subdivision of the Ministry section (M1–6) spoke of the calling of the whole people of God that derived from God calling all

52. The Church of North India is not wholly Reformed. It came about as a union of the Anglican Church of India, Pakistan, Burma and Ceylon; the United Church of Northern India (Congregationalist and Presbyterian traditions); the British Baptists of Northern India, the Churches of the Brethren in India, the Methodist Church, and the Disciples of Christ. Nevertheless, the CNI is a member church of WARC.

of humanity to be God's people. God's calling came to Israel, and with the foundation of Christ's life, death, and resurrection, a community is called and sent by the Holy Spirit to be witnesses.[53]

The second subdivision (M7–18) discussed the interrelatedness of the whole people of God with ordained ministers, that while God called the entire community, ordained ministers are needed to remind the whole community of God's call, to serve and build up the community with the ministries of Word and Sacrament, and to strengthen its witness.[54]

The third subdivision (M19–33) recognized a variety of forms of ordained ministry in the New Testament Church, but by the second and third centuries, the document noted the establishment of a threefold pattern of ministry consisting of bishop, presbyter, and deacon, and in succeeding centuries, this threefold pattern underwent change.[55] It summarized that bishops preach the word, preside at the sacraments, provide pastoral oversight over an area they are called to serve, and serve as a visible witness of the continuity and unity of the Church catholic.[56] Presbyters serve as pastoral ministers for local congregations.[57] Deacons attest to the Church its diaconal ministry, its servant service to the world.[58] This third section lifted up the personal, collegial, and communal dimensions of the Church's whole ministry.

The fourth subdivision dealt with the notion of apostolic succession and apostolic tradition (M34–38). It noted that the Church's continuity in the apostolic faith and apostolic tradition were the primary signs of apostolic succession, while at the same noting that many communions have practiced this historic continuity through the personal episcopate. In churches that do not have bishops, BEM urged those churches to "appreciate the apostolic succession as a sign, though not a guarantee, of the continuity and unity of the Church."[59] The BEM urged those churches that do have the personal episcopate to recognize that

53. *BEM*, 20 (M1)
54. Ibid., 22 (M12-M13)
55. Ibid., 24 (M19)
56. Ibid, 26 (M29)
57. Ibid., 27 (M30)
58. Ibid, 27 (M31)
59. Ibid., 29 (M38)

the apostolic faith has continued in those churches without the personal episcopate.[60]

The fifth subdivision on ordination (M39–50) highlighted the liturgical actions of the *epiclesis* and the imposition of hands, both of which indicate that ordination is a gift of the Holy Spirit. BEM noted that Jesus Christ is the "true ordainer and bestows the gift (of ordination)."[61] The BEM summarized what ordination is:

> Properly speaking, then, ordination denotes an action by God and the community by which the ordained are strengthened by the Spirit for their task and are upheld by the acknowledgment and prayers of the congregation.[62]

The sixth and final subdivision (M51–55) will not be included in this chapter as we are interested here in the responses of the Reformed churches to the meaning of ordination and church orders vis-à-vis the calling of the whole people of God. M51–55 discussed what elements would be necessary for further discussions in order to move towards mutual recognition of ministries. These ecumenical implications will be considered in the final chapter of this book.

Most of the responses applaud BEM's affirmation that the ministry of Christ is for the whole people of God. But, disappointment is expressed that BEM stopped short of following through on the implications of such an affirmation. Instead, various Reformed churches were left with the impression that the non-ordained ministry (laity) were being subordinated to a helping position vis-à-vis the ordained ministry:

> ". . . inappropriate that the subsequent discussion treats so fully the ordained ministry and so minimally the ministry of all members of Christ's Church"[63]

> "Ministry of the whole people of God "relegated to second place."[64]

> "Having affirmed the ministry of the whole, the text proceeds as if the ministry of the church is carried out by the ordained

60. Ibid., 29 (M37)
61. Ibid., 30 (M39)
62. Ibid., 40 (M30)
63. Ibid., vol. 4, 161
64. Ibid., vol. 2, 157

> alone. The role of those who are notordained appears to be reduced to that of mere 'supporters' of ministry."[65]

The critiques of the subordination of the non-ordained ministries of laypersons were accentuated by the Reformed churches' impression that BEM was clericalizing church orders.

Reformed churches criticized as what they perceived as BEM prescribing the threefold form of ministry as the norm for the whole Church. While acknowledging in M19 that there is no set pattern of ministry in the New Testament and various patterns of ministry existed in the changing contexts of the early Church's mission, M22 goes on to say, ". . . nevertheless the threefold ministry of bishop, presbyter and deacon may serve today as an expression of the unity we seek and also a means for achieving it."[66] The Reformed churches saw in this statement BEM's overvaluing the episcopal polity at the expense of presbyteral and congregational forms of church orders. The Church of Scotland observed that the threefold form of ministry does not account for the recognition made at a 1927 consultation in Lausanne of the three kinds of polity – episcopal, Presbyterian, and congregational.[67] The United Church of Christ in Japan (UCCJ) noted that the Ministry section began with the calling of the whole community, but then the rest of the Ministry section focused on the ordained ministry.[68] The UCCJ saw that the Ministry section was not helpful in Kyodan efforts to examine contextual issues as "bilevel ministry, its qualification examination system, and ministry by the mentally disabled."[69] The Evangelical Church of the Congo was prepared to recognize all forms of ministry of all the churches who obeyed and confessed Jesus as Lord. [70] The Presbyterian Church in Cameroon recognized "the one ordained ministry of the pastor" while recognizing the common calling of all the baptized, from which the ordained pastor is called.[71] The Cameroon Church extended an olive branch, stating that it could live with an episcopally-ordered church so long as such a church does not discount the legitimacy and

65. Ibid., vol. 2, 282

66. *Baptism, Eucharist and Ministry*, 24.

67. Thurian, *Churches Respond*, vol. 1, 96.

68. Thurian, *Churches Respond*, vol. II, 289–290.

69. Ibid., 290.

70. Thurian, *Churches Respond*, vol. V, 168.

71. Thurian, *Churches Respond*, vol. I, 82

credibility of the Cameroon Church's ecclesiastical standing.[72] The United Reformed Church in the United Kingdom regretted that there was no mention of the Reformed eldership.[73] The Presbyterian Church in Ireland (PCI) went further in its objection. It saw the BEM tilting towards the "Catholic" with the center of ministry at the eucharistic celebration at the expense of the "Reformed" center at the proclamation of the Word.[74] The PCI observed, "[a] threefold ministry can so easily degenerate into a three grade ministry."[75] The United Church of Canada left no ambiguity in its response, characterizing the Ministry section as "less mature" than the baptism and the eucharist sections, and then concluded, "First, the text is clericalist. Second, the text is sexist."[76]

The Reformed Churches preferred to link apostolic tradition and apostolic succession. If apostolic succession can be broadly defined as historical continuity in expressing the apostolic tradition through the faithful preaching of the gospel, administration of the sacraments, and where koinonia and diakonia are practiced, then churches like the Reformed Church in Hungary[77], the Mission Covenant Church of Sweden[78], and the Presbyterian Church of Wales could adopt those terms for their ecclesiological understandings. Such an understanding recognizes that "apostolic succession" broadly defined focuses not so much on the name of the office (bishop) nor the specific office-bearer, but on the continuation of the early apostles' teaching in and through the Church throughout all time. The broadening of definition would not negate the validity of episcopacy as a sign of the succession of apostolic traditions, but such broadening would indicate that the episcopacy is not the only way the apostolic tradition is transmitted. The Church of South India (CSI) saw that apostolic succession should be linked to the life and witness of the whole church, not to episcopal offices, though CSI affirmed that episcopacy is an essential feature of the Church's heritage, but not a guarantee of ensuring apostolic succession.[79] For the

72. Ibid., 84.
73. Ibid., vol. 1, 107
74. Ibid., vol. 3, 215.
75. Ibid, 217.
76. Ibid., vol. 2, 283
77. Ibid., vol. 5, 163
78. Ibid., vol. 2, 320ff
79. Ibid., vol. 2, 78.

Union of Welsh Independents, as an example, they see the apostolic tradition as the "contents of the New Testament" and accenting faithfulness to apostolic truth as more essential than the official doctrine of apostolic succession.[80] The Church of North India (CNI), which accepted the threefold ministry," urged that more clarification was necessary in defining the function and place of the office of deacon. The CNI indicated that the threefold pattern of ministry must parallel the threefold function of ministry. It further noted that the broad interpretation of apostolic succession in BEM in relation to the apostolic tradition was a helpful step; in the CNI episcopacy as a concept was embraced but the particular interpretation of what was meant by episcopacy was given great latitude among its members.[81] The Presbyterian Church of Korea desired the weight to be on the content of the apostolic tradition "through the Holy Spirit, especially as found in the New Testament" when speaking of apostolic succession.[82]

The Reformed churches' understanding of ordination related to their call for a broadening of the threefold form of ministry and apostolic succession as they related to the apostolic tradition. If ordination is about calling and setting apart persons with Holy Spirit-endowed charisms for the edification of the Church, then the threefold pattern of ministry prescribed by M22 may limit ordination to ministers/clergy/bishops, or, at its worst, create a bifurcated caste system ordered hierarchically with bishops occupying the top tier and presbyters and deacons at the lower tiers. The Reformed churches across the board affirmed that Jesus Christ is the Head of the Church and the prime bishop who authorizes the calling and sending of the Church.[83] Ministers share in Christ's priestly, prophetic, and kingly ministry, not represent nor substitute for him. The United Reformed Church in the United Kingdom proposed that the pattern for ministry should be fashioned after the "missionary task of the church."[84] This would mean that the apostolic ministry commissioned by the Lord to the Church and enabled by

80. Ibid., vol. 3, 280–281.

81. Thurian, *Churches Respond*, vol. 2, 73.

82. Ibid., 164.

83. The Presbyterian Church of Canada wanted BEM to go further and state that Christ is the sole possessor of ministry and authority in the Church. (see Ibid., vol. 2, 156ff)

84. Ibid., vol. 1, 108.

charisms of the Holy Spirit would result in manifold gifts that were apostolic. Thus, apostolic tradition and apostolic succession would be interrelatedly linked to the apostolic function of the church. In this sense, the functional understanding of episcopal, presbyteral, and diaconal would shift the spotlight from the specific offices and office bearers of those titles, but would describe the various tasks carried out by the Church in its apostolic mission. The Church of South India (CSI) took issue with what it considered as the insular-orientation, and professionalization of the ordained ministry. It urged a "world-oriented concept of ministry" rather than the task of just building up of the Church. With regards to professionalization, the CSI noted the challenge it faced with its Hindu context of professional ministers; in the CSI, particularly in its rural congregations, the gospel was being proclaimed by ordinary people. CSI was appalled at the ease at which persons who lack authority were granted the privilege to preach, yet churches are unwilling to license individuals to preside at the eucharistic table. The CSI urged that notions of apostolic succession should be linked to the wholeness of the Church's life and witness.[85]

The Presbyterian Church of Rwanda (PCR) took a harder stance, almost outrightly rejecting the Ministry section, indicating that it "would have to be fundamentally revised before we could accept them (Eucharist and Ministry sections)."[86] The PCR thought that the Ministry section was not based on Scripture, that there ought not to be a distinction between the laity and ordained ministries, and wondered aloud that if the ministry of the apostles was not "tied" to the sacraments, then the PCR could not see why M was tying the ordained ministry to the sacraments. The PCR's response, moreover, stated that "[t]he apostolicity of the church is not based on apostolic succession but on apostolic preaching."[87] An additional objection raised by the PCR was the Ministry section's seeming assertion that the ordained ministry derived its authority from ordination and not the word of God. That the word of God is connected to a community meant that the ordained ministry was interrelatedly connected to a community "bound up with the

85. Thurian, *Churches Respond*, vol. II, 78.

86. Ibid., vol. III, 185.

87. Ibid., 184.

community and with the function fulfilled in, by and in the name of the community."[88]

The Waldensian Evangelical Church of the River Plate (Uruguay) affirmed M1–7 on the calling of the whole people of God, but strongly objected to the Ministry section's focus on the ordained ministry, specifically the office of bishop, and what it saw as the Ministry section's reliance upon the ordained ministry as the sign of unity and life of a community rather than on Jesus Christ.[89] It noted discrepancies that while the Ministry section acknowledged the multiplicity of church orders in the early church, the BEM seemed to favor the threefold pattern of bishop, presbyter, deacon. The Waldensian Church was careful in stating that it was not opposed to the threefold pattern for, in many ways, they, too, have that same pattern, but they were concerned that that threefold pattern was being prescribed as the norm for all churches.[90] An additional concern was raised over the Waldensian Church's perception that the BEM wanted to lift up ordination as a third sacrament, thereby defining and conditioning eucharist and baptism to itself.[91] It stated that the emphasis should not be on the hierarchical ordering of the Church, but that the Church continue the apostolic tradition through witness and service. In its concluding remarks, the Waldensian Church called attention to the reality that so many human beings are suffering from hunger and exploitation, and that what the world needs is a Church in solidarity with the poor, with all those who suffer, and in this way, churches will find their unity in Christ, who was one with all who suffered. What the world doesn't need, the Waldensian Church underscored, was "internal hierarchical reinforcement."[92]

The Church of Jesus Christ in Madagascar (CJCM) briefly objected to the Ministry section while also open to learning more about what was meant by "succession in the apostolic tradition."[93] The CJCM felt that too much emphasis was placed on the ordained ministry, noting that more pages were expended on ministry alone, than on the Eucharist and Baptism sections combined, expressing its perception that

88. Ibid., 184.

89. Ibid, 121–124.

90. Ibid., 123.

91. Ibid., 126.

92. Ibid., 127.

93. Ibid., 187.

BEM seemed to suggest that the ordained ministry was the guarantor of the "perfection of the sacrament and not Christ who is the master of the feast."[94] The Madagascar church believed that the whole community, together with the ordained, all participate in ordination.

The Church of Christ in Thailand, a united church of Presbyterian, American Baptist and the Disciples of Christ, expressed an openness to learn more about baptism, eucharist, and ministry. It noted how the language of BEM was too difficult for ordinary people to understand and sounded "unlike Protestantism but rather like the language used in the early centuries of the church."[95]

The Evangelical Church of the River Plate (Argentina) noted that the threefold pattern of ministry was a way to see the unity of the apostolic faith and the unity of the Church, but not the only way. It urged that the Ministry section should take more account of the ordering of ministries as found in Reformed churches.[96]

The Evangelical Presbyterian Church in Ghana (EPCG) noted that the authority of the ordained ministry comes from the triune God, who confers ordination through the action of the community because the triune God acts in and through the community. Ordination is linked to the life and witness of the community.[97] The EPCG emphasized that "Jesus is the ordainer" and that when differences about this confession are overcome "recognition can be given by all to all kinds of ordained people as participants in the ministry of Christ."[98]

The Presbyterian Church in Sabah (Malaysia) was a relatively new church and so made few comments. It acknowledged that the Lord Jesus Christ is the "leader of the church" who endows the Church with many gifts. The witness of the gospel is the task of every member, with the ordained ministry as a proper means for "administering the word of God and the sacraments."[99]

This brief survey of Reformed churches' responses to the Ministry section of the BEM document showed the various emphases that Reformed churches saw in ordination and church orders. Far from

94. Ibid., 188.
95. Ibid., vol. V, 174.
96. Ibid., 177–178.
97. Ibid., vol VI, 102.
98. Ibid., 103.
99. Ibid., 133.

speaking univocally in their responses, the Reformed churches responded to specific issues that mattered for their particular contexts. This lends credence to the aim of this book, namely, that actual contexts must be valued and empowered to shape and articulate their own understanding of church orders and ordination in conversation with the wider Reformed tradition and the Church catholic.

The Presbyterian Church (U.S.A.) Response to the Ministry Section of the BEM

The extensive response of the Presbyterian Church (U.S.A.) to the BEM involved a year and a half process of consultations and studies in General Assembly-level units and committees, judicatories at all levels, three selected congregations from each of the 16 synods, as well as theological seminaries. A coordinating committee on ecumenical relations prepared a draft paper based on the compiled responses, then a separate writing team consisting of staff and elected members involved with ecumenical, theology and mission matters wrote the final response that was sent to the General Assembly.

The PC(U.S.A.) response to the Ministry section celebrated the emphasis of the ministry of the whole people of God, and affirmed the special role that the ordained ministry has in preserving and transmitting the apostolic tradition to succeeding generations.[100] The response, however, expressed concern that while it agreed with the functions of the threefold pattern of the ordained ministry, the BEM's focus on the eucharistic nature of the ordained ministry and the "eucharistic communities" in which they serve seemed to clericalize the whole community. The PC(U.S.A.) noted that the Presbyterian and Reformed traditions have upheld the parity of lay and clergy in the nurture and governance of the Church, and not restrict those functions to the ministry of Word and Sacrament.[101]

With regards to episkopé, the PC(U.S.A.) found helpful the BEM's discussion over the personal, collegial, and communal dimensions of the ordained ministry, but sought to shift the focus from the personal episcopacy in the minister representing Christ as the BEM does, to more of the minister as representing and serving the whole people of

100. Thurian, *Churches Respond*, vol. III, 199.

101. Ibid., 200.

God. The PC(U.S.A.) would have liked to see those three dimensions applied to the whole people of God in their common ministry and not just a clerical understanding.[102]

The PC(U.S.A.)'s response was consonant with other Reformed churches' responses to the Ministry section of the BEM, particularly in its emphasis on ministry for the whole people of God. Ironically, the methodology by which the PC(U.S.A.) response was developed and generated begs the question to which this book addresses. While the PC(U.S.A.), like other Reformed churches as we have noted, called for a democratization of church orders contra what was perceived as BEM's clericalization of church orders, yet the very method employed by the PC(U.S.A.) to respond was from an upper-tier methodology at the General Assembly level. Granted, the Faith and Order Plenary Commission of the WCC, in transmitting the BEM document to churches requested a response from the highest governing body of each church, yet the PC(U.S.A.)'s response was a sort of clerical methodology as mostly presbyters (ministers and elders) in the various councils, committees, and task forces crafted the official response of the PC(U.S.A.).

Just as with other Reformed churches' responses, the PC(U.S.A.) upheld the importance of the ordination of women. It recognized that while the absence of the ordination of women in other churches is not necessarily a bar for mutual recognition of ministries among churches, the PC(U.S.A.) noted that the BEM did not do enough to challenge those churches to seriously consider candidates for ordination regardless of race, gender, or sociological grouping.

With regards to next steps, the PC(U.S.A.) noted several areas that it needed to explore, particularly, at the time of the submission of its response, the PC(U.S.A.) was three years into living into the reality of the reunion of the northern and southern branches of its predecessor bodies. The response highlighted that any discussions about bishop, presbyter, and deacon needed a cautious approach because of strong feelings and connotations within the PC(U.S.A.) over the term "bishop" and "episkopé" and due also to the lack of a clear understanding of what ordination is: "In our church we have ourselves been very unclear about the nature of ministry and of ordination."[103] The PC(U.S.A.) would like to see more work in relating the apostolic ministry with the ministry

102. Ibid., 200.

103. Ibid., 202.

of the whole people of God. It noted the tension between apostolic continuity and proper ordination as necessary for the church, but not at the expense of neglecting the gifts of the Holy Spirit that are given to the Church to make the Church alive to serve.[104]

The PC(U.S.A.) urged a methodological consideration similar to what this book is calling for. The PC(U.S.A.) noted the importance of exploring questions of ministry through Scriptural teachings and principles, as well as Scriptural interpretations throughout the ages particularly in early church sources, but that also "should involve the commitment to discern what God is doing today and to take seriously what according to Scripture God has promised to do."[105] In other words, a theology of ministry needs to be "eschatological not only traditional."[106]

When I compare the PC(U.S.A.)'s response to the other Reformed churches, there is agreement on the following themes and issues, which may serve as features of a contour of an "official" theology of presbyteral ordination. First, the triune God is the One who calls, the One who ordains, the One who endows the Church with the task of ministry, and the One who provides the gifts for ministry. The triune God is the focal point of the Church, in its being, in its doing – worship, service, mission, witness, and faith. The triune God is the creator, initiator, and provider of the call to ministry.

Second, the call of God is to the whole people of God, which means every person has a calling to serve God, the community of faith, and the world. The Reformed churches, generally, and the PC(U.S.A..), specifically, have underscored this point, that God's call is for all persons of faith, but within that called community, are particularly called persons to serve and order the whole people of God.

Third and related to the second is that the ministry of Word, sacrament and service belong to the community, with the ordained ministry as having a derivative calling belonging to the community, to build up the community for its service and witness in and to the world. Ordination as understood by the PC(U.S.A.) and Reformed churches' documents I referenced above sees the inextricable connection of the ordinand, ordination and community, both the local community and the Church catholic. This means that those who are ordained are not

104. Ibid, 203.

105. Ibid., 204.

106. Ibid. 204.

ordained merely to an office, but to a function that is responsible to a community. That is why when one is ordained to the ministry of Word and Sacrament, it must be done only when a call to a particular validated ministry has been issued and received.

Fourth, the act of ordination belongs to the community of God's people, who respond to God's call, as expressed in the gathering of God's people, the imposition of hands and the *epiclesis,* or the prayer of invocation inviting and affirming the presence of the Holy Spirit to bless the gathered assembly and the ordinand. The liturgical gestures of gathering, laying on of hands, and praying show the Reformed emphases of the related roles of God and the community, and the divine-human dimension of ordination as the gathered community sees itself as mediating the blessing of God, or, at the very least, represents the presence of God and plays a critical role in petitioning for God's blessing.

Fifth, the ordering of the Church and the naming of offices are consequences of the Church's task in faithfully following the apostolic faith and participating in the apostolic faith. The PC(U.S.A.)'s and Reformed churches' emphasis on mission and the apostolic faith places church orders and patterns of ordered ministry in service to that mission.

Sixth, the threefold pattern of ministry—minister, elder, deacon— is one sign of the continuity of the apostolic tradition and unity in the Church, but not the only sign and not the primary sign. Both the PC(U.S.A.) and the Reformed churches, in their emphasis on God's mission through the Church, place church orders and the ordering of ministries in service to the apostolic mission. Consequently, that while the threefold pattern of ministry has traditionally characterized Reformed church orders, the responses of the PC(U.S.A.) and the Reformed churches demonstrate an openness to the names and patterning of ordered ministries provided that the nomenclature and orders are in keeping with the apostolic mission given to the Church. In the midst of the multiplicity and diversity of ministry expressions, the PC(U.S.A.) and Reformed churches highlight that Jesus Christ is the uniter of differences

Seventh, the PC(U.S.A.) and the Reformed churches sought to extend the personal, collegial, and communal dimensions of ministry beyond the specific offices, and related to the ministry of the whole people of God. Extending these three dimensions to the Church's ministry would enable the Church to see what aspects of its life are personal, collegial, and communal that are not exclusively tied to position or individual personalities, but that the life of the Church itself is composed of individuals who are united to one another in a common faith through one baptism, and mutually accountable to and responsible for one another.

Lastly, the PC(U.S.A.) and the Reformed churches see that issues of justice in the world (hunger, poverty, exploitation, gender) should be highlighted in the Church's understanding of mission and the means to unity with other churches, and not overshadowed by differences in hierarchical structuring of Church orders. Connected to the Reformed emphasis on the Church and the Church's ordering of ministries in service to mission, Reformed churches see the key to ecumenical unity in joint efforts in addressing social and moral problems in the world. What has plagued ecumenical unity has been the lack of convergence over issues of church orders and theologies of ordination, not only within the Reformed family of churches, but also with other Christian traditions.

The PC(U.S.A.) and Reformed churches' documents surveyed above have these seven characteristics in common. Can these serve as a basis for a theology of presbyteral ordination in the PC(U.S.A.)? An emphasis on the priority of God, the mediating role of the Church, the inclusive ministry of the whole people of God, and church orders in service to Christ's service in the world through the Church may go a long way in bridging the theological divide over this question of ordination and church orders.

While the Reformed tradition has sought to have a univocal definition to what is meant by ordination and which pattern of church orders is best suited for a Reformed-brand of ministry, the kaleidoscopic features of a theology of presbyteral ordination outlined above seem to gravitate towards a multivalent, multivocal understanding of theologies of ordination and church orders. This book advocates for a methodology that would enable the Reformed tradition to hold in tension multiple theologies of ordination and church orders as understood by the gathered community at all levels of the Church.

We are now ready to direct our attention to two, relatively recent attempts at understanding the nature of church orders and ministry.

Presbyterian Church (U.S.A.) General Assembly

The highest governing council of the PC(U.S.A.) is the General Assembly. Prior to 2004, the General Assembly met annually; now it meets biennially. Elected commissioners, an equal number of clergy and lay elders, from the 172 regional presbyteries are sent to constitute a General Assembly. The number of commissioners any one presbytery can send depends on the number of communicant members within the bounds of that presbytery.

In 1992, the 204th General Assembly ordered the publication of a report titled *A Proposal for Considering the Theology and Practice of Ordination in the Presbyterian Church (U.S.A.)*[107] following a 1986 proposal (or overture) from the Presbytery of Carlisle calling for a study on "the Theology and Practice of Ordination." It must be noted that the action of the General Assembly was to commend the report for study by the whole church, but the Assembly did not approve the report. According to one respected denominational staff leader who was present at both the 1992 and 1996 General Assemblies that considered the first report and a subsequent, abbreviated report, debates over human sexuality had dwarfed careful consideration of this report, and with some radical changes the report was proposing as we will see, commissioners felt that the early 1990s was not the time to change concepts of church orders when the ordination standards had to be clarified and dealt with in the midst of calls from some circles within the church to broaden the ordination standards to include homosexual persons.[108] We will discuss this report first.

In 2006, the 217th General Assembly received and adopted The Final Report of the Theological Task force on the Peace, Unity, and Purity of the Church.[109] We will discuss that report in the second part of this section.

107. *A Proposal for Considering the Theology and Practice of Ordination to Office in the Presbyterian Church (U.S.A.).* [hereafter "1992 Proposal"]

108. E-mail correspondence with the Rev. Dr. Joseph D. Small, director of the Office of Theology Worship and Education, General Assembly Mission Council of the Presbyterian Church (U.S.A.), October 26, 2009, wherein he shared, "Remember: throughout this period (1990s), ordination was a hot topic. . . So any constitutional changes were viewed with suspicion."

109. *The Final Report of the Theological Task Force on Peace, Unity, and Purity of the Church.* [hereafter "PUP Report"]

The 1992 Proposal[110]

The Task Force that developed the 1992 Proposal consisted of respected PC(U.S.A.) church leaders including Robert W. Henderson, author of The Teaching Office in the Reformed Tradition; J. Frederick Holper[111], then professor at Austin Presbyterian Theological Seminary and now professor of worship emeritus at McCormick Theological Seminary; the late C. Benton Kline, president emeritus of Columbia Theological Seminary.

The 1992 Proposal lifted up a master image of "God Service" in viewing ordination, offered a working definition of ordination, and then applied the master image of "God Service" to particular offices of ministry, employing the three ministry dimensions as outlined in the BEM, viz. personal, collegial, communal.[112]

The report noted that while those who are baptized are called to ministry and those who are called to ordained ministry are not called to "power, honor, or status," nevertheless discussions in the Presbyterian Church over ordination and ministry have started from questions over power and powerlessness. Thus, the 1992 Proposal lifted up the following working definition of ordination:

> Ordination is an act of the church in which the church orders its life by identifying and authorizing persons for offices of leadership and service in the ministry and governance of the church.[113]

Wilton noted three implications from this working definition of ordination:[114]

- "Ordination is an act of the church"
- "Ministerial office has to do with leadership and service"
- "Ordination has to do with the ministry and governance"[115]

110. We will rely on the summary of the 1992 Proposal as found in Wilton, "*As One Who Serves*", 286–313.

111. *supra* Ch. 1, n. 1

112. Wilton, *As One Who Serves,* 287.

113. *A Proposal,* 16, cited in Wilton, *As One Who Serves,* 288.

114. Wilton, *As One Who Serves,* 289–290

115. *supra* Ch. 1, n. 7 on Andrew Melville's view of ordination for in Wilton's estimation this definition is more than a Melvillian view of jurisdictional function for the ordained ministry, for the 1992 Proposal calls for the pastoral-liturgical functions to

The working definition lifted up the tension between notions of leadership and service; with the master image of "God Service" the 1992 Proposal sought to frame leadership in terms of servant leadership, using the model of Jesus's act of footwashing in the context of table fellowship.[116]

The notion of "God Service" was a foundational concept and an enduring hallmark of the 1992 Proposal. It was an English translation of the German *Gottesdienst*, literally translated "God-service" but commonly referred to as "worship service," linking the pastoral-liturgical dimensions of ministry service. The use of that term for the master image had several implications:

- It followed the model of Christ
- God-service is freely chosen, the way of Christ, so as not to oppress or force anyone to servanthood
- God-service includes a whole range of ministries, not just ministry of Word and Sacrament
- God-service empowers the disenfranchised in the Church
- God-service affirms the three dimensions of ministry – personal, collegial, communal

In a third section of the offices of ministry, the 1992 proposal expanded the working definition of ordination:

> Ordination is an act by which those God calls to necessary, representative offices of leadership in God Service are identified and authorized for their work. The word ordination is derived from the word "order." In ordination the church orders itself for the ministry of God Service, authorizing and inducting women and men with particular gifts to equip and lead it in its service of God's reign in the world.[117]

This expanded definition identified three, though not necessarily chronological, elements necessary for ordination:

1. "Testing of the inner call"
2. "Election by the community"
3. "Ratification by a governing body"

be shared by all three ordained offices (minister, elder, deacon).

116. Wilton, *As One Who Serves*, 300.

117. *A Proposal*, 51 cited in Wilton, *As One Who Serves*, 301.

The 1992 Proposal then proposed a number of suggestions for changing the existing church offices. The office of Minister of Word and Sacrament, thought to be too focused on the local context, was proposed to be renamed "Minister of the Gospel" with proclamation of the Word as the prime responsibility, followed by community formation, governance leadership, prophetic witness in the world, and the service of font and table.[118] The Minister of the Gospel would take three forms: Ministers of Word and Sacrament, Ministers of Education, and Ministers of Pastoral Care. Then, in contrast to past and present practice, all ministry offices, including that of the ordained minister, would be members of the local congregation (presently ministers are members of the regional presbytery and serve as moderator of the local session), thereby bridging the gap between the ministry of the whole people of God and ordained ministers.

With regards to the office of elder, the 1992 Proposal celebrated the fact that the ruling elder or lay elder has been a unique contribution of Reformed churches to ecumenical discussions.[119] In that one office, the whole community's ministry for God Service is represented as they are laypersons elected by the local congregation and ordained by the local session. They are responsible for ministry oversight, discipline and governance. Yet, the 1992 Proposal noted, that elders have increasingly been called to serve in paid staff positions in higher governing bodies and mission agencies of the Church. It, thus, proposed that some flexibility should be given whereby elders might potentially be elected and installed into those staff positions, instead of service, first, in the local session, which has been the traditional locus of service.[120]

With regards to deacons, they represent in a voluntary, official way, the ministry of the whole people of God, who have taken on the official function and role to be in solidarity with those who are powerless.[121] The 1992 Proposal suggested that rather than deacons being installed into office since they do not have the authority to vote in the local governing body, that they be commissioned.[122]

118. Ibid., 302–303.

119. *A Proposal*, 81 cited in Wilton, *As One Who Serves*, 307.

120. *A Proposal*, 86–87

121. Wilton, *As One Who Serves*, 310.

122. Ibid., 312.

As mentioned earlier, the 1992 Proposal was commended for study by the whole Church but was not officially approved by the General Assembly and, therefore, has no official standing in the PC(U.S.A.). In commending the 1992 Report for study, the General Assembly invited the church at all judicatory levels to send their input over the next four years. What emerged from the four-year study was an abbreviated booklet titled, "A Ministry of Service: A Guide to the Meaning of Ordination and Church Office in the Presbyterian Church (U.S.A.)" that was submitted to the 208th General Assembly (1996).[123]

The value of the 1992 Proposal for our purposes and for any future attempts at articulating an understanding of presbyteral ordination for the PC(U.S.A.) is in the added features that the 1992 Proposal introduced in constructing the contours of a theology of presbyteral ordination when we compare the 1992 Proposal with the PC(U.S.A.)'s response to the Ministry section of BEM. The following features were noteworthy: "God service" as a master image, but particularly the rendering of *Gottesdienst* for "worship service" which would be akin to the Eastern Orthodox notion of the whole of life as *leitourgia*. This understanding of liturgy would expand Reformed ecclesiology regarding the essence of the Church's being and doing as grounded and propelled by worship, that at its core, the Church is all about worship. Thus, any discussion about the Church, its mission, its patterns of church orders, and the rite of ordination must be viewed through the lenses of the Church's worship.

Second, the 1992 Report pointed to the proverbial elephant in the room. Ordination is about power and authority, and the authorization that a community gives to those ordained to exercise responsibility for and on behalf of the community. For officeholders, ordination provides a privilege of governance over persons and a community that can translate into exclusive or inclusive actions, which serve either to sustain the officeholders in their positions of authority or to open access to more potential officeholders.

Third, the 1992 Report called for a flexibility of the manifestations of the offices of minister, elder, and deacon as they relate to the three dimensions of ministry–personal, collegial, communal. The 1992 Report privileges the three ministry characteristics and not necessarily the

123. "*A Ministry of Service: A Guide to the Meaning of Ordination and Church Office in the Presbyterian Church (U.S.A.).*"

offices themselves, in keeping with the Report's main thrust of "God service." What is important for the Church, the Report sought to assert, was to live into the notion of "God service" in its personal, collegial, and communal dimensions in whatever form or manner the Church saw fit. Far from setting aside the traditional Reformed threefold pattern of minister, elder, and deacon, the Report lifts these, but also called for flexibility and invited study on whether the offices and nomenclature themselves were the primary issues, or whether they were secondary or subsidiary to the more important question of what was understood to be the Church's ministry and mission, for which patterns of ordered ministry were instituted.

The 1992 Proposal was not approved but commended for church-wide study and therefore has no official standing in the PC(U.S.A.) except as one study resource among many. From 1992–2006, the PC(U.S.A.) continued debates on ordination standards and human sexuality, with each succeeding General Assembly after 1992 receiving no less than three overtures calling for Assembly debate on ordination standards.

The 1992 Report and the subsequent abbreviated version in 1996 ("A Ministry of Service" booklet) both followed similar methodologies. Both booklets lifted up "official" sources of Reformed theology but did not include liturgical sources as resources for a theology of ordination. In fact, the 1996 booklet included questions for reflection after each section and encouraged readers to discuss the questions in a large or small group. Yet, nowhere among any of the study questions was there an invitation to review the questions before, during, or after worship, or to view the questions in light of liturgical texts, or even within the context of an actual ordination service. The 1996 booklet, instead, invited readers to respond and react to theological statements contained in the booklet, rather than experiencing theology-in-action in an actual ordination service.

Then, in 2001, the 213th General Assembly called for a special task force, composed of widely respected ministers and elders in the Church, to create a framework for church-wide spiritual discernment over issues of deep disagreement: biblical authority and interpretation, Christology, ordination standards, and power. The Theological Task Force on the Peace, Unity, and Purity of the Church (PUP) was directed to bring a report to the 217th General Assembly (2006). We now direct our attention to the PUP Report.

The 2006 PUP Report[124]

The 2006 PUP Report was not tasked to develop a common definition of ordination. In fact, the PUP Task Force's methods of mutual discernment, dialogue, worship, bible study and theological reflection were regarded as of greater importance than trying to solve the theological and ecclesiastical issues of the Church for the PUP Task Force were composed of twenty respected church leaders who came from different parts of the theological spectrum. The modeling of mutual respect was seen as a great stride in dealing with the differences in the Church.

The whole PUP Report was a 50-page glossy booklet of 1,386 lines. The section on ordination was less than one page, occupying 21 lines. In contrast to the 1992 Proposal that lifted up a working definition of ordination, the PUP Report pointed to the following insights of the PUP Task Forces' study of ordination:

- Servant leadership as modeled by Christ[125]
- Reformed tradition emphasizes the common Christian vocation of the whole community, and certain members of the body are called by God through the Church to nurture the body for spiritual growth and mission[126]
- Ordained officers are required to adhere to "confessional, governance, and disciplinary standards not required for membership"[127]

The PUP Report concluded this section on ordination with the following observation:

> Beyond these themes, Scripture does not provide a thoroughly developed theology of ordination, and a theology of ordination has not been clearly and consistently articulated in the development of Reformed and Presbyterian doctrine.[128] As one might expect, then, ordination has been a source of some confusion and a matter of controversy in our history. From the outset of American Presbyterianism to the present, denominational con-

124. I served as a minister commissioner of the Presbytery of Elizabeth to the 217th General Assembly (2006).

125. *The Final Report,* 19 (lines 553–556)

126. Ibid., 19 (lines 558–560)

127. Ibid., 20 (lines 563–564)

128. At this point, the PUP Report had a footnote referring readers to the 1992 Proposal.

> flicts have often centered on matters of fitness for ordination. The current controversy regarding issues of human sexuality and ordination is the latest example of this recurring pattern.[129]

What garnered the most committee and plenary floor debate at the General Assembly was the so-called "Recommendation 5" of the seven recommendations of the PUP Task Force. The first, fourth, sixth, and seventh recommendations were innocuous in their effect: recommendation 1 dealt with urging every PC(U.S.A.) member and governing body to see the oneness we have in God and to recommit to that unity;[130] recommendation 2 urged all governing bodies, congregations and groups to follow the mutual discernment and study processes modeled by the PUP Task Force;[131] recommendation 3 commended the PUP Report to the Church;[132] recommendation 4 urged that the Committee on the Office of the General Assembly and other governing bodies and entities "explore the use of alternative forms of discernment and decision-making"[133] to complement parliamentary procedure; recommendation 6 urged the Assembly to consider no more constitutional amendments or additional authoritative interpretations on issues such as Christology, biblical interpretation, essential tenets, and sexuality and ordination" for the remainder of the Assembly's proceedings, and urged the use of judicial proceedings as a last resort when all efforts towards mediation and reconciliation have failed.[134]

Recommendation 5 addressed the debate of ordination not through theological rationale *per se* but through ecclesiastical and constitutional mechanisms focused on national standards that are applied by governing bodies based on their local contexts and their discernment of individuals, on a case-by-case basis, for fitness for office based on national ordination standards.[135] By doing so, the PUP Task Force left unanswered what is meant by presbyteral ordination and church orders, and instead shifted the focus to ordaining bodies (local sessions in the case of the ordination of elders and deacons; regional presbyteries

129. Ibid., 20 (lines 565–572)
130. Ibid, 32 (lines 930–939)
131. Ibid., 33 (lines 964–968)
132. Ibid, 34 (lines 995–997)
133. Ibid., 35 (lines 1022–1027)
134. Ibid, 43 (lines 1307–1317).
135. Ibid., 35 (lines 1048–1072)

in the case of ministers) to apply the national ordination standards. The PUP Report magnified a Reformed principle, namely that the whole Church sets the standards and the local governing body applies and implements those standards.[136] It provided the flexibility that if candidates for ordination expressed a conscientious objection, or scruple, over the constitution of the PC(U.S.A.), then it was up to the ordaining governing body to determine whether:

1. The scruple constituted a failure to adhere to "essentials of Reformed faith and polity"[137]; and
2. The declared departure effectively barred the individual from ordained office

Yet, in order for a governing body to determine whether a scruple constitutes a failure to adhere to Reformed essentials and whether such departure constitutes an effective barring from ordained office would require theological lenses as to what constitutes the nature of ordination.

For what the PUP Report lacked by way of addressing the absence of a consistent and coherent theology of ordination, it made up for by providing a framework that assists this book in tracing the contours of a theology of presbyteral ordination. Because all seven recommendations of the PUP Report were approved (Recommendation 5 was approved with amendment), that is the official policy of the Church. That being said, there still is no "official" definition or theology of presbyteral ordination, but what the PUP Report did provide for our purposes is the official location at which such a theology of presbyteral ordination may be developed and implemented, namely the ordaining governing bodies in its relationship with the personal ordinand, the collegial presbyteries, and the communal nature of the whole Church.

Because there is no formally approved official definition of ordination from the PC(U.S.A.) General Assembly, we will need to direct our attention to two sources: confessional documents and *The Book of Occasional Services* to assist us in locating a common, official understanding of ordination. We turn our attention to those sources in the next chapter.

136. Ibid, 36–37 (lines 1082–1092)

137. Ibid, 36 (lines 1063–1065)

THREE

Creeds, Confessions, Constitution

IN ADDITION TO OFFICIAL actions by the General Assembly, the Constitution of the Presbyterian Church (U.S.A.) provides a source in which we can glean a theological understanding of presbyteral ordination.

The Constitution of the PC(U.S.A.) is composed of *The Book of Confessions and The Book of Order.* [1]

The *Book of Confessions* includes the following documents: The Nicene Creed, The Apostles' Creed, The Scots Confession, The Heidelberg Catechism, The Second Helvetic Confession, The Westminster Confession of Faith, The (Westminster) Larger Catechism, The (Westminster) Shorter Catechism, The Theological Declaration of Barmen, The Confession of 1967, and A Brief Statement of Faith-Presbyterian Church (U.S.A.)

The Book of Order consists of the following divisions: Foundations of Polity, Form of Government, Directory for Worship, Rules of Discipline.

In this chapter, we are interested in seeing what the constitutional documents say of presbyteral ordination and church orders. *The Book of Occasional Services,* the sole liturgical resource in the PC(U.S.A.) that contains a liturgy for the ordination of ministers of Word and Sacrament and a combined liturgy for the ordination of elders and deacons, will be of interest to this book as it embodies liturgically the principles set forth in *The Book of Order.*

1. *The Constitution of the Presbyterian Church (U.S.A.), Part II, Book of Order, 2011–2013* , F-3.04. (hereafter "BoO")

Just as we did in the previous chapter where we compared the PC(U.S.A.)'s official response to BEM with that of other Reformed churches' responses, we will compare the selected confessional documents in the PC(U.S.A.) *Book of Confessions* with other Reformed confessions from around the world.

We will, then, conclude this chapter in discussing the nature of confessions in the Reformed tradition, and how the regard afforded to confessions both assists and hinders our search for a coherent, consistent theology of presbyteral ordination.

The Book of Confessions of the Presbyterian Church (U.S.A.)[2]

The 11 creeds, confessions, and catechisms that compose *The Book of Confessions* are ecumenical and span from the early church to 1983. The Nicene Creed and the Apostles' Creed provide the necessary tethering of the PC(U.S.A.) to the Church ecumenical and the Church catholic.[3] The other creeds, confessions and catechisms express the 16th century Protestant Reformation principles of *sola gratia, sola fidei* and *sola Scriptura* – in common with the Lutheran and Zwinglian traditions—then narrow to express the specific Reformed strand of the Reformation with such central themes as the sovereignty of God, God's election, covenant life in the church community, stewardship of God's creation, and doing and seeking justice in the world.[4]

The present BoC was the result of the 1983 reunion between the southern Presbyterian Church in the United States (PCUS) and the northern United Presbyterian Church in the United States of America (UPCUSA) when the doctrinal standards of both branches were merged. At the time of reunion, the only document not part of the BoC

2. *The Constitution of the Presbyterian Church (U.S.A.), Part I, Book of Confessions.* [hereafter "BoC"] In these footnotes, with the exception of the Preface to the BoC titled "Confessional Nature of the Church Report" where Roman numerals are used for page numbers, I will utilize the numbering annotation system contained in *The Book of Confessions* in which sections of a creed, catechism, and confession have a numerical designation rather than the page number. So, for instance, while the entire text of the Nicene Creed is found on page 3 of *The Book of Confessions*, the three articles of the Creed are each designated 1.1, 1.2, 1.3.

3. *BoO*, F-2.03

4. Ibid., F-2.05

of the UPCUSA was the PCUS' standard of the Westminster Larger Catechism.[5] The Brief Statement of Faith-Presbyterian Church (U.S.A.) was adopted in 1991 as a specific provision in the Articles of Agreement that formed the basis of reunion eight years prior that directed a new statement of faith be developed.[6]

In the creeds and confessions, the PC(U.S.A.) "declares to its members and to the world who and what it is, what it believes, and what it resolves to do."[7] While the BoC as a whole and the individual creeds, catechisms, and confessions are standards for faith and life, they are "subordinate standards in the church, subject to the authority of Jesus Christ, the Word of God, as the Scriptures bear witness to him."[8] The BoO cautions that while the confessional statements are subordinate standards to Scripture, they are not to be "ignored or dismissed." In keeping with the Reformed principle *ecclesia reformata, semper reformanda secundum verbum Dei* ("the church reformed, as the church is always being reformed according to the word of God"), the BoO asserts that the Church is open to reforming its doctrinal and polity standards out of obedience to Jesus Christ and the leading of the Holy Spirit.[9]

When we comb the 11 confessional documents, only two speak explicitly and directly to an understanding of church orders and ordination: the Second Helvetic (Swiss) Confession and the Confession of 1967. Even the Heidelberg Catechism, regarded as the best known and most widely used confessional document in the Reformed tradition, more than Calvin's own Geneva Catechism,[10] has no specific section dealing with ordination or church orders. While the Nicene's classical ecclesiological markers of one holy catholic apostolic are helpful in describing the nature of the Church, or the Scots Confession's delineation of what constitutes a true church with the so-called *notae ecclesiae* (notes or marks of the church) – "true preaching of the word of God. . . the right administration of the sacraments of Christ Jesus. . ."ecclesiastical discipline uprightly administered,"[11] those ecclesiological issues

5. *BoC*, xxi.

6. Rohls, *Reformed Confessions*, xiii.

7. *BoO*, F-2.01

8. Ibid., F-2.02

9. Idem.

10. Barth, *The Theology of the Reformed Confessions*, 14.

11. *BoC*, 3.18

are helpful in understanding the larger framework of, in the words of a present ecumenical document now before the World Council of Churches, The Nature and Mission of the Church, and how church orders and ordination relate to the Church's life and witness. But our specific focus in this examination is to discover any explicit statements that express *a* or *the* Reformed theology of presbyteral ordination as found in the confessional documents in the BoC.

The Second Helvetic (Swiss) Confession (1561)

The Second Helvetic Confession was written in 1561 by the Zurich reformer, Heinrich Bullinger, at the personal request of Elector Frederick III of the Palatinate, who had wanted a confession of faith for his private use.[12] It was not until the end of 1565, that Bullinger sent the confession to Frederick, who subsequently published it for general use. In the accompanying letter, Bullinger indicated that the confession was in agreement with all those who confess the true faith "everywhere in all the churches of Germany, France, England, and of other regions and rulers," appealing to no other authority than to holy Scripture, to which the confession agrees ("*congruit*").[13] The very first section of the Second Helvetic Confession, like other contemporaneous confessional documents, begin with a section on Scripture, setting the standard of the holy canon over and against Roman Catholic standards of papal and conciliar decrees. It was in this polemical context that the Second Helvetic, in particular, expressed Reformed theology.

Chapter XVII in the section on the Church focused discussion on what the true Church was by saying what it was not when compared to the Roman Catholic Church. There was no mention of God's calling the whole people of God for service, witness, and mission. The first lines are an opening salvo across the bow of the Catholic Church's notion of saints as the Second Helvetic adamantly asserted that the term "saints" as is referred in the third article of the Apostles' Creed referred to all of the "assembly of the faithful called or gathered out of the world" by God, and not the specially canonized individuals of the Catholic Church.[14]

12. Barth, *The Theology of the Reformed Confessions*, 13–14.

13. Ibid. 14.

14. *BoC*, 5.125

The Second Helvetic went on to correct ecclesiological understandings vis-à-vis the Catholic Church with regards to, for instance, the term "catholic" as meaning universal;[15] distinguishing between the "Church Militant" and the "Church Triumphant;"[16] Jesus Christ as the sole head of the Church not the pope is the guarantor of order;[17] the signs of the "true church" being the "lawful and sincere preaching of the Word of God as it was delivered to us in the books of the prophets and apostles"[18] and "participat[ion] in the sacraments instituted by Christ, and delivered unto us by his apostles, using them in no other way than as they received them from the Lord;"[19] not all who are in the Church are of the true Church;[20] and that unity is achieved not by external rites "but rather in the truth and unity of the catholic faith."[21]

Interestingly, while the Second Helvetic concluded this section on the Church with a caution that "we must be very careful not to judge before the time (the eschatological time of Christ's judgment)," the Confession justified its critique of the Catholic Church for "we must be vigilant lest while the pious snore the wicked gain ground and do harm to the Church."[22]

Chapter VIII was the section on "Of the Ministers of the Church, Their Institution and Duties." The Second Helvetic affirmed that ministers have always been used by God while the Church is still on earth (cf. the Church Militant and the Church Triumphant) for "gathering or establishing of a Church" and for "governing and preservation of the same."[23] That while God can and has used other means to call humanity to salvation, God has specially chosen ministers to proclaim God's salvation, and therefore, ministers are to be regarded as "ministers of God."[24] This section cautioned ministers to maintain the healthy tension of their ministry with the "secret power of the Holy Spirit" so that

15. Ibid, 5.126
16. Ibid, 5.127
17. Ibid, 5.131, 5.132
18. Ibid., 5.134
19. Ibid, 5.135
20. Ibid., 5.139
21. Ibid., 5.141
22. Ibid., 5.140
23. Ibid., 5.142
24. Idem.

while the latter effects salvation in the hearts of people, this was not to diminish the importance of the ecclesiastical ministry and God's prerogative in utilizing the former for God's purposes in the presence and power of the latter.[25]

The Second Helvetic linked the Church's ministry and ministers to Old Testament messengers and to Christ himself. God called patriarchs, to whom God employed angels to deliver divine messages, as well as Moses and the prophets.[26] Then, in the fullness of time, God sent Jesus Christ as "the most perfect teacher of the world," and so, together with Christ, God deployed apostles and teachers of the Church to the people of the New Testament.[27] The ministers that replaced the apostles may be called bishops, elders, pastors, and teachers, but the Second Helvetic stopped short of prescribing these terms as the norms.[28] The Confession recognized subsequent introduction of other ministers such as "patriarchs, others archbishops, others suffragans; also metropolitans, archdeacons, deacons, subdeacons, acolytes, exorcists, cantors, porters, and I know not what others, as cardinals, provosts, and priors; greater and lesser fathers, greater and lesser orders" and then concluded the following:

> But we are not troubled about all these about how they once were and are now. For us the apostolic doctrine concerning ministers is sufficient.[29]

Thus, there was some latitude in the Confession's understanding of church orders, provided that any offices carried out the essential function of preserving and teaching the apostolic faith.

In terms of ministers' election, selection and ordination, the Second Helvetic prescribed that candidates for ministry should only be called by the Church, not by the individual will of the candidate, and that in doing so, the Church must carefully and orderly elect the minister. The qualifications to be a minister had less to do with the ability to carry out certain tasks and functions, and more to do with the character and uprightness of the candidate:

25. Ibid., 5.143–5.144
26. Ibid., 5.145
27. Ibid., 5.146
28. Ibid., 5.147
29. Ibid., 5.148

> Not any one may be elected, but capable men (sic) distinguished by sufficient consecrated learning, pious eloquence, simple wisdom, lastly, by moderation and an honorable reputation, according to the apostolic rule which is compiled by the apostle in 1 Tim. Ch. 3, and Titus, ch. 1.[30]

In relation to ordination, the Second Helvetic prescribed that elders were to ordain ministers with public prayer and the imposition of hands. Interestingly, the reason affixed to the laying on of hands was not the invocation and blessing of the Holy Spirit, or to express support of the community for the ordinand, but to guard against those who did not receive the corporate sign and "who go off of their own accord, being neither chosen, sent, nor ordained."[31] The Second Helvetic, of course, denied any sacrament status to the rite of ordination of ministers, but ordination, along with repentance and marriage, were regarded as "profitable ordinances of God."[32]

The Second Helvetic distinguished between priests and ministers. Priests were all the believers by virtue of Christ's call for all to offer sacrifices of praise and thanksgiving; ministers were servants of Christ, who is the "only priest forever," and stewards of God's mysteries as they attended to teaching and administering the sacraments.[33] The authority and power of ministers are derivative from the absolute power of Christ, who entrusts, as a homeowner to the house steward, to the minister the "keys" to do what the Lord prescribes from the word of God, in governing the Church by proclaiming the forgiveness of sins.[34] Ministers were to exercise their power equally with other ministers, in humility, seeing to the governing and preserving of the Church.[35] Working collegially with other ministers was key not only to the proper function of the Church, but also to mutual discipline and accountability when ministers gathered in synod.[36]

Word and sacrament were the chief duties of ministers. Ministers were to teach and preach the Gospel of Christ, and attend to the proper

30. Ibid., 5.150
31. Ibid., 5.151
32. Ibid., 5.171
33. Ibid., 5.153–5.155
34. Ibid., 5.159
35. Ibid., 5.160–5.161
36. Ibid., 5.167

administration of the sacraments. These functions included correcting and removing false doctrine, providing pastoral care, encouraging the Church in its witness towards the poor; in other words, the minister assumed the pastoral-liturgical, governance, and diaconal functions of ministry.[37] Recalling the Donatist controversy at the time of St. Augustine, the Second Helvetic, in keeping with the principle that God is the initiator and provider of salvation and uses ministers as servants and stewards of God's purposes, maintained that "even evil ministers are to be heard" because the efficacy of the sacraments and of sound preaching were not dependent on the good or evil of the minister, but totally on Christ's word.[38]

Our brief examination of the Second Helvetic Confession demonstrated the clear anti-Roman Catholic intent of its authors. The Confession sought to define Reformed ecclesiology, generally, and church orders, specifically, through highlighting differences with Roman Catholic Church ecclesiology and polity.

The Confession of 1967 (C67)

C67 was the outcome of a proposal to the 168th General Assembly (1956) of the United Presbyterian Church in the United States of America (UPCUSA) that requested a revision of the Westminster Shorter Catechism. The 170th General Assembly (1958) proposed, instead, the development of a new, briefer statement of faith that addressed the Church's role and responsibility in the midst of contemporary issues in the turbulent 1960s such as civil rights, the Cold War and a nuclear arms race, and American nationalism. A committee was appointed and a draft was presented to the 177th UPCUSA General Assembly (1965) where the committee's draft was debated, amended, taking into account feedback that local and regional governing bodies had submitted. A new committee of fifteen was appointed to consider additional revisions, and at the 178th UPCUSA General Assembly (1966), the revised draft from the committee of 15 was considered, debated, and approved, and transmitted to the regional presbyteries for their ratification; more than 90 percent of presbyteries ratified the new confession, and at the

37. Ibid., 5.163

38. Ibid., 5.166

179th UPCUSA General Assembly (1967), the Confession of 1967, or commonly called C67, was adopted.[39]

C67 was framed around 2 Corinthians 5:19, "In Christ God was reconciling the world to himself." The Confession was divided into three parts: (1) "God's Work of Rec-onciliation," which consisted of three subsections: "The Grace of Our Lord Jesus Christ," "The Love of God," "The Communion of the Holy Spirit;" (2) The Ministry of Reconciliation," which consisted of two subsections: "The Mission of the Church," and "The Equipment of the Church;" and (3) "The Fulfillment of Reconciliation."

Ordination and church orders were discussed in the second section titled "The Ministry of Reconciliation" under the subsection, "The Mission of the Church." C67 defined the Church as God's "reconciling community" deployed into the world and entrusted by God with "God's message of reconciliation" by sharing in the healing of conflicts and hatred between human beings, and linked the Church to Israel's and the apostles' call to similarly heed God's call to be agents of reconciliation in the world.[40] The life, death, resurrection, and *parousia* of Jesus Christ provide the reason and pattern of the church's mission.[41] As with Christ's life, the church carries out God's mission in common community with other human beings. As with Christ's suffering and death, the Church is to be sensitive to the needs and suffering of humanity and to see the face of Christ in the lives of other human beings. As with Christ's crucifixion, the Church apprehends God's judgment on inhumanity and injustice afflicted on humanity by human beings. As with Christ's resurrection, the Church holds to the promise that God is bringing about renewal and transformation in the world and that God will defeat all injustice and evil.[42]

C67 focused its discussion of church orders and ordination on the reconciling mission entrusted to the Church by Jesus Christ. C67 recognized that the structuring and ordering of the Church have varied in different times and places depending on what the mission requires for that temporal-spatial context.[43] Far from endorsing or prescribing

39. BoC, 252
40. Ibid., 9.31
41. Ibid., 9.32–9.33
42. Ibid., 9.32
43. Ibid., 9.34

a particular ordering or patterning of ministry, C67 asserted that the unity of the church "is compatible with a wide variety of forms, but it is hidden and distorted when variant forms are allowed to harden into sectarian divisions, exclusive denominations, and rival factions."[44] Hence, any structuring, patterning, or ordering that does not reflect a reconciled community obscures and, in fact, hinders unity. C67 placed the responsibility of the ministry of reconciliation on the whole community, guided and gifted by the Holy Spirit, and from whom certain members were called, trained, and authorized for the ordering of the community's life and witness.[45] Such persons were to be set apart by ordination "or other appropriate act and thus made responsible for their special ministries."[46] Again, the emphasis was placed on the function of ministers to assist the community to carry out its reconciling role, and the definite linkage of ministers to the calling community.

The structuring, ordering, and functioning of the church were regarded as "instruments of mission" and were to be subjected to reform and revision as the mission and ministry of reconciliation required it. C67 recognized that different ordering of ministry have been used at the service of mission and therefore, "none can claim exclusive validity."[47] In speaking about presbyterian polity, far from discussing presbyters as an office or function, C67 underscored the common responsibility of all church members for this common ministry of reconciliation and what it saw as an essential character of that polity being the "organic relation of all congregations in the church." In a concluding summary of church orders, C67 asseverated that:

> Every church order must be open to such reformation as may be required to make it a more effective instrument of the mission of reconciliation.[48]

C67 not only expressed the necessity of flexibility in service to the church's mission of reconciliation when it pertained to church orders, but it also applied such latitude to the exercise of the various gifts God has equipped the Church to carry out its mission. The second section

44. Idem
45. Ibid., 9.38–9.39
46. Ibid., 9.39
47. Ibid., 9.40
48. Idem

of the second part was titled "The Equipment of the Church," in which C67 named preaching, teaching, praise and prayer, and the two sacraments (baptism and the Lord' Supper) as the gifts that God has given the Church to carry out its ministry of reconciliation. But, the confession also affirmed that

> the church is obliged to change the forms of its service in ways appropriate to different generations and cultures.[49]

What is most central to C67 was to have the Church witnessing to Christ's transforming, reconciling work in the world, and not being too stuck on internal discussions of church orders, structures, and operations. While concepts of dynamic equivalence pertaining to issues of inculturation were surely part of the calculus in C67's call for ecclesiastical and ecclesial flexibility, what was most pressing for C67 to assert the necessity and urgency of such latitude was the even higher priority of being Christ's faithful, reconciling, witnessing community in a fragmented and hurting world in every time and place; in doing so, the Church, like Christ in an analogous way, dies to itself for the sake of the world. This can be seen in the penultimate closing lines of the confession:

> With an urgency born of this hope (God's reign in the world), the church applies itself to present tasks and strives for a better world. It does not identify limited progress with the kingdom of God on earth, nor does it despair in the face of disappointment and defeat. In steadfast hope, the church looks beyond all partial achievement to the final triumph of God.[50]

The Confession then ends with the words of Ephesians 3:20–21.
C67 gave careful attention to the nature and mission of the Church. C67 seemed to advance the notion that what was most important for the Church was reclaiming its identity as the sent witness of Christ, to be an agent of reconciliation. This is not at all surprising seeing that many of the members of the drafting committee were Barthian scholars. C67's aim, as with Barth and Barth's successors, sought flexibility in church orders while emphasizing the essence of the Church's reconciling mission as derivative of Christ's own work of reconciliation in the world.

49. Ibid., 9.48

50. Ibid., 9.55

This book will recapitulate those key themes in Chapter 7. But for now, we note that C67 and the Second Helvetic Confession, the only two confessional documents in the BoC that directly speak to issues of church orders and ordination, differ among themselves in their emphases and content in addressing these issues. C67 concerned itself with the Church's mission vis-à-vis Christ's own reconciling mission; the Second Helvetic Confession sought to differentiate Reformed polity vis-à-vis Roman Catholic polity in 16th century Switzerland.

The Book of Order of the Presbyterian Church (U.S.A.)

The other constitutional document of the PC(U.S.A.) is *The Book of Order*, which is divided into four sections: The Foundations of Presbyterian Polity (designated F in BoO citations), The Form of Government (G), The Directory for Worship (W), and The Rules of Discipline (D). Recently, the principles of an ordination service, as well as the constitutional questions that are propounded to ordinands and to presbyters being installed, were moved from The Form of Government section to The Directory for Worship. We must note that a principle of Presbyterian polity is that the church is not a confessional church, nor a church of a directory; that is, while the PC(U.S.A.) and other Reformed churches have confessions, as we saw in the previous section, the confessions are standards that guide and inform the Church and its officers; likewise, The Directory for Worship delineates specific duties of governing bodies and officers when it comes to the ordering of the church's worship and principles of Reformed worship, and, therefore, it is not a service book with standardized rubrics, rituals and prayers.[51]

The BoO lifts three core principles for the Church's ministry and its offices, or ordered ministries. The first is that the Church's ministry derives from Jesus Christ, who gives and entrusts the ministry to the Church. Second, ministry among all church members and officers are to be exercised mutually under the lordship of Christ . Lastly, because Christ serves as the basis for all the whole ministry of the Church, all ordered ministries exercise servant leadership modeled after Christ's own.[52]

51. BoO, Preface to Directory for Worship

52. Ibid., G-2.0101

A careful tension is kept in the emphasis on both the Church's whole ministry and the specific ministry of ordained officers. The PC(U.S.A.) maintains the use of the offices of presbyter (ministers of Word and Sacrament and elder) and deacon.[53] The BoO recognizes that while the ministry of the Church is one, it takes on a variety of forms by emphasis of particular tasks and skills, and even the ordering of the offices. For instance, those ordained to serve as ministers of Word and Sacrament may be called, in addition to local congregational contexts, to serve as hospital chaplains, seminary professors and administrators, judicatory officials, specialized ministry positions, and other non-congregational settings; the common principle being that the ministry of the Word and Sacrament, or, in the case of the office of elder, as it were, the ministry context may emphasize particular aspects of the whole ministry of the Church.[54]

In somewhat differing emphasis to the Second Helvetic Confession, the BoO emphasizes the ability of officers to carry out functions, and secondarily lifted up the uprightness of character needed for the call. In a section titled "Gifts and Requirements," the BoO underscored that God gives gifts to deacons, elders and ministers of the Word and Sacrament to carry out their specific duties and then adds: "In addition to possessing the necessary gifts and abilities, natural and acquired, those who undertake particular ministries should be persons of strong faith, dedicated discipleship, and love of Jesus Christ as Savior and Lord."[55] Recapitulating the aforementioned principle of the ordained offices linkage to the community, persons who are chosen to be ordained officers can do so only with the "approval of God's people and the concurring judgment of a council of the church."[56]

The BoO underscores that ordained leadership and ordination are about service, not power, patterned after Jesus Christ's own servant ministry.[57] It would be appropriate for us to quote, *in toto*, the constitutional provision defining ordination, in The Directory for Worship:

> In ordination the church sets apart with prayer and the laying on of hands those who have been called through election by the

53. Ibid, G-2.0102
54. Ibid., G-2.0103
55. Ibid., G-2.0104
56. Idem.
57. Ibid., G-14.0110

> church to serve as deacons, ruling elders, and teaching elders. In installation the church sets apart with prayer those previously ordained as deacons, ruling elders and teaching elders, and called anew to service in that ministry.[58]

We can note certain principles from these two definitions. First, the calling of the Church occurs through the act of electing; ordination follows that election whereby the same community that elected also confirms that election through ordination, in which those elected persons are set apart with laying on of hands and prayer. Second, what designates the distinctive features of ordination versus election are the corporate prayer and the imposition of hands.

With these principles, there is ambiguity, still, in other respects. First, whereas the PC(U.S.A.) response to the Ministry section of BEM as well as the Second Helvetic and C67 place the initiation of call upon the triune God in Jesus Christ through the Holy Spirit, the Directory for Worship definition does not mention the call of God upon the ordinands, with God's call being mediated through the voice or calling of the Church. This definition presented by the BoO leaves the impression that the Church is some sort of calling job agency that employs persons and calls them. There is no explicit mention of the divine initiative in calling, let alone any mention that grounds the calling of the ordinands with their common baptismal calling shared with the whole Church.

The service of ordination (and installation) focuses on worship and the Church's mission. The Directory for Worship recommended that the service occur on the Lord's Day, in that part of the worship service that responds to the proclamation of the Word.[59] That ordination is an act of the Church in service to Christ, the service of ordination is to lift up what it means to serve Christ, the joy of serving him through the mission and ministry of the Church, and include a sermon appropriate for the occasion.[60]

Because ordination occurs in the worshipping assembly of God's people, we direct our attention to the *Book of Occasional Services.*

58. Ibid., W-4.4001
59. Ibid., W-4.4002
60. Ibid., W-4.4001b

Book of Occassional Services of the Presbyterian Church (U.S.A.)[61]

The BOS was the final volume to complete *The Book of Common Worship* (BCW), which was published in 1993. When the BCW was published, the idea for a "Book of Occasional Services" was developed that would serve as a "trial use resource, which will include ordination and installation services, in harmony with the Study on the Theology and Practice of Ordination, together with other occasional services for use by congregations, presbyteries, synods and the General Assembly."[62] The 1992 study on ordination, while not formally approved by the General Assembly but endorsed as a study resource, was a primary theological resource for the shape and content of the ordination liturgies contained in the BOS. Recall that the 1992 ordination study proposed the master image of "God Service" and linked ordination to baptism. Even though the BOS, like the BCW, are not directory books and therefore are not authoritatively normative for PC(U.S.A.) occasional services, as the sole and primary liturgical resource offered by a program unit of the PC(U.S.A.), the ordination liturgies in the BOS provide a helpful source for this project in comparing the theological content and shape of the liturgies to the stated theological definitions offered by the constitutional documents, viz. the BoC and the BoO.

The ordination liturgies in the BOS emphasize the community and calling of the whole people of God. In contrast to the 1970 *Worshipbook* of the UPCUSA that had one liturgy that could be used for any ordained office for either a service of ordination or installation, the BOS has two liturgies—one for the ordination of minister of the Word and Sacrament and one for elders and deacons—with a separate prayer each for elders and deacons in the combined liturgy of those two offices.[63] But in almost every instance, with the exception of the prayer during the imposition of hands and certain rubrics, the shape and content of the ordination liturgies for presbyters and deacon were nearly identical. Holper noted that ecclesiological discussions from Vatican II, ecumenical convergence documents in the WCC Faith and Order

61. *Book of Occasional Services: A Liturgical Resource Supplementing the Book of Common Worship, 1993.* [Hereafter "BOS"]

62. Ibid., 1.

63. Holper, "Ordination as Ritually Thick," 26.

Commission, and the Consultation on Church Union have shifted the focus from hierarchy to speaking about ministry in terms of the calling of the whole baptized community of God. The BOS does this not primarily through theological instruction (although there is plenty of theology in the BOS' statement on ordination in the rite), but through the "evocative pattern of words and gestures" to include the community in the act of ordination.[64] An added characteristic of the BOS is that the community is invited to see the whole rite as the ordination liturgy, and not merely a certain portion after the sermon (cf. The Directory for Worship's prescription that the service of ordination be done as a response to the proclamation of the Word).[65]

The baptismal linkage in orientating the assembly to their common calling with one another and with the ordinand can be detected in several places in the ordination liturgies. The opening sentences come from Galatians 3:27, "As many of you as were baptized into Christ have clothed yourselves with Christ" to which the assembly responds with the words from Ephesians 4:4, "There is one body an done Spirit, just as we were called to the one hope of our calling." When the minister candidate is presented to the assembly by the moderator, he/she indicates "In baptism, N. and N. were clothed with Christ and are now called by God through the voice of the church . . ."[66] to which the community responds: "We remember with joy our common calling to serve Christ, and we celebrate God's particular call to our brothers and sisters."[67] The service proceeds with the Call to Worship, Opening Prayer, Confession and Pardon, Declaration of Forgiveness, The Peace, A Canticle or Hymn, Prayer for Illumination, Scripture readings, an Anthem, The Gospel Reading, Sermon, Hymn, and then the formal service of Ordination and Installation.

The ordination service proper connected the gathered community to their baptismal calling and to the church universal. The "Statement on Ordination and Installation" begins:

> We are all called into the church of Jesus Christ by baptism, and marked as Christ's own by the Holy Spirit. This is our common calling. . .Within the community of the church, some are called

64. Idem.

65. *BoO*, W-4.4002

66. *BOS*, 11.

67. Ibid., 12.

> to particular service as deacons, as elders, and as ministers of the Word and Sacrament.[68]

This statement on ordination served to tether the community and the ordained officers to one another, to their common calling to serve in the world, and to the triune God. The ordinand is presented with the following:

> Representing the one, holy, catholic, and apostolic church, the session of N. church (in the case of ministers, "the Presbytery of N. by means of this commission")now ordains N. and N. to the office of elder/minister. . . [69]

This statement reminded the assembly that the gathered assembly is tethered not only to one another but to the Church catholic in every time and place by virtue of the unity of the Spirit of Christ in baptism. This is followed by a reaffirmation of the baptismal covenant, followed by anointing with oil, in which chrismation is applied with the words: "N. child of the covenant, I sign you with the cross that you may remember your baptism and be thankful."[70]

This is, then, followed by the propounding of the constitutional questions required by the BoO. In chapter 6, we will see how one particular case study saw the connection of the constitutional questions with their baptisms.

This is followed by the prayer of ordination, in which the ordinand kneels facing the congregation with the presbyters standing behind him/her, and at the appropriate time, the presbyters will lay hands on them. After a prayer from the moderator, the congregation also offers a corporate, invoking the blessing of God upon the ordinand. Then a declaration of ordination is made, followed by a welcome to the ordinand to the ordained ministry, then a charge to the newly ordained (and in the case of elders and deacons, a charge to the congregation). The BOS prescribes that the ordination conclude with the celebration of the Eucharist to connect baptism, eucharist, and ministry in one unified rite.

What we find, indeed, in the BOS is, in the words of Holper, a "ritually thick"[71] liturgy of ordination that expresses a robust theology

68. Ibid., 19.

69. Ibid., 19, 53

70. Ibid., 23, 56

71. Holper, "Ordination as Ritually Thick," 30. Holper urged that "[i]n order for

of presbyteral ordination not through dogmatic theological statements or definitions, but through the enactment of ritual in words, movement and gestures of the entire assembly.

If the BOS is the liturgical expression of the official theology of the BoC and the BoO, we can affirm areas of continuity, and areas of inconsistency:

- The BOS, like the BOC, highlighted the initiative of God in calling officers; the BoO emphasized the Church's calling the officers and downplays God's call
- All documents affirm that officers are called to assist the Church in its witness, to carry out particular tasks and functions
- Emphasis on service
- Emphasis on the ministry of the whole people of god
- Prayer and the imposition of hands are key to ordination
- The common calling in baptism is highlighted in the BOS, is implicit in the BoO, implicit in C67, and absent from the Second Helvetic
- The mutuality and interdependence of ministries among the ordained ministers, and that which they hold in common with the whole Church are emphasized in the BOS, the BoO, C67, and, to some, degree, although muted in Second Helvetic
- Second Helvetic focused on the character of the ordinand; C67, the BoO, and the BOS emphasize the function and calling of the ordinand
- BOS, like Second Helvetic and the BoO, emphasize the public nature/prayer and imposition of hands as the distinctive elements of ordination; C67 glosses over the ordination rite and refers to it as well as "or other appropriate act" in the Church's act of setting apart ordained ministers at the service of the Church's ministry of reconciliation

Thus, what we find in this comparative analysis is that the BOS, as a liturgical and theological expression of the theology of the BoC and the BoO, drew from the main characteristics that those documents present

these rites to be celebrated with integrity, they need to become sources for reflecting on the church's calling and the shape of its ministries need to take."

with regards to ordination and church orders, neither privileging one document over the others, nor doing anything at variance with any one of them or all of them as a whole.

Other Reformed Confessions: A Survey

Because in the Reformed tradition, one church is an expression of the universal Church but is itself not the universal Church, it is important that we see the perspectives of other Reformed churches on this question of presbyteral ordination through their confessional documents. Just as we did with the BEM in comparing the PC(U.S.A.)'s official response with that of the official responses from other Reformed churches, we will survey the confessional documents of other Reformed churches from the 16th century to the 20th century, and then conclude in comparing the key characteristics of presbyteral ordination and offices that those other Reformed churches lift up with that of the PC(U.S.A.)'s core principles, and see where the PC(U.S.A.)'s "official" definition of presbyteral ordination may be modified.

In this section we will survey the explicit statements of 23 Reformed confessions from the 16th and 17th centuries on the matter of presbyteral ordination.[72]

Zwingli's Sixty-Seven Articles (1523)

In the section "On the Priesthood," Zwingli set out three principles.[73] Paragraph 61 rejected the Catholic notion of the indelible character (*character indelibilis*) endowed upon priests in ordination, saying that there was no scriptural foundation for that doctrine. This was to indicate that there was nothing magical that occurred to the priest's character or disposition; Zwingli wished to maintain that ordination was not so much about the transformation of the ordinand as it was about the ministry of Christ through the Church, to which the ordinand was set

72. We will rely upon Dennison, Jr., *Reformed Confessions of the 16th and 17th Centuries in English Translation* for all of the 16th and 17th century confession in this section, except for the last three confessions – the French Confession of 1559 and the Belgic Confession of 1561, the Irish Articles of Religion of 1615—none of which were included in Dennison's volume.

73. Ibid, 8.

apart to serve. Paragraph 62 asserted that the only priests that scripture recognized as legitimate were those who "proclaim the word of God." Connected to Paragraph 62 was Paragraph 63's provision that those who proclaim the word of God, scripture enjoins all people to "show respect by giving them physical sustenance."[74]

In short, Zwingli sought to assert that the ordained ministry was in service to the word of God, in its function, purpose, and content.

Confession of the East Friesland Preachers (1528)

Three specific articles in the Confession spoke to God's initiative and the derivative, but critical function of Word and Sacrament in the divine economy.[75] Article 7 of the Confession asserted God's internal work in people as "powerful, prophetic, and necessary" for salvation and assurance of one's salvation, referring to preaching and baptizing as "His preaching" and "His baptizing." Article 8 was quick to state that, nevertheless, the "external work" of the Church's ministry of Word and Sacrament were "profitable" in provoking people to act, such as in witnessing. Finally, the ninth article affirmed the importance of preaching in convicting people of their sin, and, thereby, revealing Christ.

Thus, the East Friesland Preachers' Confession emphasized divine initiative and the importance of the Church's responsibility that is derived from God's action.

William Farel's Summary (1529)

Guillaume "William" Farel joined Calvin in Geneva in 1535. In Chapter XVI of his *Summaire*, Farel asserted that the church's purpose and foundation are to be found in the 'true union of faith in our Lord Jesus, hearing and believing His holy voice."[76]

The *Summaire* went on to say that everyone in the Church is equal, with each member serving one another, especially those who were tasked to interpret and teach Scripture, they did so not for themselves for the "edification of others." The task of pastors, according to Chapter

74. Idem.

75. Ibid., 46.

76. Ibid, 66.

XVII of the *Summaire* was to use the "keys of the kingdom of heaven"—-the Word of God, the gospel—-so that the Church, depicted as the shepherd's pasture, may hear and discern the shepherd's voice.[77]

Chapters XXXIV and XXXV of the *Summaire* discussed what was expected of "good pastors" and the power and authority of pastors. With regards to characteristics of a good pastor, the shepherd was the master image in reminding pastors that Jesus Christ is "[t]he good, true, and faithful shepherd over all" who offered himself to serve all. Thus, all other pastors, who are shepherd-designees who serve on behalf of Christ, were to attend to Christ's flock (the Church), drawing the sheep to Christ and "by all means to live according to the good and holy will of God, by sound doctrine and an example of the good life."[78] Regarding the power and authority of pastors, such power was to be directed towards edifying the Church and instructing the Church by the Word of God, and pastors were to attend to careful study of the Scriptures because through faithful, pure, and simple teaching and preaching of the Word of God, people will live holy lives and follow Christ.[79]

Zwingli's Fidei Ratio (1530)

Zwingli completed this confession on July 3, 1530 as his response to the Diet of Augsburg and the Augsburg Confession. Neither the Diet nor emperor Charles V read the document since it arrived at the Diet by courier on July 8. Johann Eck (1486–1543) polemically responded to Zwingli, calling him "a Turk, a Tartar, a Hun." This confession was never officially adopted but has been included in all major works on Reformed confessions as representing the mature views of Zwingli.[80]

In the tenth article of Zwingli's confession, he asserted the divine initative and purpose in the call and function of pastors.[81] The work of prophesying and preaching, Zwingli stated, were critical and necessary for the preaching of "apostles, evangelists and bishops" enabled the Holy Spirit to give faith to hearers to believe, and even then, when

77. Ibid., 66–67

78. Ibid., 90–91

79. Ibid., 91–93

80. Ibid., 112–113

81. Ibid., 132

people did not believe, it was due to the absence of the Holy Spirit, as it were, a sign of the wrath of God.

As to the function and task of ministers, Zwingli regarded them as key to imparting a divine sense of love, justice, and equity to people, thereby assisting the laws and magistrates in maintaining order in society. Ministers were to teach, preach, baptize, administer the Lord's Supper, visit the sick, feed the poor, and study and interpret Scripture. Then Zwingli took one last swipe in this section at bishops, whom he described as "born bread eaters" and whom he and others in his company regarded as "a useless burden on the earth and illegitimate" comparing them to "goiters and hunchbacks" that burden the body.[82]

Confessio Tetrapolitana (1530)

The Tetrapolitan Confession, named after the four cities of Strasbourg, Constance, Memmingen, and Lindau on whose behalf Martin Bucer wrote, was outlined after the Augsburg Confession and presented by Bucer at the Diet of Ausburg on July 11, three days after Zwingli sent his *Fideo ratio* to the same Diet. The *Tetrapolitana* came at the heels of the failed Marburg Colloquy (October 1–4, 1529), which failed to reach a consensus among the Reformed, Lutherans, and Zwinglians on the doctrine of the Eucharist. Zwingli rejected the *Tetrapolitana*, Luther stayed with the Augsburg, and, consequently, the four cities were isolated. The *Tetrapolitana* has been regarded as the first Reformed confession.[83]

Concerning the Church and its ecclesiastical orders, its only power is for "edification," and therefore, those who are called to serve do so as "ministers of Christ and stewards of the mysteries of God." In being servants of the Lord, the role of ministers is likened to that of the apostles, the efficacy and sufficiency of their work was of God.[84] What constituted a legitimate minister (named in the *Tetrapolitana* as "bishops, teachers and pastors") was their divine commission to be sent, which meant that ordinands have "received the power and mind to preach the Gospel and to feed the flock of Christ, and also the Holy Ghost who cooperates—i.e. persuades hearts." The confession went on

82. Idem.

83. Ibid., 139

84. Ibid., 153–154

to state that ministers were sent to care for the flock and faithfully feed the flock, naming the ministers as "bishops, elders and pastors."[85]

In relation to the offices of the Church, the *Tetrapolitana* identified the role and offices of ministers. The confession named the various "offices of ministers" as ones to whom were charged specific functions "in word and doctrine" and through their service and in their person, they represent the Church, "so that who hears them is correctly said to hear the Church," a sort of *in persona ecclesiae.*

The Bern Synod (1532)

The Bern Synod convened from January 9–14, 1532 with 230 delegates, among whom were William Farel and Wolfgang Capito (1478–1541). Capito, a Reformed ally and friend of Oecolampadius and Zwingli, fortuitously arrived in Bern, where a Synod had been called by the city magistrates to calm religious and political tensions. Capito drafted 22 articles in preparation for the Synod. In 44 articles, the Synod overwhelmingly reaffirmed Bern's commitment to the Reformation, which would influence Basel, Lausanne, and Geneva in their reforming efforts.[86]

That the Bern Synod was a forum to uphold the power and authority of the civil magistrates in religious matters while allowing criticism of the same, the Bernese articles stipulated the relationship of ministers with the city, with the expectation that the minister and preachers in that canton would "comport themselves in doctrine and life" based on the Reformation principles that Bern adopted four years earlier with the Ten Theses of Reformation (Bern Disputation) of 1528.[87]

The Bern Synod lifted up the role of ministers and the divine initiative. The synodical action recognized ministers as occupying an interdependent but distinctive role in society vis-à-vis the civil magistrates; both were regarded as "servants of God," but the ministers and preachers, specifically, were to be considered "ambassadors of Christ, servants of the Spirit, and stewards of the mysteries of God."[88] Chapters two through ten of the Bernese Order asserted the centrality of Christ

85. Idem.

86. Ibid., 226–227

87. Idem.

88. Ibid., 233.

in doctrine, proclamation, life, the Church, the sermon, and the knowledge of sin and grace.[89]

Because the Church and civil government are both in service to God, the Bernese Order stated the proper relationship of ministers and civil magistrates. In Kuyperian fashion, the Bern Synod viewed the proper spheres of sovereignty between the Church and State, with ministers aiding the State in maintaining order and creating a just society where the commandments and prohibitions of Scripture and the derived principles from Scripture were to shape and govern civil laws.[90] In cases where magistrates need to be corrected or scriptural principles need to be advocated, ministers were duty-bound to speak truth to power.

With regards to the function of ministers, the Bern Synod focused on the minister's personal, collegial and communal responsibilities. Ministers were to attend to careful study of Scripture, diligent preparation for teaching and preaching, and confer with other ministers about the meaning of Scripture.[91]

The concluding chapter of the Bern synodical order emphasized the personal uprightness of the minister. The order urged modest apparel be worn by ministers in public. Married ministers were to be faithful to their wives, and single ministers were to be chaste and pure in heart. Ministers were to be sober in ingesting libations or being seen in bars, and "renounce all coarse vices."[92]

Waldensian Synod of Chanforan and Waldensian Confession of Angrogna (1532)

The Waldensians (Vaudois), people who embraced the preaching of Peter Waldo (ca. 1173-ca.1205/18), settled in the Angrogna ("very heart of the Valleys") region in the province of Provence along the Durance River in the 14th century. When the Reformation emerged in Germany and Switzerland, the Waldensians got word of it and sent their statement of faith to Bucer, Capito and Oecolampadius wherein the Waldensians

89. Ibid., 234–239

90. Ibid, 264–265

91. Ibid., 267–272

92. Ibid., 275–276

asked questions. The responses of the three Reformers inspired the Confession (Declaration) of the Synod of Chanforan (September 1532) and the Confession of Angrogna (December 1532).

In the ninth declaration of Chanforan, the laying on of hands was declared to be unnecessary. Acknowledging, though, that the apostles and patristic fathers employed the practice, the Chanforan synod could not see the necessity for the rite. But it, concluded, "nonetheless, because it is an external thing, let everyone feel free to do it or not to do it."[93]

Regarding the behavior of ministers, the Chanforan declaration addressed the issues of travel and caring for the minister's family. Surprisingly, the Declaration contained no specific roles or functions of ministers as in other confessions. The 22nd declaration sought to assert that the minister was a servant of the church and therefore "ministers of God's Word must not travel from place to place, without a greater benefit for the church." But, thankfully, the Declaration allowed ministers to feed their families, seeing that such acts did not go "against the apostolic sharing (of goods)."[94]

The Waldensian Confession of Angrogna (1532) was a brief confession of faith written by the "pastors and heads of families of the valleys of the Piedmont assembled at Angrogna on December 12, 1532."[95] The Angrogna Confession, while not explicitly naming the Roman Catholic Church, sought to distinguish the Waldensian Reformed churches and ministers from the Catholic Church and ministers by disregarding those who conducted and approved "auricular confession" (article 7), and those who prohibited marriage calling such teaching "the doctrine of the devil" (article 13). Of the 17 articles in this brief confession, only the 15th article dealt with ministers, and even then, the issue in that section was in relation to the transfer of "ministers of the word of God" and such transfer should ordinarily not occur unless there was "some great good to the Church."[96]

93. Ibid., 279–289

94. Ibid., 281

95. Ibid., 282

96. Ibid., 285

The Bohemian Confession (1535)

This Confession was more Lutheran than Reformed, but has gained a place among Reformed confessions. The Czech edition of 1535, called *Confessio Fratrum*, was fully titled, "Confession of Faith and Religion of the Barons and Nobles of the Kingdom of Bohemia presented to the most serene and invincible king of the Romans, Bohemia, etc. at Vienna, Austria, in the year of our Lord 1535." A final version of this confession was presented to Emperor Maximilian II (1527–1576) and approved by the Bohemian Diet on May 17, 1575.[97] The Unitatis Fratrum (Union of the Congregations of Bohemian Brethren) emerged in 1467 as an independent, spiritually and biblically centered fellowship that provided an alternative to the Utraquists[98] and the Roman Catholic Church.

The Bohemian Confession prescribed the manner in which ministers were to be ordained. In seeking the proper manner of ordination and installation through the "order of the Lord and the Apostles," the Confession asserted that only "pious and faithful ones be called from among the people, men (sic) full of faith and blameless, having the gifts necessary for this ministry."[99] Ministers were to have an upright character. Then, in careful detail, the Confession indicated that after ministers were duly chosen and elected, after the "Seniors" (presumably those acting as the church elders) offered prayer, the imposition of hands in the assembly was to occur.[100] The Confession prescribed that "none are indeed permitted to function in the office of a priest unless, as is proper, they are called and installed according to these precepts."[101]

Concerning the ordained ministers, all functions were to be grounded in the holy Scripture. Ministers were to care for the souls entrusted to them, offering the word ands sacraments, giving attention to "reading, to exhortation, to doctrine." The preaching of the Word of

97. Ibid., 298–299

98. The Utraquists was a fellowship that grew out of the Hussite Revolution, or "First Reformation," when Jan Hus (1369–1415) was martyred at the Council of Constance in 1415. The Utraquists got their name from the fact that they gave laity both the bread and the cup (*sub utraque specie*, "under the one kind and the other"); they were nicknamed *sub utraque* Calixtines (Lat. *calix*, "cup"). See Ibid., 297.

99. Ibid., 315

100. Idem.

101. Idem.

God "is a ministry instituted and commanded by Christ,"[102] and, therefore, according to the Confession, was regarded as 'the most important of all among us, since it is seen as the thing which contributes more to salvation and is more necessary than the sacraments themselves."[103]

The Lausanne Articles (1536)

The ten articles contained in The Lausanne Articles were the ten theses that Guillaume Farel (1489–1565) proposed in an October 1, 1536 sermon at the heels of the abolition of the Mass by the Lausanne Council. Pierre Viret (1511–1571), who arrived in town at Farel's invitation, joined Farel in preaching and teaching, urging the Lausanne citizens to embrace the Reformed faith. The Lausanne Council called for a public disputation so that crowds could hear the Reformed faith explained.

The Lausanne articles addressed ecclesiology by distinguishing the Reformation churches from the Roman Catholic Church, without explicitly naming the Roman Church. The articles lifted the principles of *sola Scriptura* and *solus Christus*, rejected all other "ceremonies" except the Lord's supper and baptism as ones "instituted by Christ." Then, in the fifth article, Lausanne asserted that the only acceptable ministry of the Church were the "preaching of the Word and the administration of the sacraments."[104]

The First Helvetic Confession (1536)

Also known as the Second Confession of Basel (to distinguish it from the First Confession of Basel of 1534), the First Helvetic Confession served to unite Protestants in the German-speaking Switzerland. The original vision of Bucer and Capito was to unite the Reformed and Lutherans in preparation for the ecclesiastical council at Mantua in 1537 summoned by Pope Paul III (1468–1549). Seven Swiss cities—Zurich, Bern, Basel, Schaffhausen, St. Gall, Mühlhausen, Biel—urged the Reformed parties to meet at Basel on January 30, 1536; Martin Luther also expressed hope for a *modus vivendi*. The Reformed delegates to the

102. Ibid., 318

103. Idem.

104. Ibid., 340–341

Basel conference were Heinrich Bullinger (1504–1575), Samuel Gyrnaeus (1539–1599), Oswald Myconius (1488–1552), Leo Jud (1482–1542), and Kaspar Megander (1495–1545), with Bucer and Capito as advisors. They were to develop a confession that would serve as a Lutheran-Reformed consensus. Even though such a consensus did not emerge, the First Helvetic paved the way for Bullinger's more influential Second Helvetic Confession.[105]

In its statements on ecclesiology, the First Helvetic underscored divine initiative and the critical responsibility of ministers. The Confession asserted that people belong to the Church through the Word of God and "external rites, instituted by Christ Himself" but such belongingness, in consequence of their salvation secured by Christ's death, resulted by "a singular privilege of God."[106] Connected to this, then, was the First Helvetic's assertion that ministers were "fellow workers of God," by which was meant that God worked through the ministry of human ministers to reveal God's self, to remit sin, convert people to God, and comforting them. In no uncertain terms, the efficacy of these works belonged to God, with the outward work attributed to the ministers, and even then, the recipients of the efficacious work of God were determined by God's divine choice and wisdom.[107]

With regards to the power and authority of the Church, the First Helvetic discussed the "power of the keys." The Confession identified the word of God and the "shepherding of the flock" as the "power of the keys" and that such power and authority was to be entrusted only to those elected to ministry. Interestingly, this section spoke of such election occurring either "by the calling of God *or* by the certain and experienced suffrage of the church. . . ."[108] This was either clarified or corrected in the subsequent section titled "The Election of Ministers" in which the minimum eligibility requirements for the ordained ministry was being skilled in "divine law" and having an upright character, theological education, and certified by the Christian magistrate on behalf of the Church. This section went on to say that God's choosing was confirmed by the church's vote and the imposition of hands by the elders.[109]

105. Ibid., 342–343

106. Ibid., 347

107. Idem.

108. Idem (my emphasis)

109. Ibid., 348

The Christ-centered, Christ-derived ecclesiology of First Helvetic also shaped its pastoral theology. Jesus Christ was identified as "the true Head and Pastor of His Church," an implicit swipe at the Roman pontiff. The Confession acknowledged that pastors and teachers serve at the prerogative of Christ, and that the ordained are "pastors in name only, least of all a Roman head."[110] The function and role of pastors was to care for the Church through preaching, teaching, and prayer. The First Helvetic, continuing its polemic against the Roman Catholic Church, asserted that pastors had a special duty to defeat Satan and all that sought to cripple the Church.

Calvin's Catechism (1537)

The French Reformer, John Calvin (1509–1564) remained in Geneva under threat by his colleague Guillaume Farel, who wanted Calvin's help in establishing the Reformed church in that city. The first edition of Calvin's *Institutes of the Christian Religion* had been completed and published in March 1536 in Basel; it served as the outline for his Catechism, which Calvin wrote and condensed into a briefer volume so that children could understand. Farel and Calvin spoke to the Petit Conseil on January 16, 1537 about the benefits of "catechizing" children in the "Fondements de la religion Chrestienne."[111]

Calvin accented his pastoral theology upon the ministry of the word. Pastors are to teach and nurture the church in public and in private with "pure doctrine, administer[ing] the sacraments, and by their good example. . . ."[112] As with contemporaneous Reformed confessions' discussion on the keys of the kingdom (an explicit critique upon the Roman Catholic Church's assumption of the Matthew 16:19 statement of Jesus handing the keys to Peter to bind and loose things on earth as it will be done on heaven), Calvin asserted that welcoming or rejecting a pastor was tantamount to welcoming or rejecting Christ, but that such power to effect transformation in people's lives and in the world was not due to the minister but solely limited to "the ministry of the word."[113] Calvin continued: "For Christ has not given this power properly to

110. Idem.

111. Ibid., 353

112. Ibid., 388

113. Ibid., 389

these men (sic) but to his word, of which he has made these men (sic) ministers." Thus, pastors must rely upon the word of God, and preach and teach what is contained in the word of God lest they be regarded as "pernicious wolves, they are to be chased away."[114]

Geneva Confession (1536/37)

It is disputed as to whether the Geneva Confession was solely written by John Calvin, or Guillaume Farel, or co-authored by the two of them. The Confession was written at about the same time the 1536 edition of Calvin's *Institutes* were published, and when Calvin began to write his ecclesiastical ordinances and catechism. Both Calvin and Farel hoped that the Geneva Small Council would adopt the Confession for the city and bind all Genevan citizens to swear to uphold it lest those who did not would not be admitted to the Lord's Supper. In the election of 1538, their opponents won and they were driven from Geneva.[115]

The Confession's clear ecclesiology was that the both the Church and her officers were to uphold fidelity to the markers of a true church. Both the Church and ministers were to proclaim the word of God faithfully and to administer the sacraments according to Christ's institution. Failing to do that, the Church or the pastors who did not remain faithful and true to the word of God were to be disregarded and summarily dismissed.[116] The power and authority of the Church, and therefore, of the ministers of the Word resided in the Word of God, entrusted to them by Christ. To hear and receive a minister of the Word were tantamount to hearing and receiving Christ Himself.

Waldensian Confession of Provence (1543)

This Confession was presented to Cardinal Sadoleto (1477–1547) to persuade him that the charges lodged against the Waldensians of Provence were false. The document was then forwarded to King Francis I of France (1494–1547) when he held control of the Piedmont region and the Parlement in Turin in 1544. King Francis I had previously

114. Idem.

115. Ibid., 393–394

116. Ibid., 400–401

suspended an edict issued by the local court (parlement) of Aix-en-Provence that called for the execution and razing of Waldensian villages, and instead ordered an investigation into the "life and character" of the Waldensians.[117]

Like other contemporaneous confessions, this Confession emphasized the upright character and doctrinal orthodoxy of ministers. The Confession recognized both bishops and pastors as "ministers of the church" who "ought to be irreproachable in life as well as doctrine. In citing the example of Aaron, Moses' brother, as an example of a selfless leader, the Confession lifted up the master image of shepherd tending to Christ's flock, and thus, the exemplary character of all ministers was necessary for be a good example to the flock "in word and conversation, in love, and in faith, and chastity."[118]

Waldensian Confession of Mérindol (1543)

As mentioned above, the Mérindol edict was issued on November 18, 1540 by the Aix-en-Provence *parlement* designating the Waldensians in that area as enemies and calling for their eradication. King Francis I of France granted authority to the *parlement* (local courts) to quell Waldensians and others considered "heretics" in order to prepare for an invasion of the Piedmont region and northern Italy against Francis I's rival, Holy Roman emperor Charles V (1500–1558).[119]

Mérindol's pastoral theology placed a high standard on the character and doctrinal commitment of ministers and pastors. It was expected that ministers of the church, like the Provence Confession, would be examples to their flock by being "faithful in word, conduct, love, and faith, and to surpass others in purity, by preaching the Word of God and by persevering in true doctrine."[120] For Mérindol, this high standard meant at least two things: pastors who did not faithfully tend to Christ's flock with right doctrine and careful teaching of the word of God were to be removed; secondly, the realm entrusted for ministers of the church was the Church, not what Mérindol saw as some pastors

117. Ibid., 446–447

118. Ibid., 448

119. Ibid., 446–447

120. Ibid., 462

assuming or attempting to usurp the power of princes and civil magistrates, calling it a "derelict[ion] of duty."[121]

Calvin's Catechism (1545)

The 1545 Catechism was a Latin version of the 1541 catechism, released on November 28, 1545. In a letter to the pastors of East Friesland on November 27, 1545, Calvin stated that he made the Catechism in Latin for children were being schooled in the *lingua franca* of 16th century Europe, and, thus, the Reformed faith would have a broader and deeper exposure and appeal.[122]

Of the 373 question-and-answers in Calvin's Latin catechism, only four specifically dealt with church orders, and even then, addressed only the role of pastors in teaching and the sacraments, or the Word and sacrament. In question 307, the minister would ask the children, "Is it necessary, then, that there should be pastors?" at which the children were to respond, "Yes" and the rest of the answer included the belief that the Church should hear what the pastor teaches for to reject the pastor and their teaching was to effectively reject Christ and separate oneself from the Church.[123] Then, with regards to the sacraments, the Catechism, within the wording of question 368, mentioned that pastors, "who are appointed to dispense the Sacraments" were not to admit just anyone to the Lord's Supper if the pastor deemed an individual to be "entirely unworthy," but even then, the answer to question 371 concerning hypocrites asserted that pastors cannot necessarily and readily exclude anyone who the pastor subjectively determined to be entirely unworthy "but must wait until God has revealed their iniquity."[124] In the final question-and-answer, number 373, the minister asked, "Then there ought to be some order and polity regarding this (if the pastor has been warned of someone being unworthy to partake of the Lord's Supper)," at which the children were to respond that the Church must have order, and that those who were appointed to tend to the spiritual life of the Church, viz. the pastors, should be given the "authority of the Church" to "refuse communion to those who are quite unfit, and

121. Ibid., 462–463

122. Ibid., 467–468

123. Ibid., 510

124. Ibid, 519

to whom communion cannot be given without dishonouring God and scandalising the faithful."[125]

The picture that we obtain from Calvin's catechism is of pastoral leadership akin to a shepherd possessing the full trust of stewardship granted by Christ to care for the flock in Word and Sacrament. This was to be done with a gentle firmness, to root out all those who appeared to be counterfeit believers, and the Church, likewise, was expected to receive the authority, discipline, and teaching of their pastors who were entrusted and empowered to care for them.

Juan Diaz's Sum of the Christian Religion (1546)

Juan Diaz (†1547) of Toledo, Spain converted to the Reformed faith in 1532 while studying Greek and Latin literature in Paris. He traveled from Paris to Geneva to study with Calvin, and when in 1546 he traveled to Strasbourg to be with Martin Bucer, he was requested to accompany Bucer and Claude de Senarcleus to represent Strasbourg at the colloquy of Ratisbon. Diaz's twin brother, Alfonso, who at the time was a member of the Roman Curia, got word of Diaz's attendance at Ratisbon and arranged for him to be assassinated. Diaz's "Summary of the Christian Faith" was dedicated to Lord Otto Henry, Palatine of the Rhine, who had officially endorsed the Lutheran Reformation in 1542. While not a confession of faith, Diaz's "summary" represented the beliefs of 16th early 16th century evangelicals in Spain.[126]

Diaz's ecclesiology centered on the word of God and sacraments, with assistance from the civil magistrate. In speaking about the mode of governing the church, Diaz underlined the cooperative spirit between "a pious prince or magistrate" and "a faithful minister or pastor." A prince was pious if he governed with a desire to please God and recognized his authority as coming from God. A minister was deemed faithful if the minister was "vigilant and faithful in the ministry of the Word and in instructing the children in the catechism." Diaz saw that when the civil and ecclesiastical leadership functioned with faithfulness and credibility then the administration of the church will be taken care of, and that both spheres can attend most especially to the education of

125. Idem.

126. Ibid., 520–521

children in schools, for in Diaz's estimation, schools are the "breeding ground of the church and the republic."[127] Diaz saw that the principal purpose of the Church was to care for the poor, to provide alms by the ministry of deacons, and to care for the sick. He saw the importance of the civil leadership providing protection so that the ministry of the Word could flourish and rid society of vices and evil. Thus, Diaz, in the final section of the "Summary" called for people, in society and in the Church, to embrace the Word of God so that the right pastors, magistrates, and princes will be chosen as the Word unleashes its power, and, therefore, both the state and the church will be run orderly and both will flourish.[128]

Confession of John à Lasco (1551)

John à Lasco (or Jan Łaski, 1499–1560) was a Polish Reformer who renounced his Catholic bishopric when he came to the Reformed faith under the tutelage of Erasmus, Zwingli, and read Luther's writings. When he settled in Emden in East Friesland, à Lasco was appointed by Countess Anna von Oldenberg to serve as superintendent of the Protestant churches in her realm until Emperor Charles V, in 1548, imposed the Augsburg Interim, forcing the Countess to allow a compromise that enabled a rebirth of Catholicism in her region; à Lasco had no choice but to flee, so he sought refuge from King Edward VI and Thomas Cranmer in England. In July 1550, the Privy Council established a "Stranger's Church" in London, consisting of French, Dutch, and Italian refugees, and appointing à Lasco as its superintendent. À Lasco's confession was the basis for admission into the church; its authorship may have been a joint project of several unnamed individuals or could have been from à Lasco's single pen.[129]

The Confession recognized three ministries of the Church: Word, sword, and poor. The Confession envisaged the civil and ecclesiastical leaders as within the general umbrella of the "Church of Christ," all of whom are "ministers and custodians" of Christ's laws. Ministers of the Word had the solemn responsibility of teaching and preaching

127. Ibid., 525

128. Ibid, 526

129. Ibid., 551–552

the Word of God, governing the Church "along with its presbyters," "obstruct[ing] the mouths of adversaries," and that through an orderly and faithful ecclesiastical government the Church's divine character will be maintained "not through the rule of the clergy" but through the godly example of the ministers who "having been set part for this by the Holy Spirit."[130]

Ministers of the sword were the civil magistrates who secured the purity of the Church against internal and external enemies. They were to maintain peace so that the ministries of the Church could be conducted unhampered, as well as discipline heretics and punish those who "heedlessly neglect, defile, or attempt to abolish" the "institutions of Christ" in the Church.[131]

The deacons were to attend to collecting and distributing alms to the poor.

What we find with à Lasco's confession was a broader definition of what it meant to be the Church for in his context, the jurisdictional lines between church and state were permeable and sometimes blurred. The responsibility of tending to the health of the Church and society lay in ministers of the word, sword, and poor. It was no wonder that the 19th century Dutch Reformed theologian, Abraham Kuyper, used à Lasco's confession as a resource for Kuyper was the one who developed the doctrine of sphere sovereignty, envisioning all of creation as under God's sovereign lordship with various "spheres" designating specific responsibilities, with all spheres interrelated and dependent upon one another in the horizontal relationships, while seeking direction from the vertical relationship with God that all the spheres had.

Large Emden Catechism (1551)

When John à Lasco was made superintendent of the Protestant churches in Emden, he wrote a catechism for those churches and then carried it to England when he sought refuge there in 1550.

In 250 question-and-answers, the Catechism addressed church orders in Q/A 134 and 135, and in that, spoke about the necessity of priests. Question 134 asked whether priests were anointed by God's

130. Ibid., 575

131. Ibid., 576.

command, to which the Catechism responded that anointing of priests was unnecessary for its use in the Old Testament was to presage the coming of Christ; with Christ's incarnation and ministry, anointing was no longer necessary. Question 135 asked whether there, therefore, were any more priests, to which the Catechism provided two responses: first, that ordained ministers are called priests in Scripture but that there are no longer any "externally anointed priests" since all external sacrifices have been completed by the eternal priesthood of Christ; second, Christ has been specially anointed by the Holy Spirit, being set apart from "all his brothers." These brothers were designated as all those who were "now consecrated through his completeness as Kings and Priests in the Spirit of the Lord,"[132] viz. ordained ministers.

À Lasco's brief theology of church orders drew the inextricable link between the status and role of Christ's eternal, efficacious priesthood and the temporal, derivative priesthood of ordained ministers.

Vallérand Poullain's Confession of the Galstonbury Congregation (1551)

Vallérand Poullain, or Vallerandus Pollanus (1520–1557), was the second successor (after Pierre Brully) to Calvin's band of French refugees in Strasbourg when Poullain was invited by Bucer to serve as pastor. Poullain's congregation settled in Glastonbury, Somersetshire in England for a short time following Emperor Charles V's adoption of the Augsburg Interim in 1548, but fled England after Queen Mary's persecution against Protestants. Poullain's Glastonbury congregation finally settled in Frankfort. Poullain developed a liturgy for his Strasbourg congregation, translated it into French, and the French edition that was published in London in 1552 contained the Confession of Faith used by the Glastonbury congregation.[133]

The Galstonbury Confession's ecclesiology lifted up several common Reformed themes. First, there was an emphasis on the true church consisting of all those who subscribed to right doctrine, who partook of the Sacraments instituted by Christ, and who observed the wholeness

132. Ibid., 617

133. Ibid, 643–645

of the Christian faith; in other words it highlighted the *nota ecclesiae*—the marks of the church—Word, Sacrament, discipline.[134]

Second, the Confession emphasized that the Church and the Church's ministry were kept vital by the presence and power of the Holy Spirit, that in the Spirit, the Church and her ministries live, move and have their being.

Third, without using the previously used terms "keys of the kingdom" as other confessions used, the Glastonbury Confession asserted that remission of sins and hope in the resurrection life of Christ are given in the Church, and that the ministry of the Word and Sacraments is the primary means through which those benefits are mediated.

Fourth and last, the Confession's ecclesiology extended the three *nota ecclesiae* to four "tokens whereby the Church is distinguished."[135] The Confession identified the ministry of the Word in teaching and preaching as the first token. In a change from usual Reformed expositions of marks of the "true" church, this Confession asserted the second token to be "the simple invocation of the one God through Christ alone." In its explanation of this second token, the Confession seeks to ward off violations of the Second Commandment in the worship of God, whereby the Church relies upon "the commandments and devices of men, or of themselves, than to the commandment of the living God."[136] The third token was the sacraments and the four token was ecclesiastical discipline.

Like previous contemporaneous confessions, the Glastonbury Confession envisaged "a twofold ministry" involving an ecclesiastical ministry and a "political" ministry, or the interrelated service of church and state; the former employing Word, sacraments and discipline; the latter utilizing the sword and laws to ensure peace and justice in society to enable the ministry of the Word and sacraments to flourish.[137]

Rhaetian Confession (1552)

The Rhaetian Confession was so-named because of the name of the region in eastern Switzerland, bordering Austria and Italy, from the

134. Ibid, 658

135. Ibid., 659

136. Idem.

137. Ibid., 661

ancient Tuscan settler, Rhetus; Rhaetia is modern-day Graubünden. The Rhaetian Free State, also known as the Republic of the Three Leagues in Old Free Rhaetia, attracted Protestant refugees, including Waldensians. Calvin's and Bullinger's influence came to the region. This Confesssion was approved in 1552 by a Reformed synod. In 1553, it was sent to Bullinger for his endorsement; Bullinger's Second Helvetic Confession would supersede the Rhaetian Confession.

In its first word about the role of a minister, the Rhaetian Confession spoke of baptism. A minister, the Confession asserted, was the only one who should confer baptism since a minister was entrusted by the Lord to preach, and that the Lord had specifically authorized apostles and ministers to baptize people and not just anyone so that the Lord's name and authority would not be taken lightly.[138]

In speaking about the qualifications and calling of a bishop and minister, the Rhaetian Confession lifted a high standard of education and the ability to teach and preach. The Confession used the term "bishop" and "preacher" interchangeably, placing the bishop as a local congregational preacher. The Confession cautioned against any hasty calling, electing, and imposition of hands upon candidates for bishop, requiring that corroborating letters from outside witnesses attest to the piety, faithful teaching, and abilities of the bishop candidates. The candidates were to be thoroughly examined by the Three Leagues of Rhaetia, so that the churches would be able to separate out mere rhetoricians from true preachers, the former being ones who could speak well about any "common tradition" but not have a grounding in human knowledge and Scripture. Thus, the Confession maintained that no one would be called to serve as preacher in Rhaetia "if he (sic) has not learned anything of fine literature and fine arts or, in the very least, does not understand the Latin language" for it was believed that preachers should be on par or exceed the knowledge of those outside the Church.[139]

Lastly, the Confession emphasized the necessity of collegial relations in ministry. Those who were chosen to serve as a bishop/minister in the Rhaetia region were not to neglect "fraternal gatherings" in synod. In fact, the Confession stipulated that if a bishop had three consecutive

138. Ibid., 684

139. Ibid, 690

absences from synodal gatherings, then disciplinary actions should be taken to address the chronic absenteeism.[140]

Interestingly, the Confession's final lines were words about the minister's responsibility in baptism. The minister was to enroll the names of the children who were baptized, along with the names of the children's godparents, in the parish books, "just as we often decreed."[141]

The Gallican (French) Confession of 1559[142]

Also known as the Confession of La Rochelle because of its adoption by the Seventh National Synod of the French Reformed Church in 1571, the French Confession of 1559 was the product of Calvin's collaboration with his Genevan colleagues (Theodore Beza, Pierre Viret, among others) as they revised an earlier 1557 version from French evangelical Protestants and presented the 1559 version to the first National Synod in Paris.[143] Calvin had been called upon by a group of French evangelical Protestants to formulate a draft confession for presentation at the Paris Synod. Persecutions that broke out in September 1557 in Paris prompted a group of evangelicals to prepare a brief statement of their beliefs to serve as an apology to King Francis I of France. They had also sent correspondences to Swiss Reformers requesting some intervention on their behalf with the French government.

Of 40 articles in the French Confession, it was remarkable that six articles dealt specifically with church orders. Article XXV asserted the necessity of the existence and function of pastors, calling the ordering of the Church "sacred and inviolable," and that when pastors faithfully teach, the Church had an obligation to receive them and listen.[144]

In denouncing the legitimacy of the Roman Catholic Church, Article XXVIII spoke of the two markers of the true Church—word and sacrament—while holding in tension the legitimacy of those baptized in the Catholic Church. The Confession emphasized, in a negative way, that where the word of God's authority was not acknowledged and

140. Ibid., 691

141. Idem.

142. *The French Confession of 1559*, trans. Ellen Babinsky and Joseph D. Small (Louisville, KY: Office of Theology and Worship, 1998)

143. Gerrish, "An Introduction," 19–20.

144. Ibid., 13

received and where the sacraments were not used in the right manner, then the credibility of the Church was to be put into question. It called the church of the papacy as one that "corrupted, bastardized, falsified, or annihilated altogether" the sacraments. But the Confession also conceded that there was some "small trace of the church" still left in the papacy and that because the efficacy of baptism does not depend on the minister, that those who convert from the Catholic Church to the Reformed faith were in no need of rebaptism.[145]

Article XXIX proposed a three-fold pattern of ministry: pastors, elders, and deacons. The Confession saw these orders of the church as functioning to insure the teaching and preaching of "pure doctrine," to correct evil and vices, to provide alms for the poor, to gather God's people for worship, and to equip the Church for ministry.[146]

Articles XXX and XXXI discussed the equality of all pastors and the calling of all church officers, respectively. With regards to the parity of pastors, they were to exercise their power and authority collegially with other pastors as they all serve under one "sovereign and universal bishop, Jesus Christ."[147] The Confession asserted that a church officer's legitimate authority and power to exercise the office was tethered to their legitimate election by the Church "as God permits." What the Confession does not delineate was what constituted God's authorization in election, whether the Church's election was tantamount to God's voice, or whether a specific process was envisaged that constituted the manner in which God would permit the selection of the candidate; such questions were left unanswered by the Confession. The Confession recognized the rare and extraordinary circumstances where God raised up leaders without a duly called election when the Church was in a state of emergency, but the *modus operandi* of church order, asserted by the Confession, was that all pastors, elders, and deacons were to be elected.

Finally, in Article XXXII, the Confession asseverated local, communal discernment of a flexibility of options for the right and appropriate church order suitable for a given context. The Confession called it "good and useful" for all elected church officers to determine together the polity for the whole church, with the caveat that such determination was not to be at variance with anything that Jesus Christ has ordained.

145. Ibid., 14

146. Idem.

147. Idem.

Then it concluded, that such a stipulation did not discount "distinctive local regulations required by particular circumstances."[148]

Noteworthy in the French Confession are two distinctive characteristics. First, the Confession does not prescribe the norm by which election of church officers was to be conducted, nor is the manner of ordination even addressed or what even constitutes a proper mode of ordination. Second, while the threefold form of ministry—pastor, elder, deacon—are mentioned, what seems to be of greater importance in this Confession is the fact that the Church is ordered, that the church officers work together, that the functions of ministry are faithfully attended to, and that great latitude was granted for the collegia of officers to discern and determine what was suitable for their given contexts. That the Confession obtained synodal approval, and was the product of collaborative work involving Calvin and other Swiss Reformers as they considered the 1557 brief statement of faith of the Paris congregation, are instructive for our purposes when we discuss not only the nature of Reformed confession, generally, but what methods were being prescribed and what methods would be helpful in our present context in crafting a theology of presbyteral ordination.

Belgic Confession (1561)

Continental Calvinism and churches that are Reformed orthodox in character subscribe to what is called The Three Forms of Unity—the Canons of Dordt, the Heidelberg Catechism, and the Belgic Confession. Of these three, only the Belgic Confession contained explicit statements on church orders. The *Confesio Belgica* was written by the French Reformer Guy de Brès (†1567) for the Churches in Flanders and the Netherlands, and adopted by a Reformed Synod in Emden in 1571 and the National Synod of Dordt in 1619.[149]

Article XXX addressed the government of the Church. The Belgic Confession asserted that the Lord had instituted ministers or pastors to preach the Word of God and administer the sacraments, and that together with the elders and deacons, govern the life of the Church, insuring the teaching and preaching of true doctrine, the correction

148. Idem.

149. Schaff, *Creeds of Christendom*, 383.

of false doctrine and messengers of the same, and providing care and comfort for the poor.

As to the calling of ministers, elders and deacons, the Belgic Confession urged that no person enter the ordained ministry in haste. Article XXXI prescribed that the election of officers by the Church be done lawfully, viz. according to the Word of God, and that ordinands ought to wait for God's calling so as to be assured of God's call and not by one's own subjective sense of call. Ministers are equal to one another and ought to treat one another as equals for they are ministers of Christ and, therefore, serve under "the only universal Bishop and the only Head of the Church."[150] Because those who are elected by the church as "ministers of God's Word" and elders were called by God, the Church should highly esteem them and receive them.

The Irish Articles of Religion (1615)

The Irish Articles of Religion were probably composed by Archbishop James Ussher (then professor of divinity in Dublin) and adopted by the archbishops and bishops in convocation at the Irish Episcopal Church and approved by the Viceroy in 1615, four years before the Synod of Dordt. These Articles served as an accurate gauge of the "prevailing Calvinism" in the Irish church, as well as a link between the Thirty-Nine Articles of the Church of England and the Westminster Confession of Faith, serving as a primary source of the latter.[151]

The Irish Articles, in classic Reformed formulation, drew a distinction between the visible and invisible church. To distinguish the true visible church, the Irish Articles lifted up the Reformed *nota ecclesiae* of faithful preaching of the Word of God and administration of the sacraments, as well as utilization of the "authority of the keys" (discipline).[152]

Those who serve as ministers of the Word and Sacrament derive their authority and power from God. Paragraph 71 stated that only those properly sanctioned, commissioned, and sent by likewise duly authorized ministers have the full blessing to serve as ordained officers.[153] God granted to ministers the power and authority to forgive sins and

150. Ibid., 422.

151. Ibid., 526.

152. Ibid., 538.

153. Ibid., 539.

pronounce forgiveness, in the name of God, to those truly repentant of their sins.[154]

20th Century Reformed Confessions: A Quick Survey

Continuing our journey to provide a comparative analysis of the PC(U.S.A.)'s constitutional definitions of church orders and ordination with that of other Reformed confessions, we fast-forward to the 20th century, while noting the paucity of 18th and 19th century Reformed confessions, due in large measure to Enlightenment critiques. Theologian Jan Rohls noted:

> The confessional doctrinal systems collapse under the storm of Enlightenment criticism, and the Reformed churches adjust themselves to this development by either totally abandoning their confessions, reworking them, or formulating new ones.[155]

We direct our attention to a representative sampling of 20th century Reformed confessions from member churches of the World Alliance of Reformed Churches.

Common Comprehension of Faith (1967)-Council of Churches of Indonesia

"A Common Comprehension of Faith (1967) from the Council of Churches in Indonesia, although not officially adopted at the 1980 General Assembly at Tomohon, Sulawesi, asserted that the Church and its ministry were reflective of and participate in Christ's threefold office of prophet, priest and king.[156] The Indonesia statement of faith went on to say that the Lord was the One who raised up leaders through the calling of the Holy Spirit, that the offices of service (used interchangeably for "ministry") were to be used for the equipping and edification of the Church, and that all offices were equal to one another.

154. Idem.

155. Rohls, Preface to *Reformed Confessions*, 5.

156. Vischer, *Reformed Witness Today*, 36–37.

Basic Confession of the Karo-Batak Protestant Church (1979)

The "Basic Confession" of the Karo-Batak Protestant Church in Indonesia described the essence of the church, using the Nicene markers, as "holy, one and catholic" but conspicuously left out "apostolic."[157] The Confession's ecclesiology indicated that the Church's function was to glorify God in worship, especially Sunday worship, and to engage in ministry of "witness (marturia), unity (koinonia), and service (diakonia)." Then, in the concluding subsection on ecclesiology, the Confession stated that God appointed officials, with a citation to Ephesians 4:11, for the orderly conducting of the forms of ministry mentioned above.

Confession of the Church of Toraja (1981)

The 1981 Confession of the Church of Toraja proposed a Christ-centered, Christ-constituted, Christ-oriented ecclesiology. In the brief section on church orders, the Toraja Confession saw the ministers of the Church as specially appointed governors through whom Jesus Christ governed the Church. The function of the officers was to equip and order the Church so that the whole people of God can carry out their ministries in the world. The Confession asserted that the status, role, and function of the minister depended on his (sic) appointment by Christ and the degree to which the minister served obediently and faithfully.[158] The Toraja Confession stated that the "Catholic Church" was present where the Word of God was taught and proclaimed "in an orderly manner," where the two sacraments were administered, where the apostolic function of the Church was done, and where discipline was exercised; this, the Confession defined, constituted the community of the one people of God.[159] Neither this Confession, nor any of the previous statements from the Indonesian churches prescribed specific church offices nor the manner of selection and ordination of officers.

157. Ibid., 41.

158. Ibid., 55.

159. Idem.

New Confession (1972) of the Presbyterian Church in the Republic of Korea

The 1972 New Confession of the Presbyterian Church in the Republic of Korea stated that the theology, polity, and organization of the Church existed to enable the right, faithful, and useful functioning of the Church. With regards to the "institutionalization" of the Church, the Confession saw church orders as necessary to insure the Church's "effective missionary work."[160] Church officers are to teach and preach the Gospel, administer the sacraments, and provide pastoral care. The Confession noted that those called to serve as officers had to have "specialized training" and have the ability to "act with authority." Then, the Confession concluded the section on church offices by reminding that people are redeemed for the purpose of becoming a part of the priesthood of God and the holy community of God, and evidence of one's faithful membership in that priesthood was engaging in the missionary task of the Church.

A Declaration of Faith (1967) – Congregational Church in England and Wales

"A Declaration of Faith (1967)" of the Congregational Church in England and Wales viewed ministry in two aspects: ministry of witness and service as embodied by the corporate ministry of the whole Church in its work in the world, primarily through the mission of local congregations; and the ministry of "those set part to lead the Church" through worship, teaching, preaching, ordering and equipping.[161] The Declaration viewed the true embodiment of God's grace when the Church, collectively and as individual members, "cares wisely and deeply for the lives of individual men and women" and for the well-being of the common good, as well as when those who are church officers lead and equip the Church in its faith and life.[162]

In addressing the issue of church orders and ordination, the Declaration noted the deep disagreements over normative ordering of church offices. In doing so, the Declaration asserted that God still

160. Ibid., 82.

161. Ibid., 145.

162. Idem.

uses the divided Church to carry out ministry. The Declaration stated that divisions over church orders threaten unity and that the Church gets into trouble when "one and only one mode of authorization" is desired as the norm for all church orders, calling such divisions "an offence against Christ and his Gospel."[163] There is no particular ordering of ministry, the Declaration asseverated, that can insure the fidelity of the Church to the Lord's calling. No matter what ordering of ministries there are, the Declaration maintained that those who are called to serve as church officers are to be carefully trained and "appointed with due solemnity" with the recognition of the whole Church.[164]

Basis of Union (1965) – Ghana Church Union Committee

The "Basis of Union" provided the theological framework for union discussions among the Presbyterian Church of Ghana, the Evangelical Presbyterian Church of Ghana, the Accra Diocese of the Church of the Province of West Africa (Anglican), and the Methodist Church of Ghana.[165]

The "Basis of Union" used the master image of body to describe the Church and its officers. Because of the Church's union with Christ, every member shares in the ministry of Christ, with the Church as being the continuation of Christ's ministry in the world.[166] The Church was sent into the world as the triune God sent Christ into the world. Through the presence and power of the Holy Spirit, testifying of the same Gospel, and receiving and giving the same apostolic tradition, the Church continues the apostolic mission. Within the body of the Church, church officers are set apart by ordination, serving as an "organ" of the body with Christ as the head; the church officers are called by God to equip the Church for ministry. The Basis of Union asserted that the ordained ministry is a gift of God to the Church, that God calls individuals to the ministry of Word and sacrament, and that through ordination, they are set apart for ministry. The Basis envisioned ordination as the act by which the Church, through prayer, confirmed the call of God and accepts the one who is being called, and in ordination God bestows God's

163. Ibid., 145.

164. Ibid., 146.

165. Ibid., 270.

166. Ibid., 276.

grace to enable the ordinand to serve. Because ordained ministers belong to God's community, they serve the community through teaching, preaching, administering the sacraments, discipline, and pastoral care; unfaithfulness or neglect of these core functions would "endanger the good order and witness of the Church" and, consequently, necessitate the Church withdrawing the minister's authority.[167]

The Basis of Union proposed two sets of ministry offices: ordained ministry and ministry of the laity. Under ordained ministry, the Basis of Union proposed bishops, pastors, and deacons. Under the ministry of the laity, there would be elders, lay preacher, and catechist. Interestingly, while elders were recognized to serve in higher governing bodies, serve in the local governing body, and share in pastoral care and oversight of the local church, elders were categorized with ministry of the laity; whereas deacons were designated as assistants to the pastors, and that a pathway to becoming ordained as a pastor would be through service, first, as a deacon.[168]

Constitution (1965) – United Church of Zambia

The United Church of Zambia's Constitution emphasized the responsibility of the whole church in its ministry as the priesthood of all believers. The ministry of the whole church—in its priestly, pastoral, and prophetic dimensions—derives its authority from and reflects in its life and work the ministry of the risen Christ.[169]

The Constitution envisaged two offices of ministry: ministry of the laity and ordained ministry. Under the ministry of the laity, the Constitution recognized the offices of lay preacher, elder, evangelist, deaconess, steward, and other lay ministries recognized by the regional presbytery.[170]

In terms of the ordained ministry, the Constitution did not delineate the names of specific offices under the category of ordained ministry, but addressed the general category of ordained ministers. The Constitution understood ordination to be the act by which God, responding to the Church's prayers, bestowed and assured the ordinand

167. Ibid., 277.

168. Ibid., 280.

169. Ibid., 298–299.

170. Ibid., 299–300.

of God's grace to serve. Ordination included the Church's acceptance of the ordinand for ministry. The ordained ministry derives its power, authority, status, and function from Christ and the apostles through the Holy Spirit.[171] The ordained ministry is to serve for the whole Church and not for itself, preaching, teaching, providing pastoral care, prayer, and exercising collegial governance for the order, life, and witness of the Church.[172]

The Constitution proposed a process for selection of candidates for the ordained ministry and the manner of ordination. Ordinands were to undergo a period of preparation and training, which included a time of service as a lay preacher; securing a commendation from the local, district, and regional judicatories, passage of tests required by the national Synod; and a period of time as a probationer and licentiate, during which time theological education and working under the supervision of an ordained minister are undertaken.[173] Ordination was to occur at a special called meeting of the national Synod for the sole purpose of ordination, after the prescribed time of service as a licentiate. Ordination involved prayer and imposition of hands.[174]

Basis of Union – Church of South India (1941)

The Church of South India grounded the Church's derivative ministry to the constitutive ministry of Jesus Christ. The ministry of the whole people of God continues Christ's priestly work through the Church's life and word. The ordained ministry, the Basis of Union stated, was given by God, called by God, and set apart in the Church to serve in and for the Church, through Word and Sacrament in order to lead God's people in worship and prayer, to call sinners to repentance, to provide pastoral care, to preach and teach the Gospel, and to administer the sacraments.[175]

The Basis of Union proposed that ordination was God's answer to the Church's prayer. In ordination, God and the Church act: God grants grace and assurance to the ordinand of the calling to serve and enables

171. Ibid., 300.

172. Ibid., 301.

173. Ibid., 302.

174. Ibid., 303.

175. Ibid., 329.

the ordinand to fulfill the service; the Church prays to God and accepts the ordinand for the specific form of ministry to which the ordinand is being called.[176]

The Church of South India proposed that there are three dimensions in the life and ordering of the Church: episcopal, presbyteral, and congregational. This was a somewhat different ordering than the classical threefold form of ministry of bishop, presbyter, and deacon. Here, the Church of South India placed the diaconal ministry upon the whole congregation; how a congregation cared for its members, insured the preaching and teaching of pure doctrine, the ordering of worship – all of these functions were to be done by the congregation in partnership with the pastoral leadership; how specifically such ordering of ministries was to be done in the congregational context was left open.[177]

The presbyterate, as envisioned by the Basis of Union, was akin to the early church presbyter, which functioned as the local church pastor. Presbyters were expected to share in the governance of the Church alongside bishops and lay members. They were to be the "dispensers of His (God's) Word and Sacraments" and edify and equip the Church for ministry.[178]

The Basis of Union remained open to flexible understandings of the episcopate. The Church of South India envisioned bishops to be "chief pastor and father in God" by providing oversight and care for Christ's flock. The Basis of Union did not commit the Church of South India to any one understanding of the episcopacy, but held to two key principles. Firstly, that the Church of South India agreed that the episcopacy as a form of polity existed since the early church, in that sense its use of the episcopacy can be considered as continuing in the historic episcopacy. Secondly, the Church of South India saw the episcopacy as a necessary office that, in its status and role, was needed for the "shepherding and extension" of the Church.[179] Moreover, ordination of presbyters was to occur with the imposition of hands by both bishops and presbyters, and the consecration of bishops was to be conducted by at least three bishops.

176. Ibid., 329.

177. Ibid., 330.

178. Ibid., 330–331.

179. Ibid., 332.

Constitution (1965)—Church of North India/Pakistan

For the Church of North India/Pakistan (CNI), ministry was entrusted to the Church by God, and therefore, the ordained ministry functions as part of the whole body.[180] In ordination, God responds to the Church's prayer, by granting and assuring the ordinand of God's grace to fulfill the special tasks that the ordinand is being commissioned to. Because the ordained ministry derived its authority, power, status, and function from Christ and the apostles, empowered by the Holy Spirit, the ordained ministry is sustained by Christ in the Church. A minister represents the Church to the whole, as the minister also represents the whole to the Church.[181]

In terms of church orders, the CNI prescribed the classic threefold form of ministry: bishop, presbyter, deacon. The CNI delineated the manner of ordination: a bishop ordained deacons through prayer and imposition of hands; bishops and presbyters ordain other presbyters through prayer and imposition of hands; at least three bishops and, in cases where the Diocese so desires and chooses, presbyters consecrate other bishops with prayer and imposition of hands.

The CNI emphasized the collegial and communal character of the selection, training, and appointment of ministers, as well as in all matters of general governance. The Diocesan Council was to oversee the process of training and education of candidates for ministry, who would have served a probationary period as deacons. The appropriate committee of the Diocese would then recommend the probationer to the bishop for ordination and appointment.[182] In terms of episcopal oversight and the episcope of the Church, this was to be done not only personally by the bishop, but in tandem with the collegial and communal ministries of other bishops, presbyters, deacons, as well as within the overall ministry of the Church.[183]

180. Ibid., 359.

181. Idem.

182. Ibid., 364–365.

183. Ibid., 365.

The Nature of Confessions in the Reformed Tradition

In the previous subsections, we looked at the constitutional documents of the PC(U.S.A.)—*The Book of Confessions* and *The Book of Order*—as well as the *Book of Occasional Services*, which is the liturgical resource that implements through the church's ordination liturgies the principles of ordination outlined in the constitutional documents. We have also surveyed confessional documents not contained in the *The Book of Confessions* but which come from the 16th and 17th Reformed heritage as well as 20th century confessions from Reformed churches from various parts of the globe.

What we see in juxtaposing these documents is a varied tapestry of ideas. *The Book of Occasional Services* represents the more mature expression of a Reformed theology of presbyteral ordination as it wove the various aspects of:

- God as the initiator of the Church's calling, and, consequently, of the Church's officers;
- Baptism as the ground of all ordinations;
- Ordained officers being called in and by the Church's voice, and, therefore, are responsible for the life, faith, and witness of the Church community;
- Emphasis on the whole ministry of the whole people of God and their participation in the life, faith, and witness of the Church community as well in the corporate participation in the act of ordination;
- Ordination involves the primary action of God and the cooperative/confirming action of the Church

When we compare these key components in the BOS with that in the BoO, for instance, we get a sense that the BoO is more concerned about governance and the essential role of the Church's role in calling, while downplaying baptism and Christ's constitutive role in one's call. Rohls noted how the Second Helvetic Confession distinctively divided the notion of priesthood to ministry, indicating that the priesthood belonged to the general responsibility of all Christians, while the ministry designated the ordained ministry.[184] According to Rohls, Second Helvetic

184. Rohls, *Reformed Confessions*, 239.

connected the "particular office of ministry" (minister) to the function (word and sacrament). Rohls commented that in the ecclesiology of Second Helvetic and the French Confession, right preaching and right administration of the sacraments are tied to the public office of ministry: "Its status as the fundamental particular office of ministry in the church results from the fact that right preaching and administration of the sacraments are the necessary and sufficient conditions as well as the marks of the true church."[185]

Second Helvetic recognized one ministerial office, under which the various functions of the Church are assumed. The one ministerial office of Word and Sacrament assumes the names and function of other offices such as bishop, pastor, teacher, elder.[186] The Confession does not divide the functions of the Church's ministry into different offices because in Second Helvetic's conception, the one office (ministry of word and sacrament) is the necessary and sufficient condition as well as the mark of the true church. Yet, this office is not the only function of the Church. As we saw with Calvin's Geneva Catechism and as we will see in the next chapter in our discussion on Calvin, whereas in the former he echoed Second Helvetic's proposal for the singular office of ministry of Word and sacrament, Calvin in his *Institutes* as well as in his *Ecclesiastical Ordinances* will propose a four-fold pattern of ministry of pastor, teacher/doctor, elder and deacon. When compared to the French Confession, which Calvin influenced, and its notion of three orders of pastor, overseer and deacon, we would need to view these offices not as offices, as such, but as functions. Likewise, the Belgic Confession spoke of three ministerial offices: pastor, elder, and deacon.[187]

All the confessions and constitutional documents were in agreement in rejecting any notion of a hierarchical view of Reformed church orders. Even in those churches, such as the Church of South India or the Church of North India, that adopted an episcopate, there is no sense that the bishop has autocratic powers; in fact, there were sufficient constitutional safeguards to insure that the bishop's power always remained in check by a collegia of episcopal and presbyteral officers. In Geneva, the Consistory consisted of pastors and elders; in the geographical contexts of the French Confession and Belgic Confession, the pastors,

185. Ibid., 239.

186. Ibid., 240.

187. Ibid., 240–241.

elders, and deacons constituted the church senate.[188] Thus, in the Reformed churches, governance is conducted on a collegial fashion, with functions distributed among three or four offices.

The calling, election, and ordination of officers differed depending on church-state status. In Geneva, the civil magistrates had to confirm those whom the Church elected. In the case of the Belgic Confession, the community elected the ministers of God's Word, the elders and the deacons. In the PC(U.S.A.), the congregation elects elders and deacons, and the local session ordains; in the case of ministers, a ministry context issues a call, but the presbytery ordains.

We also see different emphases upon whom should be called to ordained ministry. The early 16th century confessions and the 20th century confessions from churches in the Global South emphasized the upright character of the minister, whereas later confessions, and particularly the constitutional documents of the PC(U.S.A.) emphasized the function of the ordinand and the ability of the minister to carry out tasks appropriate to the ministry of Word and Sacrament. Early 16th century confessions, such as Farel's *Summary* or Zwingli's *Fidei Ratio* carried the shepherd image and shepherding theme forward to underscore the significance of the ordinand's character and outward comportment in complement to the tasks, abilities, and functions attendant to the office. With regards to elders or presbyters, the upright character requirement is downplayed and the emphasis is on the functioning ability of the elders, with numerous confessions, when discussing elders, do so by stipulating the governing relations elders were to have vis-à-vis ministers.

As for the act of ordination, what is involved in ordination differs. Some confessions, as we have seen, leave the question open as to what is involved in ordination. Calvin's ordinances for Geneva were cautious about the imposition of hands in ordination lest superstitious ideas proliferate among the faithful. The Second Helvetic, as well as the BOS, the BoO, and other confessions, stipulated that ordination involved prayer and laying on of hands.[189] In all confessions that spoke explicitly about ordination, ordinands are connected to a community and are called to service in a particular community. This is in contrast to the Roman Catholic Church notion of absolute ordination that confers the

188. Ibid., 247.

189. Ibid., 250–251.

office of priest to the ordinand, which may not necessarily be to a local ministry context.[190]

What is the nature of the confessions in the Reformed tradition? The late Jack Stotts, former president of Austin Presbyterian Theological Seminary, wrote that the Reformed tradition holds to an "open" rather than a "closed" confessional tradition. He summarized:

> A closed tradition holds a particular statement of beliefs to be adequate for all times and places. An open tradition anticipates that what has been confessed in a formally adopted confession takes its place in a confessional lineup, preceded by statements from the past and expectant of more to come as times and circumstances change. Thus, the Reformed tradition—itself a wide river with many currents—affirms that, for it, developing and adopting confessions is indeed an obligation, not option. . . . This "occasional" nature of a Reformed confession is as well a reminder that statements of faith are always subordinate in authority to scripture.[191]

In his 1923 lectures on the theology of the Reformed confessions at the theology faculty at the University of Göttingen, Karl Barth noted several key principles about the nature of Reformed confessions:

- Confessions emerged from a particular church, in a particular context, in a particular time – such particularity was the pathway to universal ecumenicity, in that while a confession did not explicitly seek ecumenical recognition for its statements, ecumenical appeal was the "quiet and distant goal for which one prayed and for which one ultimately worked;"[192]
- Each confession is a "singular work." None of the writers of the confessions sought to write a confession for all of the Reformed churches.[193]
- Confessional unity comes not by doctrinal uniformity in the confessions, but by adherence to the notion that doctrine in the church must be grounded on Scripture, which "defines not the confessional unity but the confessional freedom of the particular

190. Ibid., 251.

191. Stotts, "Introduction: Confession After Barmen," xi.

192. Barth, *The Theology of the Reformed Confessions*, 11.

193. Ibid., 12.

churches in their relationships to each other;"[194]

- Unity would be achieved not from above, as with some sort of "coordinating agency," but through horizontal and parallel relationships where freedom of movement was encouraged and differences were allowed so as to further critique and conversation. Barth noted Calvin's coining of the term "pia conspiratio" (godly compact) to describe the "fraternal and peaceful agreement" that linked the freedom of one another in the Reformed family;[195]
- One could write, if one were able and capable, one's own confession, but one could not insist that one's own confession was *the* Reformed position on the matter;[196]
- Only the early church ecumenical creeds are of a "higher order" and, thus, no Reformed statement is designated a "creed" but is called a Confession, Catechism, Consensus, Theses, Declaration, Article, or Summary;[197]

Barth concluded the following on the nature of Reformed confessions:

> The Reformed confessions are and desire to be nothing other than mere human confessional acts, over against which the revelation of God in Scripture also stands constantly as a given. . . . They are measures, significant actions, one might even say solemn gestures, carried out by believers or by those chosen by believers for the sake of the good order and edification of the community of God on earth. They are made available for examination, to prove themselves, and for discussion. They bear the marks of the occasional, of relatedness to a specific time and situation, of the unique. . . .They are all emergency measures, temporary bridges upon which one can proceed, necessitated by

194. Ibid., 13. At this point, Barth noted how 16th century Reformed communities were labeled as "Confessionists"(Confessionistae) because of the many personal and local confessions; the Reformed were content to be labeled as such. Barth further noted how Calvin's imposition of the French Confession of 1559 upon the French church was not akin to the pope's will being imposed but that it was rather a "fraternal and friendly form of help from church to church." (13)

195. Ibid., 14.

196. Ibid., 16.

197. Idem.

> the 'rationale of the times' (temporum ratione), without really being certain whether or not they will end in thin air.[198]

Yet, as the BoC affirmed, the confessions are standards not to be taken lightly, but to be heeded, taught, studied, and received for guidance for they are testimonies of faith of a tradition of faithful believers in many places across time.

Thus, the confessions in the Reformed tradition, both those that we have examined in the BoC, as well as those belonging to various Reformed churches in the 16th, 17th, and 20th centuries, while they speak with varied voices, sometimes with common patterns and themes, on this question of church orders and presbyteral ordination, because confessions themselves are isolated, unique, temporal expressions of a particular people's understanding of God's call and work in their context, the confessions, for this project's purpose, serve as a guide and not a norm. In other words, in support of the methodology that this book is proposing in terms of a Reformed theology of presbyteral ordination, we are supported and validated both by the diverse expressions that emerge from local church communities and from the nature of confessions themselves, namely they are not normative nor are they prescriptive for all times and for all places, but serve as a "higher order" resource to understand what one stream or current in the river, as it were, articulated a theology for a given moment.

Whether we speak of confessional and constitutional documents, or ecclesiastical and conciliar statements, we must include in the conversation the key theologians who directly or indirectly influenced the thoughts and theologies contained in those documents. While the writings of theologians cannot, in and of themselves, represent the whole of the Reformed tradition or *the* Reformed position on any given issue or doctrine, still their writings have influenced Reformed thinking. We now direct our attention to six representative theologians of the Reformed tradition, from the 16th century and the 20th century. It is their voices that we seek to listen to now.

198. Ibid., 20, 37.

FOUR

Reformed Theologians: A Survey

In this section, we will survey the thoughts of a representative sampling of theologians in the Reformed tradition from the 16th to the 20th centuries—John Calvin, Martin Bucer, Francis Turretin[1], Friedrich Schleiermacher, Karl Barth, and Thomas F. Torrance—as they discuss ordination and church orders.

The Reformed tradition began in the 16th century with that strand of the Protestant Reformation that took root in Switzerland (Basel, Zurich) and then to France.[2] Reformers took issue with the medieval Church's theological and liturgical tradition that emphasized sacramental efficacy through sacerdotal agency, specifically notions of Eucharistic sacrifice at the expense of the *semel pro semper* atoning work of Jesus Christ. They were concerned with at least four principal things:[3]

1. Although Francis Turretin was not included in the Field Site questionnaire, Turretin is being included here in order to gain the perspective of a theologian in the 17th century Reformed orthodoxy tradition. Jürgen Moltmann, who was included in the line-up of theologians in the Field Site questionnaire, will be brought into our discussion in the concluding chapter as his recent thoughts on ecclesiology are in line with Chapter Seven's concern for ecumenical implications moving forward. Note that this section seeks to hear from perspectives of the Reformed tradition's past, and in that light, all six of the representative theologians examined here are no longer living but alive to Christ.

2. Former WARC President and Princeton Seminary theology professor emerita Jane Dempsey Douglass observed that to do Reformed theology was to do so "in continuity with the classical Reformed theologians of the sixteenth century like Calvin and Bullinger, for example, and with the confessions of that tradition" in Douglass, "What is Reformed Theology?," 4.

3. Spijker, *The Ecclesiastical Offices*, 16–17.

- The Thomistic understanding of the *potestas ordinis* (power of order) that empowered priests to administer the sacraments and the *potestas jurisdictionis* (power of jurisdiction) that made believers worthy to receive the sacrament as both were linked to the church's power of the keys;
- The understanding of Christ being re-presented, and thus, re-sacrificed at the altar;
- The linking of sacramental grace with one's consecration into the priesthood, and therefore, the role and function of the Church;
- The opus-operatum framework that linked sacerdotal action with sacramental efficacy, virtually endowing both the sacraments and the priesthood with an objective-instrumental character, and, thereby opening up the way for priestly abuses in view of the essential significance given to priests as necessary and sufficient human instruments to vocalize the Words of Institution and enact the precise liturgical gestures in order to properly consecrate the sacramental elements.

These four theological points found liturgical expression in the high sacerdotal view of ordination as found in the pre-Reformation pontificals for the ordination liturgy:[4]

1. Eucharist
2. Presentation of Candidates and final enquiry
3. Litany and Special Clauses
4. Admonition to Ordinands
5. Imposition of hands by presbyters (in silence)
6. Bidding and Collect
7. Consecratory Prayer
8. Placing stole over the right shoulder of the candidate
9. Vesting with the chasuble
10. Bidding
11. Consecration

4. Ainslie, *The Doctrines of Ministerial Order*, 157.

12. Singing of Veni, Creator
13. Anointing of ordinand's hands
14. Delivery of "instruments" of ministry – chalice and paten
15. Second imposition of hands by the bishop alone with exsufflation
16. Kiss and Pax
17. Special Blessing
18. Exhortation

This eighteen point *ordo* was derivative of the four-point theological principles referenced above.

The Reformers, in emphasizing God's prior action and the derivative response of the Church, reduced the ordination liturgies to include, at maximum, fasting, prayer, examination of ordinand, sermon, imposition of hands, questions to ordinand and people, exhortations to ordinand and people, and a welcome. The Reformers sought to limit the potential avenues for superstitious practices and superfluous interpretations, while retaining the features of the *ordo* that included the whole community or which highlighted the role of the Word of God (sermon), or both.

We now direct our attention to the two principal theologians of the Reformed tradition in the 16th century—John Calvin and Martin Bucer—and their successors.

John Calvin (1509–1564)

Three years ago, Reformed churches all over the globe celebrated the quincentennary of Calvin's birth, a testament to the enduring influence of Calvin's theological insights upon the life and witness of the Reformed tradition for the last 500 years.

Born and schooled in France, Calvin studied at the University of Paris and law at Bourges and Orléans. It was at Paris that he encountered the renaissance humanists, Erasmus and Jacques Lefèvre d'Etaples, whose methods and pedagogy influenced him greatly, particularly humanism's *ad fontes* approach to scholarship, involving careful study of

Latin, Greek, Hebrew, classical literature, patristic writers, and the arts.[5] Calvin relied upon Scripture, as well as patristic writers' commentaries of Scripture and interpretations of early church practices, in much of his theological treaties and his own commentaries on Scripture.

It was at the University of Paris, under the influence of both Erasmus and d'Etaples, that Calvin's spiritual formation occurred.[6] Both Eramus and d'Etaples were committed Catholic humanists, seeking to reform the Church, not destroy it, convinced that only through the Bible can the Church be reformed, so said d'Etaples, the Bible was "the only truth that saves."[7] It was during this time that Calvin published his first edition of his theological treatise, Institutes of the Christian Religion.

The spirit of religious toleration was quickly dissipating by the early 1530s in Paris, leading Calvin to move on to Geneva, exiled from Geneva to Basel, to Strasbourg, and then re-invited back to Geneva. Calvin met Guillaume Farel when he was traversing through Geneva, and was forced to remain there. Both Farel and Pierre Viret were introducing the Reformed tradition in that city and wanted Calvin to join them. Farel and Calvin sought to have the Geneva council govern the city by Scriptural principles, and have the council cede the authority of excommunication to ministers.[8] In one such instance, Farel and Calvin insisted on fencing the Lord's Table from a man who had not heard preaching in a month, was seen in public gambling, and had joked to acquaintances that confession was for the "papists." For this, the Geneva Council, with the support of Anabaptist allies, exiled Farel and Calvin.[9]

Calvin traveled to Basel, then was invited by Martin Bucer to serve in the Strasbourg Church, alongside Wolfgang Capito and Matthew Zell.[10] Calvin's time in Strasbourg with Bucer would be very influential on his thoughts, as we will see in the next section on Bucer. He expanded the *Institutes* during his time at Strasbourg.

Three years later, Calvin was invited back, and reluctantly accepted to return to Geneva on September 2, 1541, calling the city a

5. Bouwsma, *John Calvin*, 9–10.

6. Ibid, 12.

7. Ibid., 13.

8. Ibid., 19–20.

9. Idem.

10. Ibid., 21.

"great abyss" because of the political and religious intrigue that he knew awaited him. During the tumultuous years he spent in Geneva after his exile, Calvin devoted the rest of his life and time there in diligent study of Scripture and the publication of his commentaries.[11] Prior to his return to Geneva, he also issued a *Draft Ecclesiastical Ordinances* for the ordering of the life and worship of the Genevan church.

Calvin's discussion of church orders and ordination emerged from his ecclesiology. He discussed orders and ordination in book 4 of his *Institutes* titled, "The External Means or Aims by which God invites us into the society of Christ and holds us therein." Upon the Church, therefore, was laid the responsibility and task, enabled by God, to summon the world through its ministries, with ordained ministers having the responsibility to equip the church through proclamation and teaching of the word of God.[12] Calvin viewed the preaching of the gospel and administration of the sacraments as the "power of the keys" by which forgiveness of sins was declared to all those who abided in the "communion of the church."[13] He went further in asserting that the mutual relationship of pastor to church, or teacher to pupil, as a bond that "fosters mutual love more fittingly."[14]

Calvin suggested a four-fold pattern of ministry for the Geneva church. In upholding the Reformed emphasis on the church's ministry of the Word and Sacrament, he saw that ministry divided into four offices: pastor, doctor, elder and deacon.[15] In practice, the office of doctor was merged with pastor seeing that a pastor could also be a doctor,[16] but Calvin was also careful to delineate that the office of doctor was a distinct office that had the important roles of training future pastors as well as securing the purity of the Church's doctrine.[17]

11. Ibid., 28.

12. Calvin, *Institutes*, 1017.

13. Ibid., 1036.

14. Ibid., 1054.

15. Calvin, *Draft Ecclesiastical Ordinances*, 58.

16 von Allmen, *Le Saint Ministère*, 169–170.

17. Calvin, *Draft Ecclesiastical Ordinances*, 60. The definitive writing on the teaching office of doctor remains Henderson, *The Teaching Office in the Reformed Tradition: A History of the Doctoral Ministry* (Philadelphia: The Westminster Press, 1962). Henderson contended that the doctrine of the teaching office or the office of doctor was formulated by Calvin during his stay at Strasbourg. Calvin was involved in both the ecclesiastical and educational sectors of Strasbourg, receiving a part-time lecturer

In speaking of the four-fold pattern of ministry, Calvin viewed the patterning of ministry as, in Small's terms, "undivided plural ministry." That is, each of the offices exercised various aspects of the ministry of the Word and Sacrament tasked to the Church by Jesus Christ, such as preaching, teaching, administration of sacraments, government, almsgiving, but that all of the offices functioned together towards the common calling given to the Church. Calvin considered the preaching office as sacred and a "singular benefit upon men (sic)" to be given the privilege to proclaim the word of God.[18] Calvin indicated there were permanent and temporary offices, which we will see below, but of all of them, pastors and teachers were offices the church "can never go without," and that between the two, the pastoral office included all the functions entrusted to the Church.[19]

The calling of pastors required a careful process of collegial and communal relations.[20] For Calvin, it was important to maintain the role of the whole people of God in selecting their pastors, while at the same time, enabling the collegium of pastors, what Calvin called the Company of Pastors in Geneva, to discern, select and welcome into their fold a future colleague in their midst. The Company of Pastors was the body to which elected and ordained pastors would have membership, within which they would be encouraged in ministry, collaborate through study, prayer and discussion, and receive as well as offer mutual discipline and fraternal correction. The named candidate would then be presented to the congregation for their confirmation vote.[21] In this way, both the collegium of pastors and the whole church had ownership and participation in the selection of the pastors. The Consistory, composed of lay elders and the ordained ministers, served as the ecclesiastical court to persons summoned there by the Genevan city council; the Consistory had the ability to adjudicate only ecclesiastical issues, not anything that fell under the civil jurisdiction.

appointment from 1539–1541. (pp. 39–41) Henderson summarized Calvin's view of the office of doctor: "that Calvin regarded the doctorate as part of the church's ministry, that he regarded it as a function distinct from the pastorate, and that he conceived of it as functioning in an academic arena." (41)

18. Calvin, *Institutes*, 1055.

19. Ibid., 1057.

20. Calvin, *Draft Ecclesiastical Ordinances*, 58.

21. Calvin, *Draft Ecclesiastical Ordinances*, 59; Calvin, *Institutes*, 1066.

In speaking of pastors and elders, Calvin discussed a double-presbyterate. In combing relevant passages of the New Testament and patristic writings, Calvin latched onto the term "presbyter" and spoke of two presbyters: pastors or ministers, and elders. In other places, Calvin was free in interchangeably using the terms "pastors," "ministers," or "bishops."[22] The coordinate function of pastors and elders was to provide for the spiritual welfare of the church and to govern the church together. Calvin was clear in saying that pastors belong to a local community, that they are called to and by a community and must focus their ministry on a local context, in contradistinction to what he saw as the perceived abuses in the Roman Catholic Church of priestly ordinations to the order of priests and not to a particular context or parish.

While connecting the undivided plural ministry of the double-presbyterate, Calvin was careful to delineate and distinguish the differences in function of ministers and elders. Calvin used key Scriptural texts to speak of temporary and permanent offices, indicating that those New Testament offices that were necessary for establishing the Church were the temporary offices, while the ones needed to maintain the Church through government, liturgical and pastoral leadership, were the permanent ones.[23] So, in his conception, the four-fold offices embodied the permanent, timeless functions of the Church: proclamation of the Word, administration of the sacraments, discipline, diaconal service. Without these, core functions and the offices attendant to them, the Church would not survive; the Church would cease being the Church.

Ministers carry in their offices all of the other functions of the other three, even as their primary function was Word and Sacrament, while elders functioned for government and spiritual discipline. Ministers of Word and Sacrament, in Calvin's conception, gave primary, though not exclusive, attention to preaching and teaching the word of God, study, prayer, administration of the Sacraments, pastoral care, and collegial relations with other ministry colleagues. This did not prevent

22. Calvin, *Institutes*, 1060, 1069–1070. Elsewhere, Calvin unambiguously asserted that "the name *bishop* is common to all the ministers of the Word, inasmuch as he (St. Paul) assigns several bishops to one Church. The titles, therefore, of *bishop* and *pastor*, are synonymous" [Calvin, *Commentaries on The Epistles of Paul the Apostle to The Philippians, Colossians, and Thessalonians*, 23.] He made the same assertion in his commentary on 1 Timothy 3:1, 8; Titus 1:5, 7. [see Calvin, *Commentaries on The Epistles to Timothy, Titus, and Philemon*, 75, 85, 290, 293–294.]

23. Ibid., 1056–1059.

nor did it limit ministers to just these core functions for ministers were responsible to insure, with the elders, that the church was governed well and the spiritual discipline of the church was maintained. Likewise, the pastors worked alongside the deacons in attending to the infirmed and poor.

Elders had their primary and exclusive role in government and church discipline.[24] What was significant in the Reformed tradition's exposition of church orders in the 16th century was in granting to lay leaders core functions of church governance and spiritual discipline. While Calvin early on will identify the whole church as responsible for those two functions, he distinguishes the office of elder as the one that was primarily charged to insure that ecclesiastical affairs were maintained and provide oversight over the spiritual well-being of church members.[25] The term "ruling elder" used in American Presbyterian-

24. For a comprehensive study on the exegetical history of the key Scriptural verses that Calvin relied upon in explicating his understanding of the office of elder see McKee, *Elders and the Plural Ministry: The Role of Exegetical History in Illuminating John Calvin's Theology* (Geneva: Librairie Droz S.A., 1988). In her study she examined the Reformed understanding and Calvin's understanding of Romans 12:8, 1 Corinthians 12:28, and 1 Timothy 5:17. With regards to Romans 12:8, Calvin understood that as laying the foundation for "one who rules" in the ecclesiastical realm and one who was focused on moral discipline (50–51). Here McKee noted Bucer's important, singular contribution in establishing the office of elder through that verse, as well as providing the first cross-reference to 1 Corinthians 12:28 with the latter's discussion of "governor" in verse 28c, translated "forms of leadership"in the New Revised Standard Version (Lat. *gubernationes*, Gr. κυβερνησεις), prompting Reformed moves to distinguish the lay elders from the Christian magistracy. With regards to 1 Corinthians 12:28, Bucer and Calvin distinguished between the Latin word *opitulationes* (translated "forms of assistance" in the New Revised Standard Version) and *gubernationes* (translated "forms of leadership" in the New Revised Standard Version). According to McKee, Calvin and Bucer designate the former to mean alms officers or deacons and the latter to mean officers of discipline, a distinct office from the pastor or bishop (76). With regards to 1 Timothy 5:17, Calvin interpreted in two ways: the text provided the validation of the permanent necessity of the office of presbyter in the church; secondly, Calvin understood the text to distinguish between two kinds of equal presbyters – a lay colleague who served alongside the pastor but whose primary ministry was that of ecclesiastical discipline and government. (103–104).

25. Calvin, *Ecclesiastical Ordinances*, 63. In his commentary on Romans 12:8, Calvin was careful to not only distinguish elders as ones who ruled others by exercising discipline, but distinguished elders as ecclesiastical rulers from magistrates, stating unequivocally, "Paul does not speak of all kinds of rulers, for there were then no pious magistrates; but of the elders who were the correctors of morals" [Calvin, *Commentaries on The Epistle of Paul the Apostle to the Romans*, 463.] Calvin made a similar point in his commentary on 1 Corinthians 12:28 in comparing the ecclesiastical elders to

ism was an effort to carry over Calvin's notion of spiritual oversight, "rule" not as in monarchical governance but rule as in a measuring rod, wherein elders, together with ministers, were to measure or check on the spiritual health of members and exhort, encourage, chasten, correct, or in extreme cases, excommunicate unruly, unrepentant members.

Calvin saw the act of ordination as connected with God and with the community. While he did not condemn the use of laying on of hands during ordination, he did not encourage it either, but noted the historical use of it dating back to the early church.[26] He noted that he did not number ordination as a third sacrament, in large part because he could not see where Christ instituted that rite for all Christians, whereas baptism and the Lord's Supper were given to the whole Church and were necessary for every believer. He noted that the efficacy of laying on of hands, while historic, depended upon the work and presence of the Holy Spirit.[27] Ordination, for Calvin, was God's act for God calls and God provides the gifts for God's call; in other words, just as God has freely chosen human beings to carry out God's salvific work in the world, God calls upon the Church to confirm those individuals whom God has called to service in ministry. Ordination is God's call and the Church's confirmation of that call as the Church, through the discernment of the Church and its officers, calls individuals to serve for and in the community.

Of primary concern to Calvin, as with other contemporaneous Reformers, was for the Church to determine whether an ordinand had a legitimate calling from God to serve in the Church. Calvin distinguished between the external call and the internal, secret call; the former designated the voice of God as confirmed by the election of the assembly whereas the latter designated an individual's inclination,

the early church's senate that had the purpose of "keeping the people in propriety of deportment" and so he concluded that the government (Lat. *gubernationes*) in the text designated presbyters "who excelled others in gravity, experience, and authority." [Calvin, *Commentary on the Epistles of Paul the Apostle to The Corinthians*, 416–417]

26. Calvin, *Institutes*, 1067.

27. Calvin, *Commentary on the Acts of the Apostles*, 238, in which he stated " . . . we gather that the laying on of hands is a rite agreeing unto order and comeliness, forasmuch as the apostles did use the same and, yet that it hath of itself no force or power, but that the effect dependeth upon the Spirit of God alone; which is generally to be thought of all ceremonies."

motivation, and will to prepare for the ministry.[28] In speaking about the means of selecting, Calvin underscored that the "how" of the process was not primarily the processes and procedures, although he discussed that, but he desired for the selecting body to observe and possess "religious awe" in the act of choosing the ordinand.[29] Calvin believed that the community's examination of the ordinand was the "principal thing."[30] The examination consisted of inquiring from the ordinand their knowledge of Scripture, and secondly, whether they were "fit and proper" to communicate the word of God "edifyingly" to the people. The ordinand was required to confess the faith of the Church and, in private, to be examined as to the ordinand's knowledge of and fidelity to "the doctrine of the Lord."[31]

The second part of the examination concentrated on the ordinand's habits, character, and conduct to insure that the ordinand was of sound mind and a character of integrity.[32]

In discussing ministers and elders, Calvin also sought to clarify the distinct, but related relationship of the Church with the civil magistrates. Because church-state relations in the 16th century were permeable and in Elsie McKee's terms "coterminous," Calvin like his contemporaries found it necessary to clarify where the State's powers began and where it ended, and what was the role of the Church vis-à-vis the State. Calvin saw the civil magistrates as a necessary component of God's work in society in that civil magistrates, when functioning according to God's design for civil government, restrained evil, but it did so through the instruments available to civil authorities, namely coercion. What the civil government could do was to restrain or deter bad behavior, not instill repentance in the heart.

For matters of the heart, Calvin saw that as an essential task of the Church, and that primarily through its ordained officers, was to work alongside the civil government, not under it, to restrain vices in society

28 Ibid., 1062–1063.

29. Ibid., 1063.

30. Calvin, *Draft Ecclesiastical Ordinances*, 58–59.

31. "The doctrine of the Lord" designated an examination of a ministerial candidate's knowledge and adherence to Scripture and the Reformed interpretation of Scripture, most notably the Genevan Confession of 1536, written by Calvin for all citizens of Geneva and intended for their strict adherence.

32. Ibid., 59.

through the "power of the keys" in the ministry of Word and Sacrament and church discipline. Thus, in contrast to his Zwinglian and Catholic opponents who sought to blur the lines between the Church and State with the Church seeking to overcome the power of the State, Calvin saw that the Church must focus on ecclesiastical and spiritual matters. The Genevan Council saw it differently; it sought to sustain its power and authority over both civil and ecclesiastical matters.

Martin Bucer (1491–1551)[33]

The Strasbourg Reformer, as noted above, heavily influenced Calvin's thought.

We see the currents of where both Reformers shared similar views, such as their emphasis on the Church's union with Christ. Bucer's ecclesiology had two main features: the communion of the saints with one another and with Christ, and the person and work of the Holy Spirit.[34] It was his firm belief in both doctrinal realities that propelled his deep passion to seek the *via media* throughout most of his theological career, seeking to bring a rapprochement with the Lutherans and Reformed parties, particularly over the issue of the Eucharist. Bucer viewed the Church as the gathering of those redeemed in Christ, and in the Church believers formed a communion with Christ by the vivifying power of the Holy Spirit, Bucer applied those two doctrines to his views on church orders and ordination. He saw the ordained ministry as necessary for the life of the Church for he described the church as a fellowship gathered by the Holy Spirit composed of "clergy, ministers and people."[35]

Bucer established the theological basis of ministry upon the incarnation of Jesus Christ by linking the work of the Holy Spirit in an actual concrete congregation. Christ uses the ministry as a means of effecting

33. Martin Bucer's views on ordination can be found in *De ordinatione legitima ministrorum ecclesiae revocanda, D. Martini Buceri scriptum nostris temporibus perncessarium* (The very learned lectures of the distinguished Dr. Martin Bucer on the epistle of Paul the Apostle to the Ephesians, delivered at Canterbury in England in the years 1550 and 1551"); and *De vi et usu sacri ministerii, explication Martini Buceri* ("Commentary of Martin Bucer on the power and practice of the sacred ministry")

34. Stephens, *The Holy Spirit*, 174; also Van'T Spijker, *The Ecclesiastical Offices*, 354–355.

35. Wright, *Martin Bucer*, 57.

God's salvation in the world, and thus, just as God's presence was made real in the human Jesus, God's presence in Christ is manifested or mediated through the ministry of the Church and the tasks carried about, among others, by ministers.[36]

Because the Church is a communion of believers in union with one another and with Christ by the Holy Spirit, the church's ordered ministries belonged to the community as God's gifts to the community. Bucer saw that God called believers together to serve in the world, and that being a communion believers were to show this with mutual love and service with one another in worship, the Eucharist, the community's life, godly exhortation and discipline.[37] To order and enhance the community's life and witness, God gave the community gifts for ministry and gifts of office.[38] Christ is the "great Minister [who] does everything in the church, and to that end gives his servants a task and the power to fulfill it."[39] Bucer was careful to insure that in both the selection, election, ordination, and service of the ordained ministries, the Church was a full participant, whether it be through the elders who were laypersons, or through the Church's confirmation in the electing of the presbyteral leadership. Bucer was careful to seek the *via media* in speaking about the *vocation* of God, concerned that God's prior and originating call was underscored while showing that it was to the congregation that God in Christ has entrusted the words of God and given the Holy Spirit to the people of God in order to discern the will and mind of God in the selection of ministry leadership. Thus, Bucer sought to ensure that the ministry offices had authority derived from Christ to proclaim the word of God in a congregational context, while enabling a congregation to exercise its freedom as it discerned and followed the Spirit of Christ in the work of selection and ordination. In this way, it can be said "the minister and the congregation therefore jointly bow their heads before him who calls and enables."[40]

36. Van'T Spijker, *The Ecclesiastical Offices*, 379, 383.

37. Van'T Spijker, *The Ecclesiastical Offices*, 359–361, 367–368.

38. Unlike Calvin, Bucer included discipline as a third *nota* of the church. (see Ibid., 155). McKee noted that for both Bucer and Calvin, Ephesians 4:11–12 provided *the* textual support for the plurality of ministries of the Word (see McKee, *Elders,* 151, 155).

39. Van'T Spijker, *The Ecclesiastical Offices*, 366–367.

40. Ibid., 395.

Bucer envisioned a four-fold pattern of ministry, but like Calvin, combined the office of pastor and doctor. Van'T Spijker noted von Allmen's conclusion that Bucer saw the office of doctor as a specialization within the presbyterate to assist pastors with insights gained from study in the pastors' work of "care of souls."[41] Bucer saw the offices of pastor, elder, and deacon as undivided plural ministries of the whole Church. Bucer had no problem using the term "bishop" in speaking about pastors, though he understood that to be the elected president of the collegium of presbyters. Pastors/bishops were called "ministers of the Spirit," and with that term designated them as ones possessed and used by the Spirit (which Bucer used until the 1530s) or ones who possess and impart the Spirit (a complementary meaning that Bucer adds after the 1530s).[42]

In the act of ordination, he saw prayers of the congregation and the imposition of hands as essential elements, although, like Calvin, he was wary about the perceived superstitious interpretations that might be attributed to the laying on of hands.[43] Bucer was careful in pointing out that there was no automatic conveyance of the Holy Spirit by virtue of laying on of hands, but he was comfortable with the notion that the sacramental act of laying of hands was somehow connected with God's action of calling, equipping and sending.[44] As a sacramental sign, the imposition of hands, while not officially a sacrament, found its signification when connected to the words of promise and congregational prayers, thus, with the entirety of the ordination service.[45] Bucer, like his other contemporaries, formulated much of his ecclesiology as a negative reaction to the Roman Catholic Church and the medieval sys-

41. Ibid., 421.

42. Stephens, *The Holy Spirit*, 177.

43. Bucer discussed the imposition of hands as a practice used not only in ordination but also confirmation and reconciliation of those who have greatly sinned against the church. He asserted that the act of laying on of hands belonged primarily to bishops and presbyters. (Ibid., 59.) This point also raised in Stephens, *The Holy Spirit*, 193. Puglisi noted Bucer's statement that the imposition of hands signified "a disposition to assume in a holy manner a particular charge in the Church" and the "communication of the Holy Spirit" in entering that particular charge. Puglisi further noted that the imposition of hands was done in the presence of the Lord as the ordinand received the guarantee that the Holy Spirit would enable and assist the ordinands in fulfilling their responsibilities. (see Puglisi, *The Process of Admission to Ordained Ministry*, 46).

44. Stephens, *The Holy Spirit*, 195.

45. Van'T Spijker, *The Ecclesiastical Offices*, 407–408.

tem of church orders and Eucharistic sacrifice that they inherited. The careful examination of ordinands within the context of an ordination service was one such correction as Bucer sought, with the participation of both ordained leaders and congregational representatives, to insure that those so elected, ordained and duly commissioned to the ordained ministry were persons who were upright in character, who possessed the right doctrine according to the Reformed tradition, and who was able to carry out the necessary functions and tasks of the Church's ministry.[46]

The whole Church was present and involved in ordination as a rite as well as a process. Bucer's ordinal followed the Reformed Eucharistic celebration as the framework for ordination of new ministers, with an emphasis on *diakonia* rather than Luther's emphasis on priesthood. In both cases, Bucer and Luther saw the importance of the community's role and responsibilitiy.[47] This included an examination of the qualifications of the ordinand, a trial sermon, an election by the community, and confirmation by the civil magistrates.[48] The examination was conducted by a committee consisting of elders, the ministers of the Word, professors, representatives from the congregation, and representatives from the civil government; thus both the congregation was represented, and, through the collective voice of the presbyterate, theological educators, congregational and civil representatives, the will and mind of Christ might be better discerned.[49]

Six new readings were added to the Lutheran rites to show Bucer's understanding of the ordained ministry. Ephesians 4 and Titus 1 were required readings that showed his concern for the organization and basis of ministries; then there were optional readings between Matthew 28, John 10, John 20, or John 21, showing Bucer's emphasis of the personal qualities and character of the ministers.

46. In his *De Ordinatione Legitima* (On Restoring Lawful Ordination), Bucer had the bishop asking the congregation the following question in the ordination of presbyters:

> "but yet yf there be any of you, which knoweth any impedimente, notable cryme in any of them, for the whiche he oughte not to be received into this holy ministery."

[quoted in Van De Poll, *Martin Bucer's Liturgical Ideas*, 167.]

47. Puglisi, *The Process of Admission to Ordained Ministry*, 52.

48. Ibid., 41–42.

49. Van'T Spijker, *The Ecclesiastical Offices*, 400.

Then, continuing the Reformed concern that those who were candidates for ordination where thoroughly and properly examined by the whole church no less than the collegia of presbyters, the ordination service proceeded to a testing and exhortations. The assembly was given the opportunity to present any valid claims that might potentially disqualify the ordinand from office. If there were none, then exhortations were give to the ordinand, describing the pastor as a shepherding minister, a teaching on God's sovereign act and our dependence on God, and a final exhortation that the ordinand seek the Holy Spirit and conform one's life to that of Christ.[50]

The ordination was followed by another examination as to the ordinand's understanding of ministry, and then this was followed by another exhortation by the principal ordainor, or a representative from the collegia of presbyters. Then a silent prayer was offered by the community, followed by a prayer of ordination[51] from the presbyter (without imposition of hands), who was then joined by other presbyters, who then laid their hands upon the ordinand. Worship continued with a profession of faith and the Eucharistic celebration.[52]

The ordination prayer expressed Bucer's ecclesiology and church orders. The Church manifested the goal of God's salvation for the Church becomes the instrument through which the world is gathered. Thus, ministers are called and sent to serve this mission in building up the body of Christ, and thus, the power and ability to serve comes from the risen and glorified Christ, conceived as a continuation of Christ's ministry.[53] The prayer had an eschatological tone in its assertion that the Church through its ministers gathered and continues to gather "all who here and everywhere call upon your holy name."

During the epicletic portion of the ordination prayer as well as the benediction prayer that followed, the congregation and the presbyters invoked the blessing, guidance and protection of the triune God in leading the Church and the ordinands in their ministry, as they, empowered by the Holy Spirit who unites all of God's people in all times and places,

50. Puglisi, *The Process of Admission*, 43.

51. For the full prayer of ordination, see Ibid., 46–47.

52. Ibid., 44.

53. Ibid., 47–48, 52.

are used by God to fulfill God's work of building up of a people from the old covenant, into the new, inaugurated at Pentecost.[54]

Bucer's perspective on the episcopate came into full view in the fact that there was only one installation rite. There was no separate installation for bishops and presbyters. For Bucer, the bishop and presbyter were one, with the former designated as an elected presbyter, presiding over the collegia of presbyters as an equal with responsibilities to preside, convene and provide pastoral care and oversight. Thus, Bucer saw the plural ministries of the Church as essentially bishop/presbyter and deacons, or for the sake of specificity: bishop/superintendent/presbyteral president, presbyter-pastor (could be doctor), presbyter-lay elder, deacon.[55]

Francis Turretin (1623–1687)

Francis Turretin was a professor of theology at the Academy of Geneva, a representative of what has been called "Reformed orthodoxy," and who presented his systematic theology in the "elenctic" form, which involved refutation of points through a question-and-answer format.[56]

Turretin's ecclesiology, which shaped his doctrine of church orders and ordination, centered on three aspects of the term "church." The primary aspect was the ineffable action of God in electing some from humanity to be believers in Christ, called the "invisible church." A second aspect was the "external church" or what he called "a society of persons called by the preaching of the gospel to the profession of one faith, communion of the same sacred rites and observances of the same order." A third aspect was the governmental assembly of rulers and pastors, "who are furnished with a lawful calling and the power to preach the word in it, administer the sacraments and exercise holy discipline, so that all things may be done decently and in order to the glory of God and the public edification of all."[57]

In speaking about church orders, Turretin does not deny the legitimacy of bishops. For him, at issue for the Reformed churches as he saw it was not the "distinction of order or of polity" but the degree to

54. Ibid., 49.

55. Ibid. 50–51.

56. Turretin, *Institutes of Elenctic Theology*.

57. Ibid., 8–9.

which bishops were regarded as a higher order than other presbyters, as in the Roman church. He acknowledged the presence of bishops in "many Protestant and Reformed churches" who chose to have a bishop that acted as a preeminent presbyter among pastors, with titles such as "superintendent bishops, overseers, deans, inspectors," for the purpose of "preservation of good order." To the latter, he objected, saying that Christ did not institute the superior authority and power of bishops nor was it part of ancient apostolic practice, but was created by the Roman church.[58] In concluding his thoughts on the episcopate, Turretin noted that Scripture's references to bishop were synonymous with that of the office of presbyter, from which he inferred that bishops were first presbyters, and then elected by their fellow presbyters to serve as a moderator or president of the presbyterate.[59] While saying this, he noted that the apostle Paul does not mention the office of bishop in the apostle's enumerating of offices in Ephesians 4 because, as Turretin contended, bishops were a *primus inter pares* in degree, not in kind, and in that, to maintain order and convene the other pastors.

For Turretin as with his 16th century forbears, the general ministry of the Church and the particular ministry of the ordained officers originate from and are constituted by God's purposes and call. God calls people to salvation, and sovereignly chose to effect salvation through the ministry of human beings, primarily through the teaching and preaching of the gospel.[60] Turretin called pastors "ambassadors. . .stewards and dispensers of mysteries in the house of God. . . soldiers of Christ. . . laborers in the field."[61]

In discussing the nature of God's call to service, Turretin delineated the various aspects of call. He distinguished between the general call of God given to all believers, and the special call given to candidates for ministry. He then distinguished between the internal call of God in an ordinand's heart, and the external call that was issued by God through the instrument of the church.[62] Then, he further subdivided the external call by distinguishing between the immediate call of God (as when God comes to individuals directly as with the calling of the apostle Paul),

58. Ibid., 200.

59. Ibid., 201–202.

60. Ibid., 211.

61. Idem.

62. Ibid., 215–216.

or the mediate call of God (through the instrument of the church). He further made a distinction between ordinary and extraordinary call; the former designated the ordinary means that God used to call people through the mediating voice of the church or an assembly, whereas the extraordinary call was directly from God for a special purpose, such as in the case of the apostles where they had a special commission to establish the New Testament church in their encounter with the Lord in his earthly ministry.[63]

Turretin saw the electing of pastors as involving four parts: God's originating call, the presbyterate's selection, the civil magistrate's confirmation, and the whole church's consent and reception of the pastor.[64] Turretin refuted the Roman church's practice of having a single bishop selecting a pastor, and instead wanted to maintain the balance of the presbyteral collegium discerning who would join them in the ordained ministry, while insuring the voice of the people in the process as well as the essential role of the civil authorities in the coterminous milieu of Church-State relations at the time. Turretin insisted that the power of the keys was entrusted to the whole church and that by the whole church having the final word on the election of a pastor, it indicated that the pastor was called to serve the whole church.[65] He employed scholastic categories in speaking of the presbyteral, civil, and community participation: *formaliter* with regards to the presbytery in examining, electing, and ordaining; *eminenter* with regards to the Christian magistrates in approving and confirming, and *virtualiter* with regards to the whole Church in consenting, admitting and receiving.[66]

Like Calvin and Bucer, Turretin spoke of the temporary and permanent offices given by Christ. Turretin saw in Scripture that the foundational offices of evangelists and apostles were "extraordinary" and "temporary" whereas that of pastors were "ordinary" and "perpetual" in that the latter was always necessary for the governing and continual ministry of the Church.[67]

In speaking about ordination, Turretin only addressed the issue of re-ordination of those who left the Roman church to join the Reformed

63. Ibid., 217.

64. Ibid., 225.

65. Ibid., 234.

66. McNeill, "The Doctrine of the Ministry in Reformed Theology," 87.

67. Ibid, 232.

churches. He noted that while ordination was not a sacrament, reordination was not indicative of the invalidity of a former priest's call, but it was an act of "reformation and purgation. . . so that what is wicked and Antichristian may be separated from what is good and Christian."[68] He argued for the validity of the Reformation ministry and all those ordained in the late medieval church by virtue of their fulfilling Christ's command, rejecting false doctrine, and having the necessary gifts attendant to the office.[69]

Turretin, like Calvin and Bucer, asserted the distinction between ecclesiastical and civil powers and jurisdiction. In doing so, Turretin sought to critique the Roman church in what he saw as the papacy trying to assume to itself powers that appropriately belonged to the State. Turretin saw that the Church was instituted by God to attend to spiritual affairs, to a "sacred government and order."[70] With regards to ecclesiastical power, the Church had at its disposal three things: the power of imparting knowledge of the articles of faith through teaching and preaching; the power to create constitutions and canons for the good ordering of the church; and the power to discipline.[71]

What we see in this brief survey of Turretin is that, just like Calvin and Bucer, his ecclesiology involved Christ as head of the Church and the Church as the assembly of God's elect translated into a view of church orders as involving an ordered society of elect believers who were tasked to be obedient and faithful to the Lord and which had divisions of labor in the discharging of the essential functions and tasks of the Church.

Friedrich Schleiermacher (1768–1834)

Schleiermacher was a Reformed preacher with several churches such as at Stolp in Pomerania and the Charité Hospital in Berlin, a tutor to the family of Count Dohna-Schlobitten, a founding professor of theology at the University of Berlin, a university pastor and professor at the University of Halle, and a member of the Evangelical Church of Germany.[72]

68. Ibid., 243.

69. McNeill, "The Doctrine of the Ministry," 88.

70. Ibid., 274.

71. Ibid., 281.

72 For a summary of Schleiermacher's career see Redeker, *Schleiermacher: Life and*

Schleiermacher rejected the ecclesiology of the Enlightenment as well as what he called "old Protestantism." He felt that the former viewed the Church as only an association, just as a state and family, seeing the Church as a "juridical and social category." As an association, therefore, the Church functioned to nurture piety, to instruct and for moral education. He also rejected old Protestantism's emphasis that the Church was essentially an institution of receiving grace for salvation.

Schleiermacher, instead, proposed that the Church was a community of faith and life.[73] He viewed the community as preceding the individual but composed of free individuals who, together, constituted a christologically-pneumatologically constituted and centered community. Thus, the Church was established by Christ and continues through the work of Christ through the Spirit. In contrast to older Protestantism's emphasis on the preached Word of God and the administration of the sacraments, Schleiermacher saw these elements not as constitutive of the Church's being, but as essential means by which Christ through His Spirit in the communal life of the Church established, maintained, and animated the Church in its life and witness; for Schleiermacher, the founders of the Church were Christ and his Spirit.[74] Recall the Reformers' assertion that the identification of a true church was one in which the Word of God was faithfully preached and taught, and where the sacraments were administered in accordance with Christ's institution. He differed with the 19th century confessional movement that asserted that dogmatic confessions, more so than the gospel, were constitutive of the Church and served as expressions of an association's will and beliefs and, therefore, binding upon its members. Schleiermacher held to the belief that individual consciences could not be legislated or dictated to, and that unity in the faith could not be achieved through creedal decrees or statements.[75]

He viewed the role of Church and State as occupying distinct, but related goals. He sought to secure the Church's freedom and prerogative at deciding upon spiritual and ecclesiastical matters. This came to a head when in 1817 a serious theological and liturgical dispute erupted over the Prussian king Friedrich Wilhelm III's desire as a Reformed

Thought, trans. John Wallhausser (Philadelphia: Fortress Press, 1973)

73. Ibid., 188.

74. Idem.

75. Ibid., 189.

believer to celebrate the Lord's Supper with his Lutheran wife. On October 30, sixty-three clerical officials from Berlin, including pastors and the entire theology faculty of the University of Berlin, gathered at the Berlin synod with an official declaration that, in one swoop, set aside the historic theological differences over Lutheran and Reformed interpretations of the Lord's Supper, called for churches and individuals to recognize Christ more than the "disputed incidentals," and saw that in the words of Christ "every individual can become aware of his full conception."[76] Throughout this time, while Schleiermacher was more than willing to assist the Prussian king as a means to advance unity among the Lutheran and Reformed churches and even participated in discussions on ecclesiastical union and drafted papers on united worship forms, Schleiermacher was concerned that any attempt at liturgical or confessional uniformity would have two unbeneficial effects: the flattening of real differences between Lutheran and Reformed ecclesiologies and a coerced unity through confessions. For him, while confessions were important in expressing the theology of forbears as well as the present, Schleiermacher believed that the Church was not something individuals decided to form by getting together, nor was it a union of individual believers; rather he saw the divine foundation of the Church through Christ and his Spirit, not through confessional formulations.[77]

Then in 1822, royal encroachment into the Church's affairs came through a liturgical dispute. At issue was Friedrich Wilhelm's desire to have a liturgy he and his advisors developed to be introduced into the Church; only a sixth of the Prussian clergy agreed to accept the king's liturgy.[78] The conflict concluded seven years later through a rapprochement in which the government *allowed*, through liturgical commissions, the use of certain portions of orders of worship among churches in individual Prussian provinces. In exchange, Schleiermacher was granted the freedom to use pericopes of the king's liturgy for Schleiermacher's congregation, but was not obligated to it by the letter. He demanded not to be obligated to chrismate as prescribed by the liturgy, nor recite the Apostle's Creed, nor offer prayers with his back to the congregation; in

76. Idem.

77. Ibid., 191–193.

78. Ibid., 195.

other words, he wanted to avoid anything that might be interpreted as a return to the Roman Mass.[79]

Schleiermacher saw the Church as a work of Christ in the Spirit. He envisioned two concentric circles: the outer circle was where the "called" were, individuals who come together to first receive and hear the preaching of the gospel; the inner circle was designated the place for the "elect" where those in the "called" outer circle receive the work of the Holy Spirit, were regenerated in the heart and then become part of the inner, "elect" circle, becoming a mutually interacting community.[80] Schleiermacher saw that the work of calling and electing was the work of Christ through the Spirit as the Spirit used the Word of God for "self-communication" and "self-presentation." As the Spirit works in an individual, Schleiermacher asserted the importance of an individual responding as "the recollecting and developing organ of Scripture," i.e. in accordance with Scripture lest "unchristian personal claims and separatist influences would break the fellowship in pieces."[81]

Individual responses to the Holy Spirit's internal work are linked to the Word of God and the ministry of the Church. Because individual responses to the Holy Spirit "must be traceable to the view of Christ in Scripture," the lives of individuals are "an offering to others of the Word of God" and therefore, are related to Christ's prophetic ministry, which serves as the foundation of the Church's ministry.[82] Schleiermacher spoke of the general, indeterminate ministry of all Christians, and urged that the distinction between the general and ordained ministries not be so sharp of a distinction and not impermeable. He sought a "both/and" arrangement of affirming the necessity to be open to what the Spirit will do in terms of ordering the Church and designating certain forms for certain times in the life of the Church, but also acknowledged the need for there to be a "division of labor" for the different gifts present in the Church in order for there to be "maximum of activity."[83]

Schleiermacher avoided speaking about definite forms of ministry, but discussed the relationship of the public ministry of the Church, the

79. Ibid., 198–199.

80. Schleiermacher, *The Christian Faith*, 533–534.

81. Ibid., 613.

82. Idem.

83. Ibid., 614.

clergy, and their relationship to those outside the Church.[84] He spoke of the public, general ministry of the Church as the external aspect and the clergy as the internal aspect, finding the origin of the clergy in the task differentiation that occurred with the apostolic commission, the appointment of Matthias as the twelfth apostle to replace Judas and upon whom the apostolic and diaconal functions were given by the Eleven, and the appointment of diaconal aides such as Stephen to attend to table fellowship while the apostles conducted the proclamation of the Word. Schleiermacher regarded this interrelatedness between the apostolic and diaconal ministries as the internal ministry of the Church emanating from and accountable to the external ministry of the Church, as the whole Church was accountable to Christ in the Scriptures.[85] The differentiation of labor and tasks was essential lest communication of the gospel would be "isolated and sporadic in character, and to all appearance fortuitous."[86] Thus, Schleiermacher concluded that not only the Church's worship, but also the public ministry, the ministers, and all those to whom they minister were always "subordinate on the one hand to the unity and identity of the Spirit in both (Church's public service and worship), on the other to the fact that both are directly dependent on Scripture."[87]

Church leadership consisted of edification in common worship, and government in discipline and ordering of the communal life.[88] He noted that pastoral work consisted of assisting the whole congregation in being community with one another, and that those who were lagging or "immature" had to become more receptive to the edifying

84. Schleiermacher designated a theologian as one who has "primarily cultivated knowledge concerning Christianity" and clergy as one who has "primarily cultivated activity which pertains to Church government" in Schleiermacher, *Brief Outline*, 6. But he noted later that both clerical and theological activities are "overlapping and coordinate." (138)

85. Ibid., 615. In §267 and 268 of *Brief Outline*, Schleiermacher noted that differentiation between the laity and clerical leadership occurred as the Church as a community matured and needed distinct formations of leadership lest the community devolve into mere relations between individuals or consist in "free-floating elements [that] could never operate as a whole" but needed leadership "for the purposes of stabilizing and advancing the community." See Schleiermacher, *Brief Outline*, 136.

86. Ibid., 616.

87. Ibid., 619.

88. Schleiermacher, *Brief Outline*, 142.

and regulative aspects of the Church's life through "quickening of religious consciousness" and then through "awakening into motivation for action."[89]

With respect to ecclesial authority and church polity, Schleiermacher noted the emergence of the Evangelical Church. He asserted that the Evangelical Church came about as a result of two tendencies: a differentiation of clergy and laity leadership, and what he called "discretionary," or the freedom of individuals to influence the whole. Thus, when a community issues a declaration, such a declaration or confession served as an "expression of the present spirit and disposition of the community," which was balanced with the free discretion of an individual or individuals who may seek to effect something new into the community's will and spirit.[90]

Schleiermacher concluded his discussion on ecclesial power in noting that the role of church government was to do two things: to preserve the received tradition of the "preceding epochs" while protecting the expression of spiritual discernment and innovation in the present. He viewed the exercise of "free spiritual power" as the source of necessary church reforms in every age, but he also advocated for some way that "free spiritual power" and ecclesial authority could find a rapprochement without diminishing the conviction of reforming agents.

Schleiermacher's advocacy for the necessary roles of ecclesial guardians and ecclesial reformers connects well with the aims of this project. He understood the importance of tradition and what prior ecclesial communities determined for their context what was appropriate and faithful for God's call upon them. At the same time, he saw the critical role of individuals within a community who may offer the voice of God's Spirit from the periphery, a necessary contribution to revitalize and reform the tradition. This project has similar aims in its advocacy for a methodology that accounts for both the "official" sources of theology in the Reformed tradition while including the voices of actual, local communities in theological discourse.

89. Ibid., 149.

90. Ibid., 158.

Karl Barth (1886–1968)

Arguably regarded as the greatest theologian of the 20th century, German theologian Karl Barth clarified Reformed orthodoxy's emphasis on the sovereignty of God, and on the other hand, provided a counterweight to what he regarded as Schleiermacher's neo-Protestant emphasis on the individual and the individual's experience of religious consciousness.[91] In doing so, Karl Barth hoped to shift the spotlight to the God-man, Jesus Christ, by and through whom God and humanity are known, and in whom the Church lives, moves and has its being.[92]

Whereas Calvin and Calvinists spoke of justification and sanctification as the two-fold benefits (*duplex beneficium*) of God's election and therefore the outcomes of God's eternal work, Barth saw that God's election, enacted through justification and sanctification, was for the purpose of electing us into the Church's vocation, which was to be witnesses of and for Jesus Christ. Stacy Johnson clarified Barth's thought on this point by proposing that Barth saw vocation as the lived experience of humanity as they sought to follow the call of Christ. What

91. Barth, with Emil Brunner, felt that Schleiermacher had subjected the Word of God to mere religious activity where the point of theology was to mediate religious consciousness and a pious life. Thus, in Schleiermacher's world, according to Barth, the human being "is left master and subject even of theology. Christ is only a predicate, a foreign body, a correlate of experience; God is wordless, ineffable, mysterious, nonobjective, *nuda essentia*, heartless, a neuter, an 'x,'" but, said Barth, even though his theology (Barth) "looked from above" and Schleiermacher "from below," Barth acknowledged that Schleiermacher was a "christocentric theologian." [in Tice, "Interviews with Karl Barth and Reflections on His Interpretations of Schleiermacher," 50, 55] In his interview with Tice, Barth acknowledged: "I always accepted him within the *communion sanctorum*, not as a heretic." (49)

92. See DeVries, *Jesus Christ in the Preaching of Calvin and Schleiermacher*, especially pp. 64–65, 97, 98–99, wherein DeVries dispelled the notion that Schleiermacher was less christocentric than either Calvin or Barth. On the contrary, says DeVries, "Schleiermacher, in the tradition of his Reformed forbears, puts the Word of God at the center of his whole system of theology" (98) DeVries showed how Schleiermacher, in fact, carried Calvin's Christology to a more understandable and coherent point by finding in the proclamation of the Word of God the *christus praesens* (Christ present) and that to speak of the "Word of God" was not to confine Jesus to the Scriptural text nor to the atoning transaction between Christ and the Father, but rather "Word of God," according to DeVries' interpretation of Schleiermacher referred to the "totality of his (Jesus Christ) to the disciples, including his submission to death on the cross. This Word saves not by imparting information, but by uniting the disciples with Christ. Words, in general, are what make intimate human relationships possible. Jesus' Word, then, is the instrument that mystically unites him with the disciples." (97)

this meant for Barth was that justification was presupposed because Christ's work of reconciliation was accomplished once *pro nobis* (for us). Sanctification was the consequence in that Spirit applies the work of redemption *in nobis* (in us). Vocation was the "historical fulfillment of election,"[93] serving as testimony of God's redemptive purposes and goals for our existence.

For Barth, as Johnson understood him, election and vocation were part of a "dynamic continuum" in which God elected humanity in Jesus Christ, but through the "exigencies of history" the way that prior election by God was experienced by humanity varied so that the lived experience of some was to hear and follow the call of Christ (vocation) and for others, they either did not hear the call or disobeyed the call; for Barth vocation was to live in service to Christ.[94] In contrast to Calvin and Calvinism's attention to election with regards to the eternal destiny of individuals to eternal life or damnation,[95] Barth shifted the spotlight with regards to election towards service and how God's call was experienced, received and responded to existentially.

Barth linked baptism and eucharist. In speaking of the confirming role of the sacraments, Barth underscored God's prior action and the sacraments as witnesses to God's work in Christ insofar as God uses the sacraments for that purpose. He stated: "In themselves, baptism and the Lord's Supper are creaturely, human practices like others."[96] But with the work of the Holy Spirit, the sacraments confirm faith to the gathered congregation which partakes of the sacraments. Barth referred to baptism as the sacrament of initiation, *sacramentum initiationis*, in its confirmation of the origin of faith and its past establishment in Christ; and the Lord's Supper as the sacrament of nourishment, *sacramentum nutritionis*, in its confirmation of "endurance" of faith, and its proleptic renewal.

93. Barth, IV.3.2, 484 cited in Johnson, *The Mystery of God*, 145.

94. Ibid., 146.

95. Barth noted that just because some may hear and respond to the vocation to live as a Christian it should not follow that we see the world as a rigid dichotomy of Christians and non-Christians for Christians are to have the posture of "an unlimited readiness to see in the aliens today the brothers of tomorrow." (Barth, IV.3.2, 494) When referencing Barth's *Church Dogmatics*, I will use the standard abbreviation, CD; the form, IV.3.2, designates volume 4, part 3.2, and so forth.

96. Ibid., 97.

In 1968, Barth articulated a "radically new view" of the sacraments in *CD IV/4*, which he sought to publish separately from the rest of the *Dogmatics*. The overall structure of *CD IV/4* was to, first, describe God's work of reconciliation in Jesus Christ – the Lord as Servant (IV/1), the Servant as Lord (IV/2), and the True Witness (IV/3); then, second, to describe the free response of humanity with its public starting point at baptism, continuing in the life of prayer, and sustained by the Lord's Supper (IV/4).[97] His chief concern was the following:

> My own concern is rather with the man who ought to come of age in relation to God and the world, i.e., the mature Christian and mature Christianity, its thought, speech and action in responsibility to God, in living hope in Him, in service to [in] the world, in free confession and unceasing prayer. As I see it, baptism with the Spirit and fire relates to the commencement of liberation for this Christian and churchly responsibility, and baptism with water relates to the entering of Christians and the community upon its discharge.[98]

Yocum summarized the significance of Barth's sacramental modification:

> The distinction of these two moments as a properly divine act of liberation and a properly human act of confession in gratitude is the signal development of Barth's sacrament theology that occurs in *CD IV/4*.[99]

Barth's departure from historic, orthodox theology of the sacraments was vitiating the term "sacrament" in describing baptism and the Lord's Supper. In doing so, Barth removed a category and important locus for effective divine-human action.

Barth's exegetical and theological methods led him to modify his sacramental theology in denying a sacramental place for baptism and the Lord's Supper.[100] In *CD/IV*, Barth exegeted the term musterion

97. Migliore, "Reforming the Theology and Practice of Baptism," 499–500.

98. CD IV.4 cited in Yocum, *Ecclesial Mediation in Karl Barth*, 146.

99. Ibid., 146.

100. In his preface to CD IV.4, Barth largely credited his son, Markus Barth, and the latter's exegesis of biblical passages:

> "A word must be said about the relation of this book to that of my eldest son, Markus Barth (*Die Taufe ein Sakrament? 1951*), who is by far my superior in specialized New Testament studies. I am surprised how easily exegetical and systematic theology has overlooked this work. Not so the aged father of its author! When my son was studying the literature available

(mysterion) from which the early Church translated that to the Latin "sacramentum," noting that "mysterion" as used in the New Testament denoted an event in the world in time and space of something that God alone brought to pass, and in distinction with other events, remained a mystery to human comprehensibility due to its origin.[101] New Testament instances which evidenced *mysterion* included the presence and divine allowance of demonic and ungodly powers in the midst of God's total sovereignty, or the reality of the cross as described in 1 Corinthians 2:7, which is concealed to some but revealed to others. Barth concluded, "Whether in the singular or plural the New Testament uses the term exclusively with reference to God's work and revelation in history, not to the corresponding human reactions."[102] This led Barth to describe Jesus Christ, the Revealed Word of God, as the only sacrament, for He uniquely attests to and reveals the triune God.

God sent Jesus Christ into the world, and the Holy Spirit sends and empowers the Church; the Church, therefore, participates and shares in Christ's work of transformation in the world. What this means for Barth was that the purpose of one's salvation was to participate in this outward orientation of one's calling, and such a calling is to be discovered not as an individual but in the community of the Church. Wilton summed up Barth's concern, and that of the 16th century Reformers: "For the Reformers, where the gospel is, there Christ is; and where Christ is, there is the Church."[103] Thus, God created the Church through Christ in the Holy Spirit precisely because of the Gospel.

For Barth, then, the church's ordering of ministry is at service to Christ's mission-orientation. The Church's vocation is to be sent, to be Christ's witnesses in the world. Jesus Christ is the head of the Church and the Church is animated by the work of Christ's Spirit, therefore the urgent call of the Church is to be faithful to the missionary tasks

---

at the time, he had to tell me kindly but firmly that 'not one stone was left upon another' of my 1943 work. This has been more or less my own finding too. In face of the exegetical conclusions in my son's book, I have had to abandon the 'sacramental' understanding of baptism, which I still maintained fundamentally in 1943, in so far as the reference is to the work of the candidates and the community which baptizes them." in Barth, *CD*, IV.4, x.

101. Barth, *CD* , IV.4, 108.

102. Ibid., 108.

103. Wilton, *As One Who Serves*, 321.

and functions of being a called out community, and not a focus on the names, number, and ordering of church offices.[104] Barth saw the call of God to believers as a communal calling, where the ministry belonged to the whole community as they discovered their calling in Jesus Christ, and as they mutually discerned the work of the Holy Spirit in ordering their life together. Thus, Barth was indifferent about offices, and underscored function at the service of Christ's mission when it came to discussing ecclesiology.

The Church is the "sent" witness of God to bear testimony of God's on-going work of reconciliation in the present world. It is important to emphasize that the present work of witnessing and attesting on the part of the Church is not to supplement nor complete the work of reconciliation accomplished at Golgotha and the empty tomb.[105] Rather,

104. Even though Barth is open to all forms of church orders in service to the Church's vocation of being Christ's witness in the world, Barth, in his characteristic fashion, shifted the focus not upon the Church's orders and offices, but upon Christ's *munus triplex* (the classical Reformed paradigm of Christological offices: priest, king, prophet). See Philip Butin's discussion of this in Philip Butin, "Two Early Reformed Catechisms, The Threefold Office, and the Shape of Karl Barth's Christology," 195–214. Butin noted Barth's use of the *munus triplex* in the framework of Barth's doctrine of reconciliation in CD IV, as Barth saw the exposition of the *munus triplex* in the Apostles' Creed as found in both the Geneva Catechism and the Heidelberg Catechism. For the *munus, triplex*'s applicability to Christ's work of reconciliation, the priestly office corresponds to justification, the royal office corresponds to sanctification, and the prophetic office corresponds to calling and vocation (Butin, Idem., 201). In doing so, Barth successfully linked Christology and pneumatology, as Butin summarized, " . . . believers not only receive and appropriate the benefits of Christ's threefold office through the Spirit; beyond this and yet included in it, we are joined by the Spirit to Christ in the exercise of that threefold office" (Butin, Idem., 211).

Recently, Butin drew the implications of the *munus triplex* of Christ's offices/ministries to the Church's shared ministry in Christ by speaking of the priestly, royal, and prophetic dimensions of the Church's own ministry [see Butin, "Christ's Ministry and Ours," unpublished paper submitted to the Ecclesiology Colloquium, May 11–13, 2009, Glen Ellyn, IL (March 28, 2009). Used with permission from the author] With regards to the priestly dimension, Butin calls for the church to become "places of welcome, acceptance, and reconciliation for all." (Butin, Idem., 15.). With regards to the royal dimension, the Church's exercise of power and authority should be reoriented towards the central truth that Christ is Lord and Head of the Church, and, therefore, emphasize the "ministry of the whole people of God" (Ibid., 17). With regards to the prophetic dimension, the Church is called to understand, share, and embrace "the whole mission of the triune God for a whole world," what Butin called "a fully-orbed biblical understanding of salvation" (Ibid., 22–23).

105. Hunsinger, "The Dimensions of Depth," 157. Here Hunsinger re-presents Barth's famous images of a circle with a center and periphery, and an ellipsis with two

the cross and resurrection provide the motive, basis, content, shape, and capacity for the Church to carry out the witness so that the whole world may know that Jesus is Lord and live out that credo with integrity and consistency. Baptism is God's gift, therefore, to the Church for in baptism the Church is united to Christ, participates in his work (here the term "co-operation" is appropriately used), to be with those with whom Christ dined, helped, and loved.[106] What Barth set out to do in his exposition of baptism was to establish that the initiation of Christian existence and its presence and work in active vocation originates *ab ovo* the history of Jesus Christ. Hartwell quotes Barth: "the *nativitas Christi* is the *nativitas homini christiani*: Christmas Day is the birthday of every Christian!"[107]

The expression of the Church's mission and identity belong to the interrelated responsibility of "mission" and "theology." In his 1932 lecture given at the Brandenburg Mission Conference in Berlin, titled 'Theology and Mission in the Present Situation," Barth spoke of his understanding of what "mission" and "theology" were and their relationship to each other. He conceived of "mission" as the work of the Church out in the world to bear witness of Christ to "heathen [sic]" who did not know of Christ and His saving work for them; "theology" as he understood it was critical reflection by the Church for the Church to insure the purity of the Church's mission: the why, how, and what. Both were needed, shaping and informing one another. One of the most important contributions that Barth made in speaking of the Church's mission and identity was the notion that the Church's sent-ness into the world originated from the doctrine of the Trinity: i.e. the "divine self-sending, the sending of the Son and of the Holy Spirit into the world. . . ."[108] This was in keeping with Barth's baptismal theology that placed in

foci. The former refers to salvation accomplished in the perfect tense, which means its present and future tenses are modes of receiving and participating in what was accomplished in the past. The latter refers to the Christ event that took place in the perfect tense, but the present and future tenses come alongside the perfect tense – either supplementing or fulfilling the process. Barth's position is the former; Calvin's, Wesley's, and Luther's *sola fide* would fall into the second category, according to Hunsinger. The perfect tense of Christ's work has already accomplished the present tense of justification, regeneration and sanctification. T.F. Torrance calls this "the dimension of depth." see Hunsinger, *idem*, 161.

106. Barth, "Baptism and Evangelism," 40.

107. Herbert Hartwell, "Karl Barth on Baptism," 16.

108. Barth, "Die Theologie und die Mission in der Gegenwart" (Theology and

the foreground the Church's vocation and very existence stemmed from Christ's own calling to be the Sent One, the Witness, or the Sacrament of the triune God.

Barth spoke of baptism as our ordination. In the fourth and final fragment of the CD, Barth discussed his baptismal theology and spoke of baptism with the Holy Spirit as "the beginning of the new Christian life which is and remains a real beginning" and described that one's authentic and faithful discharge of any institutional office in which one served was whether or not one had received the charismata of the Holy Spirit through and in the community and whether, first and foremost, one was the "recipient and bearer" of love.[109] Because baptism was an act of obedience in response to God's gracious work in and through the community, the charismata that the Holy Spirit gives in one's vocation was to be used in and through the community for the Church's mission in the word. He indicated later in fragment four that "[t]he baptism from which he (a Christian) comes was as such a consecration or ordination to take part in the mission which is committed to the whole Church."[110] In that same section, he noted the "marching orders" that were given to "pastors, elders, priests, deacons, deaconesses, bishops and even the pope as *servus servorum Dei*" and asserted that while these individuals occupied ecclesiastical orders with specific functions, they exercised those functions within the "framework of the mission of the community." He then concluded, "[b]ut all those baptized as Christians are *eo ipso* consecrated, ordained and dedicated to the ministry of the Church. They cannot be consecrated, ordained, or dedicated a second, third, or fourth time without devaluation of their baptism."[111]

In summary, for Barth, the particularity and specificity of church orders existed in service to the overall mission of the Church. He sought to demythologize the sacraments, viewing baptism as an individual's response to Christ's call and God's prior work in the life history of Jesus Christ in the power and presence of the Holy Spirit, and with the regenerating work of the Holy Spirit, one became endowed with spiritual

Mission in the Present Situation), 9. I'm grateful for the English translation provided by Darrell Guder and for he sharing this piece with me.

109. Barth, *CD*, IV.4, 38.

110. Ibid., 201.

111. Idem.

gifts, and through baptism assumed the Church's missionary vocation, namely to be witnesses in the world.

Thomas F. Torrance (1913–2007)

The late theologian Thomas F. Torrance held a distinguished chair in Reformed theology at the University of Edinburgh. He was prolific in writing on such topics as Reformed theology, theology and science, ecumenical theology, and completed the monumental translation of Karl Barth's Church Dogmatics into English.

Torrance gave careful attention to a Reformed theology of ordination that was Reformed, catholic, and evangelical.[112] Analyzing the Old Testament, Torrance discovered a twofold priesthood: a royal priesthood of the whole people of Israel initiated by circumcision, and within that royal priesthood there was an "institutional priesthood" in the house of Levi, and within that tribe, the house of Aaron. The institutional priesthood was to serve the royal priesthood, and the latter was to serve the saving purposes of God to all nations.[113] Likewise, Christ is the only priest, who invites and calls a people for Himself to share in His priesthood. The corporate priesthood (equivalent to the royal priesthood of Israel in the Old Testament) refers to Christ's body, the Church, and within that there is a particular priesthood set apart to edify the whole body. Torrance cited M. Schmaus in describing the ordained ministry as the "scaffolding" of the Church. Thus, from the time of Pentecost in Acts 2 to the final parousia of Christ, the Church is served by the ministry of Word and Sacrament. Torrance sees the corporate priesthood of the Church as arising from baptism as individuals are incorporated into the body of Christ there, and the particular priesthood of ordained ministry emerges from the ordering of the eucharistic fellowship in which bishops, presbyters, and deacons (or the fourfold Reformed system of minister, elder, doctor/teacher, deacon) serve one another and the people, as Christ serves them. As such, the ordained offices are ordered and validated as Christ's real presence is

112. Here I will briefly sketch Torrance's proposal in *Royal Priesthood: A Theology of Ordained Ministry.*

113. Ibid., 81.

made known in the Eucharist. Thus, the ordained ministry is grounded and centered in the eucharistic celebration.[114]

Throughout Torrance's discussion of ordination, Torrance emphasized the dual nature of ordination, with the primacy of Christ as the One, who through the Spirit, calls those to be ordained, as the call is issued and confirmed through the act of the Church.[115] Christ gives the word to the Spirit, who then teaches the Church what the risen Lord has said. Because Christ first called and commissioned the apostles and from them the New Testament ministry took shape, when the Church ordains it does so in obedience to the apostolic witness and teaching as testified in Scripture, and does so within the sphere of the apostolic commission and mission that Christ established when He founded the Church.[116]

Torrance stated his definition of ordination and the significance of the laying on of hands. Because Christ is the one who ordains, Torrance defined ordination as where ordinands "are all consecrated through participation in Christ's self-consecration on our behalf," and here Torrance re-emphasized that because Christ was with His disciples at the Last Supper as He consecrated Himself, so, too, ordination has a direct linkage to Eucharistic celebration because those who are ordained and commissioned to be sent out to minister the Word with and for others must do so as ones who share in Christ's own consecratory, prior act.[117] Ordination involves both a setting apart, a commission, an authorization and a blessing to an ordinand to serve in the order of Word and Sacrament; thus the ordained officer is a servant, and therefore, the minister and ordination are both "subordinate to the Word and Sacraments which it serves."[118] In reading the Scriptural testimony, Torrance saw that the laying on of hands was an essential feature of ordination in that it bore witness to the apostolic connection of the Church with the commission and mission of the apostles, it was an act of commissioning ministers to the ministry of Word and Sacrament, and it was an act of prayer invoking the Holy Spirit to endow the ordinand with gifts

114. Ibid., 82.

115. Torrance, "Consecration and Ordination," 242.

116. Ibid., 242–243.

117. Ibid., 241.

118. Ibid., 246.

to fulfill the function to which they were being ordained.[119] Torrance noted that the Westminster Form of Church Government had the laying on of hands before prayer, whereas the First and Second Books of Discipline of the Church of Scotland, following the teachings of both Knox and Calvin, have the laying on of hands after the prayer. The BOS of the Presbyterian Church (U.S.A.) places the epiclesis concurrent with the laying on of hands. Thus, Torrance observed that this ordering showed that the "primary element in ordination is the epiklesis."[120]

Torrance saw that the ministry of Word and Sacrament was the primary order. That is to say, Christ has entrusted to the whole Church the ministry of Word and Sacrament, to which ordained officers are responsible to insure that the Church is properly equipped to carry out that mission. He asserted that the goal/end of ordination is the ministry of Word and Sacrament. He stated, "[t]he order of the presbyteral ministry is not only the highest order, but in the strict sense the only order of the ministry. Other so-called orders are either for the assistance of this order or for the convenience of maintaining unity and concord and discipline among those so ordained."[121] Torrance saw that while the presbyteral ministry had priority in terms of function, the principle of parity of ministers maintained that all are equal, none subordinate to the other offices, all subordinate to Christ and to the Word, but all differentiated in their functions and tasks.

This brief survey of Calvin, Bucer, Turretin, Schleiermacher, Barth, and Torrance confirm, as in the previous chapters, that the Reformed tradition is wide and varied in its theological emphases with regards to church orders and ordination. While the 16th century Reformers appealed to patristic sources to validate hermeneutical readings of key Scriptural passages, theological themes, or ordination practices, the Reformers did so with a clear agenda to remedy the perceived abuses that they saw from the medieval Church.[122] Bradshaw noted that two in-

119. Ibid., 240.

120. Ibid., 251.

121. Ibid., 247.

122. Contrary to the Reformers' insistence, Bradshaw asserted that "[r]ather than trying to force the New Testament and apostlic testimony to fit into one single mould, therefore, the evidence is better served by the presumption of the probable existence of varied patterns of leadership in different early Christian communities, and also a variety of influences in bringing those patterns about." Quoted from Bradshaw, *The*

novations that the Reformers read into the patristic sources and which they instituted in their theological writings as well as liturgical reforms were the insistence that God's call is determined in and through the whole church and, thus, the whole people of God should be involved in some form or fashion in the selection of the ordained leadership; second, that ordination was ultimately God's work and not just an act of the Church.[123] The Reformers saw that those serving in the Roman Catholic Church were unfit and unqualified to serve because of what they perceived as priests who were serving as servants of the pope and not of Christ, and a sacerdotal system that was, in itself, without Scriptural warrant. Consequently, the Reformers underscored the significance of the participation of the whole Church from the confirmation of the election to the ordination itself, enabling public and private examination of the ordinand's character and doctrine, with the thought that transparency and public scrutiny would weed out those who did not have a genuine call to the ministry.[124]

From Turretin, we see Reformed orthodoxy's highly anti-Roman Catholic tendency, as Turretin and his contemporaries sought to safeguard the ordained ministry against any superstitious or unscriptural elements from infiltrating the Church's ministry. They did this by insuring that ministers possessed the right doctrine and possessed the necessary skills at proclaiming the word of God.

Schleiermacher sought to hold in dialectical tension, as was characteristic of his theological method, the necessity of tethering the Church's witness to the Scriptural tradition, while allowing for freedom of individuals to serve and discern the will of God as the Holy Spirit worked in them.

Barth emphasized the life history of Jesus Christ and the Church's identity as the missionary witnesses of Christ. That being the case,

---

Search for the Origins of Christian Worship, 194.

123. Bradshaw, "Preface," The Process of Admission to Ordained Ministry," xxi.

124. Bradshaw concluded that for the 16th century Reformers, "ordained ministry was for them less about the exercise of particular powers and functions and more about placing in positions of leadership men (sic) whose whole character and conduct of life would be exemplary to their congregations." (Idem., xxii) This is the same conclusion that we drew from the confessional documents in the previous chapter above, noting, too, that later confessions, as with more contemporary theologians, the emphasis became more on the functions and powers of the office and the ability of ordinands to exercise that than the character and conduct of life of the ordinand.

Barth muted discussions on church orders and equates baptism and ordination, seeing in the former the individual's obedient response to God's call to participate in the Church's vocation to be witness.

Torrance located the constitutive essence of church orders in the Eucharistic celebration for it is there that the Church is united to Jesus Christ, and from the table, the Church shares in Christ's priestly work in the world.

In terms of method, which is the chief concern of this book, Calvin and Bucer, characteristic of the Renaissance humanism of their day, used patristic and Scriptural sources in what some may consider as *eisegesis* through the hermeneutical lens of reformation of the medieval Church. Calvin's and Bucer's writings on church orders and ordination do not indicate whether they directly applied or relied upon their own pastoral experiences in developing their theologies of church orders and ordination. What was arrived at theologically was then put into practice through liturgical reforms at Strasbourg, Geneva, and England. Turretin, likewise throughout his *Institutes of Elenctic Theology*, after each question and accompanying refutation, cited patristic sources and early church practices coupled with Scripture. Schleiermacher's methodology, as was evident from his *Brief Outline* was to combine theological thought with sciences, seeing in both the necessity for practical theology in actual church practices. Barth and Torrance used scriptural and patristic sources with the hermeneutical lens of Jesus Christ as the agent of God's work of reconciliation in their understanding of the Church's vocation.

When we compare the methods employed by and the theological outcomes from the "official" sources of Reformed theology (conciliar statements, constitutional documents, representative theologians) that we have seen in this chapter and the previous chapters, we begin to see the tapestry of Reformed thought when it comes to presbyteral ordination and church order. We have noted in this chapter and in the previous ones the various emphases and key themes that each of the "official" sources produce. What emerges, as a preliminary conclusion, is that there has never been nor can there be, a one and only Reformed theology of presbyteral ordination. If we follow the lead of Reformed forbears, we can safely conclude that the Reformed tradition values diversity and multiplicity of voices as each generation of Reformed Christians discerns for their spatio-temporal context what is the will and mind of Christ for His Church. This lends credence to the aim of this project in calling for sustained engagement with the whole people of God as they encounter one another, the received tradition, and the triune God in the context of an ordination service.

The various and diverse outcomes of our examination in the previous chapters validate the central thesis of this book, namely, a new methodology is needed in discovering and articulating a more comprehensive Reformed theology of presbyteral ordination. Such a methodology would need to account for three features that have been consistently present in the "official" sources of Reformed theology:

- God's action and the Church's response
- The participation of the whole people of God
- The Church exists to share/participate (or continue) the ministry of the triune God through Jesus Christ in the Holy Spirit

These three features are not themselves a theology of presbyteral ordination but can be regarded as core features or contours of one.

Because God and the Church primarily meet one another in worship, the Church's liturgy and liturgical action are essential in understanding and appreciating the diverse meaning of an ordination liturgy. Ordination involves people—the ordinand, the presbyteral collegiums, the congregation, family and friends, and the Church in all times and places—and thus, we are interested in the theologies that are expressed, formed, enacted, and critiqued by people as they are touched by God and as they interact with God through the Church and the tradition they receive.

We direct our attention to methodological considerations and the relationship of liturgy, theology, and ritual.

FIVE

A Complementary Methodology

We get little discussion of the actual "doing" of ordination and receive abstract descriptions of what ordination is, what imposition of hands accomplishes, and theologies of church orders that prescribe more than they describe. The hitherto employed methodologies in the Reformed tradition can be described as a "distanciation" of a text, in Paul Ricoeur's critique of structuralism, or as Graham Hughes summarized Ricoeur's use of the term: "its separation from the subjectivity of its utterer or author and from the momentary event of its utterance."[1] Thus, the "official" sources of a Reformed theology of presbyteral ordination engage their act of discovery and articulation separated from the actual rite ordination and from the very assembly that is ordaining.

Such an adamant critique is lodged against the extant and prevailing methodology precisely because the current debates over ordination in the Presbyterian Church (U.S.A.) have sought to understand ordination through umbrella-like theologies or absent a consensus, through ecclesiastical judicial rulings to compel obedience and compliance with set standards. Unlike baptisms and celebrations of the Eucharist where the observance and celebrations are more regular and part of the rhythm and pattern of ecclesial life in a local congregation, ordination is a different matter for ordination is, by definition, an "occasional" service, and so what we get in ordination is an episodic, synchronic, snapshot of a particular gathered assembly.

1. Hughes, *Worship as Meaning*, 26.

Below, we critique the prevalent methodology in the Reformed tradition and offer a complementary approach, one which accounts for the local assembly and the actual rite of ordination alongside the "official" sources of theology. A complementary methodology may not necessarily yield altogether different outcomes than the "official" sources of theology; in fact, a complementary method that takes seriously the localized formation and expression of theology may actually confirm themes and elements of which "official" theological sources speak. In areas where there is discontinuity or inconsistency between "official" sources and embodied, localized sources, those may be areas of needed dialogue, study, and a re-appraisal of the tradition as well as local practice and local understanding. In both cases, a complementary methodology that includes local contexts as valued partners in theological discourse will go a long way in being faithful to the consistent Reformed insistence on the inclusion of the whole people of God.

Critiques of the Current Methodologies in Reformed Theology

George Lindbeck critiqued the two common approaches of understanding the relationship of religion and doctrine. The first, what he called the "cognitivist" or "propositionalist" approach, emphasized the character of doctrine and theology as "informative propositions or truth claims about objective realities." Thus, religion is regarded as a philosophy or science where precision is the goal; the implications of doctrinal precision would mean that if something was regarded as true, then it was true always and forever, and likewise something that was regarded as false was always and forever false.[2]

The second approach, what Lindbeck called the "experiential-expressive" perspective, viewed doctrine as "noninformative and nondiscursive symbols of inner feelings, attitudes, or existential orientations."[3] This means that an experiential-expressivist views religion as expressive symbols of experience, and that all religions, though possessing diverse religious experiences, share common core experiences. Lindbeck, citing

2. Lindbeck, *The Nature of Doctrine*, 16.

3. Idem.

Bernard Lonergan, noted: "It is this experience which identifies them as religions."[4]

Lindbeck proposed an alternative approach, what he called the "cultural-linguistic" perspective.[5] This approach looked at those aspects of religion's semblance to languages and their similarity to cultures (seen as "reality and value systems. . . idioms for the construing of reality and the living of life").[6] Thus, religions are regarded, in this approach, not as depositories and purveyors of doctrine nor as objectifications of religious experience, but as "communal phenomenon that shapes the subjectivities of individuals" whereby it possesses a "vocabulary of discursive and nondiscursive symbols together with a distinctive logic or grammar" in which "its doctrines, cosmic stories, or myths, and ethical directives are integrally related to the rituals it practices, the sentiments or experiences it evokes, the actions it recommends, and the institutional forms it develops."[7] Lindbeck, in contrasting the cultural-linguistic approach to the two other approaches, calls the former "intrasemiotic or intratextual" because in order to understand terms or what "God" signifies to a community, one will need to see its immanent usage, how the term is used within a system and how the usage shapes reality and experience, rather than the cognitivist approach that seeks to establish a precise doctrine or proposition of the term or of understanding its experiential meaning.[8]

Lindbeck saw the ecclesial actions of the Church, primarily worship, as first-order discourse about the divine. Contrasting the cultural-linguistic approach to the cognitivist-propositional approach, Lindbeck saw the former as using doctrinal statements and theology "through prayer, praise, preaching, and exhortation" as mere ordinary religious language to shape lives. He saw the latter's attempt to nail down the

4. Ibid., 31.

5. For an adept analysis and critique of Lindbeck's work, see Chapter 2 of McGrath, *The Genesis of Doctrine*, particularly McGrath's assessment that Lindbeck's "cultural-linguistic" perspective has an instrumentalist view of language, viewing doctrine as a regulating agent over religion, as grammar does towards language. Lindbeck's approach, however, provides a pragmatic scaffold for this book's framework in critiquing the Reformed tradition's reliance upon doctrinal categories that appear abstract, not accounting nor appreciating particular local, cultural-linguistic contexts.

6. Ibid., 18.

7. Ibid., 33.

8. Ibid., 114.

divine with precise theological statements as having rare "ontological import" because what ends up happening is that the cognitivist-propositional perspective tends to speak through assertions about the divine and really do not offer anything concerning the veracity or facticity of the divine; the subject matter of which cognitivists speak of in an abstract, disembodied fashion shape adherents performatively through a community's action of "worshiping, promising, obeying, exhorting, preaching."[9]

We find an additional critique against the prevailing cognitivist-propositionalist approach in the Reformed tradition in the contemporary sacramental theologian Louis-Marie Chauvet. The counterpart to Lindbeck's cognitivist-propositionalist nomenclature in Chauvet's work is what the latter calls, borrowing from Heidegger, the "onto-theological" approach. Chauvet, like Heidegger, critiqued the Scholastic metaphysics represented by Aquinas with Platonic and neo-Platonic roots. At issue was the metaphysical understanding of the relationship between entities, or "that which is," and being, "the being the entity is."[10] Metaphysics could not fully explain what being is, such that the Platonic system conceived of a representation of being as a common property to all entities, a "foundation-being" or an "uncreated being" (Aquinas) or "its own cause" (*causa sui*), or what can be called an "onto-theo-logic."[11] The ontological difference between the natural world, human beings, and the metaphysical world (with the "uncreated being" as the summit of the metaphysical world) was represented as something "outside language" with language employed as "pure instrument."[12] The Christian God became identified with the "unmoved Mover" or in Heidegger's terms, the "most entity of entities."[13] While analogy provided a tool by which it became possible to speak of God, Aquinas, like the Neoplatonists and Dionysius before him, asserted that human beings could not completely articulate nor understand what God is; what can be said of God is what God is not and God's relationship with the natural world. Thus *deus absconditus*, God-hidden, was maintained based on the metaphysical emphasis of ontological difference between

9. Ibid., 69.

10. Chauvet, *Symbol and Sacrament*, 26.

11. Ibid., 27.

12. Ibid., 36.

13. Quoted in Ibid., 37.

humanity and God. At most what can be said was that "God is simply postulated. . . outside of language" and, thus, ontological, metaphysical thought preceded language.

When it came to the sacraments, the Thomistic schema sought to overcome the difference between the sign and the thing signified through categories of instrumentalism and causation. Through the mode of signification, the sacraments mediated grace, and thus, Aquinas harmonized the *signum* and *causa*, thereby seeking to overcome difference "while recognizing the impossibility of complete homogeneity."[14] The implications for theology and theological language are that human beings become the effecting agents for the divine being, or in Boeve's description, "such a scheme turns theology into idolatry, a speculative attempt to take hold of God and God's grace"[15] and collapse the ontological difference of God and humanity into sameness. Chauvet described attempts to use the sacraments as instruments to produce God's grace as the objectivist model, and the use of the sacraments as instruments to transmit God's grace already given by God in daily life as the subjectivist model.[16] Chauvet proposed an alternative whereby we do not master the sacraments, but where the sacraments serve as God's means of mediation in ordering us.[17]

Using the metaphor of gift/return-gift and the paradigm of human communication with language as mediating relationships, Chauvet proposed an alternative to the prevailing onto-theological scheme.[18] Chauvet proposed that the sacraments are symbols of mediation of an event and a relationship: of God and human beings encountering one another; such a proposal affirmed the value of corporeality of the sacraments, demonstrating that it is in the body (the God-man Jesus Christ) that God meets human beings in their physical bodies, in our physical existences, in the body of Christ (the Church). Chauvet emphasized that the ecclesial triad of Christian identity—Scripture, sacrament, and ethics (like the Reformed *notae ecclesiae* of Word, sacrament, discipline)—are all expressions of the relationship that God graces us, gifts

14. Ibid., 17–18.

15. Boeve, "Theology in a Postmodern Context," 7.

16. Chauvet, *The Sacraments*, xiv-xix.

17. Chauvet, *Symbol and Sacrament*, 338.

18. See Boeve, "Theology in a Postmodern Context," 10–12; also Chauvet, *The Sacraments,* 121–122.

us with God's love and presence as believers express this relationship among each other. Chauvet asserted that when we name God, we address God by noting the distance, God's withdrawing absence, the difference that allows for divine-human discourse to occur based on the reception of the gift of God's grace wherein we have an "intense experience of this otherness and graciousness"[19] in the body, what Mitchell called "the primary relationship space" where ritual touches the bone, flesh and blood.[20]

Thus, our communication with God is not immediate, as was conceived under the onto-theological scheme of Scholasticism, but mediated. So that while the referent and subject of this symbolic mediation is "extra-linguistic" (God), the mediated relationship is witnessed to "intra-linguistically" in the Christian tradition.[21] Mitchell observed that Chauvet's move enabled "yielding not causes and objects, being and presence, completion and closure, but rather counter-experiences of bedazzlement, of astonishment at events we cannot comprehend,"[22] resulting in a robust, dynamic relational encounter. Summarizing Chauvet's agenda as underscoring "communication between subjects" Souletie put it this way:

> The relationship of humans with God in *Symbol et sacrament* is made explicit in the symbolic exchange that operates in the ecclesial action. It is the exchange that is found favored here through a rapport with what is exchanged. The symbolic relationship to God effects itself at Easter through the withdrawal of the absent. God is made present in the exchange when the church reads the Scriptures, celebrates the sacraments, or practices charity.[23]

While ordination in the Reformed tradition is not considered a sacrament but is sacramental, Chauvet's contribution to our discussion is relevant in his ringing critique of the onto-theological framework that has understood sacraments as sign, emphasizing difference, and causality. Umbrella-like theologies of ordination stipulated from upper-tier

19. Chauvet, Symbol and Sacrament, 338.
20. Mitchell, "Rituality and the Retrieval," 207–208.
21. Boeve, Idem.
22. Mitchell, "Rituality," 222.
23. Souletie, "The Social Sciences and Christian Theology After Chauvet," 193.

official sources seem disembodied and detached from local practices, local assemblies that engage Scripture, sacraments, and ethics in the rite of ordination and in the ecclesial worship and witness of a particular ministry context. Chauvet's point would force the Reformed tradition to face the question, "what then is the difference between baptism and ordination?," a concern that Barth raised in his doctrine of reconciliation. Is the Reformed tradition's insistence on some overarching, yet unknown and unseen theological understanding of ordination an effort to seek uniform compliance? Or is it an effort to sustain an ontological, causal, but latent assumption that ordination and church orders as conceived by the Reformed tradition are indispensable to what it means to be Reformed, that somehow the three-fold or four-fold church orders and the emphasis on laying on of hands with the accompanying interpretations of that act have become non-negotiable elements without which no one can conceive a future of Reformed mission and witness without them?

If the former, then ecumenical liturgical scholar Gordon Lathrop, in his observations of the future implications of Chauvet's work on the liturgical and ecumenical movements, is on point in calling for a "critique of power, calling always for the greatest transparency in any exercise of authority" because in a liturgical-ecumenical ecclesiology, "the only important authority is the authority to announce the mercy of God and call the community to service and love," to which Lathrop called for an appreciation of and study of local liturgical assemblies, in citing Schillebeeckx, Lathrop indicated that local assemblies are always at the same time in communion with the "more-than-local";[24] Lathrop's call would support the methodological contention and proposal of this book.

If the Reformed tradition's methodology has ossified around an abstract understanding of church orders and interpretations of what ordination is, then Chauvet's critique is on point, as is this book. What presently prevents the opening up of the gates for the whole people of God to serve in service to Christ through the Church? Is there a latent assumption that ordination grants an ontological, causal change in an ordinand to enable one to serve? While the Reformed tradition has maintained a historical consistency of rejecting the Catholic notion of the *character indelibilis* of the consecrated priesthood, can the rigidity

24. Lathrop, "'Is that your liturgical movement?,'" 108–109.

with which we in the Reformed tradition have held up church orders and ordination show that we may regard the threefold pattern of ministry as possessing some sort of *character indelibilis*? If so, then confession and transparency are what is called for and a re-examination of the tradition's understanding of church orders and ordination is needed at all levels. At the very least, an ironic outcome may result: a necessary reformation of the Reformed tradition itself!

Additionally, we note the observation of liturgical scholar Graham Hughes in his discussion of Peircian semiotics and the intended meanings of signs as opposed to their received meanings. Hughes spoke of the iconicity and indexicality of worship; the former denoted to what degree worshippers identified a similitude of what was done in worship's frontier to the far side, whereas the latter has to do with "truthfulness or authenticity" or "thoughts matching words." He called Peircian iconicity Firstness, in that it had the widest possibility of imaginative meanings tethered by the chosen sign-vehicle connected to its object.[25] So for instance, when the church gathers for worship to be in the presence of God, the spatial contents and orientation are set in such a way that the church has to imagine what worship must be like from God's perspective.

Indexicality designated Secondness because it is directly connected to the factuality of the worship act. Indexicality is concerned with the meaningfulness of actions or utterances. Like an index finger, the indexical sign directs our attention to the sense of an object; to put it colloquially, the indexical dimension has to do with truth in advertising, the synchronizing of thoughts and actions. Hughes used the example of worship leaders and how they themselves must be worshippers in order to authentically lead an assembly to worship.[26]

Hughes described Peirce's third concept, similar to Chauvet's sense of symbol, as symbolic signification. The symbolic dimension "interprets and disciplines" an experience of worship's frontier "in the name of tradition." Thus, the symbolic dimension, like Lindbeck's culturali-linguistic model, teaches worshippers the grammar and language of the tradition, in this case the Christian tradition.[27]

25. Hughes, *Worship as Meaning*, 148–170.

26. Ibid., 170–176.

27. Ibid., 176–177.

Thus, the three dimensions in Peirce's taxonomy—iconicity, indexicality, symbolic signification—enable us to see the various dimensions of meaning in worship. Iconicity directs our attention upward towards transcendence through imagination. Indexicality informs worshippers that there is meaningfulness in the contents of worship and there is an intended meaning, the signs are "meant." The symbolic dimension denominates the particular tradition of worship by locating the language of worship with an identifiable context.[28]

Hughes illustrated this process of meaning-making with the following diagrams. The first graphically described a divergence of what was intended/meant to what was received and effected:[29]

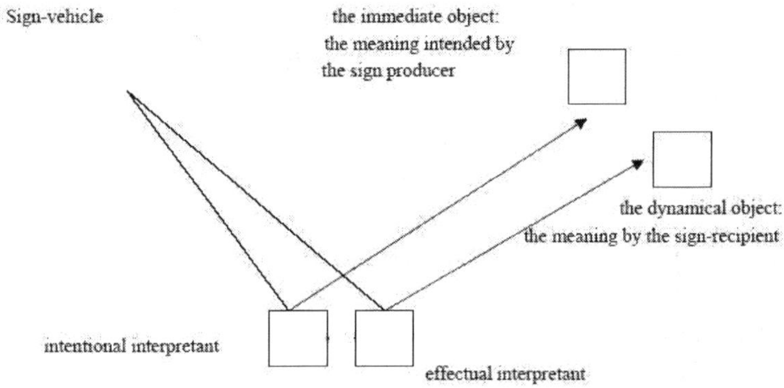

The second diagram depicted the place of convergence, which then allowed for discourse and dialogue to occur, on shared understandings as well as areas of discontinuity or critique:[30]

28. Ibid., 183.
29. Ibid., 146.
30. Ibid., 147.

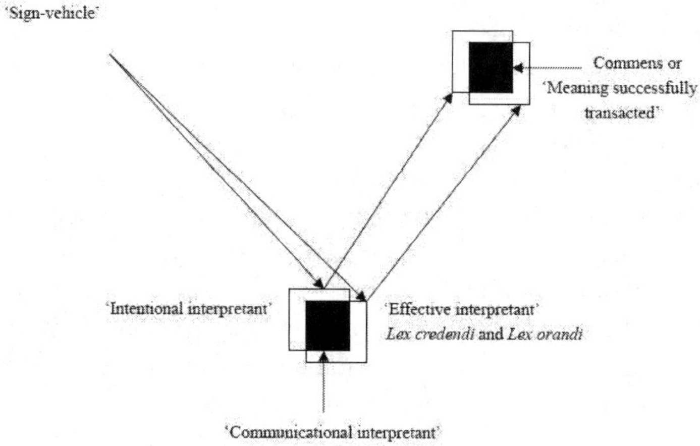

This book seeks to demonstrate the need for a methodology that allows and enables an examination of the intended and effected meanings of ordination by the whole people of God at all levels, to allow such discourse and communication to occur to see where there are areas of agreement and areas of critique and disagreement. The upper-tier theology focused so much on abstract theological definitions of church orders and ordination would benefit greatly hearing from and learning whether the "official" sources of theology are being understood and received as intended by the recipients (who themselves are the producers when ordinations occur in local assemblies), and if so/if not, why and how? Such an approach would take seriously that all are producers of meaning as all are recipients of meaning for all belong to the living tradition of the Reformed Christian faith.

Hughes's explanation of the interplay of iconic and indexical levels of meaning for the interpretant demonstrated the levels and degrees of meaning-making. Underlying the multiplicity of desired and actual meaning when a given system deploys signs to an interpretant, is the wide and deep ecology of traditions and systems that an interpretant already possesses and belongs to when participating in a ritual system, like a worship service.

Lawrence Hoffman spoke of the four dimensions of meaning in a ritual system. He called the four dimensions the private meaning, the official meaning, the public meaning, and the normative meaning.[31] Private meaning denoted the "idiosyncratic interpretations" akin to Aidan Kavanagh's Mrs. Murphy, his prototype of a baptized layperson in the pew who he regards a primary, private and idiosyncratic theologian.[32] Official meaning denoted the definition provided by "experts" who have studied a ritual and, consequently, issued a definition or statement about its meaning, to which other experts agree.[33] Public meanings denoted the consensus of ritual participants even though the consensus may not necessarily be the "official" meaning from the experts. Normative meaning was what the rite did in forming and shaping the values, attitudes and viewpoints of ritual participants as they leave the formal worship event, the context of the rite, and re-enter the world.[34]

The interplay of private, official, public, and normative dimensions of meaning in Hoffman's taxonomy demonstrated the complexity of meaning-making, and the multiplicity of theologies that result when particular human beings gathered in community are valued as equal collaborators in theological discourse. The Reformed tradition has often settled for official meanings. Hoffman lent credence to this book's advocacy for a methodology that takes seriously the ecology of meaning-making in a ritual system, such as an ordination service.

Lindbeck, Chauvet, Hughes, and Hoffman spoke about the internal meaning or meaning-making that occurs within a community, or at the very least, the interior understanding that is being internalized and

31. Hoffman, "How Ritual Means"

32. Kavanagh, "Response," 322.

33. Paul Bradshaw noted that Hoffman's "official meaning" could be further subdivided to include the intentions of the original compilers/producers of liturgical rites, as well as the subsequent meaning attached to those rites by later ecclesiastical authorities. See Bradshaw, "Difficulties in Doing Liturgical Theology," 189.

34. Ibid., 82; see footnote 7 in that reference for the quote of Ronald Grimes and his observation that the normative meaning is "paradigmatic" in the ritual's capacity to "form values and guide activity outside the context of the rite itself."

negotiated among worship participants in their encounter with God and with divine things. Before we get to the matter of ritual that Hoffman spoke about, we will direct our attention to the field of liturgical theology as a helpful resource in arguing for a complementary methodology to discover and articulate a Reformed theology of presbyteral ordination. Because in ordination, as in any time and place when the Church worships, God and people are encountering one another, we must focus on the act of worship in ordination and the theology that is at the same time expressed in ordination, being expressed in ordination, and being formed and created in the act of ordination. Broadly speaking, we agree with Paul Hoon's assertion that in worship there is a divine-human dialogue occurring where God's self-revelation in Jesus Christ is met by the human response; such is the act of worship.[35]

Liturgical Theology: An Assessment

The statement, *ut legem credendi lex statuat supplicandi* (truncated to: *lex orandi, lex credendi*), attributed to the fifth-century Christian writer and student of St. Augustine of Hippo, Prosper of Aquitaine,[36] is often quoted in the field of liturgical theology for it neatly summarized what is at stake in the relationship of liturgy and theology. That the "law of prayer" (lex orandi) established the "law of belief" highlighted the priority of the worshipping community's actions as shaping and forming

35. Hoon, *The Integrity of Worship*, 77.

36. Paul De Clerck unmasked the true meaning of the adage within its fifth century C.E. historical, textual, and liturgical context. In summary, the adage was within a longer pericope, contained in a document called the *Celestinian Capitula*, written during the time of Augustine's defense of grace contra semi-Pelagians. The lex orandi in the adage, ut legem credendi lex statuat supplicandi, designated primarily the "inviolable decisions of the blessed Apostolic See" that are attested to by tradition through the apostolic fathers, and through sacerdotal rites celebrated around the world, and these three, constituting the law of prayer, all testify to God as the author and giver of grace. Consequently, the passage continued by urging prayer for the whole human race so that God's grace may draw people such as "infidels. . .idolaters. . .the Jews. . .heretics. . .schismatics. . .the lapsed. . .the catechumens" so that the conversion of these groups would validate the earlier claim that God is the author and giver of grace, and would, thus, justify the Church in prayer. See De Clerk, " 'Lex orandi, lex credendi,'" 178–200. A summary of this is also found in Wainwright, *Doxology*, 224–229 and in Bradshaw, "Difficulties in Doing Liturgical Theology," 186–187. Wainwright is a representative liturgical theologian who holds to the mutual influence of the Church's lex orandi and lex credenda. On this point, see Wainwright, Idem, 218.

theological understanding. Theology is regarded not as an *a priori*, abstract category developed outside of the gathered people of God in worship and then imported into the liturgy to shape and, eventually serve as criteria for subsequent critique; instead theology emerged and was expressed within and from the worship life of the Church, and in a general sense, theology is the worship event. Liturgical theology in its purist form as articulated by the pioneering work of the late Orthodox theologian, Fr. Alexander Schmemann, regarded liturgy itself as the primary locus of doing theology.[37] Schmemann's successors, Aidan Kavanagh[38], David Fagerberg, Gordon Lathrop and Kevin Irwin, saw the doing of worship by the Church as primary theology (*theologia prima*) and the post-worship reflection and interpretation as secondary theology (*theologia secunda*).[39] Irwin added tertiary theology (*theologia tertia*) to this taxonomical nomenclature to designate the ethical, spiritual, and moral implications and dimensions of liturgy[40], what Saliers called *lex vivendi* (law of living) or *lex agendi* (law of intention-action).[41]

Fagerberg placed special emphasis not only on the worship event of the Church as the primary locus for doing theology, but that the act of worship was itself primary theology. In contrast to academic theology (secondary theology, or what I have called "upper-tier" theology) that employs the deductive method of investigation by having ready-set criteria of theological principles and then proceeds to study materials with worship as one object of investigation, Fagerberg described liturgical theology as concerned with the Church in its encounter with God and how the Church's "adjustment," to borrow Kavanagh's description[42], to God's presence and action is itself theology being generated, formed,

37. Schmemann, *Introduction to Liturgical Theology*, 14–15.

38. Kavanagh, *On Liturgical Theology*. 74; Fagerberg, *Theologia Prima*, 41; Irwin, *Context and Text*, 46.

39. Dwight Vogel proposed six "provinces" of theological discourse concerning liturgy: theology of worship, liturgy as theology, theology of liturgy, theology in liturgy, theology because liturgy, and liturgy and life. [Vogel, "Liturgical Theology" *Primary Sources of Liturgical Theology*, 4.] For our purposes, we will employ Vogel's "liturgy as theology," "theology in liturgy," and "liturgy and life." These specific provinces match the narrative approach that this book advocates, which seeks to capture the lived experiences of participants in the moment of the event and after the event has taken place.

40. Irwin, *Context and Text*, 46.

41. Saliers, *Worship as Theology*, 187.

42. Kavanagh, *On Liturgical Theology*, 74.

shaped, and expressed. Liturgical theology examines texts, the contexts of those texts, the structures of the liturgies, the histories of the liturgies, for as Fagerberg cited liturgical historian Robert Taft, it is critical to understand liturgy "in motion, just as the only way to understand a top is to spin it."[43] This is not at all to discount secondary theology and post-worship reflection. What liturgical theology appreciates and seeks to lift up is that because academic, upper-tier theology is conducted in service and at the service of the Church's ecclesiological identity and witness, and because the Church is the Church precisely because it is a "worshipping community,"[44] to borrow Singaporean liturgical theologian Simon Chan's descriptor, theological engagement and reflection must privilege the Church's worship for it is within the context and content of worship that God's community gathers to hear and receive Word and Sacrament, and thus, encounter the triune God; worship is not the exclusive location of the divine-human encounter, but worship is the primary locus.[45]

Liturgical theology is justified both by its Trinitarian implications and the divine-human communication that occurs by the Trinity's movement towards the Church in and through the liturgy. Trinity scholar Catherine Mowry LaCugna drew out the implication of liturgy for trinitarian theology in three (!) ways: first, in liturgy God and people one another, an encounter that doctrine attempts to articulate; second, because the Trinity is not speculative by practical (seeking to be in relationship with human beings and which provides a model for human relationships as well), then trinitarian theology is necessarily linked to liturgy for liturgy "is the ritual action by which we live and

43. Fagerberg, *Theologia Prima*, 41.

44. Chan, *Liturgical Theology*. Chan asserted that "worship is what distinguishes the church as the church," and as such, establishes the church's foundational identity. (42) He went further in saying that the aim of the Church's mission was to gather individuals to become a worshipping community, not to save people. (45) Kavanagh insightfully compared liturgical theology's correction of the proper place of academic theology with that of the philologist's relationship with language: philologists can no more control linguistics which properly belongs to the social transaction and interaction of speech in communities and societies, than can academic theology master theology which properly belongs to the whole people of God, i.e. the Church. (Kavanagh, *On Liturgical Theology*, 83–84)

45. Kavanagh, *On Liturgical Theology*, 75, where he cited Schmemann in establishing that in worship the Church is being itself, wherein the sources of theology are playing their part as sources.

enact faith in the triune God who is the ground of all relationship;" and thirdly, theology can glean insights from liturgical disagreements and disputes.[46] LaCugna designated *oikonomia* as God's saving acts in history and *theologia* as the mystery of the triune God. That liturgy is a *locus theologicus* of God's *oikonomia*, it is through the remembering and celebrating in liturgy that the Church experiences the *theologia* of the triune God.[47]

LaCugna's work buttresses one of the central theses of this book. This project seeks to widen traditional Reformed methodologies by asserting that meaning-making occurs in worship precisely because, as LaCugna pointed out, the liturgy of the Church is a *locus theologicus* in which God and Church meet, and through which God mediates the narratives of the Christian faith in word, sacrament, prayer, and song.

Fagerberg, Schmemann, Kavanagh, Irwin, and Lathrop understand liturgical theology to be about elucidating the making and meaning of theology in worship in the entirety of the liturgical rites, gestures, actions, words, texts, songs, prayers alongside with the post-worship reflections and accounts of the rites, what Fagerberg called "a record of the theology transacted by a liturgical community."[48] Kavanagh privileged Mrs. Murphy's account of her encounter with God's presence for her "language illuminates the chaotic landscape through which I must pick my professional way with the narrow laser-like beam of precise words about words and concepts. . . what she does is so much harder to do than what I do."[49] Lathrop asserted that liturgical theology focuses attention on the church—the gathered assembly that is at once

46. LaCugna, "Can Liturgy ever again become a Source for Theology?," 2.

47. Ibid., 6–7. Michael Aune called for a Trinitarian-based, Trinitarian-centered ecclesiology becoming the new starting point of liturgical theology and not the adage lex orandi lex credendi nor the common term leitourgia. He saw as problematic what he called the Schmemann-Kavanagh-Fagerberg-Lathrop hegemony in the field of liturgical studies and their reliance on those concepts. Aune asserted that it was time to demythologize if not retire altogether those concepts for they envisage the Church's liturgy as a thing rather than as a relationship, what he called the "theological reality" of the triune God working in history. Hence, Aune would find a strong ally in LaCugna for his cause. [For Aune's critique, see Aune, "Liturgy and Theology," 46–68; for Aune's alternative proposal, see Aune, "Liturgy and Theology: Rethinking the Relationship—Part II," 141–169.]

48. Fagerberg, *Theologia Prima*, 155–156; Kavanagh, *On Liturgical Theology*, 87–88; Lathrop, *Holy Things*, 8–9.

49. Kavanagh, "Response," 323.

a representative of the one holy catholic apostolic church but in and of itself not the "catholic" church but is linked to the "catholic" church. Thus, the task of liturgical theology in Lathrop's view is "to interpret the meaning of the assembly is to interpret what links these voices—but the assembly itself, not the interpretation, remains the link."[50]

What is important to note, as we move forward, is that liturgical theology's task is not only to elucidate and discover the meaning-making that occurs as the Church worships in a particular context, but to see how and if the particularity of a given context shares a common identity with the one holy catholic apostolic church, as well as to see areas of dissimilarity as a means for further reflection, dialogue, re-assessment, and, possibly reform. Liturgical theology's task connects with this book's advocacy of juxtaposing the "official" sources of Reformed theology with the enacted "lived" sources of Reformed theology in ordination services, and allowing the two sources to interact with one another.

Irwin helpfully reinterpreted "text" as the source of liturgical theology's study. Liturgics as a discipline concerned itself primarily with liturgical texts such as ordinals, sacramentaries, and the like. Irwin advanced the meaning of "text" to mean liturgy's context, where context becomes the "text" to study. Here Irwin meant "context" in three ways. First, context means the evolution of a rite and the evolution of meanings of a rite. Second, context means the setting of and performance/execution of worship and its various liturgical elements, as well as how liturgical participants experience the liturgy. This would be akin to our discussion of Peircian iconicity and indexicality above. Third, context means the contemporary and theological milieu of liturgical rites and how they may be adapted to particular ecclesial and societal settings. Thus, context in these three dimensions becomes the "text" of liturgical theology.[51] This tripartite understanding of context clarifies the task of liturgical theology and will serve as a guide in the methodology being advocated for by this book.

Lathrop, in his characteristic perspicuously poetic style, named the context of liturgical theology's task. He queried the simple but insightful, "What do you need for a church?" to which he replied, "People,

50. Lathrop, Idem.

51. Irwin, *Context and Text*, 54–55.

of course. People are primary."[52] He went on to say that the Church has things—written liturgies, bread, cup, Bible, water, sanctuary—and that people say and do, they perform with the things, they engage the things, and that through the "juxtaposition" of people, places, and things, we will see theology in the making. In toto, the people, places and things are the " 'words' that the assembly uses to speak of God."[53]

Moore-Keish used liturgical theology in support of ritual studies with two key critiques. Citing liturgical scholars Mary Collins and Gordon Lathrop in their call for appreciation and examination of particular liturgical acts, Moore-Keish, writing as a Presbyterian scholar concerned about the Reformed tradition's emphasis on abstract doctrine concerning the Eucharist, pointed to the need for theology's work to see, feel, hear, think, experience the worship of God's assembled people in actual, particular practices. She critiqued Fagerberg's ambivalence of appreciating actual liturgical practice due to his distinction between liturgy (content of worship elements, rubrics) and *leitourgia* and his judgment that not all of worship is *leitourgia*.[54] Fagerberg, like Schmemann and Kavanagh, speak in abstractions, seeking some sort of fundamental logic and grammar to the Church's liturgy, but not concretizing it. Instead, Moore-Keish recommended following the lead of Lathrop in his call for examination and study of the diachronic structure of the Church's worship: the juxtaposition of the gathered people in prayer, song, bath, bread, cup, Scripture. This, Moore-Keish argued, are not abstractions but actual, concrete things that serve as guiding principles

52. Lathrop, *Holy Things*, 87.

53. Ibid., 90. Melanie Ross critiqued Gordon Lathrop's construction of the ordo through his emphasis on juxtaposing binary opposites in his criticism of megachurch worship structures and his followers who, in turn, criticize the Free Church, a move, Ross contended, shared methodological kinship with structuralism's emphasis on seeing the whole as more than the sum of the parts and the reduction of structural relations to binary opposites. Ross lodged her critique on along two lines: structuralism assumes that the theorist knows better than the subject being studied, and second, there is no agreement among liturgiologists on what constitutes the ordo. Instead she called for a methodological move from structuralism to hermeneutics, which emphasizes "the event nature of worship,. . . meaning in the context of relationship. . . [and] the interpreter's 'lived experience.'" Ross, thus, arrives at the same point as Moore-Keish in calling for a hermeneutical methodology even though Ross critiqued Lathrop's method and Moore-Keish lauded his. [see Ross, "Joseph's Britches Revisited," 528–550.]

54. Moore-Keish, *Do This In Remembrance of Me*, 74–75.

and criteria for discovering and articulating what Lathrop called "pastoral liturgical theology."[55]

The other critique leveled against liturgical theology is its reliance on structuralism. Moore-Keish, citing Mary Collins and ritual anthropologist Victor Turner, critiqued Kavanagh's call for the use of structuralism's approach in searching for the "deep structure" of a liturgical system, hoping to articulate the common threads of diverse liturgical practices. Collins and Turner saw that when structuralism was used in isolation of the particular cultures and contexts of liturgical theology's study, the particularities and differences can potentially be elided and general, abstract statements can be made about particular practices and contexts.[56] Thus, they prescribed liturgical theology needing to account for particular liturgical practices, noting the structures of the practices within the given cultural context in which they are enacted.[57]

Paul Marshall added an additional critique against liturgical theology. Marshall saw that liturgical theology wrongly demarcated primary theology and secondary theology with adherents to liturgy as *theologia prima* as defining too narrowly what qualified as *theologia prima* and not seeing in that concept more "interactive or multivalent" elements.[58] Here Marshall saw that scholarship in the field of liturgical theology have not adequately accounted for the activity of worship planning and those who plan worship, such as preachers, musicians and artist.[59] Liturgical theologians have focused on liturgical rites, to the exclusion of Protestantism and Protestantism's emphasis on the ministry of the word. Lastly, Marshall saw in liturgical theology's emphasis on liturgy as almost a living thing with human beings as passive receivers who experience liturgy's power as reinforcing systems of oppressions.[60] The complementary methodology which this book advances and the four

55. Ibid., 76.

56. Ibid., 82–83.

57. Bradshaw indicated that what may pass as a movement by liturgical theologians to go from liturgy to doctrine may, in most cases, be a cover for an actual movement from doctrine to liturgy to doctrine in that the liturgical theologian has already decided beforehand what theological theme(s) or ideas to argue and then locate that theological doctrine in its liturgical expression. See Bradshow, "Difficulties in Doing Liturgical Theology," 187.

58. Marshall, "Reconsidering 'Liturgical Theology,'" 135.

59. Ibid., 129–131.

60. Ibid., 146–147.

case studies in the next chapter lift up preaching and the preacher as essential elements in the shaping and articulation of a Reformed theology of presbyteral ordination.

Following Moore-Keish's lead on the methodology she employed with regards to her study of the Eucharist, we direct our attention briefly to ritual studies and narrative theory as allied fields to liturgical theology as we seek to advance a complementary methodology for the development and articulation of a Reformed theology of presbyteral ordination.[61]

Liturgical theology provides a rationale for the methodology this project advances, but to a certain point. Marshall rightly asserted that over-privileging the power of the liturgy may actually undermine the constitutive and significant role of the gathered assembly, where they become passive receivers of liturgy's power. Liturgical theology corrects traditional Reformed source methods in the former's assertion that meaning-making occurs within the Church's worship, and that the triune God encounters the Church in and through the liturgy. But, liturgical theology does not adequately address the particularity and the value of human beings in a given context.

While liturgical theology as an academic field began with Schmemann's call for a closer examination of the undivided, ancient Church's Tradition as an inviolable source for the Church's rule of faith and the rule of prayer[62], liturgical theology in the Reformed tradition, as we have seen, consists of a multiplicity of sources and strands of the tradition. That liturgical theology sought a return to the patristic texts, this project agrees with that proposition but balances that approach to Irwin's own observation that text and context are not limited to paper documents, but must include people, places, and things.

61. James Empereur, too, called for liturgical theology to use interdisciplinary fields such as ritual studies to go beyond the bruta facta of raw data of liturgical celebrations in order to understand the ways human beings "interact symbolically and celebrate by means of ritual" [Empereur, *Models of Liturgical Theology*, 8–9, 13, 45. In Empereur's model scheme (institutional, mystery, sacramental, proclamation, process, therapeutic, and liberation), the Reformed tradition would belong to the "proclamation model" and our methodology would advance the "therapeutic model" but we note that Empereur urged the use of all models so that they can be "mutually self-correcting." Thus, where the Reformed proclamation model is impoverished by its lack of accounting for the human experiencing of God's presence and call in ordination, this book proposes a complementary methodology that will enable the Reformed tradition to do just that.

62. See Schmemann, 14–16

The fields of ritual studies and narrative theory will assist in this effort. This project values the role of the rite of ordination itself, the sum of all its elemental parts and each part. Included and critical to the rite of ordination are the human persons gathered in an ordination service, called by God, seeking to encounter God, and desiring to celebrate God's work in the life of the Church and in the life of the ordinand.

Ritual Studies and Narrative Theory: Their Possibilities

Ritual studies and narrative theory are cognate fields of one another and of liturgical theology. As interdisciplinary fields in the social sciences, ritual studies and narrative theory seek to unearth the rich meaning of a community's engagement with culture, the world, the cosmos through people, places and things. In the case of ritual studies as it applies to rites of ordination, this involves an analysis of ordination liturgies, the performance of the liturgy in the assembly, the gestures of ritual participants, the employment and placement of symbols (cross, water, bread, cup, pulpit, paraments, table, Bible), the words and tone of prayers and songs, Scriptural texts chosen, and other elements related to liturgical space and liturgical time.

Narrative theory narrows the field of examination even further, to the human person. Narrative theory is interested in unearthing the stories, the experiences, the reflections of ritual participants, how they understand the "language games," if you will, of the ordination rite, when compared with their own experiences, demographics, and background.

The use of ritual studies and narrative theory for our analysis seeks to do what Peter Fink called the task of a liturgical theology.[63] In reflecting upon the Eucharistic rites of the Roman Catholic Church, Fink asserted that the central question for a liturgical theology was one of "credibility" and "honesty." What he meant by this was whether what the church claims is and should be happening in the church's prayer actually enacted? He put the question this way, "Under what conditions are the church's claims for its prayer to be rendered credible?" This would be akin to Hughes' indexical dimension of the degree of meaningfulness of the liturgical performance. Fink helpfully distinguished between declarative and evocative language; the former is the language

63. Fink, "Toward a Liturgical Theology," 601–609.

of control, manipulation and information; evocative language kenotically surrenders in vulnerability to the creative input of the worshipping community and to what the Spirit of God is doing among and within them.[64] The danger, Fink cautioned, of privileging declarative statements of upper-tier theological sources at the expense of the evocative input of the worshipping assembly would be to effectively present a Docetic dualism of what God really is doing versus what God appears to be doing based on human perception. Instead Fink sought the complementary input of both the declarative and evocative statements of upper-tier theological sources and the worshipping assembly as he rightly recognized the limiting conditions of sinfulness, finitude, incomplete knowledge, and a tendency for parochial agendas upon both upper-tier theological sources and the worshipping assembly.[65]

Liturgical theology needs ritual studies and narrative theory because the subject of study is people, places and things by which and with which God encounters the Church and vice versa. Ritual studies and narrative theory offer precise methods that liturgical theology speaks of. For instance, narrative theory can be considered a secondary liturgical theology because narrative theory involves gathering and analyzing the post-worship observations of participants and observers.

David Newman asserted that worship should properly be viewed as a body "that has life and movement" and because the worshipping community is a corporate body, our study should look at the nature of relationship and how the network of relationships (God with Church, Church with God, Church members with one another, Church with world) are enacted and understood through the system of ritual gestures, words, and symbols.[66]

Ritual scholar Ronald Grimes offered seven critiques of classical Christian liturgical theory as he called for the alliance of ritual studies and liturgical studies, and I would argue, liturgical theology. He critiqued classical approaches as being:[67]

- Focused solely on the intended meaning of liturgical texts when they were first constructed;

64. Ibid., 607.
65. Ibid., 608.
66. Newman, "Observations on Method in Liturgical Theology," 380.
67. Grimes, *Beginnings in Ritual Studies*, 8–10.

- Unable to self-diagnose normative practices;
- From the top-down (divine to human, synod to worshipper, mind to body) rather than accounting for the entire ecology of the theological enterprise;
- Focused on rational, cerebral, mental senses and obscuring or ignoring the auditory, olfactory, tactile, and gestural aspects of the liturgy;
- Too goal-oriented and too rigid because of precise planning rather than allowing an element of freedom and play;
- Divorced from imagination, performative drama, wherein the church becomes too serious;
- Exclusivist and seeing that as being uniquely Christian (e.g. only the ordained officers are the important actors in worship).

On this last point, Grimes insightfully queried what would be the implications if, instead of approaching the Christian faith theologically, we approached it ritologically. For instance, instead of asking, "Who are my sisters and brothers in the faith by virtue of their confession of the Apostles' Creed?" what if the question was changed to, "Are those with whom I break bread with my sisters and brothers in the faith?"

We must be cautious that characterizations and interpretations about what a ritual is doing and meaning are not too generalized or are too privileged over and against the actual context or the wider tradition. Because the idiosyncratic interpretations of ritual participants are significant and because we give careful attention to the detail of ritual actions, there is a temptation (and tendency) in employing these two methodologies for an interpretation to be taken as *the* meaning of that ritual and that context. This must be balanced with what each participant has said, what the community senses is the meaning, as compared to the universal Church community and tradition to which the local church belongs.

Catherine Bell noted that traditional, liturgical studies looked askance at methods employed by ritual theory because of the wide variance and informality of practices and input that result from such investigation. She noted that oral societies, when given texts that supposedly embody sacred truth and tradition, are forced to relate to centralized authorities, where "ritual spontaneity is devalued in favor of testifying to belief, reciting creeds, and performing choreographed mysteries in which hierarchies of official mediators dominate."[68] Instead she urged liturgical practictioners and experts to regard ritual as "the medium people usually use to recognize and defer to the authority of tradition, supernatural beings, divine right, or even, as Freud suggested, obsessive compulsion." With this she prescribed that liturgists ought to seek theoretical models to learn how rituals are developed and conducted so that the Church can "develop the theological and ecclesiastical supports needed to build coherent and authoritative liturgical communities—not just experts."[69]

Bell proposed seeing ritual as practice.[70] In contrast to prevailing thoughts that viewed ritual as "the sociopolitical mechanism by which cultural ideas and social dispositions are integrated on the one hand, and as the phenomenon that affords theorists special access to the dynamics of culture on the other" Bell proposed ritual as practice.[71] These prevailing views, espoused for instance by Paul Ricoeur and Clifford Geertz, see ritual as fulfillment of group thought and ideas, or the actions of the group/culture. As practice, ritual should be analyzed, not as an independent act from other acts that a culture does, but within its own context in the midst of a community's total action, with ritual as one among several acts. In this way, ritual observers/researchers will discover ritualization occurring: how does a community/culture distinguish a ritual act from all others, and why and how does this community/culture deem that this ritual act is the right and effective thing to do.[72] Additionally and ideally, the ritual theorist/observer would not treat ritual as an object to deconstruct based on the theorist's own predetermined methods and discourse, and thus the theorist would be the main actor; instead to regard ritual as practice is to value and appreciate

68. Bell, "The Authority of Ritual Experts," 119.

69. Ibid., 120.

70. In an earlier work, Bell laid the groundwork for ritual as practice by critiquing the thought-action dichotomy that split human thought and human action spatiotemporally. See Bell, *Ritual Theory, Ritual Practice*, especially pp. 47–54. Tom Driver regards ritual as performance. Driver sees three positive outcomes for ritual as performance: order, community, and transformation. See Driver, *Liberating Rites*, 79–106, 132.

71. Bell, *Ritual*, 80.

72. Ibid., 81.

the ritual and ritualization that are being unfolded before the witnessing senses of the ritual theorist/observer.[73]

Here, we note that Bell seems to suggest that it may be possible (and desired) for the ritual theorist/observer to not carry their preconceived theories, methods, assumptions, and goals into the ritual situation. Can the theorist/observer be totally discounted from the total ecology of meaning-making that occurs within a ritual context even as the theorist observes and is physically located within the ritual, granted as an observer? Witvliet cited Thomas Kuhn's pioneering work on paradigm as it related to observation analysis in the former's caution about too quickly integrating ritual studies into liturgical work: "observation is theory-laden; meanings are theory-relative; facts are theory-dependent."[74] That the views and experiences of the theorist/observer is part of the ritual being analyzed also points to the critical difference between a theorist/observer who is a pastoral liturgist and a theorist who is a social scientist. Whereas the social scientist describes what is being observed, the pastoral liturgist's role is not only to describe but to prescribe as well.[75]

Second, seeing ritual as practice enables the ritual observer/researcher to appreciate the value and primacy of the body. It is the physical, human body that moves, gestures, speaks, responds, receives, gives, eats, laughs, dances. The body interacts with a given spatio-temporal environment and within that ecology, the body is designating the special, I would even say, the hallowed, character of the environment in which the ritual is taking place.[76] The body that engages in ritual practice does so not with an "intellectualist logic" but does so with an "implicit and rudimentary" logic, one that is "ceaseless play of situationally effective schemes, tactics, and strategies" or, to cite Bourdieu, "the intentionless invention of regulated improvisation."[77]

Thirdly, regarding ritual as practice enables the ritual observer to see that the ritual derives authority outside or beyond the immediate

73. Bell, *Ritual Theory, Ritual Practice*, 54.

74. Witvliet, "For our own purposes: the appropriation of the social sciences in liturgical studies," Liturgy Digest, 6–35 reprinted in Bradshaw and Melloh, *Foundations in Ritual Studies*, 22. (Page citations are from the reprinted edition.)

75. Ibid., 24–25.

76. Bell, *Ritual*, 82.

77. Bell, *Ritual Theory, Ritual Practice*, 82.

situation and context. Through ritualization, ritual "agents" designate through differentiated movements and deployed schemes and strategies how they regard, value, and respond to powers that are eternal, transcendent and autonomous.[78]

In seeing ritual as practice, Bell asserted that ritual constructs, rather than expresses relationships of authority and submission. Rather than communicating certain meanings and values that are expressions of culture, ritual as practice attends to the practices that shape and form those patterns of meanings and values. Thus, ritual as practice is interested in both the synchronic, as well as the diachronic (historical) practices as past and present converge and meaning-making occurs, as ritual agents see themselves as not only reproducing traditional meanings and practices, but also reinterpreting, and, in fact, transforming those received values.[79]

Because we are studying the rite of ordination which involves obvious displays of power, authority and control as to those who are "ordained" and those who are not, we note Bell's word about the notion of ritual as a tool for social control and ideological education and compliance. Bell challenged such notions, urging, instead that ritual be seen as an activity that "constitute a specific embodiment and exercise of power,"[80] that is to say, for our purposes, that a rite of ordination is a snapshot instantiation of *a* power relationship because to a great degree, ritualization requires the external consent of the participants while "simultaneously tolerating a fair degree of internal resistance."[81] Thus, ritual cannot be totally seen as a tactic or method for coercion. The critical question would be, is the power dynamic that is being embodied in a particular rite of ordination negative, imposing and constraining to individual and communal freedom?

78. Bell, *Ritual*, 82.

79. Ibid., 83.

80. Bell, *Ritual Theory, Ritual Practice*, 170.

81. Ibid., 221. We should note the related, but distinct relationship of the terms "ritual" and "ritualization." Ritual scholar Tom Driver helpfully clarifies this by noting that both involve improvisation and repetition. They differ in that ritualization focuses on developing new forms through which expressive behavior can emanate, while ritual focuses on already known, "richly symbolic pattern of behavior," less on the making and more on the "valued pattern and its panoply of associations." Driver cited Ronald Grimes, "Ritual begins with ritualization." See Driver, *Liberating Rites*, 30.

Ritual theory as it relates to a study of rites of ordination provides a valuable resource in ritual studies' view of liminality. Borrowing from Arnold van Gennep's notion of rites of passage—separation, margin (or *limen*, "threshold" in Latin), aggregation—ritual anthropologist Victor Turner developed further the concept of liminality to designate that stage wherein the ritual subject, or "passenger," experiences ambiguity, they are "neither here nor there; they are betwixt and between the positions assigned and arrayed by law, custom, convention, and ceremonial."[82] Using catechumenal neophytes as examples, Turner observed that those in the liminal stage are passive, humble, having to obey authority, made naked (either figuratively or literally), so that it was "as though they are being reduced or ground down to a uniform condition to be fashioned anew and endowed with additional powers to enable them to cope with their new station in life."[83] As presbyteral ordinands—ministers especially, but also elders—can attest that preparation for ordination is akin to a liminal stage of belongingness in the body of Christ for one is in the in-between stage of being a layperson to being a recognized church leader with significant responsibilities. Turner's insight into this liminal stage validates the necessity for appropriating ritual theory for this book's methodology. Turner saw the dialectic nature of the liminal stage as essential for formation, as he noted that liminality involves statusless-ness in the midst of ritual elders who have status, homogeneity in preparation and differentiation in functions, states of equality (e.g. parity of ministers, priesthood of all believers) and inequality (clerical vs. lay; presbyters vs. deacons vs. the rest of the Church). In this tension of opposites, Turner observed that each "constitute one another and are mutually indispensable."[84]

Preparation for ordination and ordination itself are liminal stages in one's ecclesial role. An ordinand is neither a layperson nor a ritual elder; she is in the in-between stage of negotiating roles, as she, together with the Church community, discern together the call of God, and in what form and in what location the call will materialize. Ordination necessarily involves a human person, with all the complexities and interwoven narratives that any one human being possesses. When we

82. Turner, *The Ritual Process*, 94. Reprinted as Turner, "Liminality and Communitas," 74. (Page citations are to the reprinted edition.)

83. Ibid., 75.

84. Ibid., 76.

multiply that tenfold or one hundredfold to include those numbered in a gathered assembly, there's an enhancement of theological discourse.

As we desire to examine the human element as an active participant in the meaning-making of the ordination process and the ordination rite, a new methodology is required which will enable us to locate the participant within their cultural, social, theological, and affective context. Chase observed that the added value of the narrative approach is to account not only of past events, but to also "express emotions, thoughts and interpretations."[85] In contrast to policy and doctrinal statements, narrative puts the spotlight on the narrator/self as the protagonist and values the uniqueness of each human and human action and not just their "common properties."[86] Questions which are neglected by the "official" ecclesial definitions of ordination include: Why ordination? What elements were significant for you? What did you obtain from the ordination rite? What now enables you to fully minister to the whole people of God when prior to your ordination you could not? What thoughts were going through your mind before, during and after your ordination service?

These and other related questions are premised on the classical notion of Reformed theology: *ecclesia reformata, semper reformanda secundum verba dei* ("reformed and always being reformed according to the word of God"). That is, that each local community contributes to the reforming and re-forming of the Church as they themselves are formed by the word of God. This means that the articulated theological reflection of an ordained minister as they have understood it going into their ordination and after the rite has happened are as important as the published ecclesial definitions offered by ecclesiastical documents or assemblies.

Narrative theory as a method alongside ritual studies will assist us greatly. One of the key interests of narrative theory is the stories told, shared, and enacted. Narrative theory can be considered secondary liturgical theology for it involves reflection upon the worship event. Narrative theory also values the role of the participant-observer-interviewer as he plays a vital role in the meaning-making that occurs in an ordination service. Narrative theory will enable us to closely analyze what has been shared and why, what Chase calls "biographical

85. Chase, "Narrative Inquiry," 656.

86. Ibid., 657.

particulars as narrated by the one who lives them."[87] What emerges for us are living persons, ordained officers, who seek to understand God, themselves, the Church, and their vocational calling while still being wedded to this nebulous notion of the "Reformed tradition" and the "Reformed" understanding of what it means to be called by God.

Through the leadership of Carl Savage and under the guidance of postmodern scholar Leonard Sweet, the Doctor of Ministry program at Drew University has advanced narrative theory for field site research.[88] Savage and company draw upon insights of postmodern and pastoral theology scholarship in regarding religious communities through the metaphor of the story narrative. Drawing upon Peircian semiotics and his use of abductive method of reasoning, the new method of narrative theory proposed by Savage and Presnell allows for multiple sensory experiences and inferences so that the senses are exposed to a wide array of experiences in the field site, what they call a "sensory banquet," in the form of stories of human experiences.[89]

The Savage-Presnell approach values the entirety of the ecological story-telling that takes place at a field site. The observer/researcher is called to be attentive to his/her own stories, experiences, background, assumptions and to intuit his/her observations and feelings. Their method urges the researcher to compare and contrast the stories told by the participants with one another, with the narratives of their communities, with that of the researcher's, essentially drawing upon as many sources as possible and entrusting that God will lead one to the "truth" of the world. [90] In comparing postmodern theology with pastoral theology, Savage and Presnell say that both seek to describe, but the latter also employs abductive logic to "hover over the faith-storied experiences human beings find meaningful, and discerning and describing these meanings so that they make sense."[91] What a community holds dear and meaningful is transmitted and received through generations of story-tellers through stories, symbols, and rituals, and as a researcher, one is privileged to receive a snapshot moment of that history.

87. Chase, "Narrative Inquiry," 651.

88. Savage and Presnell, *Narrative Research in Ministry*.

89. Ibid., 58.

90. Ibid., 59–60.

91. Ibid., 67.

Recall the previously referenced contribution of Peircian semiotics and the critical role in uncovering both the iconic and indexical dimensions of meaning. Narrative theory enables an interviewer to evoke the embedded perceptions, stories, and messages from participants.

Thus, for them, the researcher is a "story broker," who seeks to evoke from the multiple, spoken and embodied narratives the intersection of concerns and opportunities, where the researcher seeks to broker a negotiation between an unrealized potential or a negative condition and what they call a "preferred, emerging story" or what the community discerns as a positive work that God is doing among them.[92] The narrative of concern and opportunities in the four case studies in Chapter 6 will revolve around the reflections and experiences of participants with the laying on of hands as this has been identified consistently in the Reformed tradition as a critical and essential element in the rite of ordination, as well as the input offered by interviewees and survey respondents to the issue of presbyteral offices. These are narratives of concern, and have been within the Reformed tradition, as well as narratives for opportunity, as the concluding chapter will lift up, particularly in regards to ecumenical implications.

Because the process of ordination and the ordination rite involves a calling from God, the ordinand's response to that call, and a community's participation in the entirety of the process, there is an external, public dimension as well as an internal, personal dimension. In speaking about self-narrative, Bruner aptly summarizes the value of the narrative method for our purposes in explicating this external-internal dynamic:

> The object of a self-narrative was not its fit to some hidden "reality" but its achievement of 'external and internal *coherence, livability,* and *adequacy.*[93]

Chapter 6 will explore this external-internal tension in our analysis of the four case studies in Chapter 6. Suffice it to say that the stories told about one's call and a community's response to that call are a collective grappling with "coherence, livability, and adequacy" with one's self-understanding and self-identity, with a community's own

92. Ibid., 75.

93. Bruner, *Acts of Meaning*, 112. (emphasis not mine)

self-understanding, and how both the ordinand and the community come to understand their relationship to the connectional nature of the Church.

Akin to Moore-Keish's use of ritual studies to analyze the world of symbols in the Eucharistic rite, Polkinghorne supports our use of a narrative approach to enter into the meaning-making world of symbols in ordination. Polkinghorne observed:

> Human action occurs within cultural settings that maintain symbolic narrative forms for use in the articulation of action. These symbolic forms have a public character and are not the private understandings of a particular actor. Thus, an act is undertaken with the knowledge of what it will mean to the community in which it takes place.[94]

That the ordination process and the ordination rite are public and belong to and occur within a community, analysis of an ordinand's story and reflection about the process and rite must account for the ordinand's understanding of their place within the tradition and community as they borrow the handed down symbols of the Church (e.g. confessional statements, prayers, rites, creeds) and are active contributors to nuancing the meaning-making power of those symbols in a particular context. Polkinghorne's prescription of the narrative method addressed this dynamic, diachronic nature of the plots of our stories as we attempt to configure and reconfigure them into a "historical unity" of what has happened and what the possibilities are for the future.[95] The plot of an ordinand's story involves the environment of an ordinand's call (e.g. a pastor-friend, a church), preparation (e.g. seminary, field education internship), ordination (e.g. presbytery, community, denominational tradition), as well as projections of what God may be doing in their lives from the stuff of today for the stuff of tomorrow.[96]

94. Polkinghorne, *Narrative Knowing and the Human Sciences*, 144.

95. Ibid., 150.

96. Ibid., 152.

SIX

Ritual & Narrative Analysis in Action: Four Case Studies

WE PUT THE LITURGICAL-RITUAL-NARRATIVE methodology into action through analysis of case studies of four Presbyterian Church (U.S.A.) ordinations I participated in and observed: two ordinations to the office of ruling elder, and two ordinations to the office of minister of the Word and Sacrament/teaching elder. The liturgical-ritual-narrative methodology advocated by this project advances the discourse on the issue of ordination and church orders in our contemporary spirit of broad and wide communications that democratize meaning-making and provide wide accessibility to information.

I will examine these case studies by paying attention to the following:[1]

- Textual analysis of the ordination/worship liturgy (the order as well as the content);
- Phenomenological observation of the gestures, words, prayers, songs, movement of participants, liturgical space, location and placement of symbols as I experienced it both during the worship service and in post-event reflection in viewing my digital camera recording of the worship service;
- Worshippers' input through a survey questionnaire (Appendix 1);
- The narratives of the ordinand, the preacher, members of the

1. Moore-Keish, *Do This In Remembrance of Me*, 109–110.

ordaining body, and representative members of the gathered assembly through focus group-style interviews with transcription.

In the following sections, we will examine each field site one by one, then in the final section conduct a comparative analysis of the four.

Elder Ordination # 1 – Central New Jersey (EC)[2]

EC took place at a Presbyterian congregation over 150 years old in a middle-to upper-middle class bedroom community of central New Jersey. The surrounding town is mostly Caucasian; the congregation itself while mostly Caucasian has some racial-ethnic diversity. The worship attendance numbered about 150 people of all ages, which is almost the average worship attendance for this congregation.

EC occurred on Sunday, October 19, 2008 on Peacemaking Sunday. The senior pastor alerted me to the particular full and busy day this Sunday would be, that this being Peacemaking Sunday, there were congregational plans for a Crop Walk, an adult education class, in addition to the ordination and installation of an elder and a scheduled infant baptism. The senior pastor would not be preaching on this Sunday as was his custom, but he had invited a female doctoral student from Union Theological Seminary in New York to preach. She, unfortunately, could not join us for the focus groups because of time constraints.

Textual Analysis

The worship liturgy followed the five major movements described in the BoO: gathering around the Word, proclaiming the Word, responding to the Word, sealing of the Word, and bearing and following the Word into the world.[3] The community orientation of EC modified the five movements in the liturgy text by stating "we gather. . .," "we proclaim. . .,""we respond. . .;" the liturgy text does not explicitly say "sealing" or "bearing" but one can readily equate the sealing with the

2. The real names of cities, churches, and people will not be used. In all cases I will use the first initial of each. For people's names, I will use their initials. For the field sites, I will use "E" to designate elder or "M" to designate minister followed by the first initial of the city.

3. *BoO*, W-3.3202.

ordination and installation occurring after the offering, and rather than "bearing and following," the text says, "Go in Peace, to Serve in Love."

The worship liturgy involved the following elements:

- Prelude
- Introit
- Call To Worship
- Opening Hymn
- Prayer of Preparation and Confession
- Assurance of God's Love and Forgiveness
- We Give Glory to God
- Welcome and Ritual of Friendship
- A Time for Children
- Sacrament of Baptism
- First Scripture Reading
- Anthem
- Second Scripture Reading
- Sermon
- We Worship with our Offerings
- Ordination and Installation of Elder MK
  - Words of Introduction
  - Presentation of MK as Candidate for Ordination and Installation
  - Constitutional Questions to Church Leaders
  - Constitutional Questions to the Congregation
  - The Laying on of Hands and Prayer of Ordination
  - Declaration of Ordination and Installation
- Hymn of Ordination
- Prayers of the People and The Lord's Prayer
- Closing Hymn
- Benediction
- Postlude

The Peacemaking Sunday theme was expressed in several ways. The Call to Worship focused on God's work of justice in the world. The unison Prayer of Preparation and Confession was taken from South Africa, addressing injustice and poverty and asking God to send out the Church to be God's instrument of peace and justice. The Ritual of Friendship was connected with the senior pastor's welcome. The sermon titled, "Peace, Peace When There is No Peace," was delivered by a Ph.D. student of New Testament at Union Theological Seminary in New York who also served as co-founder of a para-church, non-profit ministry focused on justice issues. The offertory song during the collection of the offerings was called a "Song of Peace" (tune: Langlais). The closing hymn, "Canto de Esperanza (Song of Hope)," was played and sung to an Argentine folk melody.

Interestingly, the instructions for Laying on of Hands at the EC indicated "All previously ordained elders, ministers and deacons ordained in any PC(USA) congregation are invited forward." In the red-lettered rubrics of the BOS, the only ones designated to stand with the presiding minister at the time of the laying on of hands is to take place are other ministers of the Word and Sacrament and elders.[4] The EC's inclusion of deacons in the laying on of hands may speak to this particular congregation's openness to widening those who are involved in the act of ordination and/or the fact that two deacons were being installed (not ordained). Even then, the BOS rubrics do not stipulate that deacons are to be involved in the laying on of hands; only ministers and elders are named as situated near the elder or deacon candidate and are then instructed to lay hands on the candidates. From my friendship with the senior pastor, I know he is one who is an advocate of inclusivity in church orders and so this rubric in the EC's ordination liturgy did not come as a surprise.

Phenomenological Observations

Worshippers at EC congregated with much conversation with the playing of "Sheep May Safely Grace" (J.S. Bach) on the organ in the background as a musical prelude. The sanctuary is of an old wood, two side aisles and one center aisle in a semi-circle, sloping formation. The steps leading from the nave to the chancel area were blocked by four tables covered in blue felt upon which the hand bells for a bell choir are placed. The pulpit is to the right; the lector's lectern is to the left. An octagonal baptismal font, a marble, upright "ashtray" receptacle, stood just underneath the lectern. Hanging next to the font was a large U.S. flag. The Eucharistic table was at the top of chancel, covered with a white tablecloth and a green parament, with a chalice and a plate on

4. *BOS*, 25.

top, as well an open Bible, two vases of flowers, a golden cross, and two lit candles in two golden candleholders. Green paraments hang from the pulpit and lectern.

There was a strong sense of community and an intentionality of community participation. The Call to Worship involved congregational response; the Prayer of Preparation and Confession was offered in unison; the Gloria Patri sung in response to the Assurance of God's Love and Forgiveness was done while holding one another's hands; a Ritual of Friendship involving first the children coming to the center aisle to learn about family belongingness and then an invitation from the senior pastor to the whole congregation to hold one another's hands to signify peace and reconciliation as he led the congregation in a prayer for peace while the congregation repeated the prayer after him; and the community confessing the Apostles' Creed together.

The sermon was offered by a Ph.D. student in New Testament and a co-founder of a justice-oriented initiative. She offered examples of visiting areas where racial discrimination was taking place, food pantries for the homeless, demonstrations for non-violence, advocacy for adequate health care for all, and then called upon the congregation to work together for peace and justice in the world. The sermon was followed by the collection of the offerings, during which "Song of Peace" was sung to the Langlais tune.

The ordination service proper took place in the chancel area, near the Eucharistic table. While the BOS involves an explicit linkage to baptism within the service of ordination and installation, both in words and gestures, such as a "Reaffirmation of the Baptismal Covenant" and a "Thanksgiving for Baptism" prayer with water being poured into the font, the EC ordination service proper did not include such a linkage, either through the prayers, the litanies, or even the elder candidate MK being directed to remember his own baptismal covenant, particularly in light of the fact that an infant baptism had just occurred earlier in the worship service.

Elder candidate MK and the two deacons to be installed were called by the senior pastor to stand at the bottom of the chancel steps, facing the congregation. The senior pastor explained to the congregation the New Testament etymology of "Presbyterian" and that ordination involves calling and electing leaders from the congregation, and, thus, by their origin from the general body, all officers were equal. Elder candidate MK, the two deacons, and the senior pastor remained standing at the bottom of the chancel steps facing the congregation during the ordination litany, presentation of the candidates by the Session, and the propounding of the constitutional questions. The fact MK and the two deacons stood with the senior pastor on the base floor at the level of the pews visibly demonstrated the parity of officers.

At the appropriate time, all the previously ordained elders and deacons and myself as a minister of the Word and Sacrament, gathered around MK and the two deacons to do the laying on of hands. I was struck by the range of ages, and the great number of people from the pews and choir loft who came to fill the chancel area as we laid hands on MK. MK knelt in front of the Eucharistic table facing the tall golden cross atop the Table. After the ordination prayer, the entire gathering of ordained officers welcomed MK with hugs and pats on his back as the whole congregation welcomed him and the deacons with the singing of the ordination hymn.

I felt a sense of camaraderie with these fellow Presbyterians as we gathered in that chancel area. I noted that a few moments prior a little baby was baptized and how each one there was, at some point in all of our lives, baptized. And now MK was responding to God's call in this congregation to serve as an elder.

Survey Questionnaires

One hundred-twenty one (121) survey questionnaires were distributed during the offering by ushers and respondents were requested to fill out the questionnaire at some point during the worship service or after the worship service and deposit them in designated boxes, hand-deliver them to me, email their responses, or mail them to me. Forty-five (45) completed surveys were submitted, a response rate of 37%.[5]

Of those who responded, the general profile based on their self-identified description was Caucasian (82.22%), overwhelmingly Reformed/Presbyterian in their ecclesial heritage (60%), between the ages of 36–56 (73.33%), largely female though there were a number of male respondents, theologically moderate (46.67%), and a large number who were familiar with the constitutional documents of the PC(U.S.A.) and

5. Note: In this section, I refer to the quantitative analysis found in Appendix 2.

John Calvin. These numbers confirmed my own personal knowledge of the community and of this particular congregation having worked with them and their pastoral staff on previous projects and assignments.

Respondents had various understandings of ordination with no consensus on what ordination means. We note that over half of the respondents attended more than seven ordinations prior to EC (55.56%). The EC affirmed their prior understanding (65.63%) of what ordination means; with regards to their understanding their views, consistent with their familiarity with Calvin and the BoO of the PC(U.S.A.), held to the tripartite call of God (21.26%), the community (11.49%), and the individual (20.69%), the so-called "external" and "internal" dimensions of call and vocation. They affirmed, in smaller but still noteworthy numbers, that ordination involved sharing in Christ's ministry (12.07%) and the ordinand was becoming an officer of the denomination and the universal church (14.37%). One respondent wrote that ordination signified "[the] church officially confirming & entrusting the new titles/ roles of some [of its] members."[6]

When asked what image and/or word best described their experience of EC, some of the responses were: "spirit of unity;"[7]"business as usual;"[8] "connection, pride, tradition;"[9] "very joyful;"[10] "I became part of it;"[11]and "who can 'run' the church."[12]

Interestingly, even though an infant baptism occurred in this worship service, the linkage of ordination with baptism was not affirmed based on the results to answer 2d with regards to ordination as an extension of one's baptism (3.45%) and 2f with regards to the ordinand's

6. Respondent # C45. (Each returned survey questionnaire was coded. C45 designates that this was at field site in city C, and the 45th respondent)

7. Respondent #C3 – a Caucasian female, age 55–65, deacon, Reformed/ Presbyterian, theologically "liberal"

8. Respondent # C4 – a Caucasian female, age 46–65, layperson, Reformed/ Presbyterian, theologically "moderate"

9. Respondent #C13 – a Caucasian female, age 46–65, elder/deacon/friend of ordinand, Reformed/Presbyterian, theologically "moderate"

10. Respondent # C15 – a Caucasian female, age 55–65, family member of the ordinand, Reformed/Presbyterian, theologically "conservative"

11. Respondent # C20- a Caucasian female, age 76+, elder/deacon/friend of ordinand, Reformed/Presbyterian, self-described as theologically "mix" of liberal/ moderate/conservative

12. Respondent # C27 – a Hispanic female, age 46–55, elder/deacon/Session member, Roman Catholic, theologically "liberal"

linkage to the congregation as the baptized community (4.02%). This is consistent with what we noted above in the textual analysis that the ordination litany makes no explicit mention of baptism, and the response to question 14 about whether the connection of ordination and baptism (or the Eucharist) was made clear it was split 42.22 % and 31.11% of those who said "Yes" and "No, not really," respectively; of those who said there was a connection made between ordination and the sacraments only 12.7% said that the statement of ordination mentioned Eucharist and baptism, and 9.52% drew the connection because the baptismal font was in full view.

The laying on of hands was the most important aspect of the ordination service (30.88%). Over two-thirds affirmed that something "special" was indeed happening at the EC; what that "special" quality was had mixed responses with 15.38% responding that the Holy Spirit was empowering and blessing candidate MK (response 9b), and a tie of 11.97% of respondents indicating the Holy Spirit was blessing the community (response 9c) and candidate MK was being inducted into the rank of officers of the PC(U.S.A.) and the Church universal (response 9g).

That 10 respondents of the 45 answered "Yes" to Q11 and correctly ranked the 12 choices as the question requested, we will not spend too much time on Q12, but will note that of the respondents to Q12, there was an overwhelming affirmation (80%) that as people either participated in or witnessed the laying on of hands they felt the whole assembly was participating in the ordination service.

Whether one indicated the laying of hands as the most important aspect of the ordination service or not, respondents were queried as to what they thought the importance was of laying on of hands (Q13). A near majority indicated that imposition of hands signified the Holy Spirit empowering the candidate at that moment, with almost one-third indicating that the hands of the officers were the hands of Christ (13b) or the act was a gesture of welcome to a fellow ministry colleague (13e). Respondents affirmed that laying on of hands (17b) together with the presence of other ministers or elders from other churches (17a) both demonstrated the connection of EC with the Church universal.

Respondents were requested to write brief comments on what other occasions or events cause them to think or associate with ordination (Q18) and any other comments that they wished to express about their experience of this particular ordination (Q19). With regards to other occasions, some responses were: "commissioning of teachers for Sunday School, confirmation of youth (8th graders), baptism, sending ministers to conferences;"[13]and "when I participate in presbytery meetings and fulfill my ordination vow in doing so."[14] As for additional comments, the following response was offered: "I really enjoy the laying of hands - it makes it apparent how interrelated the members of this church are."[15]

A preliminary analysis of EC's ordination includes the following features:

- Respondents had strong sense of community
- EC affirmed their sense of ordination in the Presbyterian/Reformed tradition
- Laying on of hands was the most important aspect of the ordination service
- Laying on of hands signified the empowering presence of the Holy Spirit upon the elder candidate, as well as Christ's hand upon the candidate, and a gesture of welcome from the collegium of officers
- EC had a high regard for the ordination's connection to the Church universal and MK's connection to the body officers in the whole PC(U.S.A.) and the Church universal
- There was a muted linkage between baptism/Eucharist and ordination

As an aside, the holding of hands and the laying on of hands at EC expressed community in different senses. The holding of hands during the Children's message involved the entire community in the literal sense as they sought to experience being one fellowship around the children and imparting that experience with the children. The laying on of hands involved the blessing and authorization of the entire community in a representative sense. Members of EC were comfortable in witnessing and supporting the elders and deacons coming forward to the chancel area and laying on hands upon the ordinands on the community's

13. Respondent # C13

14. Respondent # C14 – Caucasian female, age 36–45, elder/Session member, Reformed/Presbyterian, theologically "moderate"

15. Respondent # C3

behalf. As will be seen below in the focus group interviews, the elders see the laying on of hands as especially significant in that they recalled the imposition of hands at their own presbyteral and, for some, diaconal ordinations, as connecting them to the communion of saints who have been previously ordained in the Church catholic. Hence, the holding of hands had a synchronic communal meaning for EC; the laying on of hands had both a synchronic-diachronic communal character.

Focus Group Interview[16]

The EC focus group interview involved two active/ruling elders on Session (GB and CV), the clerk of Session (AW), the newly ordained elder MK, and a previously ordained elder not presently serving on the Session (JN). The guest preacher, ET, could not attend as she was conducting an adult education class concurrent with the focus group interview and then had to leave immediately after her class session. There were attempts by the senior pastor and clerk of session to recruit two additional lay members who would serve as representatives of the worshipping assembly, but due to the busy-ness of the Peacemaking Sunday, there were no willing and able participants beyond the five who spoke with me. In addition to the five elders and myself present, a professional transcriptionist whom I retained was in attendance. The whole focus group proceeding for EC and for all subsequent focus groups in the other fields were video recorded and, likewise, transcribed.

The participants of the focus group were:

-GB, a young female ruling elder in her 30s

-CV, a female ruling elder in her 50s

-MK, the elder ordinand, a young male in his 30s

-AW, a male ruling elder, clerk of Session, in his 60s

16. Members of Elder Ordination Service of MK (pseud.), interview by author, 19 October 2008, Central New Jersey, transcription, Robert J. Cirillo, Inc, Florham Park, NJ.

References to the EC transcript will include page and line numbers in that order. For example, my name first appears in the transcript on page 2, line 2. This would appear in the footnotes as follows: EC, 2, 2.

(Note: per the stipulation of the Institutional Review Board of Drew University in their approval of the research instruments for all field site research, as well as the written consent agreement between me and my research subjects, the actual names of people are given by initials and the actual location of the ordination service and focus group interview are given as a generalized location within the state.)

-JN, a male ruling elder not on the Session, in his 60s

Members of the focus group had varying understanding of ordination prior to the ordination service, but was affirmed in their understanding by the ordination service. The ordinand, MK, viewed ordination as "the Lord bestowing upon the person service to the Church, and providing him or her with that power or knowledge and everything to worship the Lord and also to serve the Church as a whole."[17] CV asserted it was about the call, and that seeing MK ordained reinforced her ordination and helped her to remember her ordination vows. GB agreed with CV, but added that ordination is about an individual sensing and answering to an internal call, what she equates with a desire to want to serve, and that the internal call "may sometimes coincide with a need of the church or God coming down through the Church" or through someone asking a person to consider serving as an elder or deacon.[18] Both JN and SW agreed with the prior comments, with JN adding that ordination and installation was a necessary requirement of the Church, and SW added that ordination was also about taking on a new responsibility for the community as stewards of Christ and representing Christ, for he saw ordained responsibility as participating in and "to continue what was started by Christ over 2000 years ago."[19]

When asked about the source of their prior understanding of ordination, their past largely determined their present views. GB grew up in the Roman Catholic tradition and associated ordination with "becoming a priest,"[20] "authoritarian, hierarchical, paternal, a little bit misogynistic and really very set apart from the congregation as a whole."[21] This constricted view contrasted with GB's present view of ordination grounded in the whole community and the equality of officers. CV noted that she grew up in a Presbyterian household and that she grew up knowing one's place in the Church's history, and that when she became ordained she became keenly aware of how she would participate in and become a part of not only a particular congregation's history, but the whole Church's unfolding history.[22] SW, being the clerk of session

17. EC, 3, 11–15.
18. Ibid, 4, 3–10.
19. Ibid., 5, 10–11.
20. Ibid., 5, 25.
21. Ibid., 6, 11–13.
22. Ibid., 7, 7–13.

and in some sense the elder statesman of the group both in age and in title, noted the gradations of responsibility that he became aware of in first becoming a member of a church, then being ordained, and his observation that the church is responsible for itself and that by accepting the call to be ordained, an individual joins the church in its self-governance, further observing that a main principle of the Reformed faith is that we "in the Reformed tradition are responsible for making our own decisions."[23] JN attributed his understanding of ordination to personal reasons: his commitment to having his children grow up in a Church wherein the whole family was involved, a self-commitment to get more involved, and a sense of obligation to finally serve after the death of the former pastor.[24]

Both GB and CV saw MK's ordination as tied to their own personal connection with him as a colleague in ministry. Even though GB could not physically be in the sanctuary for the ordination but was part of the Session decision that certified MK ready for ordination and installation, GB knew MK more personally than the other participants and stated how she observed MK mature in faith, with ordination as a "culmination of where he should be and a calling that really came together."[25] GB added that because she was on the nominating committee that asked MK to consider serving, that his ordination was not merely about filling a gap of a responsibility in the church that needed to be done, but that it included "spiritual fulfillment" in the sense that there was a spiritual need in the church that needed to be filled and MK was being called to fill that need.[26] Later in the interview, MK said that he didn't feel his ordination was a culmination of his life and faith journey but that it was "a key point in my faith journey."[27] CV spoke of her enhanced awareness of the great responsibility it takes to be an elder, and that she "felt" that Mike was a right fit to serve as an elder: It just gave me a good feeling that this was right. It's right for Mike. It's right for this congregation. It just felt right."[28]

23. Ibid., 9, 18–20.

24. Ibid., 10, 3–11.

25. Ibid., 11, 11–12.

26. Ibid., 15, 17.

27. Ibid., 70, 22.

28. Ibid., 12, 6–8.

CV, JN, SW, and MK all viewed the laying on of hands as one of the most if not the most important aspect of the worship service as a whole and the ordination service proper. CV felt a feeling of "holiness" while everyone was laying on hands on the ordinands.[29] JN saw the laying on of hands as the powerful moment of the ordination service because of the number of people gathered and his understanding that "God's Spirit working through everybody" in the laying on of hands.[30] SW saw the laying of hands coupled with the confessing of the Apostles' Creed during the baptism as the most important aspects of the worship service because the former completed what the latter had begun earlier in the service, viz. sharing the faith that he grew up in, saying that perhaps he appreciated both pieces "maybe because of age or older or what not."[31] MK recounted how powerful the laying on of hands was in its anamnetic character of bringing to mind the story his father told him of an old family tradition in which every Easter MK's paternal great grandmother would crawl on her knees and kiss the feet of Christ's statue. As MK himself knelt before the giant gold cross atop the Eucharistic table coupled with the number of hands that were laid upon him, he concluded: "So kneeling before the cross just brought that together and as well as with everybody touching me. It just, it was so moving, so powerful."[32] Later in the interview, MK described that moment as "it was a feeling of humility. It was a feeling of empowerment. It was a feeling of camaraderie. It was a feeling of support and it was a feeling of holiness....the feeling of sort of timelessness in the fact that everything, everything seemed to work up to this point in time for me."[33] Whereupon hearing MK's account of his family, JN volunteered that whenever he (JN) serves as an usher, when he brings the collection plates forward down the aisle and he faces the giant gold cross, he is reminded of Christ's crucifixion.[34]

There were different views on what was happening at the laying on of hands. JN saw that the "spirit of God [was] being transferred amongst each other" and that the act signified a oneness of the gathered

29. Ibid., 16, 17.

30. Ibid., 17, 3–4.

31. Ibid, 17, 12–17.

32. Ibid., 18, 21–24.

33. Ibid., 70, 6–15.

34. Ibid., 19, 1–8.

and a unity of purpose in serving God.[35] GB noted that before she was ordained she empathized with those, such as a friend of hers, who thought that the laying on of hands by ordained officers upon other officers was exclusivist and elitist; now, as an elder herself, GB felt that laying on of hands was essential in communicating the connection of a wider and longer tradition to which the ordinand is connected to, and the camaraderie is expressed: ". . . it's a way of affirming to that person that they are part of a tradition, that they are part of a community, that there are people with them, they are not alone. There's a history before, there's going to be a future after them, you know, that lays ahead of them to do the work that they were ordained to do."[36] The ordinand, MK, agreed with GB's observation, seeing in the community that laid hands upon him as a ready resource for him in his service, to encourage him in his Christian discipleship, to navigate through questions; MK felt a belongingness to the community.[37] SW pointed to the connectional nature of the laying on of hands in the fact that previously ordained presbyters from all congregations are invited to lay hands, and he affirmed GB's observation that those who are not Presbyterian may see the laying on of hands as elitist.[38] CV spoke about how her growing up in the Presbyterian tradition made her sensitized to the laying of hands and so she never viewed it as exclusive; she saw laying of hands as affirming her own ordination, an act of setting someone apart for service, and an expression of collegiality towards the one being ordained.[39]

When asked about the distinct but related nature of baptism and ordination, there was greater consensus. MK saw baptism as initiation into the Church; ordination was taking a next step in indicating one's willingness and the recognition of one's willingness and ability "to be more of a servant and more of a leader for the Church as opposed to just being part of Christ's Church."[40] GB saw baptism as the *sine qua non* to being a church member, "be[ing] a worshipper, be[ing] a believer and be[ing] a follower and be[ing] a role model,"[41] but to be ordained is to

35. Ibid., 20, 3–8.
36. Ibid, 21, 3–9.
37. Ibid., 21, 14–23.
38. Ibid., 22, 20–25 to 23, 1–4.
39. Ibid., 24, 1–17.
40. Ibid., 26, 22–24.
41. Ibid., 27, 18–19.

be a leader, and, therefore, have a responsibility for the good and well-being of the whole Church. CV agreed with GB, adding the caveat, that ordination is to service in a particular way for a specified time.[42] She (CV) used the metaphor of a flock of geese with a lead goose alternating to lead the flock in a flight path formation. SW likened ordination to an inauguration, akin to the installation of a college president or senator, in which the Church recognizes those who are stepping forward and responding to the call to serve the common good.[43]

CV and GB reflected upon the wideness of the belongingness that comes with ordination. Because ordination is for life, both women saw ordination as drawing ordinands into the wider circle of the Reformed tradition and the Church universal.[44] When reflecting upon the width, length, and breadth of one's place in the tradition, CV and GB sensed the enormous responsibility that attended the ordained office.

I asked each participant to summarize ordination, as if they were to explain it to a five-year-old child. Participants viewed ordination in jurisdictional-governance terms more than the pastoral-liturgical functions of the office of elder. GB compared ordination to being sworn in to office, to become a leader "like the pastor," who attend meetings once a month, who guide the congregation, and who make decisions.[45] JN saw ordination as a call to serve the Church and "the teachings of Jesus Christ."[46] MK proposed that "ordination is accepting the responsibility to be a leader and serve for the Church."[47] CV and SW chose to pass on the question.

The focus group experienced their full participation in the ordination service at different points. JN felt there was a great sense of "community and empowerment" at the laying on of hands.[48] CV felt the propounding of the constitutional questions connected her to her own ordination vows.[49] For SW, the laying on of hands expressed the community. For GB, baptism was key because she envisioned the journey

42. Ibid., 28, 18.
43. Ibid., 31, 1–13.
44. Ibid., 33, 1–24.
45. Ibid., 35, 8–14.
46. Ibid., 35, 15–17.
47. Ibid., 35, 19–20.
48. Ibid., 36, 13–15.
49. Ibid., 36, 17–23.

of faith for the newly baptized, and how one's baptism may lead up to ordination.

I explored the question of the nature of "undivided plural ministry" that ministers, elders, and deacons share. All were unanimous in agreeing with MK's observation that the laying on of hands of ministers, elders, and deacons upon MK and the two deacons being installed brought all three offices together.[50] Interestingly, the three active elders—CV, GB, and SW—saw their roles as elders as ones who give approval for MK to be ordained, and approve a date for the ordination and installation to take place, but in the actual ordination service, they believed that their roles were no longer as elders in an official sense, that they became a part of the whole congregation and were in the congregation in a supportive function to encourage MK in his ordination.[51]

The group agreed that the reversion to terms "ruling elders" and "teaching elders" would be counterproductive to the democratic principles of Reformed polity. They felt such terms created an unnecessary hierarchy, that one should simply be a presbyter. When I explained the original meaning of "ruling" to designate lay elders' responsibility to assist in measuring the ethical and moral life of the congregation (as in gauging, like a measuring rod or ruler), they were more acceptable to the terms, but again resisted because of the common connotation of the term "ruling" with issues of power and authority, and the abuse of them.[52]

I had the group reflect upon an anti-hierarchical polity, one in which there were no official leaders, but that the whole baptized community would gather and await the leading of the Holy Spirit to reveal a leader or leaders. True to the theologically moderate position of this congregation as represented by these elders, this group saw the need for a middle ground of official offices set apart from the congregation but accountable to the congregation, representing the congregation, and in difficult cases, to discern a prophetic word for the congregation's life. They saw the necessity for offices and leadership to bring order and cohesion to a congregation's mission and government.

50. Ibid., 46–47,19.

51. Ibid., 48–49,10.

52. Ibid., 54–62.

Personal Experience as Participant-Observer

EC was a welcoming church. I had visited this congregation before; the pastor and I were friends. The setting of EC combined a traditional Reformed liturgy with the folksy, down-to-earth style of the pastoral leadership. This congregation actively participates in social justice ministries. Having EC on Peacemaking Sunday detracted from church orders and ordination, and, instead, placed the focus on peacemaking and the Church's witness in the world. I did not get a sense that EC downplayed the ordination, but, instead, emphasized the need for being a part of God's work of reconciliation in the community and the world through the children's message, the sermon, the scripture texts, and the inclusion of deacons in the laying on of hands.

I came away from the focus group interviews refreshed and hopeful for the Church. Focus group interviewees were young, middle-aged, and older adults. They welcomed a newly ordained elder who was in his thirties. They all expressed genuine joy and gladness at seeing the new ordinand become ordained, as they each and all lent their vocal support to him and as they shared experiences of nurturing him in his preparation process for ordination.

The focus group participants genuinely grappled with the questions I offered to them. For instance, they sought to understand a possible linkage between baptism and ordination, or the undivided, plural nature of the ordained offices.

Elder Ordination # 2 – upstate New York (EN)

The second elder ordination field site that we will examine occurred in upstate New York. Two elders were ordained and installed, along with four previously ordained elders who were installed, and seven deacons to be installed. The community in which EN took place was a largely Caucasian, middle-class town. Several residents were adversely affected by the Fall 2008 economic downturn. The Church is more than 200 years old. It is engaged in various community service and justice relief organizations through funding and member participation. EN occurred on Sunday, January 18, 2009 during Ordinary Time.

Textual analysis

The worship liturgy followed the standard Directory For Worship five-part movement.[53] The following order was observed:

- Welcome and Announcements
- Prelude
- Call to Worship
- Hymn
- Prayer of Confession
- Words of Assurance
- Gloria Patri
- Scripture
- Offertory
- Anthem
- Children's Time
- Scripture
- Sermon
- Silent Reflection
- Prayers of Intercession-The Lord's Prayer
- Hymn
- Ordination and Installation of Officers
    - Ordination Litany
    - Recognition of Women's Council
    - Constitutional Questions to Officers
    - Constitutional Questions to Congregation
    - Laying on of Hands
    - Unison Prayer
- Hymn
- Benediction
- Benediction Response
- Postlude

The opening hymn spoke of the historical awareness of this congregation. The hymn, "Our Founders Cleared an Open Field," was specially put to tune named after this congregation. This hymn is pasted on the back flap of the pew hymnals, and is used on special occasions,

53. BoO, W-3.3202 (gathering around the Word, proclaiming the Word, responding to the Word, the sealing of the Word, bearing and following the Word into the world.)

and is always used during ordinations, installations, and baptisms. The hymn after the "Prayers of Intercession" was "The Summons," a song about serving one another as Christ did. This hymn immediately preceded the ordination and installation service proper. The ordination and installation service proper occurred after the sermon, as a response to the Word read and proclaimed.

For the ordination and installation service proper, the liturgy basically followed the form in the BOS. The opening sentences of Scripture were printed as a responsive litany of pastor with congregation. This was followed by "Recognition of Women's Council," names of whom were printed underneath the names of the elders and deacons who were to be ordained and installed. Conspicuously missing from the order of ordination and installation was a mention of the "Reaffirmation of the Baptismal Covenant" or any liturgical, written linkage to baptism.

The ordination and installation service proper was immediately followed by a common hymn, "Here I Am, Lord."[54] This song is a common one in ordination services, as well as in worship services of judicatories. Recalling Moses,' Isaiah's, and Samuel's calls in the Old Testament as they responded to the voice of God, the song speaks to one's commitment to God's call to serve others.

Phenomenological Observations

The church building of EN had a rectangular nave of two side aisles with no center aisle. Three columns of pews were arranged theater-style. A pipe organ is situated at the rear of the sanctuary. The chancel area consisted of a pulpit, an ambo, the choir loft facing the congregation, the Eucharist table with two candlesticks on two golden candleholders upon which a paten and a chalice with the leftover bread from the previous time the congregation celebrated Eucharist were laid. A wooden Celtic cross hung on the chancel wall. There were not many decorative elements, except for red paraments that hung from the ambo and pulpit. Although this Sunday was in the liturgical calendar in Ordinary Time and therefore green paraments would usually be used, this congregation was intentional about using red paraments for the occasion of the ordination and installation of officers. A Christian flag and American

54. See Appendix 12 for the lyrics to this song.

flag stand on either side of the side door leading into the sanctuary from the multi-purpose room. The free-standing octagonal, wooden, baptismal font with cover stood just at pew level just beneath the pulpit, next to the steps leading up to the chancel. The sanctuary windows are decorative stained-glass, illuminating the whole sanctuary with natural light, augmenting the gold chandeliers inside. Simple banners bearing various themes from the Advent and Christmas seasons hung from the sanctuary walls.

As the worship begins, there is a solemn feeling as people quiet down and listen attentively to the female pastor, who greets visitors and shares community announcements. The organ played the prelude as the candlelighter, a young girl, comes forward to light the candles on the Table. About 100 people, mostly middle-aged adults, Caucasian, were in attendance.

The pastor connected the children's time message to Barack Obama's presidential inauguration that would occur two days later, and to ordination. She asked all elders and deacons who would be ordained and/or installed to stand as she made the point that all are important, all are precious in God's eyes, and that each one is needed for the Church to function well. She likened ordination to the presidential inauguration.

The chosen Scripture texts for the sermon were 1 Peter 4:7–11 and Matthew 4:18–22. The former spoke of the ethics of those who serve, and the latter spoke of Christ's calling of the first disciples. The sermon was focused on ordination, indicating that this particular Sunday is the day to ordain officers, the Sunday that begins the Week of Prayer for Christian Unity (January 18, 2009). The pastor shared her understanding of ordination and vocation. She shared that ordination is a response to God's call in which the Church acknowledges God's call upon an individual to serve the Church in a particular way. Ordination calls some from the whole body for a specific service, but that it does not get "the rest of you off the hook." Here she cited baptism, in which all have been called to serve.

In preaching about the call of the first disciples, she focused not on why they answered Christ's call, but the fact that in spite of whatever hindrances unbeknownst to us, the disciples answered "Yes" to Jesus Christ. She emphasized that God in Christ can use anyone, just as Christ called fishermen and tax collectors. Christ invites people now to be what we were meant to be. She cited Drew University professor and postmodern scholar, Leonard Sweet, in his discussion of shoes: shoes are not merely fashion statements but they speak about where our lives are directed and going, that shod with shoes we can stride almost anywhere. She connected this to Christ's call to wear His shoes, the sandals that we are unworthy to tie. She called the congregation to imagine the people whose lives have traversed the 200-plus years of the congregation's history. She summed up, "Christ's shoes become our shoes, and our shoes become Christ's shoes;" this spoke of our sharing in and continuation of Christ's ministry now.

At the ordination and installation service proper, the pastor followed almost verbatim the BOS liturgy of ordination and installation. As noted in the textual analysis above, linkage to baptism was conspicuously missing. The "Statement on Ordination and Installation" in the BOS is followed by the presentation of the ordinands by the clerk of session, then the "Reaffirmation of the Baptismal Covenant," then the "Renunciations," then the "Thanksgiving for Baptism."[55] The Reaffirmation, Renunciations and Thanksgiving were skipped and the service proceeded straightaway to the Constitutional Questions to Officers. All ordinands faced the congregation at the bottom of the chancel steps. Numbered among the diaconal ordinands were two teenage boys who appeared excited at the prospect of being ordained.

At the laying on of hands, those elders and deacons who were to be ordained were invited to kneel at the chancel steps. All those previously ordained as elders or ministers were invited to stand behind the ordinands for the laying on of hands. There was a great number of presbyters who stood behind the ordinands as we filled the chancel area. I felt a sense of being in community with this congregation. We welcomed the newly ordained and installed officers.

Survey Questionnaires[56]

Worship attendees were given a survey questionnaire as they entered the sanctuary, and were then invited to drop off the questionnaire at four different locations on the church premises, hand-deliver to me, email the responses to me, or mail them to me by postal mail. One

55. *BOS*, 19–23.

56. In this section, I will be referring to the quantitative analysis found in Appendix 3.

hundred thirty-eight (138) survey questionnaires were distributed, of which eighty-three (83) were returned and were in a form that was usable; thus, there was a 60.1% return rate.

The survey respondents were largely Caucasian (97.59%), almost evenly split between the genders, middle- to older- aged adults, raised Reformed/Presbyterian (44.58%), theologically moderate to left-of-center, and familiar with the constitutional documents of the Presbyterian Church (U.S.A.) as well as somewhat familiar with the theology and writings of John Calvin. The demographic of the respondents was representative of the general demographics of the congregation and in many ways, of the town itself, with the exception of religious affiliation as there was a large segment of Roman Catholics and Congregationalists in this particular town.

For 61.45% of the respondents, they had attended more than seven ordinations prior to EN. In their understanding of ordination prior to EN, there was a great number who indicated that ordination involved both God's calling upon an individual (19.68% or 62 responses) and an individual's response to a call (20.63% or 65 responses). This particular ordination affirmed those prior beliefs; as stated earlier, there was nothing conspicuously different from this ordination so such affirmation was not surprising. In terms of aspects of the worship service that spoke to the meaning of ordination, respondents ranked the sermon and the laying on of hands as equal in expressing the meaning. As noted earlier, the sermon was focused on ordination, made the linkage to baptism, and in many ways, served as the statement on ordination that well-articulated a meaning of ordination. The hymns were ranked second in terms of expressing the meaning of ordination. It was noted earlier that particularly the two closing hymns, "The Summons" and "Here I Am, Lord," spoke clearly about Christ's call to serve one another. The sense of solemnity in EN was experienced as joyful on the part of most respondents.

The most important aspect of the EN was the laying on of hands (Q7). The sermon was ranked a distant second. The laying on of hands was also ranked the most important aspect not only in terms of the ordination service proper, but also in the responses to the question about how they felt the assembly was "fully participating" in the ordination service. More than 90% of the responses indicated that by participating in or witnessing the laying on of hands, they felt the assembly was participating in the ordination service. Respondents also ranked the laying on of hands as the key part in the ordination service that connected EN to the universal Church (Q17). This was consistent with the 24.09% of responses for choice 13f ("There was a connection being made with the apostolic faith and the apostolic witness throughout the ages") in their understanding of what was happening during the laying on of hands.

Respondents saw the important role of the Holy Spirit in the ordination service (Q9). They were almost equal in indicating that the Holy Spirit was empowering and blessing the ordinands (14.55%), as well as blessing the gathered community (16%). This can be compared to the responses to Q13 where 31.39% of responses indicated that the Holy Spirit was empowering the ordinands at the moment of the laying on of hands.

The connection to baptism or the Eucharist was made almost equally clear by the hymns and sermon (Q15). As noted earlier, the closing hymns in particular were clear in Christ's call to join His work of service. The sermon was more explicit in stating the connection of baptism, and the equalizing effect of baptism upon the whole people of God, from whom certain persons are set apart for particular functions.

The written responses to Q10 showed this congregation's awareness of historical linkages and the presence of Christ. A sampling of comments indicating images or phrases with which respondents associated this ordination service, included the following: "connection with past & future - a link in the chain;"[57] "continuity of responsibilities;"[58] "Christ's loving arms encircling us;"[59]and "Christ laying his hands on his people."[60]

As for other times in which respondents thought of ordination, in response to Q18, many respondents indicated that they think of ordination when new ministers are ordained or received into the presbytery.[61]

57. Respondent #H1 – Female, age 55–65, Session member, Caucasian, grew up Lutheran and Dutch Reformed, theologically liberal

58. Respondent # H3 – Female, age 55–65, Observer, Caucasian, grew up Baptist, theologically liberal

59. Respondent #H30 – Female, age 55–65, Elder, Caucasian, grew up Presbyterian/Reformed, theologically moderate

60. Respondent # H56 – Male, age 46–55, Friend and Observer, Caucasian, grew up Roman Catholic, theologically conservative

61. Respondents #H2 (Female, age 46–55, Family member, Caucasian, grew up

Others were reminded of ordination when they serve the church in various capacities: "carry out work in church;"[62] "when I tire of the related work and responsibility;"[63] and "mission outreach and serving as moderator of a committee."[64] Two respondents explicitly indicated the connection they associated ordination with the sacraments: "during baptisms and communion"[65] and "baptism."[66]

Focus Group Interview[67]

I was invited to hold focus group interviews during an actual Session meeting. In attendance were the pastor JR; clerk of session JN; elders BA, KP, AH, PJ, BM, MI, DW, ML, LW, IM, RR, JS, RW, BB; newly ordained and installed elders CR and CH; and congregation member JB. Because other business of the Session was to be conducted after my focus group interview, there was not adequate time to notate the particular demographic profile of each participant. The general demographic

Reformed/Presbyterian, theologically moderate), H22 (Female, age 36–45, deacon/family/observer, Caucasian, grew up Reformed/Presbyterian, theologically conservative), H30 (Female, age 55–65, elder, Caucasian, grew up Reformed/Presbyterian, theologically moderate), H48 (Male, age 66–75, elder, Caucasian, grew up Reformed/Presbyterian, theologically moderate to liberal), H59 (Male, age 55–65, Session member, Caucasian, grew up Baptist, theologically moderate), H63 (Male, age 55–65, elder/deacon, Caucasian, grew up Brethren, theologically liberal), H65 (Male, age 46–55, elder/family, Caucasian, grew up Roman Catholic, theologically moderate), and H82 (Female, age 76+, elder/deacon, Caucasian, grew up Baptist, theologically moderate).

62. Respondent #H9 – Female, age 66–75, elder/deacon/friend, Caucasian, grew up Reformed/Presbyterian, theologically liberal and moderate.

63. Respondent #H23 – Female, age 66–75, Session member/deacon, Caucasian, grew up Reformed/Presbyterian, theologically liberal.

64. Respondent #H78 – Male, age 66–75, Session member, Caucasian, grew up Reformed/Presbyterian, theologically liberal; and H79 – Female, age 55–65, elder, Caucasian, grew up Methodist, theologically liberal.

65. Respondent #H10 – Female, age 46–55, observer/layperson, Caucasian, grew up Reformed/Presbyterian, theologically conservative.

66. Respondent #H62 – Male, age 55–65, elder/deacon/layperson, American, grew up Reformed/Presbyterian, theologically conservative.

67. Members of Elder Ordination Service of CH and CR (pseud.), interview by author, 18 January 2009, upstate New York, transcription, Action Reporting Service, Syracuse, NY. I will use the same numbering system as with the previous focus group. For this focus group, as my name first appears on page 3, line 2 of the transcript, I would designate it as EN, 3, 2 (where "E" designates elder ordination, and "N" as first initial of the actual city name).

of the Session was almost evenly split male-female, all Caucasian, and middle- to older- age adults.

PJ indicated that he grew up in the Episcopalian church. He was ordained last year, so the ordination of elders and deacons was new to him, and having all the presbyters to lay hands on the ordinands was a new experience for him. He previously regarded ordination as "just an ordination of ministers or priests and this is something new."[68] RW, who also was raised Episcoplian, agreed with PJ.

IM viewed ordination universally with particularity. He regarded ordination as connecting the ordinand and the Church "as a calling back to the time of Christ" and that as a disciple of Christ now he (IM) was continuing the service of generations before him to serve "[a]t this point in time at this church that I am here to serve the people of this church and this community. . . ."[69]

JS saw ordination as being given and receiving new responsibility as well as receiving the support and encouragement of the congregation, the pastor, and God.[70]

AH saw herself as a part of the general congregation during the ordination service, and that, for her, the ordination service reminded her, as it reminds others who serve in various capacities, of the calling to which she was tasked to do.

The newly ordained elders, CR and CH, stated that they had not hitherto regarded ordination in broad terms beyond "a public commitment and accepting a charge to an officer in the church and to be willing to serve."[71] CH added that she had thought that ordination was "just something within the family of the church. And as reading through this, I do see it differently now."[72] Both of them had previously served as deacons. They both affirmed the educative value of the focus group and survey questionnaire as they had learned about the broader dimensions of ordination.

KP concurred with CH and CR, in that she had regarded ordination as only functioning for this particular congregation and had not considered the connection to the broader Church context.

68. EN, 3, 17–18.

69. Ibid., 5, 8–13.

70. Ibid., 5, 17–20.

71. Ibid, 6, 25 to 7,3.

72. Ibid., 7, 11–13.

RR, who also grew up Episcopalian, saw that with ordination there was an added benefit: ordination "gave me a stronger feeling of responsibility that I was just not a common layman. . . ."[73]

BM, who likewise was Episcopalian before joining this particular congregation, associated ordination with all the church members participating in the church's life and witness because in the Episcopalian church "I mean, we attended church every week but that was it. I never got involved or participated in anything. . . ."[74]

ML grew up Southern Baptist. She noted how Baptists do not ordain woman so she expressed her delight that women are ordained. BA, later on in the interview, urged the focus group to note that half the session were composed of women.[75] ML underlined the importance of that aspect of ordination in which the ordinand gives of themselves to others, to the service of others. She observed, "It's very hard to sit through that, I think, without realizing that that's what you're doing when you become ordained."[76]

Clerk of Session JN saw ordination as an acknowledgment of past, present and future: one's place in the "community of faith, Christian faith, the local church, and the acknowledgment of the future of the church through your work."[77]

JB regarded ordination as an individual accepting God's call, indicating one's willingness and readiness to do the work, as well as a public recognition and affirmation of the congregational support system, i.e. the whole congregation is expressing its support to the ordinand as he/she carries out God's work.[78]

BB, who grew up Roman Catholic, was "terrified" when she was first asked to consider serving on Session because she felt unworthy to offer anything to the church. Then she came to the realization that the call was from God to serve in the church, and for her, the laying on of hands helped her to realize that "it's more than just this church, it's you know, a higher being."[79]

73 Ibid., 8, 4–5.

74. Ibid., 8, 9–12.

75. Ibid., 10–11.

76. Ibid., 9, 3–6.

77. Ibid., 9, 17–21.

78. Ibid., 10, 2–5.

79. Ibid., 10, 23–24.

On the question of what aspect expressed the essence of ordination, there were various viewpoint. IM offered that the laying on of hands served as a "[c]onfirmation of my commitment and the fact that I am like a speck of sand on a beach. I'm one of billions of people who have served Christ throughout eternity and will continue to do so."[80] JN agreed with IM but added that the hymns also had a pattern—the first hymn ("Our Founders Cleared an Open Field" served as a question, with the second hymn ("The Summons") serving as an answer, and the last hymn ("Here I Am, Lord") as the acceptance.[81] ML agreed with IM, and added how significant it was for deacons and past Session members to be included in the laying on of hands. CR saw the first scripture reading (1 Peter 4:7–11), the sermon, concluding with the laying on of hands as integrating all pieces into one, connecting the church and the ordinands "back in time, as far as back as time exists and we're all here together and we'll continue to be together going forward."[82] BB saw the laying on of hands coupled with the constitutional questions to officers that brought the whole ordination service together. AH noted that the movement of worship focused on an individual's response, until the laying on of hands when "it's wow, we're really part of this chain that goes back to not only the beginnings of this church but the beginning of the church."[83] RR noted his Episcopalian upbringing and how he had experienced laying on of hands but in the context of physical healing. When RR was ordained and hands were laid on him, he felt the presence of God and that "I was meant to be there to serve."[84] JB shared how when she was a deacon and she sat in the pews while she saw most of the congregation who were elders go up and lay hands on another ordinand, she felt a yearning to experience laying hands on someone else. KP treasured the moment that when two strong hands were on her shoulders, she imagined all the previous members of the more than 200 years of this congregation's history who had laid hands on others and who themselves received laying on of hands from others. Pastor

80. Ibid., 12, 3–7.

81. Ibid., 12, 14–18.

82. Ibid., 13, 13–16.

83. Ibid., 14, 14–17.

84. Ibid., 15, 8–9.

JR affirmed KP's observation that "I'm a part of that chain and feel the hands, which is pretty powerful."[85]

I shared with the focus group T.F. Torrance's insight that in ordination we are joined to the priesthood of Jesus Christ and the Church shares in the past, present and future ministry of Christ. Pastor JR shared how the first hymn, "Our Founders Cleared an Open Field" (a hymn written specifically for this congregation), really connected her to Jesus Christ and to the Church of all ages.[86] AH pointed to the "timelessness" of the scripture, the sermon, the Bible stories, and the hymn "Here I Am, Lord" as a personal acceptance of responsibility. RR pointed to the music's synchronous relation to the sermon. JN affirmed JR's children's message and sermon as good reminders that the whole congregation has a responsibility to answer and heed God's call to service.

I asked the focus group about the difference of and the relationship between ordination and baptism, with the pointed question, "Why then get ordained?" Newly ordained elder CH saw ordination as a necessary reaffirmation "of all my Christian upbringing."[87] CR spoke of her Baptist upbringing and how in that tradition she understood that to believe in Christ one had to come to a point at a later age to be really aware of Christ and therefore one would arrive at a point in their lives to accept and believe with what they understand. Thus, CR saw ordination as "when you're accepting an officership for something, at that point you're aware and you are consciously accepting if for yourself." CR's comments made me wonder about whether ordination and confirmation were regarded in her mind as synonymous, in which case, if the latter were emphasized, what part would the former have in her formulation of vocational formation? BA agreed with CR that ordination indicated a certain level of maturity. AH summarized that baptism is a call and ordination is a response to that call. MH saw baptism and ordination in terms of levels of participation and commitment: the former indicated that, at the very least, one who was baptized will come to church on Sunday; the latter indicated a commitment and participation beyond Sunday worship attendance. BM agreed with MH: "It's a calling to get more involved."[88] BB likened ordination to a kind of second-order

85. Ibid., 16, 22–23.

86. Ibid., 19, 11–20.

87. Ibid., 25, 11.

88. Ibid., 27, 10–11.

baptism, one in which you were more aware of things, unlike an infant baptism or a baptism as a child, where you were either unaware of the baptism or you possessed only rudimentary facts about the faith. JN was more explicit in affirming BB's point that ordination "[i]t's a difference kind of baptism."[89] Pastor JR saw ordination as being "fully committed" that baptism did not quite do in her infant baptism. She concluded, ". . . I live out my ordination as I live out my baptism."[90] AH came to the realization that the Constitutional Questions asked of a minister of the Word and Sacrament and an elder are almost identical. RR shared how he was a Baptist before becoming Episcopalian and then Presbyterian. He had been baptized by immersion and had no knowledge or recollection of his confirmation. For him, ordination confirmed baptism, "becom[ing] ordained has simply reinforced that baptism. . . ."[91]

Because so many had seen ordination as a confirmation of one's baptism, I was led to ask that if a church did a good job in living out its baptismal commitments, would ordination still be necessary? BA answered from a polity perspective, indicating that baptismal vows, while similar to the ordination vows, do not cover one's commitment to be governed by the polity of the church. CR also answered from a polity standpoint, saying that ordination was necessary as a public recognition of who the legitimate leaders and decision-makers for a particular congregation are.[92] JS agreed that ordination was necessary for a reaffirmation of faith and public recognition of who the duly elected leaders are.[93] ML saw ordination as not another layer on top of baptism, but as a humbling reaffirmation that you are a servant.[94] JB pointed to her experience that she had not been baptized up until her wedding and she came to a point when she felt, "Is it time that I could be baptized? Because for me I was missing something. . . .I was missing being incorporated, joining that greater community."[95] She then observed that when she then became a part of the larger community, she wondered

89. Ibid., 28, 15–16.

90. Ibid., 29, 13–14.

91. Ibid., 30, 12–13.

92. Ibid., 33, 19–24.

93. Ibid., 36, 9–11.

94. Ibid., 38, 2–3.

95. Ibid., 38, 17–21.

how she could use her particular gifts to serve the church. She said, "[t]hat's where I see the call and the ordination."[96]

That many associated ordination with a reaffirmation of faith, I asked how many times a service of "Reaffirmation of the Baptismal Covenant" is observed in this congregation and if more frequency of such a service would vitiate the necessity of ordination. JN replied that baptism does not necessarily make one a servant for the whole church; ordination "takes you to the next step where you are now ready to serve others not just bring it for yourself, but to take it out to others."[97] CR agreed with JN in saying that baptism does not place a particular, named obligation or task upon an individual to the community; ordination is specific in assigning function and particular in the person(s) being called.

To the question of the "undivided plural ministry" of ministers, elders, and deacons, there were various understandings of the shared, but distinct ministries of the three classical Reformed offices. CH regarded the deacons as "the workhorse" while the elders made decisions about "common goals," but both work towards the same goal. CR, who had previously been ordained a deacon, wondered why an additional ordination for the eldership was necessary. JR, who had been ordained an elder before her ordination as a minister of Word and Sacrament, saw ordination as to a specific role and responsibility.

LW wondered the difference between ordination and installation. I reflected with him that if baptism was our primary ordination, can service in the three offices—minister, elder, deacon—be initiated through installation? JS replied that replacing ordination with installation would "risk decreasing the importance of each of them."[98] IM linked ordination to communion in that when the Eucharist is celebrated ordinary elements are set aside for special use; likewise in ordination, "ordinary personage" is being set aside "for those special purposes of doing that work."[99]

Because the preacher plays an important role in any ordination, I was interested in learning from pastor JR of her thought process in developing the sermon for the EN. She indicated that for EN and for all

96. Ibid., 39, 6–7.

97. Ibid., 41, 15–18.

98. Ibid., 50, 25 to 51, 2.

99. Ibid., 51, 20–24.

other ordinations, she intentionally selects Scripture passages and crafts a sermon that addresses ordination for "it makes it more meaningful to those being ordained at the time" as well as to educate those "who may not have a clue about what happens with the ordination."[100]

Beyond the official role of the Session of approving and authorizing the ordination and installation of officers and the setting of the date of such to occur, elders saw their roles in the ordination service with various understandings. JS saw his role as to lend support to the new officers. BA, likewise, saw her role as to be supportive. AH saw her role to be an encourager.

JB, a layperson who was not ordained to any office, saw her role as being "a witness [to] what is occurring, to be a reporter."[101] She saw her role in the congregation as changing as the laying on of hands occurred; prior to the laying on of hands, she was a supporter of all of the ordinands, then as presbyters went forward to the chancel area for the laying on of hands, JB understood her role to be a witness. JB expressed a yearning feeling she gets when she sees others participating in the laying on of hands and she is unable to because of her non-ordained status.

I asked the focus group to imagine explaining ordination to my young sons (my then 5 year old son, Daniel, had accompanied me on this particular field site visit and was in the next room). JN replied that ordination is about "accepting, another step in accepting God's call because they're the community."[102] IM would explain ordination as helping the ministry of the church.

Personal Experience as Participant-Observer

EN was welcoming in that the liturgy felt comfortable because it was traditional. EN was in a congregation that prided itself on its historical place in the community and in the PC(U.S.A.). The actual liturgy and the liturgical movements were traditional, following almost exactly the pattern in the Directory for Worship. There were little attempts to nuance traditional Reformed theology or polity in the focus group interviews.

100. Ibid., 52, 17–21.

101. Ibid., 59, 21–22.

102. Ibid., 65, 16–17.

Minister Ordination # 1 – eastern Pennsylvania (MP)

The first of the two minister ordination sites that we will examine in this section occurred in an urban, middle-class, multi-ethnic neighborhood of eastern Pennsylvania. Within a few feet of the church building are homeless persons, civic offices, an arts center, and a Starbuck's®. The church is less than 10 years old; its membership is composed of persons ranging from their 20s to their lower 40s, educated, middle- to upper- middle class. The congregation meets in a large, Gothic-looking building that had been abandoned by a now defunct Presbyterian congregation. The congregation is actively engaged with social justice and political advocacy work in the city, hosting a homeless shelter, a homeless café, a "No Holds Barred" Bible study, and an active youth initiative that hosts various youth groups from all across the country for urban ministry immersion experiences. MP occurred on Saturday, December 6, 2008 during Advent.

Textual Analysis

While a "standard" worship bulletin in Presbyterian churches would be a folded or tri-folded paper with several inserts, MP's worship liturgy was a simple, black-and-white, four page, double-sided 8.5 inch by 11 inch paper, stapled.

Because MP was a minister ordination overseen by a presbytery commission but held at a local congregation, the main focus of the worship service was the ordination service.

The worship liturgy text cover expressed the main thrust and theme of this ordination service: baptism and mission. On the cover was a black-and-white photograph of a sleeping baby on his/her mother's chest, with a child standing beside the baby with one hand on the baby's head and the other on the baby's back, as another child's hand is placed on the baby's head. Underneath the photograph is the following quote from Barbara Brown Taylor's book, Leaving Church:

> If churches saw their mission in the same way, there is no telling what might happen. What if people were invited to come tell what they already know of God instead of to learn what they are supposed to believe? What if they were blessed for what they are doing in the world instead of chastened for not doing more

> at church? What if church felt more like a way station than a destination? What if the church's job were to move people out the door instead of trying to keep them in, by convincing them that God needed them more in the world than in the church?[103]

The following elements were in the liturgical ordo:

- Prelude
- Call to Worship and Welcome
- Hymn
- Prayer of Confession
- Assurance of Pardon
- Scripture
- Hymn
- Sermon
- Affirmation of Faith
- Announcement of Offering and Its Purpose
- Musical Offering
- Service of Ordination
    - Constitutional Questions to the Candidate
    - Questions to the Congregation
    - Laying on of Hands
    - Prayer of Ordination and The Lord's Prayer
    - Passing the Peace
    - Presentation of Symbols of Ministry
    - Charge to the Pastor
    - Charge to the Congregation
- Music
- Benediction

The order of worship followed the five-part movement as prescribed by the Directory For Worship of the Book of Order. The musical prelude was "O Come, O Come Emmanuel," a nod to the time of Advent as well as an epiclesis for MP. The Call to Worship underlined the inclusivity of God's call, not only as a responsorial litany, but in indicating that God's call was to "Women and men, old and young, poor and rich, weak and strong" all for the cause of peace and justice. The Prayer of Confession, from the Iona Community, continued the theme of the Veni Emmanuel in acknowledging the ubiquitous presence of God in all of creation and

103. Taylor, *Leaving Church*, 222.

in people, and expressed a contrite heart at "trampl[ing] You in creation] and "reject[ing] You in the poor." The Scripture text was from 2 Corinthians 5 and 6 emphasized God's work of reconciliation in Christ, our joining in that work, and the great cost to ourselves in being a part of that work. The Affirmation of Faith was a responsorial litany from South Africa, in which various Scripture passages serve as the congregation's gospel response to falsehoods perpetuated by powers and principalities of the world, such as:[104]

> One: It is not true that we must accept inhumanity and discrimination, hunger and poverty, death and destruction;
> **Many: This is true: I have come that they may have life, and have it abundantly.**
> One: It is not true that violence and hatred shall have the last word, and that war and destruction have come to stay forever;
> **Many: This is true: For to us a child is born, to us a son is given, in whom authority will rest, and whose name will be Prince of Peace.**

The ordination service proper as printed in the liturgical text is simple. It names the various parts and elements (e.g. Constitutional Questions to the Candidate, Laying on of Hands) and those persons designated to perform or coordinate that part, but otherwise, the text does not elaborate on what was expected from the assemblyl or what each element meant. The ordination service proper liturgy is 10 lines, single-spaced, which seemed to designate that while MP was the focal point of this gathering, the liturgical text belied that fact and, instead, for better, in my estimation, placed the ordination service within the larger framework of the Church's worship and God's call to the Church to be about the work of Christ's reconciliation in the world. The relative smallness and simplicity of the ordination service proper text seemed to communicate that what was most important was not the ordaining of the candidate, but the ministry of peace and justice that comes with that ordination and when the assembly dispersed.

104. The boldface font was used in the worship liturgy to designate the congregational response, and is used here not for emphatic purposes but in the spirit of verbatim retention.

Phenomenological Observations

MP occurred on a snowy, winter, Saturday night in an urban city of eastern Pennsylvania. The sanctuary was an old church building with homeless people wandering the streets, an arts center and school across the street, civic center a few blocks away, and a Starbuck's® adjacent to the church building.

Much of the wooden pews have been removed from the sanctuary to create a clearing where movable chairs are placed in an oval-shape setting, like the open- and close- parenthesis marks "(" and ")." In the middle of this setting is an open space where an empty wooden chair is placed, upon which is a wooden chest box/luggage. A lectern is on one end of the clearing, and a Eucharistic Table is laid on the other end opposite the lectern. Atop the Table are three large candles, three smaller candles, a flower vase, and a large closed Bible. Familiar with the pastoral leadership of this church and this new church's history, I know that the empty chair in the middle signifies those who have been excluded from the Church and society but who are loved by God and who the Church strives to serve, love, and include.

The drab sanctuary belies the life that is emerging in this place. This young adult, new church development has gathered in this sanctuary for about four years, meeting in a place whose Gothic architecture and storied past peeks from the stained glass windows and the discolored stone and overlaid paint that covers the walls. Above the oval worship space below hung suspended origami cranes, in which prayers from various homeless individuals were inscribed and lifted for the whole Church to be continually reminded of those with whom the Church serves and loves. The pastor of the Church, in sharing with the assembly what those cranes were about, called the prayer cranes "a talisman against pettiness." Next to the origami cranes are about eight suspended metal windmills installed by a local artist. This congregation embodied and valued their context.

The gathered assembly was quiet as the ordination commission entered in single-file line led by the presbytery moderator. The commission that processed in was composed of all women (three Caucasian women, one Korean woman) and two men, one of whom processed in with the commission.

I felt the holiness of the moment in that MP was occurring in Advent. The musical prelude was "O Come, O Come Emmanuel" sung by a young adult laywoman cantor from the host congregation. Her melodious voice reverberated throughout the Gothic sanctuary, creating a feeling of solemn preparation. She sung accompanied by various musical instruments.

I felt included and part of this community. I visited this community several times, and was a part of a worship consultation the founding pastor, a friend of mine, convened when this new church development was taking shape. There were many young adults. Even though I did not know the ordinand, I joined the excitement in the air as the gathered assembly wore smiles at the prospect of EW's ordination.

There was diversity in the worship leadership. The reading of Scripture was done by an African American woman elder and a Caucasian male minister. There were persons of different ages, both laypersons and ordained ministers.

The cantor ensured that those who probably were not familiar with the songs were led to the tune of the song. She would sing the first stanza, and then invite the rest of the assembly to join her in the remaining stanzas of each hymn.

The preacher, prior to offering the sermon, welcomed the entire assembly by introducing them to the worship space and how God's presence was embodied, expressed, and mediated in the various elements of the liturgical space, such as the origami cranes.

The preacher explored the past, present, and future dimensions of EW's call. He wondered how many children will meet EW as their first pastor, or the number of couples she will walk with as they get married or seek counseling. In focusing on the past, he spoke of the "how and when" of EW's calling, dating back to 1977, the year of EW's birth and baptism. The preacher spoke of baptism as setting aside EW for salvation and service. In calling her, God instilled in EW all the gifts and skills that she will need to serve in places that God will place her. As I listened to the sermon, I thought of my ordination and my present ministry context, and thought of other ministers I know who are serving in churches.

The preacher continued his sermon by walking to the wooden chest box/luggage. He gave EW a dictionary with the highlighted words "faithfulness" and "success." He exhorted her to know the difference between the two, and to share with God's people the difference for our world lives in a "success paradigm." The second gift was a music compact disc from a recording band that has its studio adjacent to this church. He critiqued the Reformed tradition as loving the mind at the expense of the heart, soul, and strength. He exhorted EW that it "takes soul to be a pastor," to not be guarded but to have passion and flair in ministry. Then he placed at EW's feet the wooden chest box/luggage and offered it to her because just as the luggage has traveled to many places, EW is being sent by God, and therefore, she was "no longer the architect of your future." He noted that the dictionary and the CD were challenges; the box was a promise. The preacher indicated that that is both bad news but more so, good news, because of the freedom that we have in God. In this freedom, EW is free to be the messenger with a message that she has received and heard. I received that exhortation for my own ministry, as I prayed for EW as she received that word.

An elder of the church invited the assembly to offer two offerings: a financial offering to assist other candidates for ministry under the care of the presbytery; and a second offering in the form of a prayer for EW so that the host church could pray for EW during the course of the week. The assembly walked up to two baskets to place their offerings, a physical act of volition and intentionality.

There was a sense of formality as the presbytery moderator formally began the ordination service proper. In the ordination service proper, EW stood at the lectern while the presbytery moderator and another minister stood on the side where the Table was located so that the ordinand was facing the wooden chest box/luggage. The positioning of the three of them demonstrated the linkage of Word and Sacrament, as the two ministers addressed the ordinand. The presbytery moderator stated that the assembled congregation was acting on behalf of a congregation that has called EW to serve as their pastor. I felt connected to that congregation in which EW would serve even though they were not physically present.

The symbols of ministry, stoles colored according to the lectionary seasons, were presented by a minister and by the ordinand's mother, who was an ordained elder. I saw this as the full circle of the baptismal emphasis of this ordination service as EW's mother presented the stoles.

Survey Questionnaires[105]

The survey questionnaire was distributed to the assembly prior to the start of the ordination service, as well as handed to attendees as they entered the church building. Receptacles were placed at the two exit doors of the sanctuary, as well as in two locations in the multi-purpose room where dinner was served after the ordination service with instructions that respondents had the option to deposit their completed surveys in the receptacles, hand-deliver them to me, mail them to me by regular postal mail, e-mail, or fax their responses.

Sixty-three (63) surveys were distributed at MP, of which thirty-four (34) were returned and were in a usable form; thus a fifty-four percent (54%) return rate.

Respondents were largely female (64.71%), young adults (ages 26–35, 61.76%), friends of the ordinand (58.54%), Caucasian (82.35%), Reformed/Presbyterian (38.24%), quite knowledgeable about the sources of Presbyterian theology and polity (Q25), and theologically liberal (64.71%). Even though 13 of the 34 respondents indicated they grew up in a Reformed/Presbyterian tradition, there was a higher combined total for respondents who indicated non-Reformed/Presbyterian traditions, including three who indicated no religious affiliation, two Roman Catholic, one Anglican/Episcopalian, one Methodist, one Baptist, three Lutheran, one non-denominational, one Jewish; and six categorized as "Other." Those who indicated "Other" responded in the blank space provided by indicating they were from a United Church of Christ (UCC) background, or "embrace the moral values of all religions," or "combined Jewish, Episopal, Quaker," or "Quaker." MP's survey results, thus, showed a great diversity in many demographic areas. Noteworthy for our purposes was the overwhelming number of respondents who indicated that MP was, at most, the third ordination service they had ever attended (choice 1a, 76.47% of respondents). Thus, MP's quantitative results can provide an almost objective perspective from persons who are largely foreign to the Reformed tradition, and who have experienced and witnessed MP through non-Reformed lenses, or for some, non-Christian, or non-religious senses.

The religious diversity showed in the diverse responses with little consensus of interpretation of ordination itself and the various aspects

105. In this section, I will be referring to the quantitative analysis in Appendix 4.

of ordination. There was no clear-cut understanding of what was understood by ordination prior to MP (Q2). Some saw it as an individual responding to a call (18.27%), others saw it as God's calling upon an individual (16.35%), or a combination of that with the ordinand becoming an officer of the Church (15.38%). Because Q2 provided an option for multiple responses, those not committed to any one way of understanding ordination had various choices. When compared to Q9 about this actual ordination, respondents viewed MP with more community orientation, indicating for instance that what made ordination special was that the gathered community represented the universal Church in blessing the ordinand (17.48%) and/or that ordination was the gathering of family and friends in celebration of the ordinand's calling (21.36%).

While not receiving a clear majority of respondents, the sermon as an element of the ordination service was by far the most significant aspect for respondents. Of those who responded to Q4 as to what aspects affirmed, enhanced, challenged, or changed their understanding of ordination, there were 23 or 16.91% of checked responses. Likewise, respondents to Q7 as to what was the most important part of the ordination service, 16 or 26.23% of checked responses indicated the sermon was most important. Respondents also indicated that the sermon made clear the connection of ordination with baptism and/or the Eucharist with 15 or 39.47% of checked responses to choice 15g of Q15.

While laying on of hands was important, it was not seen as the most important.

Q12 asked respondents to rank the top three parts of the ordination service where they felt they and the assembly were participating in the ordination service. Participating or witnessing the laying on of hands received 12 or 70.59 of checked responses, with "merely being in attendance as an attendee and witness" receiving 11 or 64.71 of checked responses, and the offering receiving 10 or 58.82% of checked responses.

Even though laying on of hands was not seen as important as the sermon, respondents were asked what they understood was happening at the laying on of hands. There was no clear consensus on what the laying on of hands meant, but the top choice was that that element was about "expression of support, blessing, and love," which received 11 or 32.35% of checked responses. The laying on of hands was ranked as the top element that exhibited MP's connection with the universal Church, with that element receiving 17 or 21.52% of checked responses for choice 17b of Q17.

Responses to Q 10 (prevailing image, word or metaphor), Q18 (other times respondent thought about ordinations), and Q19 (other comments) were not substantive aside from one word commentaries such as "woohoo" or "joyful." One noteworthy written response was a respondent, in answering Q18, commented that "confirmation"[106] was a time that she thought about communion; this, again, was indicative of the relationship of baptism, eucharist and ministry.

One person who did not fill out a survey but who spoke to me prior to the ordination service was the husband of the presiding moderator. He himself was a minister of the Word and Sacrament in the PC(U.S.A.). He shared how he had accompanied his wife to several ordination services in her term as presbytery moderator. What he found was that while there was diversity in the worship styles and settings of each ordination service, the constitutional questions propounded by the moderator were the same questions that were propounded in every ordination service not only during her term, but to all officers throughout the PC(U.S.A.). He noted that the constitutional questions show in a profound way the unity of the PC(U.S.A.).

Focus Group Interview[107]

After the ordination service, the assembly gathered for dinner in the multi-purpose hall. The focus group met after the dinner in the pastor's office. The focus group consisted of:

EW, the ordinand, a Caucasian woman in her 30s;

BG, the preacher, a Caucasian man in his mid-30s;

DH, representative of the host church, a Caucasian man in his late 30s;

106. Respondent #P21 – Female, age 36–45, minister, Caucasian, grew up in Reformed/Presbyterian tradition, theologically liberal.

107. Members of Minister Ordination Service of EW (pseud.), interview by author, 6 December 2008, eastern Pennsylvania, transcription, DiPiero Court Reporting, Philadelphia, PA. I will use the same numbering system as in the two previous sections to indicate the page and line numbers in the written transcript of the focus group interview.

EF, a representative of the host church, a Caucasian woman in her mid-30s;

LN, a representative of the presbytery, a Caucasian woman in her mid-30s;

HC, a representative of the ordaining commission, a Korean womn in her late

30s/early 40s;

AG, a representative of the ordaining commission, an African American woman in her late 30s/early 40s

When asked about the meaning of ordination, each one emphasized various aspects of what ordination is. DH described it as "an affirmation by a gathered community of one's calling."[108] EF emphasized the nurturing and sending aspects of community, "[b]ecause we're ordained into a community but also it's a community that brings individuals to the point of recognizing the call."[109] HC saw ordination as publicly responding to God's call, but grappled with understanding how that was different from responding to God's call in secular vocations without an ordination service.[110] LN spoke of ordination as setting apart an individual for "a particular calling among the priesthood of all believers,"[111] and, thus, the necessity for having ordination services within and among a community that has been "an important part of that discernment process and that journey."[112] EW saw her ordination as an affirmation of God's call, "a general invitation" to serve, in this case, as a pastor, "which is a huge gift from a new congregation to say come in here and do what God has called you to do in our presence."[113]

LN and AG discussed their understanding of their role as members of the presbytery's ordaining commission. The ordaining commission was entrusted by the presbytery to offer the ordinand support and to insure that the "particular expectations of the process are followed."[114] In addition to being the visible presence and witness of the presbytery, LN saw the ordaining commission as also representing the universal

108. MP, 3, 18–19.

109. Ibid., 4, 2–4.

110. Ibid., 10, 25 to 11,1–4.

111. Ibid., 4, 9–10.

112. Ibid., 4, 17–18.

113. Ibid., 29, 23–25.

114. Ibid., 5, 12–13.

church. BG added that the ordaining commission had the responsibility to interpret to the gathered community what was involved in calling, ordaining, and installation, but the commission had the responsibility to also interpret the gathered community to itself and to the presbytery of the particular character of this gathered community that received, nurtured, and now joined in sending the ordinand to the ordained ministry.[115] With regards to interpretive task of interpreting to the community, the ordaining commission, added BG, had the awesome responsibility of embodying in word and deed the liturgical and theological tradition and towards what end the ordination service seeks in terms of ministry and worldview, particularly in a time when, in BG's estimation, "[d]enominationalism is dead. People travel between many denominational identities in their lifetime if they ever had any at all."[116] AG saw her role as providing support as a personal friend and as representing the congregation at which EW served as a seminary intern.[117]

The focus group described the liturgical moment that best embodied the essence of ordination. LN was particularly moved by BG's sermon that focused on baptism, and that in focusing on baptism prior to the ordination service proper, the sermon laid a "wonderful foundation."[118] HC saw the benediction that EW offered as the first act of the newly ordained for "[t]hat's the first and the only moment that this ordained person could see the change because probably the next time when she gives a benediction she will be, it will be the second time and not the first time."[119] EF coupled the constitutional questions propounded to the ordinand and the laying on of hands as the singularly key elements of the ordination service proper in that the constitutional questions are public vows to God, the community, the people, the Church, that she found "both very serious but also very energizing. . . ."[120] With regards to the laying on of hands, EF viewed that in two ways: an epiclesis of blessing the candidate and "visual embodying of community and that's how the Holy Spirit works is through the community."[121] DH concurred

115. See Ibid., 6, 15–21.

116 Ibid., 6, 22–24.

117 Ibid., 30, 6–18.

118. Ibid., 8, 12.

119. Ibid., 11, 16–20.

120. Ibid., 9, 6.

121. Ibid., 9, 11–13.

with EF but nuanced the understanding of the laying on of hands by underscoring the physicality and tactility of the event and the infrequency of touching one another in Presbyterian worship; he saw the laying on of hands as a powerful, tangible way of the community blessing one another and one of their own for he felt, "I think we're very hesitant to bless people. . . It's not something that happens often."[122] AG, who shared that her congregation was going through a church budgeting process and determining spending priorities in light of the church's mission, saw the most essential element in this particular ordination when BG opened up a wooden chest box that was in the middle of the liturgical space and BG gave EW gifts, one of which was a dictionary with the highlighted words, "faithfulness" and "success," as he spoke about the difference between the two.[123]

The ordinand, EW, insightfully shared the most important aspect of her ordination service. EW reflected upon what she had heard from others about the laying on of hands as "when you experience that community but you also feel this weight and sort of what I was anticipating feeling a lot of weight on my body."[124] Instead, what she felt as hands were being laid on her was not weight but that "my head was cradled by hands. . .I felt very comfortable, like I felt like my head was being held."[125] She shared how she shared this experience of being cradled with a friend, at which her friend commented, "that's kind of like birth, like that's the first thing that gets cradled."[126] EW saw how this helped her to experience the baptismal linkage with ordination.

BG shared his sense of responsibility of a preacher for this ordination service and for ordination services, generally. He shared how there's an unspoken expectation that the sermon is "almost giving a valedictory address, a lifetime achievement award, person appreciation."[127] Instead, what he strove to do and what he attempts to do when asked to preach at ordination services is to direct the ordinand "toward Golgotha actually in a really menacing way. If you are serious about being ordained and following Jesus Christ and guiding people you are guiding

122. Ibid., 10, 1–3.

123. Ibid., 22, 3–20.

124. Ibid., 25, 19–22.

125. Ibid., 25, 23–25.

126. Ibid., 25, 2–3.

127. Ibid., 12, 9–11.

them to their death. That will not get you any applause lines. You are now being charged to invite people to relinquish themselves and no one gets a standing zero for that."[128] As for hermeneutical method in his sermon preparation for this ordination service, BG shared how he brought the question he implied—how, what, when for ministry—as the text—2 Corinthians 15—answered that question through the lens of the ambassador image. He said that by using the ambassador image and text, BG was able to connect what was "plausible and possible" for EW's ministry, and what pastoral ministry would look like if being an ambassador for Jesus Christ was truly and fully grasped, it would involve "saying and doing and performing that which Jesus Christ demonstrated for humanity the church would look very different."[129] While in his sermon for this particular ordination BG made a direct mention to baptism, in other ordination services he either explicitly mentions it or there is at least an allusion to baptism. In this case, because the ordination service occurred in the community, not in which she would serve but which participated in her preparation for ministry, BG took note of the context as a "community of preparers" who took a small part in EW's journey "from parenting on" and, thus, BG took the past, present, future aspects of God's call upon her life and wove it into her baptism and her call to be an ambassador for Christ.[130]

I queried the focus group on what difference ordination would make in EW's service seeing that one is already commissioned to serve by virtue of one's baptism. DH, referring to BG's charge to the congregation during the ordination service, indicated that in ordination the community was setting apart someone for a particular service and to serve as a leader for the community, and that in ordination "we are agreeing that she is qualified to be in that position and that is suggestive that we will subject ourselves to her."[131] DH went further in discussing ordination as "instilling an awareness in a community" that Emily is qualified and has been called, and, likewise, the congregation's presence and role in the ordination service is to agree with that affirmation, in essence saying "we will hold you accountable but we will also respect

128. Ibid., 12, 16–23.

129. Ibid., 19, 18–20.

130. See Ibid., 20, 18–22 and 21, 5–6.

131. Ibid., 14, 17–19.

you, encourage you, pray for you and support you."[132] LN spoke of baptism as one's belonging to the priesthood of all believers and the general ministry that everyone is committed to, but that in ordination, there is a call from that priesthood of all believers for some who are called to "different ministries, and some are specifically called to ministry of word and sacrament."[133] LN used the image of a wedding ceremony to describe ordination, paralleling a courtship to one's journey of faith as one responds to God's call over time. LN spoke of the "awesomeness of the task and the sacredness of the task"[134] when her status moved from being an ordained elder to being an ordained minister of Word and Sacrament, as she referred to BG's statement that ordination involves positioning an ordinand towards the cross as the ordained ministry guides a community towards their death. EF spoke of the community orientation of both baptism and ordination, and noted how in the ordination for the ministry of Word and Sacrament, the ordinand will now be baptizing others in the priesthood of all believers.[135]

In asking the focusing group to offer a simple explanation to a young child what ordination is, they used the image of a puzzle. AG said she would give a child a puzzle, and "just hold back one piece."[136] DH would use a "crossword puzzle with no clues."[137] BG indicated that EW's role, like other ministers" is to "help us work on the puzzle because "we need her help to understand how to love God and how to love each other."[138] EF observed that EW, like other ministers, cannot put the puzzle together all by oneself, but needs a community to work on the puzzle because "without their pieces we wouldn't have a very pretty picture."[139]

132. Ibid., 15, 2–4.

133. Ibid., 16, 4–6.

134. Ibid., 17, 2–3.

135. Ibid., 17, 20–23.

136. Ibid., 37, 6.

137. Ibid., 37, 7–8.

138. Ibid., 38, 6–9.

139. Ibid., 39, 3–4.

Personal Experience as Participant-Observer

MP took place in a new church development that I was quite familiar with through my friendship with the convening minister and multiple visits with this congregation. The pastoral and worship leadership were adept at connecting tradition with the urban context of this congregation, employing music and art forms that appreciated traditional hymns and songs while drawing our attention towards the Church's mission to those in need. For instance, using suspended origami cranes with written prayers from homeless individuals in the liturgical space demonstrated aesthetic adeptness in service to serving the least in society.

The convening minister, a close friend of mine, had great skill at subversively identifying pastoral-identity issues in poetic words. For instance, in describing the origami cranes to the gathered community, BG explained that the cranes were constant, visible "talismans against pettiness." In another instance, BG offered a teaching moment to EW, the ordinand, by giving EW a musical compact disc of a local artist, exhorting EW to have soul in her ministry for pastors in the Reformed tradition, in BG's estimation, needed not only mind, but soul in their vocation.

The focus group interviews were with a community of friends and colleagues. I came away from the interviews refreshed and edified. Every participant in the focus group interview was not only familiar with the Reformed tradition, but had thought about issues of ordination and church orders in great depth, and, thus, were able to engage in deeper conversation about the presenting issues, such as the linkage of baptism with ordination.

Minister Ordination # 2 - eastern Pennsylvania (MW)

The second minister ordination site we will examine came to my attention through a friend on the social utility network, Facebook®. MW occurred at a largely Caucasian, suburban, upper middle-class city in eastern Pennsylvania on Saturday, December 20, 2008, during Advent. MW was held in the sanctuary of a large, historic Presbyterian church with over 2000 members. The church is active in the community and various social justice ministries.

Textual Analysis

The textual liturgy of MW was in the traditional, prescribed form of the BOS. It was printed using Old English Text font on a tri-folded, 11 inches by 17 inches paper, with a printed picture of the exterior of the historic sanctuary on the cover, and the seal of the PC(U.S.A.) on the inside cover. I note these specifications because in many historic Presbyterian congregations, similar efforts are made in the written liturgy to display the historicity of both the particular congregation and the denominational identity and ecclesial connection of the church.

The liturgical text showed an appreciation of and cohesive integration of traditional and contemporary elements of worship. As stated above, the ordo generally followed the BOS service for "Ordination to the Ministry of Word and Sacrament"[140] but omitted some key elements such as Thanksgiving over Baptism or the celebration of the Eucharist. MW's liturgical text included the old hymn, "Holy, Holy, Holy" (tune: NICAEA) and confession of the Apostles' Creed, but also included a musical anthem and musical offertory by a jazz ensemble.

The following was the ordo of MW:

- Prelude
- Welcome and Call to Worship
- Hymn
- Prayer of Confession
- Assurance of Pardon
- Anthem
- Old Testament Reading
- Psalm Reading
- New Testament Reading
- Sermon
- Affirmation of Faith: Apostles' Creed
- Announcement of the Offering and Its Purpose
- Offertory
- The Doxology
- Prayer of Dedication
- Preface to the Service of Ordination
- Presentation of Pastor-Elect
- Constitutional Questions

140. BOS, 45–80.

- Laying on of Hands
- Prayer of Ordination
- Declaration of Ordination
- Extending the Right Hand of Fellowship
- Charge to the Pastor
- Hymn
- Comments and Benediction by the Newly Ordained Pastor
- Postlude

Other traditional elements retained by MW's liturgical text include the placement of various elements, and the song choices. MW had three Scriptural readings as prescribed by the BOS: one from the Old Testament, one from the Psalms, and one from a Gospel. The Apostles' Creed immediately followed the sermon, indicating MW's notion that the Creed is a confessional, congregational response to the Word that had been read and proclaimed. Likewise, the ordination service proper immediately followed the prayer of dedication for the offering, demonstrating that the act of ordaining was not only in response to the spoken Word in sermon, but as a continuous act of offering oneself to God. Consistent with gatherings of judicatories, as in this ordination, the song, "Here I Am, Lord" was the selected one as the closing hymn. The traditional Laying on of Hands in MW included a rubric that followed the BOS in indicating that ministers and elders would be the ones participating in the laying on of hands.

Phenomenological Observations

MW occurred on December 20, 2008, the Sunday of the week of Christmas, at a historic, suburban stone and wooden church sanctuary. Attendees gathered to the sound of jazz music in a contemporary Gothic space with stained glass windows throughout the sanctuary, and pointed arches at the side aisles. Poinsettia flowers decorated the sanctuary space. Stone steps lead up to a chancel space where a choir loft facing the congregation is situated. It appeared, then, that when the Eucharist is celebrated, a movable Table must be placed either in the space between the top of the steps and the choir loft, or at the bottom of the stairs in the nave. An octagonal, white marble font was situated just below the pulpit, but no water was in it. Members of the ordination commission processed in full regalia during the opening hymn "Holy, Holy, Holy," which, I felt was in keeping with the holy season of Advent and the solemnity of the ordination service. The mixture of jazz music at the musical prelude and then the use of organ music for the opening hymn showed an appreciation for and sensitivity of the diversity of worship styles and modes.

The female minister who offered the Assurance of Pardon read the words of the Assurance slowly, emphasizing each word, seeking to have each one understand each word and to fully embrace God's love in Jesus Christ.

At the first anthem sung by the jazz ensemble, the ordinand, a member of the ensemble, joined the group. It showed me that she was not separate from the group, that she was not being serenaded by the music group, but she was a full participant, she was enabling the whole body to worship. In this sense, she was already putting herself in service to the community.

The preacher was a young adult male minister who was a friend of the ordinand and who served with the ordinand as a seminary intern at this host church. His chosen texts were 2 Kings 6:24–31, Psalm 18:1–9a and Luke 4:14–21. The 2 Kings passage was a curious one involving a siege of Samaria by the Aramean armies in the midst of famine, demonstrated most powerfully by a woman, who as was described in verses 28 and 29 of the text, was lamenting the fact that her son was given to another woman for a cannibalistic feast. Linking the God-forsaken context of 2 Kings to what sometimes feels like our God-forsaken contemporary context, the preacher pondered whether we all think of God has left us. He clued in to the king's question, "Why should I wait for the Lord any longer?" to which Elisha the prophet, "Hear the word of the Lord. . . ." Then he directed our attention to the four lepers in 2 Kings 7 who go to the Aramean camp, and finding it empty because God had caused the Arameans to think that the Hittites and Egyptians had joined forces with Israel and therefore fled in fear, and began to eat and drink what the Arameans had left. The four lepers discover that they should not be enjoying everything for themselves because "[t]his is a day of good news" (2 Kings 7:9). He then linked this temptation to the Church's tendency to hoard things for its own gain; instead he challenged the assembly to be lepers, to bear witness of times of suffering and desperation in order to testify of God's provision and mercy.

He called upon the ordinand and other presbyters to not place trust in the accoutrements of the office, such as academic degrees and robes and stoles, but yet the preacher himself was garbed in robe and stole, preaching from a high pulpit that looked down upon the congregation. Yet his voice and mannerisms in the pulpit were cool, down-to-earth; thus what he was wearing, who he was and what he was doing had a double entendre quality that captivated me and the other assembly. It helped me to see the paradox of ordained office in our world today, where he called ministers to be lepers for the sake of Christ, yet Presbyterian ministers are highly educated, and comparatively wealthy vis-à-vis our counterparts in other parts of the world.

The presiding moderator was an elder stateswoman, an African American minister who spoke powerfully and gracefully, garbed in a red robe. If the Reformed church had a bishop or cardinal, the presiding moderator would have fit such a role.

The ordinand stood on the same level at a close distance to the presiding moderator as the Constitutional Questions were propounded. It was like an older generation passing the baton to a younger generation.

The laying on of hands and extending the right hand of fellowship to the ordinand after the laying on of hands were special with the number of presbyters present. We gathered at the stairs as the ordinand knelt at the stairs, and it looked like a big football huddle.

Proclaim the message, be persistent, and bring the good news as an evangelist by being with the people—these were the three points of the pastoral charge offered by a middle-aged Caucasian male pastor to the ordinand. The pastor was the ordinand's supervisory pastor during an internship she did at his congregation. His charge was heartfelt, as a mentor to a mentee, one family member to another.

The closing hymn, "Here I Am, Lord" was a perfect capstone to the ordination service and an excellent segue from the pastoral charge. The song is a confessional commitment to serve and be at the service of God to the world.

For the benediction, the jovial, newly ordained minister, invited everyone to hold each other's hands, to offer a silent prayer of peace for the person next to oneself, after which the new minister offered the closing prayer. This invitation helped to make the service be about community, not just the ordinand, for people to be a blessing to one another.

I would characterize MW as a "soulful" ordination service because of the smooth flow and cohesive content of the service, and the palpable passion of the ordinand, members of the ordination commission, and the preacher. The following elements contributed towards making MW a "soulful" service: blended worship and musical instruments, worship leadership who did not read scripts but who seemed to internalize the thoughts and themes of the liturgical and Scriptural texts, and a welcoming atmosphere that did not seem mechanical but appeared to be celebratory of the ordinand as the ordinand herself was receiving the support and expressing that in her words, facial countenance and gestures.

Survey Questionnaires[141]

There were eighty-two (82) survey questionnaires distributed at MW, inserted into each liturgical text/worship bulletin; thirty-six (36) were returned in a usable form, thus, a forty-four percent (44%) return rate. An invitation to fill out the questionnaire was placed in the acknowledgments section of the worship bulletin, as well as a public invitation made by the ordinand just prior to her pronouncing the benediction. Respondents were given the opportunity to submit their completed survey questionnaires at four different receptacles located at the egress and ingress of the sanctuary, as well as in the reception hall where refreshments were served after MW. Respondents were also invited to hand deliver, fax, mail, or e-mail their completed questionnaires to me.

Respondents were largely female (66.67%), ages 26–56, friends of the ordinand (50%), Caucasian (58.33%), grew up in the Reformed / Presbyterian tradition (36.11%), quite familiar with the official sources of Reformed/Presbyterian theology and polity, and theologically moderate (30.56%) to conservative (30.56%).

For more than two-thirds of respondents, MW was at most the sixth ordination service they had attended, yet their interpretation of ordination prior to MW revolved around four key understandings: God's calling upon an individual (2a), community's calling upon an individual (2b), individual responding to a call (2c), and equipping by the Church and the Holy spirit for a specific ministry/service (2g).

141. In this section I will refer to the quantitative analysis found in Appendix 5.

Respondents overwhelmingly found their prior understanding of ordination affirmed by MW (3a, 65.22%) in five key elements: the sermon (4d, 12.5%), hymns/songs (4g, 11.93%), propounding of the constitutional questions (4i, 11.36%), the pastoral charge (4k, 11.36%), and the laying on of hands (4n, 13.07%). Of those who answered "Hymns/Songs," eight respondents wrote in the space provided that the hymn, "Here I Am, Lord" was the song that affirmed their prior understanding of ordination. Likewise, respondents expected an ordination service to be joyful (6b, 96.15% of those who chose 'joyful" as their only answer) and that was what they observed of the assembly in MW (5b, 84.62% of those who chose "joyful" as their only answer). Thus, there was consistency of respondents' theological understanding and feelings prior to the ordination and what they received and understood at the conclusion of MW.

What did they understand ordination to be? The prior understanding of respondents revolved around God's call, a community's call, the ordinand's response to that call, and the equipping function of the Church and the Holy Spirit. This was consistent in what respondents saw as the essence of MW, namely the Holy Spirit empowering the ordinand and blessing her (9b, 12.58%), and the community of the gathered people were representing the universal Church in blessing the ordinand into the ministry (9e, 14.47%). But ranked even higher than these two choices was choice 9f, i.e. family and friends were gathering to celebrate a milestone in the service of the minister/elder candidate (15.72%). If we account for the fact that most of the respondents were friends of the ordinand, then the two former responses would be in keeping with the prior understanding of respondents before MW.

When we look at the top three elements that respondents saw as the most important aspects of MW, we see a difference from traditional responses to this question. While one may expect the laying on of hands as the most important aspect, responses to Q7 ranked the pastoral charge as the most important (7k, 19.4%), followed by the sermon (7d, 16.42%), then laying on of hands (7n, 11.94%). But respondents ranked the laying on of hands as the top choice of the particular element in MW that exhibited that the gathered assembly was fully participating and a part of the ordination service (12a, 72.73%).

Respondents were consistent in linking their understanding of ordination to their understanding of the laying on of hands. They saw ordination as involving the Holy Spirit, together with the Church, blessing and empowering the ordinand to service. Likewise, respondents indicated that the Holy Spirit was empowering the minister ordinand at the moment of the laying on of hands (13a, 36.11%) followed by their second choice, i.e. that the hands of the officers were the hands of Christ upon the candidate (13b, 27.77%). Respondents also top ranked the laying on of hands as the element in the ordination service that exhibited the connection of MW with the universal Church, its officers and its ministries (17b, 20.43%). The response to 17a, i.e. the presence of other ministers or elders from other churches, received 17.20%, which when combined with the response to 17b clearly indicate that respondents felt the presence and action of presbyters at MW connected this particular ordination service to the universal Church.

Written responses to Q10 regarding a prevailing word or image that expressed respondents' feelings or thoughts about MW expressed the joy they had towards the ordinand's call and being sent. A sampling of the written responses are as follows:

"joy-affirmation;"[142] "a desire to know and do God's will from a pure heart;"[143] "the sending of [the ordinand] to tell the Good News-Encouraging her to continue in the path of Jesus;"[144] "[the minister ordinand] is a gift of hope to the church;"[145] "excitement & anticipation at what lies ahead [for the ordinand] and the church;"[146] and "the joy [the minister ordinand] exudes when she shares her love of Jesus."[147]

As stated in the textual analysis, confirmed by the phenomenological observations, and re-confirmed by the survey responses, there was little connection exhibited in MW between the ordination service

142. Respondent # W3- Female, age 46–55, Friend, African American, grew up in Baptist tradition, theologically liberal.

143. Respondent # W5- Female, age 36–45, Family and Layperson, African American, grew up in Baptist tradition, theologically conservative.

144. Respondent # W7- Female, age 55–65, Elder, African American, grew up in Anglican/Episcopalian and Reformed/Presbyterian traditions, theologically conservative.

145. Respondent # W10- Female, age 46–55, Elder, Friend, Caucasian, grew up in Baptist tradition, theologically liberal/moderate.

146. Respondent # W25- Male, age 76+, Elder and Friend, Caucasian, grew up in Plymouth Brethren tradition, theologically moderate.

147. Respondent # W34- Female, age 55–65, Deacon and Friend, Caucasian, grew up in Lutheran tradition, theologically moderate.

and the sacraments of baptism or the Eucharist (14b, 52.78%, "No, not really" and 14c, 22.22%, "Not sure").

Respondents associated ordination with various other events. The written responses to Q18 included the following: "only if i feel a minister is straying from their mission;"[148] "commissioning church officers, missionaries, leaders;"[149] "commissioning mission workers;"[150] "profession of faith @ baptism;"[151] and "weddings, baptisms."[152]

Focus Group Interview[153]

I convened the focus group during the reception following the ordination service. In addition to the professional transcriptionist, the following were the participants:

-AB, the minister ordinand, a young adult, African American woman;

-SM, a member of the presbytery ordination commission, Caucasian, young adult woman minister;

-RM, a member of the presbytery ordination commission, Caucasian, middle agedwoman elder;

-RR, a member of the presbytery ordination commission, African American, middle aged woman minister;

-JM, worship participant (offered pastoral charge to ordinand), Caucasian, middle aged male minister;

-TS, preacher at the ordination service, Caucasian, young adult male minister;

148. Respondent # W10. Note 737 *supra*.

149. Respondent # W11- Female, age 55–65, Friend and Layperson, Caucasian, grew up in Reformed/Presbyterian tradition, theologically self-described as "depends on the company I'm in! who to compare myself to."

150. Respondent # W18- Male, age 17–25, Friend and Layperson, Caucasian, grew up in Reformed/Presbyterian tradition, theologically liberal.

151. Respondent # W23- Female, age 26–35, Friend and Layperson, Caucasian, grew up in Baptist tradition, theologically moderate to conservative (respondent notated "leaning here" in reference to theological conservatism).

152. Respondent # W24- Male, age 36–45, Minister, East Asian, grew up in Reformed/Presbyterian tradition, theologically conservative.

153. Members of Minister Ordination Service of AB (pseud.), interview by author, 20 December 2008, eastern Pennsylvania, transcription, Dineen Communications, Ltd., Wayne, PA.

-SN, representing the assembly at-large, Korean American, middle aged male minister;

-KS, representing the assembly at-large, African American, middle aged laywoman;

-CB, representing the assembly at-large, African American, young adult elder.

The meaning of ordination was varied among the members of the focus group. JM saw it as designating someone from the priesthood of all believers to be a "priest among the people."[154] Ordination for JM involved a time in which a "community celebrates, identifies, and confirms the one whom God has called to lead that community."[155] JM noted his Scottish heritage and his wearing of Geneva tabs on his pastoral robe for in the Scottish church the exterior tabs designated one's call for this time, a recognition of both the old and new covenant.[156] RM saw ordination as akin to Jesus washing the disciples feet, that ordination was "a call from God to service. . .not to lord over people."[157] SN spoke of three aspects of ordination: the "scriptural calling,"[158] "the personal calling,"[159] and the "community say[ing], 'That's right. God did call you.'"[160] TS critiqued ordination as "the affirmation of the professionalization of clergy persons"[161] in which ordinands are authorized to perform certain tasks hitherto unable to do without the imprimatur of ordination, and wondered whether in the act of ordaining the Church was "sort of feeding into the culture of the professionalization of all things."[162] RR agreed with SN but felt that when she was going through the ordination process she experienced it as "gate-keeping and a way to decide who's in and who's out by the continued layers that are placed on the process."[163] KS spoke of the dual natures of the discerning community who ask, on the one hand, "What is God doing with

154. Ibid., 2, 17.

155. Ibid., 2, 22–24.

156. Ibid., 3, 5–13.

157. Ibid., 7, 4–6.

158. Ibid., 7, 18.

159. Ibid, 7, 22–23.

160. Ibid, 8, 4–5.

161. Ibid, 9, 3–4.

162. Ibid., 9, 21–22.

163. Ibid., 10, 17–19.

this person" also ask, on the other hand, "What do we really think, you know, this person is about?"[164] These two questions were essential for KS because the community in and from which the ordinand is nurtured and serves double-checks an ordinand's sense of call and grapples with the ordinand's presentation of his/her call as the community discerns God's leading and direction. SM saw ordination as an "affirmation of God's call. . .and the gathered community saying, 'Amen'" to the ordinand's understanding of God's call.[165] AB, the ordinand, saw ordination as something akin to a group of people standing in a line and God "pick[ing] you out of the line almost and ask[ing] you to do something a little bit different."[166]

There was also varied understanding of the laying on of hands. JM saw this element as the body of Christ gathering "asking God's spirit to empower" the ordinand.[167] He added that laying on of hands upon the ordinand was "to pray for God's anointed, and God's protection, and God's leading in the days to come."[168] He noted that the presbyters who gathered "represent the different gifts of the Body of Christ and the supernatural promise and covenant of God's Spirit to rest upon that one. And that's the mystery and the great power that I think is celebrated."[169]

For some in the focus group, the Constitutional Questions were the most essential element in this particular ordination service. SM shared that because she has been in an interim ministry, the Constitutional Questions helped her to confront the "reworking of stuff" and enabled her to say, "These are the things that I have said 'yes' to."[170] RR, likewise, saw the Questions as not only the most essential element at MW, but also for her own ordination service because it particularized the worship service to an ordination service, and forces the realization "this is it. You know, when you finish asking these Questions, this is it. And you must be truthful. And you must be committed."[171] The Questions propounded to AB made RR remember "when I said 'yes';" thus

164. Ibid., 15, 8–12.

165. Ibid., 17, 9–11.

166. Ibid., 68, 17–18.

167. Ibid., 3, 20–21.

168. ibid., 4, 4–6.

169. Ibid, 6, 7–11.

170. Ibid., 18, 14–17.

171. Ibid., 20, 3–5.

it had an anamnetic character.[172] When I summarized to RR what she meant by describing the Questions as a "covenantal yoke," her response was, "Yeah, yeah, yeah."[173] TS agreed with RR and SM that the Questions were the most important element because the laying on of hands involved only presbyters, while the Questions propounded to an ordinand were akin to questions asked of those joining a church.[174] He

172. Ibid., 20, 20–21.

173. Ibid., 21, 2.

174 The Constitutional Questions propounded to officers are the following:

Do you trust in Jesus Christ your Savior, acknowledge him Lord of all and Head of the Church, and through him believe in one God, Father, Son, and Holy Spirit?

Do you accept the Scriptures of the Old and New Testament to be, by the Holy Spirit, the unique and authoritative witness to Jesus Christ in the Church universal, and God's Word to you? to believe and do, and will you be instructed and led by those confessions as you lead the people of God?

Will you fulfill your office in obedience to Jesus Christ, under the authority of Scripture, and be continually guided by our confessions?

Will you be governed by our church's polity, and will you abide by its discipline? Will you be a friend among your colleagues in ministry, working with them, subject to the ordering of God's Word and Spirit?

Will you in your own life seek to follow the Lord Jesus Christ, love your neighbors, and work for the reconciliation of the world?

Do you promise to further the peace, unity, and purity of the church?

Will you seek to serve the people with energy, intelligence, imagination, and love?

(1) (For elder) Will you be a faithful elder, watching over the people, providing for their worship, nurture and service? Will you share in government and discipline, serving in governing bodies of the church, and in your ministry will you try to show the love and justice of Jesus Christ?

(3) (For minister of the Word and Sacrament) Will you be a faithful minister, proclaiming the good news in Word and Sacrament, teaching faith and caring for people? Will you be active in government and discipline, serving in the governing bodies of the church; and in your ministry will you try to show the love and justice of Jesus Christ?

Do you sincerely receive and adopt the essential tenets of the Reformed faith as expressed in the confessions of our church as authentic and reliable expositions of what Scripture leads us

(in *BoO*, W-4.4003; also *BOS*, 23–25, 57–58)

For the reception of new members, either by baptism or the reaffirmation of the baptismal covenant, the Directory for Worship indicates that such persons shall make vows that:

profess their faith in Jesus Christ as Lord and Savior,

renounce evil and affirm their reliance on God's grace,

declare their intention to participate actively and responsibly in the worship and mission of the church.

declare their intention to provide for the Christian nurture of their child.

(in *BoO*, W-3.3603)

The new members are asked three questions of Renunciations, and then following

hoped that one day there will come a time when the whole assembly can answer those Questions because with the exception of the Question directly applicable to ministers, all the other Constitutional Questions can be answered by any congregant member.[175] SN likened the Questions to vows at a wedding and at a baptism, where he was confronted with the question, "All right, am I living this way? Am I living as a good minister in that regard?"[176] For him, the Questions serve as a "renewal time" for those already ordained and hear the Questions propounded again. For those being ordained, the Questions, like marriage vows, are orientated towards continual commitment into the future.

RR saw the laying on of hands and the song, "Here I Am, Lord" as the most significant aspects of the ordination service. Regarding the latter, RR noted how every time she sings that song or hears it sung, she felt "this is where we are and we're going out now to serve."[177]

KS saw the Prayer of Confession as the most essential element of MW. She indicated that the unison confession helped her to refocus not on herself or her "preconceived notions that I had come with" but on the worship service, on God's call to AB, and on God's call to the assembly.[178]

AB, the ordinand, experienced two powerful elements in her ordination service. The first was kneeling and praying in preparation for and during the laying on of hands. She recounted how the words were spoken by a pastor, "When I anoint you, I'm going to anoint your head,

---

confession of the Creed, are then asked a question of commitment:

Renunciations:

Trusting in the gracious mercy of god, do you turn from the ways of sin and renounce evil and its power in the world?

Do you turn to Jesus Christ and accept him as your Lord and Savior, trusting in his grace and love?

Will you be Christ's faithful disciple, obeying his Word and showing his love?

Question of Commitment:

Will you be a faithful member of this congregation, share in its worship and ministry through your prayers and gifts, your study and service, and so fulfill your calling to be a disciple of Jesus Christ?

(from *Book of Common Worship*, 435–436, 438)

175. Ibid., 22.

176. Ibid., 36, 3–5.

177. Ibid., 37, 14–15.

178. Ibid., 24.

but I'm going to anoint your hands." [179] Then she shared how when she got up after hands were laid on her, that she saw surrounding her looked "almost like the great cloud of witnesses. . . And it was like all those people and all the ways they had been there to support you and to recognize that this particular way you have to function. Even though it's a priesthood of all believers, but you have to function a little bit different than us."[180]

The second element that was important for AB as the ordinand was the special offertory music sung and played by the jazz ensemble, "Chasing After You." For AB, that song brought two things: first, the fact that the jazz ensemble was composed of persons of different faith traditions and one who was not a Christian spoke powerfully to AB of the ecumenism of the music that transcended any differences. Secondly, the song itself "was like a devotional practice for me when I didn't know, am I going to get ordained to [x Church]? Am I supposed to go to another church altogether? Do we need to just break loose and try to go to Chicago? Like what are we supposed to do?"[181] As I heard AB share that, I was brought back to my experience of that song during the ordination service and how I myself was touched by it and how I was prompted to chase after God as I was being pursued by God in the midst of service in ministry.

CB, a musician and the husband of AB, shared his insight in seeing his wife become ordained. He indicated that after the second hymn ("Here I Am, Lord"), he looked at the congregation and "like watching my wife marry someone else, marry Jesus. And I feel like—I felt like I was at a wedding."[182] Being married to one who was a seminarian, CB shared how AB's ministry colleagues would try to equalize themselves with him, to somehow minimize their status as ministers so as to say that there was no difference between ministers and elders; CB stated that he is "quick to be like, 'No, you're not.' I'm not up there at the Constitution questions promising anything.[183] He indicated that a minister making a vow through the Constitutional Questions sets a minister from an elder and from the rest of the Church, and he likened it to a wedding,

179. Ibid., 38, 2–4.
180. Ibid., 38, 9–15.
181. Ibid., 39, 16–20.
182. Ibid., 40, 16–18.
183. Ibid., 41, 6–8.

with the minister being the one married to Christ, observing, "I'm okay with that. To me, I don't think it robs your—we all have the same call to be a disciple of Christ, but we all don't have the same action as far as how we live that out. I think we have unique experiences in our faith."[184] He recounted how at his workplace, some of his co-workers who are cohabitating with their boyfriend/girlfriend say, "Well, it's really no different" but he tells them that there is a difference in being married, and what happens the day after the wedding. Likewise, he shared how his wife will expected to live and serve in a different way on December 21, the day after her ordination.[185]

Even though SM felt the Constitutional Questions were the most important element in MW, she felt that the laying on of hands with the accompanying ordination prayer were still the most important aspects of ordination services, generally. She characterized the act of laying on of hands as "turning back to God and saying, 'It is by Your power that any of this happens."[186]

As with the previous focus groups, I queried this focus group as to their understanding of the related difference between baptism and ordination. Prompted by a Facebook® discussion titled, "Why I Choose Not to Get Ordained," AB researched ordination in the Old Testament books of Numbers and Leviticus and discovered the pattern of God setting apart Aaron and the Levites for the purpose of "being set apart to take care of God's people."[187] AB then observed that in baptism "everyone of us needs to like work like ferociously to just tell the basic good news that Christ is the answer"[188] but that in ordination God turns to those set apart "to be about the business of taking care of these wayward people and reminding them of what it means to really serve God."[189]

KS emphasized God's prior action in calling and ordaining. She cautioned that anyone who chose to be ordained or sought to be ordained was acting out of place for God chooses and God seeks, "that's not your place."[190] As to why people should be ordained, KS asserted

184. Ibid., 41, 17–21.

185. Ibid., 42.

186. Ibid., 42, 25 to 44,3.

187. Ibid., 46, 24.

188. Ibid., 48, 4–6.

189 Ibid., 48, 14–16.

190. Ibid., 51, 12–13.

that "because God said so. God said, 'Listen, you. I want you to do X and so.'"[191]

RR distinguished baptism and ordination by referring to the universal and particular character of each. Baptism is a general call; ordination is specific. RR shared of a story titled, "The Point," in which one line says, "A point in every direction is no point at all."[192] She then shared an example of a bunch of parents with their children gathered at a pool party, where every adult comes with the assumption and expectation that the other adults will watch out for the safety of not only their own kids but yours as well. But, RR said, to insure that your child is also watched by other adults, it is best "to call someone out of the group as that being their responsibility. . . Everybody's got the same job. . .But somebody has got to be called out."[193] She noted that just because someone is called out to watch out for a particular child, that does not absolve the other adults from looking out for that child or any other, but that some specific persons need to be called out to have a specific task to point out to the gathering, "This is the point of our baptism. You know, this is the job we're supposed to do."[194]

The connection of ordination and ministry to baptism and the Eucharist were not explicitly expressed in the liturgical text nor the movement and content of the ordination service proper. AB acknowledged that the connection was not made explicit because it was assumed that because there were many Presbyterians present at the ordination service, that they would readily draw the connection between pulpit, font, and Table.[195] Secondly, in crafting the ordination liturgy, AB sensed that ecumenically some of the attendees may have gotten stuck with peripheral questions such as, "Well, what kind of a baptism are you talking about? Well, what do you mean by communion?"[196] SN agreed with AB, and added that it depends on context and whether in a particular context such explicit relationships between baptism, Eucharist, and ministry should be and can be drawn.[197]

191. Ibid., 51, 18–19.

192. Ibid., 52, 11–12.

193. Ibid., 53, 1–12.

194. Ibid., 53, 22–24.

195. Ibid., 58.

196. Ibid., 60, 15–16.

197. Ibid., 64, 10–23.

AB concluded that ordination causes people to pause. Ordination reminds the ordinand and all those in attendance that "the movement of God is big."[198] She shared how a friend grasped the significance of AB becoming a "Reverend" and "the magnitude of the set-apartness."[199] She observed that in the quotidian patterns of each lived day, we carry on with an attitude, "Yeah, whatever. Text me. Call me. You know, whatever."[200] Ordination, AB said, causes everyone to pause to consider God and God's call to service.

Personal Experience as Participant-Observer

MW took place during Advent. The decorated liturgical space where MW took place added to the festive occasion of MW. I noted already the excellent integration of traditional hymnody and jazz music, coupled with the exuberance and passion of AB, the ordinand, and the ordination commission. Because AB and some members of the ordination commissioner were friends of mine, I did not feel distant at all, but felt part of the family as I was celebrating AB's ordination.

The flow of the service felt like the Holy Spirit was carrying the whole assembly forward, from one part to the next. Each part—the reading of Scripture, the ordination prayer, the sermon, the pastoral charge—were carefully crafted that I felt this was a solemn, but joyful event. It was serious, but not somber, as I felt the gravity of the call upon AB, and as I remembered my own call to the ministry of Word and Sacrament.

The focus group interviews at MW were enriching. There were several "Aha!" moments in the focus group as several participants raised issues that helped me to consider church orders and ordination from a different vantage point. For instance, RR's example of a gathering of people in a large party and the need for a parent to designate one or two other party attendees to keep a close watch on a child while the parent steps out for a few minutes. This insight from RR on the linkage of baptism and ordination helped me to see the general call in baptism upon the Church and the particular call on specific persons in ordination. I

198. Ibid., 74, 11.

199. Ibid., 73, 24.

200. Ibid., 74, 2–3.

appreciated the insight of CB, husband of AB, in his observation that it felt like AB was being married to Christ in the same sanctuary that he and AB were married in.

Comparative Analysis of Four Case Studies

Having analyzed each of the four field sites above—EC, EN, MP, MW—through textual analysis of the liturgical texts (worship bulletins), phenomenological observations, quantitative analysis of survey questionnaires, and analysis of the transcripts of focus group interviews, we are now in a position to compare the four case studies with one another. Of interest to this book are to notate and affirm areas of commonality with the "official sources" of theology, while highlighting areas of interpretation that nuance or are at variance with the "official sources." A comparative analysis will enable us to see how much particular demographic and geograhic contexts (age, gender, racial ethnic identity, suburban/urban), ordination status (minister, elder), or theological self-identification were more likely to offer interpretations that affirmed, nuanced, or challenged "official" Reformed teaching on ordination.

As was done in the previous four sections, we will conduct the comparative analysis along the four lines of textual analysis, phenomenological observations, quantitative analysis of survey questionnaires, and analysis of the focus group transcripts.

Textual Analysis

All four field sites used the five-fold pattern of worship prescribed by the Directory for Worship and the basic pattern of ordinations for both ministers and elders. As was noted above, there was little departure from the official liturgical resources of the PC(U.S.A.), particularly in the ordination service proper, with a few notable exceptions. The inclusive nature of EC's congregation not surprisingly instructed that all officers—deacons, elders, and ministers—participate in the laying on of hands and not just presbyters.

A notable departure from the BOS liturgy for ordinations of ministers and elders was the absence of explicit linkages of ordination with baptism. The ordination liturgies for both ministers and elders in the BOS include a Reaffirmation of the Baptismal Covenant with a full Thanksgiving Prayer over Baptism. While EN and MP were the two field sites that had sermons that explicitly connected ordination with baptism, the liturgical texts of all field sites did not include any responsorial litany, prayer, or ritual act that highlighted the connection of ordination with baptism as the BOS itself prescribes and includes.

Phenomenological Observations

The difference of minister and elder ordinations highlight the difference of office. Ordination services, by definition, are occasional services. But the fact that ordination services for candidates to the ministry of Word and Sacrament are called by a presbytery for a specially appointed time in a specially designated place lends to the overall sense that the focal point of the worship service is the ordination service, whereas an elder ordination appears as an appendage to the Service of the Lord's Day in the life of a congregation. This can be seen, for instance, in the giving of symbols for ministry. The BOS includes an optional giving of symbols for both elder and minister ordinations. As expected, the two elder ordination services—EC and EN—omit the giving of the symbols in the liturgical texts as well as in ordination service itself. MP and MW included the giving of symbols in both the liturgical texts and in the ordination service itself. In EC and EN, ordinands are called from the pews, included in the ordination service proper, and then dismissed back to the pews. In MP and MW, there were processions, and in the case of MW, a procession of the ordination commission in full regalia, as well as a benediction offered by the newly ordained ministers.

The elder ordinations and minister ordinations differed in the degree of a sense of flexibility and spontaneity. EC and EN were elder ordination services with the pastor as the exclusive spokesperson of the session, and the one who followed the ordination liturgical "script." This disallowed any possible contribution from the elder ordinands to contribute to the ordination service proper aside from replying to the propounded Constitutional Questions, and receiving the laying on of hands. In other words, in the elder ordinations, the elder ordinands were limited in their participation, and were more of passive recipients. In MP and MW, perhaps due to the fact that both minister ordinands crafted the ordination liturgy and planned every element of the ordination service, there was more allowance for spontaneity, a strong sense of celebration, and an overall feeling of true collegiality among all presbyters.

None of the sites adequately employed the Table or font. EN had the Eucharistic elements of the last Sunday that congregation communed on the Table, but no reference was made to the Table, nor the elements during the course of the worship service, or at the least, during the ordination service proper. A font was present, but no reference was made to it. EC had a Table but there was no paten nor chalice. A font was present because of an infant baptism that was done on that day, but surprisingly no further word was made about the baptism during the ordination service proper. In some sense, it was a missed opportunity as the service seemed disjointed, involving a patchwork of various elements on a Peacemaking Sunday. The sermon at EC was focused on the peacemaking and justice aspects of the Sunday theme but had little connection to the baptism that preceded it, nor had little connection to the ordinations that followed it. MP had a Table, but no chalice or paten, and no baptismal font. No reference was made to the Table. MW had no Table present, and a font was present at the foot of the pulpit, but there was no reference to it.

Generational differences showed in the approach of the content and type of music employed by the minister and elder ordinations. MP and MW involved minister ordinands who were young adults in their 30s. EC involved a young adult elder ordinand, and EN involved middle-aged adult elder ordinands. But EC and EN also involved pastors who were middle-aged adults in historic congregations who also planned the entirety of the worship service. MP occurred in a historic, abandoned sanctuary, in a congregation that was a new church development that attracted so-called "twenty- and thirtysomethings" and young professions. MW occurred in a historic suburban sanctuary and congregational context but was planned by a young adult, African American woman. EC used hymns and songs played to organ music, as well as handbell choir. EN used organ music. MP had a multi-musical instrument band. MW used organ music, as well as a jazz ensemble. All field sites mostly used traditional hymns or historic hymns, but MP and MW played those hymns with different tunes, or in a context that placed traditional hymns within more contemporary music.

Survey Questionnaires

EC had 45 completed and usable surveys out of 121 distributed (return rate: 37%). EN had 83 completed and usable surveys out of 138 distributed (return rate: 60.1%). MP had 34 completed and usable surveys out of 63 distributed (return rate: 54%). MW had 36 completed and usable surveys of 82 distributed (return rate: 44%). Thus, there were 198 surveys completed in usable form of 404 distributed (return rate: 49%).

In this section, the following questions are important for this project:

1. What was the demographic profile of all field sites?
2. What were identified as the top three important elements in the ordination services, when comparing MW to MP and EN and EC?
3. What was the general profile of those who said the Laying on of Hands was the most important element?
4. What was the general profile of those who said the Constitutional Questions was the most important element?
5. With regards to Q13 ("What do you believe was happening during the laying on of hands upon the candidate?"), what was the top response for each field site and overall?

    a. Of those who responded to Q13, what percentage of the total were elders or ministers who ranked the first option as number one, i.e. "Holy Spirit was empowering the minister/elder candidate at that moment?"

    b. Of those percentage of elders and ministers who ranked "Holy Spirit was empowering the minister/elder candidate at that moment" as the number one choice, how many of those elders or ministers indicated familiarity with any of the confessional documents/theologians in Q25?
6. What were the top two responses to Q15 (if experienced connection of ordination with the sacraments was made, how was the connection made?)

Let us take each question item by item:

1. Comparative Demographics

The comparative demographics of all four field sites can be seen in Appendix 6. The graphical analysis shows the responses for each field site. Then in the fifth and sixth columns, a total of the two elder sites—EC and EN—and a total of the two minister sites—MP and MW—are made, and then overall total for all four sites in the eighth column.

Generally speaking, the respondents to the survey questionnaire at the four field sites were largely female, either ages 26–35 and 55–65, Caucasian, grew up in the Reformed/Presbyterian tradition, and leaning liberal to moderate in their theological positions. Among elders who responded, they were generally older (the 55–65 age bracket); among ministers who responded they were generally young adults (the 26–35 age bracket).

Those who responded to the survey were mostly friends of the ordinand or elders. Interestingly but not surprisingly because of the infrequency of minister ordinations, those who responded to the survey questionnaire were largely minister friends of the minister ordinand, while elders were the ones who largely responded to the survey questionnaire at the elder ordination sites.

Appendix 7 indicates the familiarity of respondents to "official" sources of Reformed theology. Of all respondents, 17.11% indicated that they were familiar with the Book of Order and 15.27% were familiar with John Calvin and his writings. Only 13.59% of overall respondents in both the elder and minister field sites indicated familiarity with the Book of Confessions. Only a mere 2.01% of overall respondents were familiar with the Book of Occasional Services. While the BoO contains much theology, it is generally regarded as the polity book of the PC(U.S.A.). What emerges from these field sites lends support to the general portrait of the ecclesial life of the PC(U.S.A.), and supported by the historical research of Holper and Walton mentioned in Chapter 1, namely that the Church views the office of presbyter through the lenses of governance and jurisdictional responsibilities, and less on the pastoral-liturgical function for elders.

2. What were the top three important elements/events within the ordination service?

This analytical question concerns responses to Q7 (the most important element/event) and Q9 (what do you understand to be happening in the ordination service). Appendix 8A shows the results of the comparative and overall tallies with regards to Q7; appendix 8B shows the results of the comparative and overall tallies with regards to Q9.

The elder ordination sites, separately and cumulatively, ranked the Laying on of Hands as the most important element/event in the ordination service. The minister sites, separately and cumulatively, ranked the Laying on of Hands as third as the most important element/event. MP ranked the sermon as the most important element, and MW ranked the pastoral charge as the most important element. In the MP focus group transcript as well as the phenomenological observations, the sermon laid out the significance of ordination and its linkage with baptism. The preacher at MP also used the occasion of the sermon to present gifts to the ordinand, which served as a stand-in for the giving of the symbols of ministry; thus the sermon in MP was all-encompassing in its pedagogical, educative, and catechetical methods and content. MW, we will recall, was attended by many friends of the ordinand. The pastoral charge offered by the minister ordinand would have been regarded by her friends as the tangible and first expression of her ordination. Still, the overall tally for all four sites as that the laying on of hands was ranked first in importance garnering 22.46% as compared to the sermon which received 16.92%. The overall low percentage of laying on of hands as the most important element in the ordination service shows an uncertainty among overall respondents that the laying on of hands was the defining moment/element in the ordination service.

Again, there was a divergence when comparing the elder ordination sites (EC and EN) with the minister ordination sites (MP and MW). The elder ordination sites tended to offer the "official" or "traditional" interpretation of what was occurring in an ordination service. Both sites ranked the work of the Holy Spirit as the number one interpretation of what occurred at the ordination service: EC ranked choice 9a ("The Holy Spirit was empowering the minister/elder candidate and blessing him/her") as the top choice, while EN ranked choice 9c ("The Holy Spirit was blessing the community gathered together") as the top choice in understanding the special nature of an ordination service. MP and MW, on the other hand, tended to see ordination as a time of celebration (choice 9f, "Family and friends were gathering to celebrate a milestone in the service of the minister/elder candidate"). While the overall ranking of all four sites ranked the work of the Holy Spirit as the top two interpretations of the special character of ordination services (choices 9b and 9c), respondents were not definitive as to what role the Holy Spirit was having in the ordination service. Additionally, when we combine the totals for the top two ranked choices, that means that respondents among all four field sites were uncertain about whether the ordination service was primarily about the Holy Spirit working in and upon the ordinand and community, but tended to see ordination service as orientated towards the community, or the community's role in connecting itself and the ordinand to the wider church, or still yet, a time to celebrate a milestone in the faith and life journey of the ordinand.

3. *What was the demographic profile of those who tended to indicate that the Laying on of Hands was the most important event/element?*

Of the 196 total respondents in the four field sites, 73 respondents chose option 7n (Laying on of Hands). Older females (age 55–65), elders, Caucasian, reared in the Reformed/Presbyterian tradition, and theologically moderate (35.62%) tended to indicate that laying on of hands was the most important event/element.

4. *What was the demographic profile of those who tended to indicate that the Constitutional Questions were the most important event/element?*

Of the 196 total respondents in the four field sites, 21 respondents chose option 7i (Constitutional Questions) as the most important event/element. These respondents tended to be middle-aged female elders (age 36–45), Caucasian, reared in the Presbyterian/Reformed tradition, and theologically moderate.

5. With regards to Q13 ("What do you believe was happening during the laying on of hands upon the candidate?"), what was the top response for each field site and overall? [LL a-b]

> *a) Of those who responded to Q13, what percentage of the total were elders or ministers who ranked the first option as number one, i.e. "Holy Spirit was empowering the minister/elder candidate at that moment?"*
>
> *b) Of those percentage of elders and ministers who ranked "Holy Spirit was empowering the minister/elder candidate at that moment" as the number one choice, how many of those elders or ministers indicated familiarity with any of the confessional documents/theologians in Q25?*

Appendix 9 shows the top responses in each of the field sites and overall as to interpretations of what was happening during the laying on of hands. EC, EN, and MW all affirmed that the laying on of hands was about the "Holy Spirit was empowering the minister/elder candidate at that moment;" thus three of the four field sites held to the traditional understanding of laying on of hands. The exception was MP. The top interpretation of the laying on of hands at MP was that it was an "[e] xpression of support, blessing and love." Those who had the traditional understanding regarding the Holy Spirit's empowering work were two-thirds elders and one-third ministers.

Appendix 10 shows an analysis that of those respondents who indicated that the laying on of hands primarily involved the "Holy Spirit was empowering the minister/elder candidate" what percentage of those respondents were familiar with the "official" sources of Reformed theology queried in Q25. The analysis shows that the two elder ordination sites (EC and EN) had more respondents who were more familiar with the "official" sources of the Reformed tradition than the minister ordination sites. Of the overall total of 66 respondents in the four field sites who ranked the empowering work of the Holy Spirit as the primary meaning of the laying on of hands, forty-four of those respondents were familiar with the "official" sources of the Reformed tradition, and of those forty-four, thirty-four came from the two elder ordination sites.

That minister ordinations are an infrequent event, those who tend to attend are persons outside of the church, particularly friends and family of the minister ordinand who may not necessarily be Reformed/Presbyterian in their ecclesial upbringing or present affiliation. Elder ordinations, because they are a part of a Service of the Lord's Day of a congregation, occur within the rhythm of a church's life and community; regularity of teaching and education would enable the instruction of the "official" understanding of laying on of hands, or at least, make more readily available the resources that would provide such instruction.

6. What were the top two responses to Q15 (if experienced connection of ordination with the sacraments was made, how was the connection made?)

Appendix 11 shows graphically the top two responses to Q15 as to how the respondents sensed the present ordination was related to the Eucharist and/or baptism. The respondents at EC seemed to regard a call to recall baptism as the linkage that was made to ordination. While no such call can be recalled by the author based on phenomenological observations as well as a review of the video recording of EC, the infant baptism during EC's worship service may have been interpreted by respondents at EC as the "call" to recall baptism. Respondents at EN, likewise, were not certain as which element made that connection with the sacraments and ordination. There was a split between the sermon, pastoral charge, hymns/songs, and a call to recall baptism. These results would confirm the presiding pastor's strong intentionality of highlighting ordination in the Service of the Lord's Day throughout various elements of the worship service. MP and MW overwhelmingly regarded the sermons as the element that linked ordination with the sacraments, with MP more so than MW. My phenomenological observations as well as the focus group interviews confirm that the preacher at MP was intentional about emphasizing the connection of ordination with baptism. I question the results of MW in respondents' seeing the sermon as the location where ordination was linked to the sacraments. In my phenomenological observations, review of the video-recording, as well as my de-briefing session with the preacher during the focus group interview, there was no mention of the sacraments in the sermon. In fact, the focus group members affirmed that the explicit mention of a sacramental relationship was understood by them as a given, and a judgment was made by the ordinand to not make such an explicit mention out of pastoral sensitivity and ecumenical concern as to the diverse persons in attendance. On the other hand, the preacher at MW, while preaching from 2 Kings 6:24–31 nd Luke 4:14–21, MW's sermon focused more on the 2 Kings passage, which involved four lepers eating and drinking in the abandoned tents of the Aramean armies. This feasting event could have been rightfully interpreted by MW respondents as the sermon linking ordination with the Eucharist.

Focus Group Interviews

Focus group participants in all four sites, by and large, affirmed traditional interpretations of ordination. They regarded ordination as a time to celebrate God's call through and in a community for a member of the priesthood of all believers to serve in a specific capacity for the common good, a corporate act of the Church to beseech God's blessing upon the ordinand to fulfill his/her office, and a continuation of a ritual act practiced by the Church universal in all times and places.

Focus group participants were also traditional in their understanding of laying on of hands and in identifying the laying on of hands as the decisive moment of the ordination service. A notable exception would be the focus group at MW, in which a number of participants noted that the Constitutional Questions at MW and in other ordination services were the significant element because of the tangible vows that are made in the propounding and answering of the Questions. EC and EN lifted up the laying on of hands as the capstone of the whole worship service where the whole assembly and the wider tradition came together, as represented by the presence of many presbyters. The ordinand at MP spoke of how she felt her head cradled like a baby coming out of a mother's womb, an imagery and interpretation that may enrich our understanding of the body's role in ordination.

Another noteworthy nuancing of the tradition was the assertion of the husband (CB) of AB, the ordinand at MW. CB shared how he saw his wife becoming married to Jesus Christ as she was being ordained through her commitment to now take on the responsibility of being a minister of Word and Sacrament. CB, we will recall, noted this in discussing the difference between his role as an elder and her role now as a minister of Word and Sacrament. That while ministers and elders are similar in many ways, the office of minister is qualitatively different, in degree and in kind, with the expectations that are attended to the office by the community.

The focus groups also saw the importance of ordination beyond a community's calling in baptism. For the focus groups, baptism provided a general call, while ordination provides a specific call. The focus group in EC, in particular, emphasized how without ordination there would be general chaos because ordination orders the community to designate specific persons to take on particular responsibilities. The parental imagery offered by RR at the MW focus group was helpful in this regard in that ordination was analogous to a parent calling upon another parent at a pool party to watch a particular child, but such a specific calling and responsibility would not vitiate the general responsibility that all other parents at the pool party have in ensuring the safety of all children.

BG, the preacher at MP, provided a needed reminder of what has been missing in ordination services. His critique that ordination services often have turned into a party to celebrate an ordinand with a sermon becoming a virtual "valedictory" speech was helpful as he emphasized that ordination should include an element of orientating the ordinand towards the cross, that ministry in the name of Jesus Christ is about sacrificial service for the community as the minister calls the community to prepare for their deaths; such a message can also be applied to elder ordinands as well.

Preliminary Concluding Remarks

When we juxtapose the comparative theological sources from these four field sites—textual analysis, phenomenological observations, survey questionnaires, and focus group interviews—we gain a common picture of local, gathered communities eager to respond to God's call in and through the lives of one of their own as he/she assumes the role and responsibility of an ordained officer.

The four field sites show an overall strong connection and continuity with the received Reformed tradition, with some notable exceptions. The elder ordination sites (EC and EN) followed the "party-line" if you will in acknowledging the laying on of hands as the key element in ordination, in seeing the laying on of hands as the Holy Spirit empowering or blessing the candidate and congregation, and in seeing ordination as both an act of God and the community responding to that call. The minister ordination sites affirmed those elements to a lesser degree, but saw ordination in largely celebratory ways, that the community that gathered, largely friends of the minister ordinands, knew the candidates through their lives and preparation process, and now, ordination was a *pro forma* ritualization of gifts and skills long-recognized by the community in the ordinand. It is noteworthy that the two minister ordination sites occurred in an urban and suburban contexts and both minister ordinands were young adults, as well as members of the focus group were young adults. The emphasis on the sermon in both the ministry sites seemed to anchor the meaning of ordination as the bridge between the ordination service proper and the entirety of the worship service, while for the elder sites, the laying on of hands was the distinctive feature that set apart ordination service from the rest of the worship service proper.

SEVEN

Conclusion

The Tsar declared a pogrom against a particular Jewish village in Russia. Being a sporting fellow, however, he invited the villagers to a debate with the Metropolitan of the Russian Orthodox Church to be conducted by sign language. Well, the villagers knew they were doomed because the Metropolitan was the champion of champions in sign language debate in all Russia. So nobody volunteered to accept the challenge except the village idiot. Without hope anyway, the village elders agreed to send him up to Moscow for the encounter.

The two debaters sat an opposite ends of a long table and the debate began. The Metropolitan held up three fingers on his right hand, and the village idiot responded immediately by holding up the forefinger of his right hand. Somewhat hesitantly, the Metropolitan then made a sweeping arc sign with his two arms extended, and the village idiot again responded by pointing to the table with his right hand forefinger. Now obviously bothered, the Metropolitan reached into his bag and placed a loaf of bread and a bottle of wine on the table. Immediately, the village idiot reached into his bag and produced an apple. With that the Metropolitan conceded defeat.

Back home the Metropolitan explained his defeat to the Tsar. He said, "I held up three fingers, symbolizing the Holy Trinity. But he held up one finger reminding me that is yet One. I then made a sweeping gesture to claim that God is universal and thus everywhere. But he pointed defiantly to the table to remind me that God is yet right here. I then produced the holy elements from my bag to symbolize God's salvation, but he produced an apple to remind me of the continuing reality of sin. It was a humiliating defeat.

Meanwhile, the village idiot also returned home and is explaining his totally unexpected victory to the gathered elders. "Well," he said, "the Metropolitan held up three fingers to say that we had three days to flee, but I told him that not one of us was going anywhere. He then made this sweeping gesture to tell me that we all had to go, but I pointed to the table to say that we were staying right here. He then took out a loaf of bread and a bottle of wine, and I showed him that I had brought my lunch too."[1]

Summary of Problem

What is told in jest, we have spent a great length looking at the mixed signals and sometimes divergent messages and interpretations of official, intended, perceived, and actual meanings. The levels and degrees of meaning and meaning-making are complex and require methodologies that welcome, value, and enable discovery of the multiplicity of understanding. This project has advocated a complementary methodology to accomplish such a goal.

While neither the village idiot nor the Metropolitan exchanged any spoken words, their bodily actions carried meaning for the doer and the receiver, as each tried to convey a message in hopes of gaining victory. It was only after the conclusion, when interpreting their intentions and their interpretations of their adversary's perceived intent to their respective communities do we see the meaning-making capacity of both individuals and their communities who hear their accounts of the gestural encounter.

This book set out to establish that the Reformed theological, textual and ceremonial tradition was impoverished by not adequately accounting for actual ritual enactment of ordination. The traditional privileging of "upper-tier" sources has left theological discourse and problem-solving in a few ecclesiastical elites, church bureaucrats, and "professional" theologians in a five century-old tradition that was founded on the principle of a "priesthood of all believers" and the accessibility of God's revealed Word for all. Numerous theological, conciliar, ecclesiastical, creedal, and confessional statements on ordination and church orders

1. This is a classic Jewish story recounted to me by Dr. Thomas Gillespie, Princeton, NJ, May 2009.

have not resulted in consistency, coherency, and convergence on these issues.

When we combed conciliar statements, the statements themselves were either varied or lacked the ecclesial authority to speak on behalf of the entire Reformed tradition. We noted in chapter 2, the numerous efforts in the mid- to late- 20th century by the WARC to grapple with ordination, but numerous studies and papers produced did not garner the official imprimatur of any of the WARC General Councils. The responses of WARC-member churches to the BEM document were varied, with each church emphasizing various aspects of the Ministry section of BEM, with overwhelming critique against what Reformed churches perceived as BEM's privileging of the threefold office of bishop, presbyter, and deacon at the diminution of the ministry of the whole people of God. In a few instances, such as the Reformed churches of North and South India, a system of bishops is used. But what has become more commonplace is to locate the episcopé (oversight function) in regional presbyteries, a synodal episcopate rather than an individual/personal bishop.

We then looked carefully and extensively at the constitutional, creedal and confessional documents of the PC(U.S.A.). Of the confessional documents in the BoC, only the Second Helvetic Confession and the Confession of 1967 directly spoke about ordination and church orders, and even then, these two tackled the issue from the temporal context of their development; the former reflected the anti-Roman Catholic tenor of its primary author (Bullinger) and of the mid-16th century in its emphasis of the marks of the offices in service to the Gospel over and against the papal system, while the latter underscored a Barthian theme of the Church's essential nature as being a witnessing community of and for reconciliation in and through Christ. The Form of Government section of the BoO focused discussion on the presbyteral offices with an accent towards polity considerations, functional tasks, and jurisdiction, and less so on pastoral-liturgical function of the two offices, or their equality in those functions; an emphasis was placed on the parity of the two offices with regards to representation and service in governing bodies. The BOS as a liturgical resource puts the best of the BoO's theology of ordination into liturgical texts and rubrics through its emphasis on and linkage with baptism, the shared responsibility of the ordained with the community, the essential participation of the community in the rite of ordination, and the direct relationship of ordination with celebration of the Eucharist in community; what the BoO lacked in theological substance, the BOS exceeded the BoO in providing a robust theological explication of ordination through the liturgical ordo and rubrics.

A survey of other Reformed confessions beyond those contained in the BoC was conducted. There we discovered a varied picture of confessional statements, some prescribing the classical Reformed fourfold office as with the French Confession of 1559, to the international sampling of confessions compiled by the WARC that exhibited diverse understanding of ordination and Reformed church orders. Many confessional documents placed the accent on linking church orders with the Church's ministry in Christ through the personal, collegial, and communal dimensions. An important note was made that there was broad agreement that the very nature of Reformed confessions was that while confessional statements provided significant expressions of belief for a particular time in a specific context in response to particular issues or topics, Reformed confessions are not intended to constrain belief or action, but to shape it, not to legislate, nor adjudicate, but to educate. In that sense, confessions, while part of constitutional documents of Reformed churches do not and cannot carry the same prescriptive and normative role as Scripture. In that sense, while confessions are authoritative, their essential intent are to enshrine commitments and beliefs within a spatio-temporal context, and therefore, limited in time and specific in scope.

To round out our survey of the "official" sources of Reformed theology, Chapter 4 briefly explored the methods and expressed theology of a sampling of six respected and renowned Reformed theologians spanning four centuries—John Calvin, Martin Bucer, Francis Turretin, Friedrich Schleiermacher, Karl Barth, and Thomas F. Torrance. As with the previous sections, these theologians lifted up various aspects of ordination and church orders. Calvin and Barth were closer in their approaches, seeing in Pauline epistles a call for a presbyteral form of ecclesiastical government, of three offices, or in some of their writings, four offices, that are linked to Christ's own ministry in and through the Church. Bucer, more than Calvin, lifted the role of the Holy Spirit in calling and animating the offices. Both Reformers framed all offices—whether the three or the four (minister, elder, doctor, teacher)—within the ministry of Word and Sacrament entrusted to the Church by Christ. Turretin, because of his spatio-temporal context, focused his writing on upbraiding Roman Catholic polity, while lifting up the Reformed understanding of offices in service to the Gospel. Schleiermacher emphasized the role of the Holy Spirit and the Church as a gathering of individuals who were given freedom to join and serve in the Church by individuals' consciousness of the Holy Spirit's leading. Along these lines, with regards to ministry and offices, Schleiermacher underscored the freedom in the Spirit in ordering various patterns of ministry for the sake of Christ's ministry. Barth saw vocation as the historical, existential reifying of justification and sanctification in one's life as part of the Church's vocation of witness in Christ. Barth addressed vocation in the fourth fragment of the CD in the section of baptism and the role of the Holy Spirit. We will recapitulate Barth's conception of baptism, ministry, and the Holy Spirit later in this chapter, but needless to say, Barth advocated for a flexibility of church offices, seeing baptism as the primary and sufficient ordination for the Church, and what mattered was not the offices themselves or the ordering of such, but that the offices were in and at the service of the Church's primary vocation, namely being Christ's witness in the world. Torrance underscored the linkage of the Church's ministry with that of Christ's royal ministry, and connected that with the Eucharistic nature of the ordained offices. We noted Butin's discussion of both Calvin's and Barth's discussion of the *triplex munum* of Christ (priest, king, prophet) , and how the threefold offices of Christ may provide a framework in discussing the tripartite dimension of the Church's ministry, and, derivatively, the threefold areas of the Church's offices, regardless of what specific titles are attached to those offices.

In Chapter 5, we posed several critiques of the prevalent methodology of the Reformed tradition. We were careful to note that one cannot discard the tradition nor of the methodologies employed by the tradition for much is gained by a thoroughgoing analysis of the "official" sources of theology. While much is gained, the tradition is impoverished for it diminishes or ignores altogether the critical contribution that local gathered communities offer in their encounter with the living God and their grappling with the received tradition. We were helped in this regard with the insights of Lindbeck's discussion of religious systems that need to be understood as cultures with their own language and rules of engagement; Hughes' discussion of the indexical and iconic meanings of symbolic action, particularly the dissonance that often occurs between messenger and receiver; and Chauvet's critical contribution in seeing the mediation of the divine-human and human-human relationships through and in the body.

Liturgical theology, ritual studies and narrative theory provided the complementary methodology to the "official" sources of theology. Liturgical theology showed how one must account for the meaning-making that occurs as the Church worships for the Church's worship is, properly speaking, primary theology; particularly with ordination, as an occasional service in the life of a congregation or a presbytery, that potentially harnesses the fullness of the Church's liturgy in Word and sacrament, one must take seriously the Church's worship *in toto* and its individual parts. Ritual studies gave clarity and specificity as to the generic aims and goals of liturgical theology. The field of ritual studies orientated us to the human aspect of a community as a gathered assembly understands itself, its identity vis-à-vis God, the Church, the ordinand, and the received tradition through the sights, sounds, gestures, and history enacted and represented in an ordination rite. Ritual studies helped us to appreciate that as ordination is the culmination of a liminal time in the ordinand's life, the Church must be attentive to the ordinand's and community's self-understanding as role negotiation occurs in the new role assumed by the ordinand, and as both the ordinand and the gathered community seek to understand the nature of God's call upon the ordained officer and upon the Church. Narrative theory, as a cognate field of ritual studies, emphasizes story-telling as a means by which participants express themselves, and a medium through which mutual understanding and meaningful dialogue occurs. In seeking the aid of liturgical theology, ritual analysis, and narrative theory, we positioned the book to analyze four field sites with the stated interest of seeing whether and how the "official" sources of theology connect with the expressed theologies represented at a gathered ordination service, pointing to areas of continuity with the tradition, while identifying discontinuities as possible areas of nuancing the Reformed tradition or providing a fresh interpretation to the tradition.

The four field sites were carefully analyzed to uncover the theological understanding and meaning-making occurring at the ordination services. Two elder ordinations and two minister ordinations provided the locales for our analysis. That two of the field sites were identified through the social networking site, Facebook®, was demonstrative of the contemporary milieu that calls for inclusion of multivalent perspectives, thus, buttressing, in some way, the principle of this book's advocated methodology, namely, that all people make meaning and must be included at the table of discourse. In addition to phenomenological observations by the author, a survey questionnaire was given to the assembly, as well as textual analysis was conducted of the liturgical texts, and focus groups interviews were coordinated involving a representative sampling of the gathered assembly. By and large, we found that all four sites were in keeping with the Reformed tradition in their use of the BOS liturgical rites, as well as in their overall interpretation of the various elements of ordination and ordination itself; at this point we ought to note that this outcome comes from respondents and interviewees who, while largely reared in the Presbyterian/Reformed tradition, were relatively unfamiliar with the "official" sources of the Reformed tradition. In varying degrees, all four sites saw ordination as involving God's call, the community's call, and a time of celebration. Overall, the four sites identified the laying on of hands as the significant element of the ordination service, with differing understanding as to what exactly was happening during that rite. All in all, the laying on of hands was described as a visible connection with the larger Church and tradition, and a sense of being supported.

As we speak of the commonalities, we also note the following differences:

- The elder ordination sites (EC, EN) tended to offer the "classical" explanations;
- The minister ordination sites tended to nuance "classical" explanations, such as likening the laying on of hands as being cradled from the womb, or ordination as a marriage of the ordinand with Christ;
- Laying on of hands was the most important feature identified by the elder ordination sites while the sermon was identified as the most important by the minister ordination sites;
- That minister ordination sites had more friends and family members of the ordinand present, ordination was regarded largely as a time of celebration;

- Ordination, vis-à-vis baptism, was seen as the final step in one's baptism, or the particularization and specification of one's baptismal calling, but even then, among the elder ordination sites, baptism was downplayed, with more emphasis placed on one's ordained status and the accompanying responsibilities that comes with that status;
- The preachers at EN and MP were more intentional about linking ordination and baptism, but none of the ordination sites included the baptismal liturgies or litanies as prescribed by the *BOS*;
- The laying on of hands and the constitutional questions were the two features identified that indicated to participants that the assembly had moved from the worship service into the ordination service proper;
- The insight of BG, the preacher at MP, that ordination should be about orientating the ordinand to the cross and his/her call to help the Church to "prepare for their deaths" was a helpful contribution to the discourse, particularly when ordinations are sometimes regarded as an inaugural party to one's career;
- Elder ordination sites understood the relationship of presbyters (minister of Word and Sacrament, and elders) as being one focused on terms of office and jurisdictional/decision-making dimensions and less on the pastoral-liturgical parity of responsibilities, willingly ceding those responsibilities to the minister;
- Minister ordination sites tended to view the relationship of presbyters as collegial in doing the pastoral-liturgical tasks, while highlighting the call of the whole people of God to serve.

The last two bullet points are instructive. The analysis of the four field sites demonstrate that the elder ordination sites (older Caucasian, suburban Presbyterian) were comfortable in presbyteral roles that placed the minister/pastor in the role of *primus inter pares*, with the elders as equal in decision-making; but in the sphere of pastoral-liturgical dimensions of the office, the elders were more than willing to allow the pastor to take the lead. In fact, in the focus group interview of the elder ordination sites, participants were in agreement that, once they formally voted to authorize a candidate's ordination, their role as elder ceased during the ordination service and they were in the pew as supporters of the candidate. Although Pauline and early church accounts of the original role of bishop in a local church would be akin to the *primus inter pares* understanding of the two elder ordination service sites, these sites were equally adamant in any proposal that had any appearance of hierarchical ordering of offices, such as a recently approved constitutional amendment to the BoO that returned the old terms, "teaching elder" (for minister of Word and Sacrament) and "ruling elder" (for lay elders).[2] We will discuss the New Form of Government (nFOG) later in this chapter.

While the elder ordination sites underlined the parity of presbyters in matters of jurisdictional governance, the minister ordination sites underscored the parity of all members to serve by virtue of baptism. This telling response by focus group participants in MP and MW demonstrate a common ministerial concern, namely the sharing of responsibilities of the Church's total ministry in the life of a congregation or judicatory.

The field sites confirm the value of including actual ordination services as sources of theology in the Reformed tradition. The field sites *in toto* confirm that the Reformed tradition finds wide acceptance in the enacted ordination liturgies of elder and minister ordinations, even as there are wide interpretations as to what precisely is occurring at key moments in ordination and in the ordination rite itself. The field sites have also shown, as we have noted, the aspects of the ordination rite that connect with the gathered assembly as being meaningful in their connection with God's movement in that event, as well as their connection with the assembly and the tradition.

Finally, the field sites affirm that the whole people of God—individually and collectively—are theologians and ought to be regarded as such. Laypersons may not all hold theological degrees or advanced training in theological method, but, like Kavanagh's Ms. Murphy, they have an encounter with the triune God and interpret that divine-human discourse through various matrices of meaning. In all four field sites, the overwhelming response by survey respondents and focus group participants were consistent with many of the statements and definitions offered by the "official" sources of the Reformed tradition.

2 *The Constitution of the Presbyterian Church (U.S.A.), part II, Book of Order, 2011–2013*, F-3.0202. Hereafter "nFOG".

This book sought, not to propose a theology of presbyteral ordination, but to prescribe ritual analysis and narrative theory, with the associated field of liturgical theology, as a complementary and necessary methodology to the "official" sources of theology traditionally and comfortably employed by the Reformed tradition. At the very least, what we have demonstrated is that the inclusion of the gathered assembly in the theological discourse has a value for the whole Church: for the professional theologian and judicatory official, this study confirms that the Reformed tradition is wide and deep, with consistent practices with diverse theologies; for the wider Church, this study affirms the diversity of theologies that constitute the Reformed tradition and the historic grappling with what it means to faithfully serve Christ in the Church and the world.

Why is a New Methodology Needed

Early twenty-first century culture is learning to adapt to Internet technology. Social networking sites, such as Facebook® and Twitter®, are demonstrative of a culture desirous for democratization of ideas, ready access to information, and inclusion of all ideas in social and theological discourse. Access and privileging of information and interpretation need to be opened to the whole people of God, valuing not just the contributions of ecclesiastical elites, but, indeed, every single member of the body of Christ. [3]

A new, complementary methodology is needed in discovering and articulating a theology of presbyteral ordination for the Presbyterian Church (U.S.A.). Formal theology from "official" sources have their limits, two of which must be noted. The first limit concerns authority. In PC(U.S.A.) polity, specifically, but Reformed polity, generally, constitutional documents (the BOC and the BoO) and ecclesiastical court decisions interpreting those documents are binding upon the congregations and ecclesial life of the Church; the theologies of Reformed theologians and conciliar statements are highly regarded but not binding. And as we saw in previous chapters, even the constitutional documents

3. See the insightful work by Whitsitt, *Open Source Church: Making Room for the Wisdom of All* (Alban Institute, 2011). Whitsitt argues that Wikipedia® serves as a paradigmatic framework of viewing our present ecclesial context of a sharing in meaning-making, democratization, mutual accountability, and shared authority.

themselves do not speak with one voice on matters of church orders and ordination; the field sites demonstrate that multichrome, multivalent character of the "official" sources of theology. We can say with certainty: there is no singular theology of presbyteral ordination in the PC(U.S.A.). This brings us to a notable, second limit of the "official" sources of theology.

The "official" sources of theology cannot account for the diversity of practices and theologies extant within the Reformed tradition, both past and present. As we have seen, the "official" sources of Reformed theology sought to prescribe a blanket theology of ordination and church orders to describe and prescribe a unified, consistent explanation of what would be the distinctive theology of the Reformed churches in those matters, but this came at the expense of the wide-ranging theologies not only in the PC(U.S.A.) itself, but as we saw in the examination of worldwide Reformed confessions, even the Reformed churches globally.

Thus, with at least these two limitations—authority and scope—the "official" sources of Reformed theology require and need a complementary methodology that takes seriously:

- actual, local, gathered assemblies
- the meaning-making that occurs in ordination services
- the reality that ordination services themselves are occasional, and therefore, any enduring explanations of what ordination means theologically must be tethered to the ecclesiological identity of the Church and its offices, as well as the sacrament of baptism, in which the triune God calls all people to service in the Church and in the world.

The methodology this book has proposed is grounded in the actual ritual practice of ordination services as a gathered assembly and the triune God encounter one another in the calling and sending of ordained presbyters.

Ritual analysis as a complementary methodology takes seriously the Church's worship and the people in worship, regarding them as *bona fide* theologians of the faith. Ritual studies sees each element and the whole of ordination as playing essential parts in the Church's theological work, as the relationship involving the Church, the ordinand, and the triune God are mediated through the ordination rite.

With regards to the limits of authority and scope referenced above, ritual analysis appreciates the diversity and multiplicity of practices and theologies. As with a modern culture characterized by the social utility network, Facebook® and Twitter®, which distinguish themselves on the democratization of and access to ideas, ritual analysis does not seek, as with "official" sources, to prescribe a specific theology to explain each and every instance of ordination rites or the theologies undergirding it. Rather, ritual analysis, together with liturgical theology and narrative theory, is open to the Church's wide and deep understanding of itself, the triune God's revelation in and through the Church and the world, and the unfolding story of the Reformed tradition, past and present.

Next Steps

This book provides a pathway for future research in several areas. Firstly, as was noted in the first chapter, the works on Reformed presbyteral ordination are sparse. There are works on Reformed church orders as we have noted previously, but this book, when added to the books of Holper and Wilton, add to the discourse by its advocacy of taking seriously the meaning-making that occurs in the ordination rite itself. Research can be undertaken, as Holper, Wilton, and I have done, in combining the findings of our works, and putting them in one volume, tracing the histories and theologies of Reformed ordination in the PC(U.S.A.) and in the Reformed churches globally.

Secondly, an ecclesiology for the Reformed churches grounded in baptism would be key to a better understanding of the linkage of ordination, church orders, and our "first ordination." In some of the "official" sources we examined, as well as notations referenced in chapter 6 in the field sites, the baptismal connection to ordination and church orders has not been adequately engaged. What would it mean if a theology of ordination and church orders emerged from, or, at least, was tethered to, our baptismal theology? Would such a methodological move enable the Reformed tradition to live into God's call to the whole people of God? Twelve years ago, Reformed worship scholar, Ronald Byars, put it aptly in the very first line of his article: "The most critical liturgical issue facing our denomination is, in my judgment, centered on the Sacrament of Baptism."[4] Byars went on to query how the Church would be different if a whole congregation, or the whole denomination, lived into the baptismal commitments made to one another and to the world. Such shared responsibility in equipping, nurturing, and sending would transform the Church's present self-identity to one in which the whole people of God , not just ordained officers, serve, in the words of the eighth constitutional question propounded to officers, "with energy, intelligence, imagination, and love."[5]

Thirdly, connected to baptism is the issue of constitutional questions and its resemblance to the vows taken at baptism. As noted in field sites EC, MP and MW, the propounding of the constitutional questions were a meaningful and significant moment for several focus group members, and 21 of 198 survey respondents counted it as the essential element in the ordination service. Future research is needed in tracing the history and theology of the present constitutional questions.[6] PC(U.S.A.) polity expert and former stated clerk of the Presbytery of Palisades, William E. Chapman, noted in his own research on this subject at my request, that the current constitutional questions "were basically those agreed upon in the Plan of Reunion, 1983." Then in a remarkable finding, strangely familiar to the tone of baptismal vows, Chapman quoted from paragraph 6 of the "Rules for Examination" of a paper titled, "The Form of Presbyterial Church Government agreed Upon by the Assembly of Divines at Westminster, Examined and Approves, Anno 1645, by the General Assembly of the church of Scotland, etc." as he found in archival papers of the late PC(U.S.A.) stated clerk, Jim Andrews, as follows:

> After the sermon, the minister who hath preached shall, in the face of the congregation, demand of him who is now to be ordained concerning his faith in Christ Jesus and his persuasion of the truth of the Reformed religion according to the Scripture; his sincere intentions and ends in desiring to enter into his calling; his diligence in prayer, reading, meditation, preaching,

4 Byars, "Indiscriminate Baptism and Baptismal Integrity" *Reformed Liturgy & Music*, 36–40.

5. *BoO*, W-4.4003h.

6. I am grateful to the staff of the Presbyterian Historical Society (Department of History) of the Office of the General Assembly of the PC(U.S.A.) in Philadelphia, PA for combing their archival records for any extant work on the history and/or theology of the constitutional questions; their research was unable to uncover any such work.

> ministering the sacraments, discipline, and doing all ministerial duties toward his charge; his zeal and faithfulness in maintaining the truth of the gospel and unity of the Church against error and schism; his care that himself and his family may be unblamable, and examples to his flock; willingness and humility, in meekness of spirit, to submit unto the admonitions of his brethren and discipline of the Church; and his resolution to continue in his duty against all trouble and persecution.[7]

That several focus group participants as well as survey respondents (in their written in comments to Q18 on other occasions they associate ordination with) associated ordination as a continuation or completion of baptism, or as a "super" confirmation, research into the constitutional questions and their possible linkage to baptismal vows would be on the mark. For instance, Reformed worship scholar, Hughes Oliphant Old, in his pioneering work on the baptismal rite in the 16th century, noted that even in Bucer's Hessian reforms, as Bucer was addressing Anabaptist concerns over infant baptism, he proposed an "evangelical confirmation" laid out in *Ziegenhainer Zuchtordnung* (order/arrangement of Ziegenhain, the site of the Synod of the Hessian Church).[8] Old noted that the proposed evangelical confirmation provided a way and means for Bucer to lay out his ideas on ministry. Moreover, Old asserted that research has shown that Bucer's overriding concern in addressing confirmation was to seek a compromise with the Anabaptists based not on the historicity of the origins of confirmation per se, but on "the medieval sacrament of confirmation developed out of the biblical rite of laying on of hands when intercessory prayer was made for someone."[9] The close relationship of ordination, confirmation, baptism, and laying on of hands would need further research and discussion in future works.

Fourthly, further research can be done on the theology of Jonathan Edwards on presbyteral ordination and church offices. Because of the necessity to place limits on the scope and number of theologians to be

7. Quoted in William E. Chapman, "Sources of Ordination Question" unpublished paper. March 3, 2009. Prepared for this project and used with permission. I am grateful to William Chapman for his preliminary research and findings, and for pointing out this passage to me.

8. Old, *The Shaping of the Reformed Baptismal Rite in the Sixteenth Century*, 210. I am grateful to Hughes Oliphant Old for directing my attention to this insight.

9 Ibid., 216.

surveyed, this book did not include Edwards as one of the key theologians surveyed in Chapter 4. Future research can comb this important Presbyterian theologian's thought on ordination. Helen Westra's book would be a good starting place for any such research.[10] Because any work that attempts to comb a theologian's thought on church orders and ordination would necessarily have to research their ecclesiology, a sustained study of Edwards's ecclesiology is much needed, as Douglas A. Sweeney notated, an area of Edwards's work that "has gone largely unnoticed by scholars."[11]

As was noted earlier, at this writing, the PC(U.S.A.) judicatories have ratified a constitutional amendment to the *BoO* called the New Form of Government (nFOG).[12] Since its charge four years ago, the Task Force sought to do two things: to simplify the current *BoO* Form of Government section that maintained the foundational principles of Presbyterian polity as found in the first four chapters of the *BoO* by combining them into a new section called the Foundations of Polity (designated by "F"), while proposing a polity structure that would be missional in character. The nFOG clarified what Small has called the "undivided plural ministries" of the three Reformed offices of minister, elder and deacon by clearly delineating that deacons belong to the "Ministry of Compassion and Service," elders (returned to the traditional nomenclature of "ruling elder") belong to the "Ministry of Discernment and Governance," and ministers (returned to the traditional nomenclature of "teaching elder") belong to the "Ministry of Word and Sacrament."[13] The nFOG asserted that ordered ministries are gifts from God to the Church to order its life so that the whole body may flourish, and that in calling certain individuals from the whole body to exercise ordained leadership, this "in no way diminishes the importance of the commitment of all members to the total ministry of the church."[14] In so stating that shared commitment by all, however, the FOG-RGA

10. Westra, *The Minister's Task and Calling in the Sermons of Jonathan Edwards*, Studies in American Religion, Vol. 17 (Lewiston, NY: The Edwin Mellen Press, 1986).

11. Sweeney, "The Church" in *The Princeton Companion to Jonathan Edwards*, 167–189.

12. See footnote 2 *supra*

13. Ibid, G-2.02, 2.03, 2.05.

14. Ibid., G-2.0102.

does not explicitly state the baptismal foundation of that communal responsibility.

The nFOG describes the nature of one's call to the ordained ministry as one that originates from the action of the triune God, "evidenced by the movement of the Holy Spirit in the individual conscience, the approval of a community of God's people, and the concurring judgment of a council of the Church."[15] The nFOG describes the service of ordination and installation as: "The service of ordination and installation shall focus upon Christ and the joy and responsibility of serving him through the mission and ministry of the church, and shall include a sermon appropriate to the occasion."[16] The nFOG appropriately retains the tripartite nature of one's call: God, community, and individual. Missing from the nFOG's description of call and ordination are Torrance's emphasis on the Church's shared work with Christ's ongoing work in the world and the Church's participation in the work of the triune God in the world, Bucer's and Calvin's emphasis on the Holy Spirit as empowering and enabling the Church and its officers in fulfilling its calling, and Barth's emphasis on baptism as our first (and primary) ordination, just to name a few.

The nFOG has directed the PC(U.S.A.) in a direction that is less legislative and more focused on shared ministry clearly defined. Reverting back to the terms, "teaching elder" and "ruling elder," carries colloquial and vernacular baggage that, in the public mindset, appears to create a hierarchy of power and responsibility, even though the nFOG clearly states that the terminological term "ruler" does not mean a lording over one's authority. But as noted in the focus group at EC and EN, where I specifically asked about reverting to those terms, there was wide resistance to that proposal, even after the author elucidated the meaning of the term. The terms themselves seem to suggest that only ministers (teaching elders) are the only ordained officers authorized, qualified, and capable of teaching in the Church. The onus will be on the whole people of God, as it should always be, to ensure that ruling elders as with teaching elders are equipped, empowered and enabled to exercise educational and liturgical ministries alongside teaching elders.

The nFOG has also charted a course where there is wide latitude on the shaping of form and function of mid-councils (presbyteries and

15. Ibid., G-2.103.

16. Ibid., G-2.0403.

synods). As of this writing, creative conversations are occurring across the Presbyterian Church (U.S.A.) on various configurations of presbyteries and synods. What the nFOG has unleashed is the permission-giving to one another to explore new and fresh ways in which structure, organization, administrative operations, and rules do not stifle creativity, but direct focus on relationships, networking, and mutual collaboration on common ministries.

Ecumenical Implications

Lessons from BEM

The Ministry section of the BEM document provided a focused means for all Reformed churches to receive a convergence document addressing *inter alia* church orders and ordination. We surveyed the responses of Reformed churches to the BEM in Chapter 2. There are lessons from the BEM process that are related to the proposals and findings of this book.

This book, as with lessons from the BEM, advocates for a multi-tiered engagement of the entirety of the Church in its ecclesial and missional life. Roman Catholic theologian, Hervé Legrand, has advocated for Roman Catholic implementation of the principles of BEM and Vatican II at all levels of the Church whereby the personal, collegial, and communal dimensions of the Church's ministry are exercised simultaneously. What this would mean would be a re-examination of the relationship of the Holy See with diocesan bishops, and diocesan bishops vis-à-vis local priests, as to the level and degree of shared governance and decision-making.[17] This is somewhat akin to Butin's proposal of comparing the tripartite dimensions of Christ's offices with the tripartite dimensions of the Church's ministry and its offices. We will have more to say about this in our discussion below about Hunsinger's proposal for ecclesiological convergence between the Reformed churches and episcopally-ordered traditions.

Kenyan theologian, Jesse N.K. Mugambi, noted that inadequate representation and participation on the part of churches in the global

17. Legrand, "Personal, Collegial and Synodal Responsibility in the Roman Catholic Church: What Convergences Are There Between Reception of Vatican II and BEM?," 105–134.

South created a BEM document that was orientated towards the global North.[18] Mugambi asserted that "[t]he majority of Christians (especially in tropica Africa) can hardly identify themselves with the document's doctrinal formulation and theological justifications."[19] Mugambi spoke of BEM's eliding of the mythical character of ritual for myth "deals with stories through which a community of faith expresses its understanding of ultimate origin, ultimate purpose and ultimate destiny." Consequently, "doctrinal formulations should include not only the intellectual abstractions of the elite but also practical applications of ordinary believers."[20] The proposal and principle of inclusion advocated by this book is in keeping with that conclusion. At the core of Mugambi's critique was BEM's inadequate address of the relationship of Gospel and Culture. Mugambi put it this way:

> But theology cannot be conducted outside the cultural matrix within which a theologian has been brought up and trained, just as liturgy cannot be abstracted from the community of faith within which it has evolved. The BEM document did not deal sufficiently with the cultural matrices within which these rituals have become central to the various faith communities of Christianity. The consensus reached and approved at Lima, was, as an abstraction, a great achievement; but as an instrument to break social barriers it was perhaps of little utility. It did not, for example, help with healing the wounds inflicted by apartheid. This could be one of the reasons why the document did not become normative among the WCC member churches.[21]

That on a global scale local the BEM document did not adequately account for actual ecclesiologies demonstrates that for a denomination such as the PC(U.S.A.), it is paramount, when speaking about ordination and church orders, that the relationship of the Gospel to the actual "cultural matrices" in which ritual has evolved be included in the discourse. Grdzelidze, citing the late Reformed ecumenist Lukas Vischer, asserted that the common understanding of authority and decision-making would be needed to effect inclusion in not only participation in decisions, but the implementation of decisions at all levels, asking

18. Mugambi, "Some Problems of Authority and Credibility in the Drafting and Reception Processes of the BEM Document," 185–201.

19. Ibid., 191.

20. Ibid., 195.

21. Ibid., 198.

the question, "despite all divergences, [how] common decisions can be taken by all world communions."[22]

Benjamin Conner noted the major critique of Catholic theologian Edward Schillebeeckx of BEM and Barth's advocacy for flexibility in church orders.[23] Schillebeeckx observed that the threefold pattern so highly advocated by the BEM (bishop, presbyter, deacon) ignored the "alternative practices" of the present church, contra the "undivided church" of the early church, causing Schillebeeckx to query whether the retention of the threefold pattern of ministry had "become so important that it can hinder the vitality of churches in the gospel." Conner observed that Schillebeeckx clearly pointed to a major limitation of BEM, namely that it was a "piece of academic ecumenical theology written in studies and is disconnected from those who are presently engaged in actual ministry."[24]

Conner noted Barth's assertion that all are ordained to the ministry of witness, even though all are not necessarily gifted to be servant-leaders in a congregation. As noted in Chapter 4, Barth includes vocation in his discussion of the Holy Spirit, and in the final fragment in book four of the CD on his theology of baptism. Because for Barth, baptism was a human response to Christ's redemptive work, all those who are baptized are already "consecrated, ordained, and dedicated to the ministry of the Church. They cannot be consecrated, ordained, or dedicated a second, third, or fourth time without devaluation of their baptism."[25] That the Spirit of Christ calls and equips the Church to be witness in baptism and the Spirit's ongoing ministration, Barth saw that while believers have various gifts and diverse tasks and responsibilities, there was to be a flexibility of church orders, with no "superior or inferior functions and tasks, nor can there be a rigid hierarchy."[26] Thus, for Barth, as with Schillebeeckx, what may be needed is vocational maximalism and structural minimalism; that is, a recapitulation of the

22. Grdzelidze, "Ecclesiology and Shared Identity," 289–313.

23. Conner, "The Ministry Section of BEM: A Cautious Critique," unpublished paper (Princeton, NJ: Princeton Theological Seminary, 2005). Used by permission. I am grateful to Benjamin Conner for his permission, and for Darrell Guder for directing my attention to Conner's paper.

24. Ibid., 26.

25. Barth, *CD*, vol. 4.4 Fragment, 201 quoted in Conner, *The Ministry Section*, 30.

26. Barth, *CD*, vol. 4.2, 631 cited in Conner, *The Ministry Section*, 31.

Church's primary vocation to be a missional witness in the world with a flexible ordering of ministries in service to that purpose.

The successor of the BEM is the present ecumenical document titled, *The Nature and Mission of the Church.*[27] Paragraph 77 of NMC speaks of the work of justice and liberation in the world as belonging to the Church's "baptismal vocation."[28] Similar to Torrance's discussion of the Church sharing in the royal priesthood of Christ, paragraph 84 of the NMC asserted that "Christians are constituted a royal priesthood called to offer spiritual sacrifices and indeed their very selves as a living sacrifice after the example of Jesus himself."[29] Paragraph 85 observed that "on the basis of the one baptism in Christ," the work of justice was incumbent upon every Christian.[30] Paragraph 86 emphasized the place of ordained officers in and at the service of the communities to which they belong while paragraph 87 of NMC noted that while the three-fold pattern of ministry existed as a general pattern in the early church, there are many patterns in churches today.[31] The NMC helpfully noted in paragraph 94 that the personal, collegial and communal dimensions of the Church's ecclesial life referred not only to "particular structures and processes, but also describe the informal reality of the bonds of koinonia, the mutual belonging and accountability within the ongoing common life of the Church."[32] The NMC builds upon the BEM by affirming key aspects of the received tradition while affirming the flexibility and diversity of forms and practices in the present time.

At the recent meeting of the Faith and Order Plenary Commission of the World Council of Churches at the Orthodox Academy at Kolympari, Crete in October 2009, where I had the privilege to serve as the representative of the World Alliance of Reformed Churches, Trinity scholar, Paul M. Collins of Cambridge University, presented a paper in which he sought to examine the level and degree to the which the NMC appealed to the lived experience of the Church.[33] He noted

27. *The Nature and Mission of the Church: A Stage on the Way to a Common Statement*, Faith and Order Paper No. 198 (Geneva: World Council of Churches, 2005)

28. Ibid., 45.

29. Ibid., 50.

30. Ibid., 50.

31. Ibid., 51.

32. Ibid., 54–55.

33. Collins, "Cognitive and Aesthetic Approaches to Theology and *The Nature and*

the use of "indicative" language to evoke a sense of aspiration, what he categorized as "objective" or "cognitive;" he also noted the use of "descriptive" language in the NMC to denote the experience of God by the Church in the present, what he categorized as "subjective" or "aesthetic." Collins cited Samartha, who observed that "[t]rue knowledge is the transformation of the knowing subject,"[34] and concluded that a revised NMC needs to "allow different approaches to the construction of doctrine to inform and transform one another [for it] could provide a means of beginning the reconciliation of different understandings and approaches in the different church traditions."[35] Collins went even further, and extended his exhortation to the ecumenical movement, generally: "The interpretation of 'experience' in the 'raw data' of 'revelation' and in the 'lived reality' of 'ecclesial communities' *lies at the heart of the ecumenical project*."[36]

As a participant in that Faith and Order Plenary Commission proceeding, I spoke on the plenary floor and in my small group of the need to account for actual, lived experiences in churches in order to understand whether and in what manner the wider Christian tradition was being received and interpreted by local communities. But even more importantly, the ecumenical movement must consider how local communities shape the living tradition. The conversation cannot merely be a top-down approach where local communities are invited to respond to a particular statement or document, but the conversation must be bilateral, involving local communities expressing their own ecclesiology as they see and live it within their own particular contexts.

The Faith and Order Plenary Commission urged the Standing Commission of Faith and Order to consider methodologies that would enable a multilateral conversation around ecclesiology. There was an overwhelming response among Plenary Commission members and observers that the NMC was not yet a convergence document, but that the next phase of NMC must necessarily include a mechanism whereby what Collins addressed, i.e. holding the aesthetic and cognitive

Mission of the Church" paper presented at the Faith and Order Plenary Commission of the World Council of Churches, Kolympari, Crete, October 12, 2009.

34. Samartha, "The Asian Context: Sources and Trends" in *Voices from the Margin: Interpreting the Bible in the Third World*, 48.

35. Collins, "Cognitive and Aesthetic," 6.

36. Ibid., 5. Emphasis is mine.

dimensions of doctrine in healthy tension, includes the different approaches to doctrinal construction by various ecclesial traditions. The ritual approach, coupled with liturgical theology and narrative theory, advanced by this book may be one means to assist in that endeavor.

Guder, Hunsinger and Moltmann in Conversation: Contours of a Proposal

Reformed missiologist Darrell Guder of Princeton Theological Seminary and leader in the Gospel and Culture Network has put forward a revolutionary but simple proposal: reversing the Nicene marks of the Church so that the Church is apostolic at its core and discovers its unity thereby – apostolic catholic holy one.[37] This would provide a new biblical hermeneutic that understands the biblical witness as pointing to the "sent-ness" of the Church, the "sent-ness" of the triune God in Christ, and the agenda of God to reconcile the world. To read "catholicity" through the lenses of apostolicity would emphasize the multi-dimensionality, multi-lingual, and multi-cultural diversity of the shape of the Gospel. The Gospel would not be enshrined in institutions and structures, but be grounded in that which is whole ("catholic"), the Christ-event of His life, death, and resurrection. To read "holiness" through the lenses of apostolicity is not to seek purity for purity's sake, but to see the community life and ethics as "potential demonstrations or witnesses" to God's rule in the Church. Guder summarized the implications for holiness from the vantage point of apostolicity: "Holiness has therefore to do with fitness for service, with usable-ness for God's mission."[38] To the mark of "oneness," apostolicity makes a prophetic critique at the altar of Christendom's "preoccupation with power and influence," the golden calf of the ecumenical movement that has placed greater faith in organizational unity through structures and councils rather than discovering the common unity in the Church's vocation as the "sent" witness of Christ. Rather than assuming unity, as did the Constantinian Church, from its position as the imperially-sanctioned Church, the Church in the post-Constantinian era must discover its unity through its apostolicity. Perhaps, then, the Church catholic will

37. Guder, "The Nicene Marks in a Post-Christendom Church," 28ff.

38. Ibid., 31.

discover with fresh vitality the One who was sent and who continually comes to encounter us, reconciling the world to God's self. Embedded in such a discovery and the journey towards it, may lie the pathway towards a Reformed theology of ordination that has as its driving force the very mission of Christ sent out to the world, with the Church following her Lord's lead, and, likewise sent, to bear witness in word, in deed, and in community, of the apostolic work of Jesus Christ.

Guder's proposal would provide an overarching and underlying framework for understanding ordination while providing criteria to assess the adequacy of any form of ministry. If the principle of vocational maximalism and structural minimalism being advanced by this book were retained, then regional and local judicatories would be in the best position to determine the precise structure, infrastructure, and nomenclature of patterns of ministry that are necessary for carrying out the Church's apostolic witness in a particular context. Such patterns may take the form of minister, elder, deacon; or it may take the form of teaching elder, ruling elder, or deacon; or still yet, it may take the form of bishop, presbyter, deacon, doctor. Guder's proposal takes the discussion beyond the divisive issue of what offices and what names, to the ecclesiological question, "What is the nature and mission of the Church?" To which, Guder answers, echoing Barth, the Church's nature and mission is to be sent witnesses to participate in the work of the triune God in the world.

Jürgen Moltmann made a similar case in grounding the identity and mission of the Church in the person and work of Jesus Christ. He proposed that just as the Church acquires her existence from Christ's history, the Church also acquires the characteristics of Christ too. So the third article of the Nicene formula – one holy catholic apostolic – is strictly speaking, an ascription to the character of the person and work of Jesus Christ, and of the idealistic aspiration of what the visible Church is to become.[39] These statements of faith are also "statements of action." They express who Christ is and what Christ's body (the Church) is to be and do. Christ is united in Himself – divine and human natures – as He is united to those oppressed and suffering from injustice. So, too, the Church, united with Christ is to seek unity among its broken members, while being united with those who are oppressed and suffering from

39. Moltmann, *The Church in the Power of the Spirit: A Contribution to Messianic Ecclesiology*, 338–361.

injustice. Because Christ's Lordship and love encompasses the whole world, so, too, the catholicity of the Church speaks of the wideness and broadness of the Church's unity and her apostolic mission.[40] The Church's holiness and sanctified life stems from Christ's own holiness, the One who was rich became poor, the One who came from heavenly glory became human, suffered, bled, and died. The Church is holy as it participates in "lowliness, helplessness, poverty and suffering of Christ."[41] Apostolicity speaks not only of the content of the Church's word established from the witness of the early church apostles, but speaks to the active mission endeavor of Christ, and, consequently, His body, to encounter and face "tribulation, contradiction and suffering." Moltmann summarized: "Its [the Church] apostolic succession is the succession of the passion of Christ."[42]

Reformed theologian and Barthian scholar, George Hunsinger of Princeton Theological Seminary, recently published a major work seeking convergence between Reformed churches and episcopally-ordered traditions on the issue of the Eucharist.[43] He addressed perennial issues of division such as real sacrifice, eucharistic presence, and ministry. In addressing the first two, he adeptly used the Chalcedonian pattern used by Barth and the doctrine of transelementation employed by Peter Martyr Vermigli in speaking about the unity-in-distinction of bread/cup and Christ's past/present work, namely that while each element was distinct, because of the work and action of the Holy Spirit, to speak of one necessarily included that which it referred. When extending this principle to ministry, Hunsinger proposed a close linkage of the Church's ministry to the asymmetrical relationship it had with the priesthood of Christ. What this would mean is that the Church's participation in Christ's ministry and life necessarily entailed that the "charism needed for ministry inheres principally in Christ himself. It belongs to the church, and to ordained ministers within the church, only as it is granted via *participation Christi*. Since no form of ministry is without the promise of its charism, Christ grants to those ordained the charism they need by giving it to them as a special form of

40. Ibid., 348–349.

41. Ibid., 355.

42. Ibid, 361.

43. Hunsinger, *The Eucharist and Ecumenism: Let Us Keep the Feast* (New York: Cambridge University Press, 2008)

participation in himself and his ministerial action."[44] Hunsinger went on to urge compromise on the part of the Reformed churches, Roman Catholic Church, and Eastern Orthodox Church, with the Reformed churches (and all churches, for that matter) accepting some form of episcopacy.[45] Likewise, episcopally-ordered traditions would affirm lay presbyters in decision-making, while reconfiguring the collegial structure of the episcopacy to accommodate all Christian traditions. Hunsinger urged that baptism be seen as the center of ordination "so that ordination becomes a further specification, for a particular ministry, of the charism received in baptism."[46] He believed that tethering church offices to baptism would prevent the temptation to distance the episcopacy away from the rest of the church.

While Hunsinger's proposal may not gain traction in the PC(U.S.A.)[47] as the current nFOG has no mention of episcopacy, what Hunsinger's proposal does do, as it relates to the thrust of this book, is to urge the Church ecumenical and the Reformed tradition to examine itself and to acknowledge "that none can be without non-trivial defect. . .[a]ll traditions need to subject themselves—through self-examination, dialogue, and prayer, under the sovereignty of the Word of God in the power of the Spirit—to the admonitions of others, and so ponder what they are called to learn from the Spirit's operation in traditions not their own."[48]

44. Ibid., 204.

45. Ibid., 321.

46. Ibid., 321–322.

47. A proposal to include some form of episcopacy in the PC(U.S.A.) and to align the PC(U.S.A.)'s polity with that of the Episcopal Church (U.S.A.) through ordination of Presbyterian ministers involving at least three Episcopal bishops was made in the national ecumenical organization, Churches Uniting in Christ (CUIC), the successor body to the Consultation on Church Union (COCU). The proposal stalled and has prevented mutual reconciliation of ministries, although a recent arrangement between the two denominations was approved by the 218th General Assembly of the PC(U.S.A.) and the General Convention of the Episcopal Church (U.S.A.), and ratified by judicatories, that now allows for ministerial exchange between the two communions under certain circumstances provided that authorization is granted by the regional presbyter in the case of the former, and the diocesan bishop in the case of the latter. I am grateful to PC(U.S.A.) ecumenical officer, Robina Winbush, for the documents and discussions of CUIC concerning the on-going effort of mutual recognition and mutual reconciliation of ministries between our two communions. E-mail correspondence, Feburary 7 and 14, 2008.

48. Hunsinger, *The Eucharist and Ecumenism*, 322.

When we put Guder, Moltmann and Hunsinger in conversation, what emerges is the very principle advocated by this book and what the complementary methodology proposed by this project seeks to do: vocational maximalism and structural minimalism. The various and diverse sources of presbyteral theology in the Reformed tradition—the "official" sources (conciliar statements, constitutional and liturgical documents, theologians' writings) and enacted/local sources—demonstrate that the Reformed churches have strived to understand themselves in relation to God's call, seeking to be faithful to that call within a given time and context, with outcomes that cannot be pinned down as constituting *the* Reformed theology on presbyteral ordination. Instead the multichromatic, multivalent image that we have seen emerge in our survey of the sources of theology show exactly what the Reformed tradition is: *ecclesia reformata semper reformanda secundum verbum Dei*, the church reformed and always being reformed according to the word of God; Guder, Moltmann, and Hunsinger call the Reformed tradition, and I would say, the PC(U.S.A.) to a needed self-examination as to the Church's regard of the centrality of the triune God's call to the Church to be witness, to find in the Lord Jesus Christ through the Holy Spirit the nature and mission of the Church, and in the triune God the necessary charism to carry out that call.

That the nature and purpose of the Church, as attested to by the tradition's "official' sources and the enacted/local sites, is mission through the framework of the church's worship, then the ordering of the church's ministry, while important, must be seen in light of the Church's engagement with God's overall mission, and as that mission is understood and discerned at the regional and local levels. What would the ecclesial life of the PC(U.S.A.) be like in the next decade if, instead of church judicial cases that center on the legitimacy of an ordinand's call or the credibility of the constitutional process in determining that call, that the denomination had, when confronted with a potential case for litigation, a multi-level conversation as to what the General Assembly, synod, presbytery, and session understand God's overall mission to be, and how it understands that general mission to be implemented and enacted at the local level? And what if that multi-tiered conversation occurred within the core framework of the Church's identity as Christ's worshipping community?

As with our Reformed forbears, reformation of the Church happens as mutual critique occurs between and within the so-called 'grassroots' and 'upper-tier' levels. This book demonstrates that the richness of the Reformed tradition, on the issue of church orders and presbyteral ordination, has a long story with many different voices telling the story; what is critical for the life of the tradition to flourish is to include and to appreciate the width, depth, length, height and breadth of the whole people of God, and, ultimately, the God who continues to call.

Appendix 1

Survey Questionnaire for Field Site Participants

Questions About Your Experience of Ordination

1. How many ordination services have you attended, not including this one?

- ☐ 0-2
- ☐ 3-5
- ☐ 5-7
- ☐ More than 7

2. *Prior* to attending this particular ordination service, what was your understanding of what ordination means? (Check all that apply)

- ☐ God's calling upon an individual
- ☐ Community's calling upon an individual
- ☐ Individual responding to a call
- ☐ Particular calling as extension of one's baptism
- ☐ Participation in Christ's own priestly calling to serve the Church
- ☐ Called from the baptized community to serve the baptized community
- ☐ Equipping by the Church and the Holy Spirit for a specific ministry/service
- ☐ Becoming an officer of the Presbyterian Church (U.S.A.) and the Church universal
- ☐ Ordering the Church's offices
- ☐ Other: ________________________________

3. *During/After* the particular ordination service, was your understanding of what ordination means: (Check all that apply)

- ☐ Affirmed
- ☐ Enhanced
- ☐ Challenged
- ☐ Changed

4. What aspects of this particular ordination service affirmed, enhanced, challenged, and/or changed your understanding of what ordination means? (Check all that apply)

- ☐ Written Liturgy/ Worship Order
- ☐ Prayers (specify which prayers): ______________________________
  ____
- ☐ Scripture texts (specify which Scripture texts): ______________
- ☐ Sermon
- ☐ Presentation of the Candidate for Ordination
- ☐ Liturgical Space (specify what aspects):______________________
- ☐ Hymns/Songs (specify which ones):_______________________
- ☐ ______________________________
- ☐ Other readings used in the service (specify): ________________
  ____
- ☐ Constitutional Questions
- ☐ Presentation of Gifts
- ☐ Pastoral Charge
- ☐ Blessing/Benediction
- ☐ Celebration of the Eucharist/ Communion (if celebrated)
- ☐ Laying on of Hands by Presbyters
- ☐ Invocation (invitation) of the Holy Spirit
- ☐ Offering
- ☐ Statement on Meaning of Ordination
- ☐ Procession of Participants
- ☐ Other:____

5. What word best describes the mood of the assembly during this particular ordination service?

- ☐ Somber/Serious
- ☐ Joyful
- ☐ Peaceful
- ☐ Sad
- ☐ Other:______________

6. What do you think *ought* to be the mood of the assembly during ordination services in general?

- ☐ Somber/Serious
- ☐ Joyful
- ☐ Peaceful
- ☐ Sad
- ☐ Other:___________________________________

7. What part of the ordination service was the most important for you? (Check only *one)*

- ☐ Written Liturgy/ Worship Order
- ☐ Prayers (specify which prayers): ________________ ________________________
- ☐ Scripture texts (specify which Scripture texts): __________
- ☐ Sermon
- ☐ Presentation of the Candidate for Ordination
- ☐ Liturgical Space (specify what aspects):____________
- ☐ Hymns/Songs (specify which ones):___________________
- ☐ Other readings used in the service (specify): _________ ______ ____
- ☐ Constitutional Questions
- ☐ Presentation of Gifts
- ☐ Pastoral Charge
- ☐ Blessing/Benediction
- ☐ Celebration of the Eucharist/Communion (if celebrated)
- ☐ Laying on of Hands by Presbyters
- ☐ Invocation (invitation) of the Holy Spirit
- ☐ Offering
- ☐ Statement on Meaning of Ordination

- ☐ Procession of Participants
- ☐ Oter:____

____

8. Did you feel or sense that something special was happening at the ordination service?

- ☐ Yes
- ☐ No, not really.
- ☐ If "No," please explain.
- ☐ Maybe

9. If yes to number 8, what do you think was happening at the ordination service that was making it special? (Check all that apply)

____ The minister/elder candidate was receiving an office and a big responsibility

____The Holy Spirit was empowering the minister/elder candidate and blessing him/her

____The Holy Spirit was blessing the community gathered together

____ The minister/elder candidate was joining the ministry of Jesus Christ and Christ's ministry through the Church

____The community of the gathered people were representing the universal Church in blessing the minister/elder candidate into the ministry

____Family and friends were gathering to celebrate a milestone in the service of the minister/elder candidate

____The minister/elder candidate was joining the ranks of other Church officers – with other ministers and other elders

____There was a connection with the apostolic faith and apostolic witness of the Church throughout the ages

____Other:______________________________________

10. What image and/or word best describes your experience of this particular ordination service? ____________________________________

11. Did you feel that you and the rest of the gathered assembly were full participants in this particular ordination service?

- ☐ Yes
- ☐ No
- ☐ Not sure, maybe

12. If yes to number 11, what were the top three parts in the ordination service that really made you feel like the gathered assembly was fully participating and a part of this ordination service? *(Please rank 1-3, with 1 being most fully participated)*

____ Participating in or witnessing the laying on of hands
____ Eucharist/Communion (if celebrated)
____Congregational Responses to Litanies and Readings
____ Hymns/Songs
____ Reading of Scripture
____ Prayers
____ Presentation of Gifts
____ Offering
____ Sermon
____ Merely being in attendance as an attendee and witness
____Other:____

13. What do you believe was happening during the laying on of hands upon the candidate?
(Rank 1-8, with 1 being the most important aspect)

____ Holy Spirit was empowering the minister/elder candidate at that moment
____ The hands of the officers were the hands of Christ upon the candidate
____The hands of the officers were the hands of the community
____The hands of the officers represented the universal Church in all times and in all places
____ The hands of the officers were welcoming a colleague into the ministry
____ There was a connection being made with the apostolic faith and the apostolic witness throughout the ages
____ Expression of support, blessing and love
____Other:________________________________

14. Was the connection and relation of ordination with Eucharist/communion and baptism made clear in this ordination service?

- ☐ Yes
- ☐ No, not really
- ☐ Not sure

15. If yes to number 14, in what ways did you feel or experience that the connection and relation of ordination with Eucharist/communion and baptism were made clear in this ordination service? (*Check all that apply)*

- ☐ Actual celebration of the Eucharist
- ☐ Statement about Ordination that mentioned Eucharist and Baptism
- ☐ The Baptismal Font was in full view
- ☐ A call to recall our own baptisms and our baptismal calling
- ☐ Hymns/Songs (specify which ones):________________________
- ☐ Prayers (specify which ones):____________________________
- ☐ Sermon
- ☐ Scripture texts (specify which ones):_____________________
- ☐ Litanies
- ☐ Pastoral Charge
- ☐ Blessing/Benediction
- ☐ Other:___________________________________

16. Was the connection of this particular ordination service with the universal Church, its officers and its ministries, made clear?

- ☐ Yes
- ☐ No, not really
- ☐ Not sure

17. If yes to number 16, in what ways did you feel or experience the connection of this particular ordination service with the universal Church made clear? (*Check all that apply)*

- ☐ Presence of other ministers or elders from other churches
- ☐ The laying on of hands
- ☐ Prayers
- ☐ Hymns/Songs
- ☐ Sermon
- ☐ Scripture texts (specify which ones):____________________
- ☐ Celebration of the Eucharist
- ☐ Constitutional Questions to the minister/elder candidate

- ☐ Words of greetings from guests
- ☐ Pastoral Charge
- ☐ Blessing/Benediction

18. Besides this particular ordination service, are there other occasions that you think of ordination? If so, when? ____________________

19. Are there any other comments you would like to make about your experience of or thoughts on this particular ordination service?

____

Demographic Information
(please circle below)

20. Gender:
- ☐ Male
- ☐ Female

21. Age:
- ☐ 17-25
- ☐ 26-35
- ☐ 36-45
- ☐ 46-55
- ☐ 55-65
- ☐ 66-75
- ☐ 76+

22. Attendance in this ordination service as: (Check all that apply)
- ☐ Minister
- ☐ Elder
- ☐ Deacon
- ☐ Ecumenical Guest
- ☐ Family
- ☐ Friend Observer
- ☐ Session Member
- ☐ Presbytery Ordaining Commission

- ☐ Layperson

23. Racial Ethnic Identity (Check all that apply)

- ☐ Caucasian
- ☐ Hispanic/Latin American
- ☐ East Asian
- ☐ Pacific-Islander
- ☐ African
- ☐ African American
- ☐ Native American/First Nation
- ☐ Middle Eastern
- ☐ Jewish
- ☐ Eurasian
- ☐ South Asian
- ☐ Other:__________

24. In what religious tradition were you raised? If you were raised in more than one, with which did you have the greatest identification?

- ☐ None
- ☐ Methodist
- ☐ Roman Catholic
- ☐ Anglican/Episcopalian
- ☐ Congregational
- ☐ Baptist
- ☐ Reformed/Presbyterian
- ☐ Lutheran
- ☐ Pentecostal
- ☐ Evangelical
- ☐ Non-Denominational
- ☐ Jewish
- ☐ Islam
- ☐ Buddhist
- ☐ Other:____________________________

25. Are you familiar with any of the following writings/books and theologians? (*Check all that apply)*

- ☐ *Book of Confessions of the Presbyterian Church (U.S.A.)*
- ☐ *Book of Order of the Presbyterian Church (U.S.A.)*
- ☐ *Book of Common Worship*
- ☐ *Book of Occasional Services*
- ☐ John Calvin
- ☐ Thomas F. Torrance
- ☐ Martin Bucer
- ☐ Karl Barth
- ☐ Jürgen Moltmann
- ☐ Friedrich Schleiermacher
- ☐ *The Church Dogmatics*
- ☐ *Baptism, Eucharist, and Ministry*
- ☐ *Institutes of the Christian Religion*
- ☐ *Report of the Theological Task Force on Peace, Unity and Purity (PUP Report)*
- ☐ *General Assembly paper, "A Proposal for Considering the Theology and Practice of Ordination in the Presbyterian Church (U.S.A.), 1992"*

26. What do you consider your theological/biblical positions and views to be?:

- ☐ Liberal
- ☐ Moderate
- ☐ Conservative

Thank you for your participation and valuable input.
You may submit this completed form to the principal investigator, Rev. Neal D. Presa, or send it to him by fax, or regular mail to:

27 Princeton Drive
Middlesex, NJ 08846
Fax: (732) 469-6293

If you prefer an electronic version of this questionnaire or if you would like to return your responses by email, you may do so through: ndpresa@yahoo.com

Appendix 2

Results of Survey Questionnaire

Elder Ordination, New Jersey (EC)

Notes About Analysis:
Some questions offered respondents the choice to select more than one choice. Therefore, the results of some questions will show an aggregate total greater than the actual number of survey questionnaires returned, and a percentage higher than 100.

Written responses in blank spaces (such as names of Hymns/Songs) or specific comments (such as in Q10, 18, 19) are not included in the quantitative analyses found in Appendices 2-5; those written responses will be discussed within the narrative sections of Chapter 6 under each corresponding ordination site.

N designates the number of respondents eligible to answer the question, or in some cases the cumulative number of ranked points.

Number of Survey Questionnaires Distributed: 121
Number of Survey Questionnaires Returned & Usable: 45
Return Rate: 37%

	How many ordination services have you attended, not including this one?		
1a	0-2	11	24.44%
1b	3-5	6	13.33%
1c	5-7	3	6.67%
1d	More than 7	25	55.56%
		N=45	100.00%

	Prior to attending this particular ordination service, what was your understanding of what ordination means?		
2a	God's calling upon an individual	37	21.26%
2b	Community's calling upon an individual	20	11.49%
2c	Individual responding to a call	36	20.69%
2d	Particular calling as extension of one's baptism	6	3.45%
2e	Participation in Christ's own priestly calling to serve the Church	21	12.07%
2f	Called from the baptized community to serve the baptized community	7	4.02%
2g	Equipping by the Church and the Holy Spirit for a specific ministry/service	17	9.77%
2h	Becoming an officer of the Presbyterian Church (U.S.A.) and the Church universal	25	14.37%
2i	Ordering the Church's offices	3	1.72%
2j	Other:	2	1.15%
2k	No response	0	0.00%
		N=174	100.00%
	During/After the particular ordination service, was your understanding of what ordination means:		
3a	Affirmed	42	65.63%
3b	Enhanced	13	20.31%
3c	Challenged	6	9.38%
3d	Changed	3	4.69%
3e	No response	0	0.00%
		N=64	100.00%
	What aspects of this particular ordination service affirmed, enhanced, challenged, and/or changed your understanding of what ordination means?		
4a	Written Liturgy/ Worship Order	13	8.61%
4b	Prayers (specify which prayers):	8	5.30%

4c	Scripture texts (specify which Scripture texts):	3	1.99%
4d	Sermon	7	4.64%
4e	Presentation of the Candidate for Ordination	21	13.91%
4f	Liturgical Space (specify what aspects):	1	0.66%
4g	Hymns/Songs (specify which ones):	10	6.62%
4h	Other readings used in the service (specify):	1	0.66%
4i	Constitutional Questions	16	10.60%
4j	Presentation of Gifts	0	0.00%
4k	Pastoral Charge	11	7.28%
4l	Blessing/Benediction	8	5.30%
4m	Celebration of the Eucharist/Communion (if celebrated)	0	0.00%
4n	Laying on of Hands by Presbyters	25	16.56%
4o	Invocation (invitation) of the Holy Spirit	7	4.64%
4p	Offering	2	1.32%
4q	Statement on Meaning of Ordination	7	4.64%
4r	Procession of Participants	3	1.99%
4s	Other:	3	1.99%
4t	No response	5	3.31%
		N=151	100.00%
	What word best describes the mood of the assembly during this particular ordination service? (some chose more than one)		
5a	Somber/Serious	13	24.53%
5b	Joyful	13	24.53%
5c	Peaceful	25	47.17%
5d	Sad	0	0.00%
5e	Other:	1	1.89%
5f	No response	1	1.89%
		N=53	100.00%
	What word best describes the mood of the assembly during this particular ordination service?		

5a	Somber/Serious	9	24.32%
5b	Joyful	8	21.62%
5c	Peaceful	18	48.65%
5d	Sad	0	0.00%
5e	Other:	1	2.70%
5f	No response	1	2.70%
		N=37	100.00%
	What do you think *ought* to be the mood of the assembly during ordination services in general? (some chose more than one)		
6a	Somber/Serious	7	12.50%
6b	Joyful	28	50.00%
6c	Peaceful	19	33.93%
6d	Sad	0	0.00%
6e	Other:	1	1.79%
6f	No response	1	1.79%
		N=56	100.00%
	What do you think *ought* to be the mood of the assembly during ordination services in general?		
6a	Somber/Serious	4	11.76%
6b	Joyful	19	55.88%
6c	Peaceful	9	26.47%
6d	Sad	0	0.00%
6e	Other:	1	2.94%
6f	No response	1	2.94%
		N=34	100.00%
	What part of the ordination service was the most important for you?		
7a	Written Liturgy/ Worship Order	2	2.94%
7b	Prayers (specify which prayers):	2	2.94%
7c	Scripture texts (specify which Scripture texts)	2	2.94%

7d	Sermon	6	8.82%
7e	Presentation of the Candidate for Ordination	9	13.24%
7f	Liturgical Space (specify what aspects):	0	0.00%
7g	Hymns/Songs (specify which ones):	2	2.94%
7h	Other readings used in the service	0	0.00%
7i	Constitutional Questions	7	10.29%
7j	Presentation of Gifts	0	0.00%
7k	Pastoral Charge	6	8.82%
7l	Blessing/Benediction	2	2.94%
7m	Celebration of the Eucharist/Communion (if celebrated)	1	1.47%
7n	Laying on of Hands by Presbyters	21	30.88%
7o	Invocation (invitation) of the Holy Spirit	4	5.88%
7p	Offering	0	0.00%
7q	Statement on Meaning of Ordination	4	5.88%
7r	Procession of Participants	0	0.00%
7s	Other:	0	0.00%
7t	No response	0	0.00%
7u	Multiple answers		
		N=68	100.00%
	Did you feel or sense that something special was happening at the ordination service?		
8a	Yes	30	66.67%
8b	No, not really.	3	6.67%
8c	-If "No," please explain.	2	4.44%
8d	Maybe	9	20.00%
8e	No response	1	2.22%
		N=45	100.00%
	If yes to number 8, what do you think was happening at the ordination service that was making it special?		
9a	The minister/elder candidate was receiving an office and a big responsibility	13	11.11%

9b	The Holy Spirit was empowering the minister/elder candidate and blessing him/her	18	15.38%
9c	The Holy Spirit was blessing the community gathered together	14	11.97%
9d	The minister/elder candidate was joining the ministry of Jesus Christ and Christ's ministry through the Church	12	10.26%
9e	The community of the gathered people were representing the universal Church in blessing the minister/elder candidate into the ministry	12	10.26%
9f	Family and friends were gathering to celebrate a milestone in the service of the minister/elder candidate	11	9.40%
9g	The minister/elder candidate was joining the ranks of other Church officers – with other ministers and other elders	14	11.97%
9h	There was a connection with the apostolic faith and apostolic witness of the Church throughout the ages	8	6.84%
9i	Other:	1	0.85%
9j	No response	14	11.97%
		N=117	100.00%
	Did you feel that you and the rest of the gathered assembly were full participants in this particular ordination service?		
11a	Yes	31	68.89%
11b	No	2	4.44%
11c	Not sure, maybe	11	24.44%
11d	No response	1	2.22%
		N=45	100.00%
	If yes to number 11, what were the top three parts in the ordination service that really made you feel like the gathered assembly was fully participating and a part of this ordination service?		
12a	Participating in or witnessing the laying on of hands	8	80.00%
12b	Eucharist/Communion (if celebrated)	0	0.00%

12c	Congregational Responses to Litanies and Readings	6	60.00%
12d	Hymns/Songs	5	50.00%
12e	Reading of Scripture	1	10.00%
12f	Prayers	4	40.00%
12g	Presentation of Gifts	0	0.00%
12h	Offering	0	0.00%
12i	Sermon	1	10.00%
12j	Merely being in attendance as an attendee and witness	5	50.00%
12k	Other:	0	0.00%
12l	No response	0	0.00%
	*This number designates that 10 people answered "Yes" to Q11 AND correctly ranked Q12 with a 1-2-3 ranking order as requested in the question.	N=10	
	What do you believe was happening during the laying on of hands upon the candidate?		
13a	Holy Spirit was empowering the minister/elder candidate at that moment	18	40.00%
13b	The hands of the officers were the hands of Christ upon the candidate	12	26.67%
13c	The hands of the officers were the hands of the community	7	15.56%
13d	The hands of the officers represented the universal Church in all times and in all places	4	8.89%
13e	The hands of the officers were welcoming a colleague into the ministry	10	22.22%
13f	There was a connection being made with the apostolic faith and the apostolic witness throughout the ages	3	6.67%
13g	Expression of support, blessing and love	6	13.33%
13h	Other:	1	2.22%
13i	No response	3	6.67%
		N=45	

	Was the connection and relation of ordination with Eucharist/communion and baptism made clear in this ordination service?		
14a	Yes	19	42.22%
14b	No, not really	14	31.11%
14c	Not sure	8	17.78%
14d	No response	4	8.89%
		N=45	100.00%
	IF YES to Q14, in what ways did you feel or experience that the connection and relation of ordination with Eucharist/communion and baptism were made clear in this ordination service?		
15a	Actual celebration of the Eucharist	3	4.76%
15b	Statement about Ordination that mentioned Eucharist and Baptism	8	12.7%
15c	The Baptismal Font was in full view	6	9.52%
15d	A call to recall our own baptisms and our baptismal calling	11	17.46%
15e	Hymns/Songs (specify which ones):	3	4.76%
15f	Prayers (specify which ones):	3	4.76%
15g	Sermon	4	6.35%
15h	Scripture texts (specify which ones):	2	3.17%
15i	Litanies	4	6.35%
15j	Pastoral Charge	9	14.29%
15k	Blessing/Benediction	5	7.94%
15l	Other:	2	3.17%
15m	No response	3	4.76%
		N=63	100.00%
	Was the connection of this particular ordination service with the universal Church, its officers and its ministries, made clear?		
16a	Yes	36	80.00%
16b	No, not really	1	2.22%
16c	Not sure	5	11.11%

16d	No response	3	6.67%
		N=45	100.00%
	If yes to number 16, in what ways did you feel or experience the connection of this particular ordination service with the universal Church made clear?		
17a	Presence of other ministers or elders from other churches	16	13.68%
17b	The laying on of hands	30	25.64%
17c	Prayers	12	10.26%
17d	Hymns/Songs	11	9.40%
17e	Sermon	5	4.27%
17f	Scripture texts (specify which ones):	1	0.85%
17g	Celebration of the Eucharist	1	0.85%
17h	Constitutional Questions to the minister/elder candidate	14	11.97%
17i	Words of greetings from guests	4	3.42%
17j	Pastoral Charge	11	9.40%
17k	Blessing/Benediction	9	7.69%
17l	No response	3	2.56%
17m	Other	0	0.00%
		N=117	100.00%
	Gender		
20a	Male	16	35.56%
20b	Female	27	60.00%
20c	Unspecified	2	4.44%
		N=45	100.00%
	Age		
21a	17-25	3	6.67%
21b	26-35	3	6.67%
21c	36-45	10	22.22%
21d	46-55	11	24.44%
21e	55-56	12	26.67%

21f	66-75	4	8.89%
21g	76+	2	4.44%
		N=45	100.00%
	Attendance Role in Ordination		
22a	Minister	0	0.00%
22b	Elder	16	21.33%
22c	Deacon	11	14.67%
22d	Ecumenical Guest	0	0.00%
22e	Family	4	5.33%
22f	Friend	6	8.00%
22g	Observer	10	13.33%
22h	Session Member	11	14.67%
22i	Presbytery Ordaining Commission	0	0.00%
22j	Layperson	13	17.33%
22k	No response	4	5.33%
	*some chose multiple roles	N=75	100.00%
	Race		
23a	Caucasian	37	82.22%
23b	Hispanic/Latin American	1	2.22%
23c	East Asian	2	4.44%
23d	Pacific-Islander	1	2.22%
23e	African	0	0.00%
23f	African American	1	2.22%
23g	Native American/First Nation	0	0.00%
23h	Middle Eastern	0	0.00%
23i	Jewish	0	0.00%
23j	Eurasian	0	0.00%
23k	South Asian	0	0.00%
23l	Other:	0	0.00%
23m	No response	3	6.67%
		N=45	100.00%

	Religious Tradition (* when more than one was chosen or when a tradition that is not listed was written in the blank space, it was counted as "Other")		
24a	None	1	2.22%
24b	Roman Catholic	7	15.56%
24c	Anglican/Episcopalian	1	2.22%
24d	Methodist	2	4.44%
24e	Congregational	0	0.00%
24f	Baptist	2	4.44%
24g	Reformed/Presbyterian	27	60.00%
24h	Lutheran	1	2.22%
24i	Pentecostal	0	0.00%
24j	Evangelical	0	0.00%
24k	Non-Denominational	0	0.00%
24l	Jewish	0	0.00%
24m	Islam	0	0.00%
24n	Buddhist	0	0.00%
24o	Other:	2	4.44%
24p	No response	2	4.44%
		N=45	100.00%
	Familiar with Writings/Books		
25a	*Book of Confessions of the Presbyterian Church (U.S.A.)*	14	15.22%
25b	*Book of Order of the Presbyterian Church (U.S.A.)*	21	22.83%
25c	*Book of Common Worship*	15	16.30%
25d	*Book of Occasional Services*	0	0.00%
25e	John Calvin	16	17.39%
25f	Thomas F. Torrance	0	0.00%
25g	Martin Bucer	3	3.26%
25h	Karl Barth	5	5.43%
25i	Jürgen Moltmann	0	0.00%
25j	Friedrich Schleiermacher	1	1.09%

25k	*The Church Dogmatics*	0	0.00%
25l	*Baptism, Eucharist, and Ministry*	0	0.00%
25m	*Institutes of the Christian Religion*	0	0.00%
25n	*Report of the Theological Task Force on Peace, Unity and Purity (PUP Report)*	2	2.17%
25o	*General Assembly paper, "A Proposal for Considering the Theology and Practice of Ordination in the Presbyterian Church (U.S.A.), 1992"*	0	0.00%
25p	No response	15	16.30%
	(*No response means None or no answer)	N=92	100.00%
	Theological Position		
26a	Liberal	14	31.11%
26b	Moderate	21	46.67%
26c	Conservative	6	13.33%
26d	No response	3	6.67%
26e	None of the above	0	0.00%
26f	Other: (multiple)	1	2.22%
		N=45	100.00%

Appendix 3

Results of Survey Questionnaire

Elder Ordination, upstate New York (EN)

Notes About Analysis:
Some questions offered respondents the choice to select more than one choice. Therefore, the results of some questions will show an aggregate total greater than the actual number of survey questionnaires returned, and a percentage greater than 100.

Written responses in blank spaces (such as names of Hymns/ Songs) or specific comments (such as in Q10, 18, 19) are not included in the quantitative analyses found in Appendices 2-5; those written responses will be discussed within the narrative sections of Chapter 6 under each corresponding ordination site.

N designates the number of respondents eligible to answer the question, or in some cases the cumulative number of ranked points.

Number of Survey Questionnaires Distributed: 138
Number of Survey Questionnaires Returned & Usable: 83
Return Rate: 60.1%

	How many ordination services have you attended, not including this one?		
1a	0-2	15	18.07%
1b	3-5	12	14.46%
1c	5-7	5	6.02%
1d	More than 7	51	61.45%
		N=83	100%

	***Prior* to attending this particular ordination service, what was your understanding of what ordination means?**		
2a	God's calling upon an individual	62	19.68%
2b	Community's calling upon an individual	37	11.75%
2c	Individual responding to a call	65	20.63%
2d	Particular calling as extension of one's baptism	18	5.71%
2e	Participation in Christ's own priestly calling to serve the Church	39	12.38%
2f	Called from the baptized community to serve the baptized community	17	5.40%
2g	Equipping by the Church and the Holy Spirit for a specific ministry/service	24	7.62%
2h	Becoming an officer of the Presbyterian Church (U.S.A.) and the Church universal	42	13.33%
2i	Ordering the Church's offices	7	2.22%
2j	Other:	4	1.27%
2k	No response	0	0.00%
		N=315	100%
	During/After the particular ordination service, was your understanding of what ordination means:		
3a	Affirmed	61	50.00%
3b	Enhanced	37	30.33%
3c	Challenged	15	12.30%
3d	Changed	8	6.56%
3e	No response	1	0.82%
		N=122	100%
	What aspects of this particular ordination service affirmed, enhanced, challenged, and/or changed your understanding of what ordination means?		

4a	Written Liturgy/ Worship Order	24	6.38%
4b	Prayers (specify which prayers):	9	2.39%
4c	Scripture texts (specify which Scripture texts):	18	4.79%
4d	Sermon	56	14.89%
4e	Presentation of the Candidate for Ordination	25	6.65%
4f	Liturgical Space (specify what aspects):	4	1.06%
4g	Hymns/Songs (specify which ones):	46	12.23%
4h	Other readings used in the service (specify):	1	0.27%
4i	Constitutional Questions	25	6.65%
4j	Presentation of Gifts	4	1.06%
4k	Pastoral Charge	23	6.12%
4l	Blessing/Benediction	23	6.12%
4m	Celebration of the Eucharist/Communion (if celebrated)	1	0.27%
4n	Laying on of Hands by Presbyters	56	14.89%
4o	Invocation (invitation) of the Holy Spirit	13	3.46%
4p	Offering	6	1.60%
4q	Statement on Meaning of Ordination	25	6.65%
4r	Procession of Participants	13	3.46%
4s	Other:	0	0.00%
4t	No response	4	1.06%
		N=376	100%
	What word best describes the mood of the assembly during this particular ordination service? (some chose more than one)		
5a	Somber/Serious	26	23.42%
5b	Joyful	43	38.74%
5c	Peaceful	35	31.53%
5d	Sad	0	0.00%
5e	Other:	5	4.50%
5f	No response	2	1.80%
		N=111	100%

	What word best describes the mood of the assembly during this particular ordination service?		
5a	Somber/Serious	16	26.67%
5b	Joyful	24	40.00%
5c	Peaceful	16	26.67%
5d	Sad	0	0.00%
5e	Other:	2	3.33%
5f	No response	2	3.33%
		N=60	100%
	What do you think *ought* to be the mood of the assembly during ordination services in general? (some chose more than one)		
6a	Somber/Serious	18	14.63%
6b	Joyful	64	52.03%
6c	Peaceful	31	25.20%
6d	Sad	1	0.81%
6e	Other:	7	5.69%
6f	No response	2	1.63%
		N=123	100%
	What do you think *ought* to be the mood of the assembly during ordination services in general?		
6a	Somber/Serious	6	11.32%
6b	Joyful	35	66.04%
6c	Peaceful	7	13.21%
6d	Sad	0	0.00%
6e	Other:	3	5.66%
6f	No response	2	3.77%
		N=53	100%
	What part of the ordination service was the most important for you?		

7a	Written Liturgy/ Worship Order	5	3.88%
7b	Prayers (specify which prayers):	3	2.33%
7c	Scripture texts (specify which Scripture texts)	0	0.00%
7d	Sermon	22	17.05%
7e	Presentation of the Candidate for Ordination	10	7.75%
7f	Liturgical Space (specify what aspects):	0	0.00%
7g	Hymns/Songs (specify which ones):	11	8.53%
7h	Other readings used in the service	2	1.55%
7i	Constitutional Questions	7	5.43%
7j	Presentation of Gifts	0	0.00%
7k	Pastoral Charge	11	8.53%
7l	Blessing/Benediction	5	3.88%
7m	Celebration of the Eucharist/Communion (if celebrated)	0	0.00%
7n	Laying on of Hands by Presbyters	38	29.46%
7o	Invocation (invitation) of the Holy Spirit	3	2.33%
7p	Offering	0	0.00%
7q	Statement on Meaning of Ordination	11	8.53%
7r	Procession of Participants	0	0.00%
7s	Other:	1	0.78%
7t	No response	0	0.00%
7u	Multiple answers		
		N=129	100%
	Did you feel or sense that something special was happening at the ordination service?		
8a	Yes	68	81.93%
8b	No, not really.	0	0.00%
8c	If "No," please explain.	2	2.41%
8d	Maybe	13	15.66%
8e	No response	0	0.00%
		N=83	

	If yes to number 8, what do you think was happening at the ordination service that was making it special?		
9a	The minister/elder candidate was receiving an office and a big responsibility	34	12.36%
9b	The Holy Spirit was empowering the minister/elder candidate and blessing him/her	40	14.55%
9c	The Holy Spirit was blessing the community gathered together	44	16.00%
9d	The minister/elder candidate was joining the ministry of Jesus Christ and Christ's ministry through the Church	31	11.27%
9e	The community of the gathered people were representing the universal Church in blessing the minister/elder candidate into the ministry	31	11.27%
9f	Family and friends were gathering to celebrate a milestone in the service of the minister/elder candidate	21	7.64%
9g	The minister/elder candidate was joining the ranks of other Church officers – with other ministers and other elders	34	12.36%
9h	There was a connection with the apostolic faith and apostolic witness of the Church throughout the ages	27	9.82%
9i	Other:	2	0.73%
9j	No response	11	12.36%
		N=275	100%
	Did you feel that you and the rest of the gathered assembly were full participants in this particular ordination service?		
11a	Yes	73	87.95%
11b	No	1	1.20%
11c	Not sure, maybe	7	8.43%
11d	No response	2	2.41%
		N=83	100%

	If yes to number 11, what were the top three parts in the ordination service that really made you feel like the gathered assembly was fully participating and a part of this ordination service?		
12a	Participating in or witnessing the laying on of hands	41	91.11%
12b	Eucharist/Communion (if celebrated)	1	2.22%
12c	Congregational Responses to Litanies and Readings	16	35.56%
12d	Hymns/Songs	24	53.33%
12e	Reading of Scripture	1	2.22%
12f	Prayers	14	31.11%
12g	Presentation of Gifts	0	0.00%
12h	Offering	1	2.22%
12i	Sermon	21	46.67%
12j	Merely being in attendance as an attendee and witness	16	35.56%
12k	Other:	0	0.00%
12l	No response	0	0.00%
	*This number designates that 45 people answered "Yes" to Q11 AND correctly ranked Q12 with a 1-2-3 ranking order as requested in the question.	N=45	
	What do you believe was happening during the laying on of hands upon the candidate?		
13a	Holy Spirit was empowering the minister/elder candidate at that moment	26	31.39%
13b	The hands of the officers were the hands of Christ upon the candidate	14	16.86%
13c	The hands of the officers were the hands of the community	11	13.25%
13d	The hands of the officers represented the universal Church in all times and in all places	10	12.04%
13e	The hands of the officers were welcoming a colleague into the ministry	13	15.66%

13f	There was a connection being made with the apostolic faith and the apostolic witness throughout the ages	20	24.09%
13g	Expression of support, blessing and love	17	20.48%
13h	Other:	1	1.20%
13i	No response	5	6.02%
		N=83	
	Was the connection and relation of ordination with Eucharist/communion and baptism made clear in this ordination service?		
14a	Yes	36	43.37%
14b	No, not really	21	25.30%
14c	Not sure	22	26.51%
14d	No response	4	4.82%
		N=83	100%
	IF YES to Q14, in what ways did you feel or experience that the connection and relation of ordination with Eucharist/communion and baptism were made clear in this ordination service?		
15a	Actual celebration of the Eucharist	0	0.00%
15b	Statement about Ordination that mentioned Eucharist and Baptism	10	9.09%
15c	The Baptismal Font was in full view	7	6.36%
15d	A call to recall our own baptisms and our baptismal calling	14	12.73%
15e	Hymns/Songs (specify which ones):	17	15.45%
15f	Prayers (specify which ones):	7	6.36%
15g	Sermon	15	13.64%
15h	Scripture texts (specify which ones):	6	5.45%
15i	Litanies	4	3.64%
15j	Pastoral Charge	14	12.73%
15k	Blessing/Benediction	12	10.91%

15l	Other:	0	0.00%
15m	No response	4	3.64%
		N=110	100%
	Was the connection of this particular ordination service with the universal Church, its officers and its ministries, made clear?		
16a	Yes	64	77.11%
16b	No, not really	6	7.23%
16c	Not sure	10	12.05%
16d	No response	3	3.61%
		N=83	100%
	If yes to number 16, in what ways did you feel or experience the connection of this particular ordination service with the universal Church made clear?		
17a	Presence of other ministers or elders from other churches	18	6.21%
17b	The laying on of hands	56	19.31%
17c	Prayers	29	10.00%
17d	Hymns/Songs	37	12.76%
17e	Sermon	41	14.14%
17f	Scripture texts (specify which ones):	13	4.48%
17g	Celebration of the Eucharist	4	1.38%
17h	Constitutional Questions to the minister/elder candidate	30	10.34%
17i	Words of greetings from guests	12	4.14%
17j	Pastoral Charge	27	9.31%
17k	Blessing/Benediction	21	7.24%
17l	No response	2	0.69%
17m	Other	0	0.00%
		N=290	100%
	Gender		
20a	Male	33	39.76%

20b	Female	49	59.04%
20c	Unspecified	1	1.20%
		N=83	100%
	Age		
21a	17-25	0	0.00%
21b	26-35	4	4.82%
21c	36-45	8	9.64%
21d	46-55	14	16.87%
21e	55-56	27	32.53%
21f	66-75	22	26.51%
21g	76+	8	9.64%
		N=83	
	Attendance Role in Ordination		
22a	Minister	1	0.82%
22b	Elder	31	25.41%
22c	Deacon	19	15.57%
22d	Ecumenical Guest	0	0.00%
22e	Family	13	10.66%
22f	Friend	8	6.56%
22g	Observer	13	10.66%
22h	Session Member	10	8.20%
22i	Presbytery Ordaining Commission	0	0.00%
22j	Layperson	25	20.49%
22k	No response	2	1.64%
	*some chose multiple roles	N=122	100%
	Race		
23a	Caucasian	81	97.59%
23b	Hispanic/Latin American	0	0.00%
23c	East Asian	0	0.00%
23d	Pacific-Islander	0	0.00%

23e	African	0	0.00%
23f	African American	0	0.00%
23g	Native American/First Nation	0	0.00%
23h	Middle Eastern	0	0.00%
23i	Jewish	0	0.00%
23j	Eurasian	0	0.00%
23k	South Asian	0	0.00%
23l	Other:	1	1.20%
23m	No response	1	1.20%
		N=83	100%
	Religious Tradition (* when more than one was chosen or when a tradition that is not listed was written in the blank space, it was counted as "Other")		
24a	None	1	1.20%
24b	Roman Catholic	9	10.84%
24c	Anglican/Episcopalian	8	9.64%
24d	Methodist	6	7.23%
24e	Congregational	1	1.20%
24f	Baptist	9	10.84%
24g	Reformed/Presbyterian	37	44.58%
24h	Lutheran	3	3.61%
24i	Pentecostal	0	0.00%
24j	Evangelical	0	0.00%
24k	Non-Denominational	1	1.20%
24l	Jewish	0	0.00%
24m	Islam	0	0.00%
24n	Buddhist	0	0.00%
24o	Other:	8	9.64%
24p	No response	0	0.00%
		N=83	100%
	Familiar with Writings/Books		
25a	*Book of Confessions of the Presbyterian Church (U.S.A.)*	35	16.28%

25b	*Book of Order of the Presbyterian Church (U.S.A.)*	45	20.93%
25c	*Book of Common Worship*	26	12.09%
25d	*Book of Occasional Services*	2	0.93%
25e	John Calvin	34	15.81%
25f	Thomas F. Torrance	2	0.93%
25g	Martin Bucer	1	0.47%
25h	Karl Barth	15	6.98%
25i	Jürgen Moltmann	2	0.93%
25j	Friedrich Schleiermacher	0	0.00%
25k	*The Church Dogmatics*	1	0.47%
25l	*Baptism, Eucharist, and Ministry*	4	1.86%
25m	*Institutes of the Christian Religion*	4	1.86%
25n	*Report of the Theological Task Force on Peace, Unity and Purity (PUP Report)*	13	6.05%
25o	*General Assembly paper, "A Proposal for Considering the Theology and Practice of Ordination in the Presbyterian Church (U.S.A.), 1992"*	6	2.79%
25p	No response	25	11.63%
	(*No response means None or no answer)	N=215	100%
	Theological Position		
26a	Liberal	24	28.92%
26b	Moderate	33	39.76%
26c	Conservative	19	22.89%
26d	No response	3	3.61%
26e	None of the above	0	0.00%
26f	Other: (multiple)	4	4.82%
		N=83	100%

Appendix 4

Results of Survey Questionnaire

Minister Ordination, Eastern Pennsylvania (MP)

Notes About Analysis:
Some questions offered respondents the choice to select more than one choice. Therefore, the results of some questions will show an aggregate total greater than the actual number of survey questionnaires returned, and a percentage greater than 100.

Written responses in blank spaces (such as names of Hymns/Songs) or specific comments (such as in Q10, 18, 19) are not included in the quantitative analyses found in Appendices 2-5; those written responses will be discussed within the narrative sections of Chapter 6 under each corresponding ordination site.

N designates the number of respondents eligible to answer the question, or in some cases the cumulative number of ranked points.

Number of Survey Questionnaires Distributed: 63
Number of Survey Questionnaires Returned & Usable: 34
Return Rate: 54%

	How many ordination services have you attended, not including this one?		
1a	0-2	26	76.47%
1b	3-5	4	11.76%
1c	5-7	0	0.00%
1d	More than 7	4	11.76%
		N=34	100%

	***Prior* to attending this particular ordination service, what was your understanding of what ordination means?**		
2a	God's calling upon an individual	17	16.35%
2b	Community's calling upon an individual	12	11.54%
2c	Individual responding to a call	19	18.27%
2d	Particular calling as extension of one's baptism	5	4.81%
2e	Participation in Christ's own priestly calling to serve the Church	12	11.54%
2f	Called from the baptized community to serve the baptized community	7	6.73%
2g	Equipping by the Church and the Holy Spirit for a specific ministry/service	9	8.65%
2h	Becoming an officer of the Presbyterian Church (U.S.A.) and the Church universal	16	15.38%
2i	Ordering the Church's offices	2	1.92%
2j	Other:	4	3.85%
2k	No response	1	0.96%
		N=104	100%
	During/After the particular ordination service, was your understanding of what ordination means:		
3a	Affirmed	18	36.00%
3b	Enhanced	19	38.00%
3c	Challenged	5	10.00%
3d	Changed	8	16.00%
3e	No response	0	0.00%
		N=50	100%
	What aspects of this particular ordination service affirmed, enhanced, challenged, and/or changed your understanding of what ordination means?		
4a	Written Liturgy/ Worship Order	7	5.15%

4b	Prayers (specify which prayers):	4	2.94%
4c	Scripture texts (specify which Scripture texts):	3	2.21%
4d	Sermon	23	16.91%
4e	Presentation of the Candidate for Ordination	9	6.62%
4f	Liturgical Space (specify what aspects):	3	2.21%
4g	Hymns/Songs (specify which ones):	4	2.94%
4h	Other readings used in the service (specify):	2	1.47%
4i	Constitutional Questions	9	6.62%
4j	Presentation of Gifts	11	8.09%
4k	Pastoral Charge	14	10.29%
4l	Blessing/Benediction	6	4.41%
4m	Celebration of the Eucharist/Communion (if celebrated)	1	0.74%
4n	Laying on of Hands by Presbyters	14	10.29%
4o	Invocation (invitation) of the Holy Spirit	1	0.74%
4p	Offering	11	8.09%
4q	Statement on Meaning of Ordination	6	4.41%
4r	Procession of Participants	3	2.21%
4s	Other:	0	0.00%
4t	No response	5	3.68%
		N=136	100%
	What word best describes the mood of the assembly during this particular ordination service? (some chose more than one)		
5a	Somber/Serious	2	4.65%
5b	Joyful	26	60.47%
5c	Peaceful	13	30.23%
5d	Sad	0	0.00%
5e	Other:	2	4.65%
5f	No response	0	0.00%
		N=43	100%

	What word best describes the mood of the assembly during this particular ordination service?		
5a	Somber/Serious	0	0.00%
5b	Joyful	19	70.37%
5c	Peaceful	7	25.93%
5d	Sad	0	0.00%
5e	Other:	1	3.70%
5f	No response	0	0.00%
		N=27	100%
	What do you think *ought* to be the mood of the assembly during ordination services in general? (some chose more than one)		
6a	Somber/Serious	1	2.38%
6b	Joyful	29	69.05%
6c	Peaceful	12	28.57%
6d	Sad	0	0.00%
6e	Other:	0	0.00%
6f	No response	0	0.00%
		N=42	100%
	What do you think *ought* to be the mood of the assembly during ordination services in general?		
6a	Somber/Serious	0	0.00%
6b	Joyful	22	81.48%
6c	Peaceful	5	18.52%
6d	Sad	0	0.00%
6e	Other:	0	0.00%
6f	No response	0	0.00%
		N=27	100%
	What part of the ordination service was the most important for you?		
7a	Written Liturgy/ Worship Order	0	0.00%

7b	Prayers (specify which prayers):	3	4.92%
7c	Scripture texts (specify which Scripture texts)	2	3.28%
7d	Sermon	16	26.23%
7e	Presentation of the Candidate for Ordination	5	8.20%
7f	Liturgical Space (specify what aspects):	0	0.00%
7g	Hymns/Songs (specify which ones):	4	6.56%
7h	Other readings used in the service	0	0.00%
7i	Constitutional Questions	1	1.64%
7j	Presentation of Gifts	2	3.28%
7k	Pastoral Charge	7	11.48%
7l	Blessing/Benediction	4	6.56%
7m	Celebration of the Eucharist/Communion (if celebrated)	1	1.64%
7n	Laying on of Hands by Presbyters	6	9.84%
7o	Invocation (invitation) of the Holy Spirit	2	3.28%
7p	Offering	4	6.56%
7q	Statement on Meaning of Ordination	2	3.28%
7r	Procession of Participants	0	0.00%
7s	Other:	2	3.28%
7t	No response	0	0.00%
7u	Multiple answers		
		N=61	100%
	Did you feel or sense that something special was happening at the ordination service?		
8a	Yes	32	94.12%
8b	No, not really.	0	0.00%
8c	If "No," please explain.	0	0.00%
8d	Maybe	1	2.94%
8e	No response	1	2.94%
		N=34	100%
	If yes to number 8, what do you think was happening at the ordination service that was making it special?		

9a	The minister/elder candidate was receiving an office and a big responsibility	10	9.71%
9b	The Holy Spirit was empowering the minister/elder candidate and blessing him/her	15	14.56%
9c	The Holy Spirit was blessing the community gathered together	11	10.68%
9d	The minister/elder candidate was joining the ministry of Jesus Christ and Christ's ministry through the Church	11	10.68%
9e	The community of the gathered people were representing the universal Church in blessing the minister/elder candidate into the ministry	18	17.48%
9f	Family and friends were gathering to celebrate a milestone in the service of the minister/elder candidate	22	21.36%
9g	The minister/elder candidate was joining the ranks of other Church officers – with other ministers and other elders	8	7.77%
9h	There was a connection with the apostolic faith and apostolic witness of the Church throughout the ages	7	6.80%
9i	Other:	0	0.00%
9j	No response	1	0.97%
		N=103	100%
	Did you feel that you and the rest of the gathered assembly were full participants in this particular ordination service?		
11a	Yes	28	82.35%
11b	No	2	5.88%
11c	Not sure, maybe	4	11.76%
11d	No response	0	0.00%
		N=34	100%

	If yes to number 11, what were the top three parts in the ordination service that really made you feel like the gathered assembly was fully participating and a part of this ordination service?		
	*This number designates that 17 people answered "Yes" to Q11 AND correctly ranked Q12 with a 1-2-3 ranking order as requested in the question.	N=17	
	What do you believe was happening during the laying on of hands upon the candidate?		
13a	Holy Spirit was empowering the minister/elder candidate at that moment	9	26.47%
13b	The hands of the officers were the hands of Christ upon the candidate	4	11.76%
13c	The hands of the officers were the hands of the community	7	20.58%
13d	The hands of the officers represented the universal Church in all times and in all places	7	20.58%
13e	The hands of the officers were welcoming a colleague into the ministry	7	20.58%
13f	There was a connection being made with the apostolic faith and the apostolic witness throughout the ages	2	5.88%
13g	Expression of support, blessing and love	11	32.35%
13h	Other:	1	2.94%
13i	No response	2	5.88%
		N=34	
	Was the connection and relation of ordination with Eucharist/communion and baptism made clear in this ordination service?		
14a	Yes	20	58.82%
14b	No, not really	7	20.59%
14c	Not sure	5	14.71%
14d	No response	2	5.88%

		N=34	100%
	IF YES to Q14, in what ways did you feel or experience that the connection and relation of ordination with Eucharist/communion and baptism were made clear in this ordination service?		
15a	Actual celebration of the Eucharist	0	0.00%
15b	Statement about Ordination that mentioned Eucharist and Baptism	10	26.32%
15c	The Baptismal Font was in full view	0	0.00%
15d	A call to recall our own baptisms and our baptismal calling	3	7.89%
15e	Hymns/Songs (specify which ones):	1	2.63%
15f	Prayers (specify which ones):	1	2.63%
15g	Sermon	15	39.47%
15h	Scripture texts (specify which ones):	2	5.26%
15i	Litanies	1	2.63%
15j	Pastoral Charge	2	5.26%
15k	Blessing/Benediction	1	2.63%
15l	Other:	2	5.26%
15m	No response	0	0.00%
		N=38	
	Was the connection of this particular ordination service with the universal Church, its officers and its ministries, made clear?		
16a	Yes	22	64.71%
16b	No, not really	5	14.71%
16c	Not sure	6	17.65%
16d	No response	1	2.94%
		N=34	100%

	If yes to number 16, in what ways did you feel or experience the connection of this particular ordination service with the universal Church made clear?		
17a	Presence of other ministers or elders from other churches	14	17.72%
17b	The laying on of hands	17	21.52%
17c	Prayers	7	8.86%
17d	Hymns/Songs	4	5.06%
17e	Sermon	7	8.86%
17f	Scripture texts (specify which ones):	3	3.80%
17g	Celebration of the Eucharist	1	1.27%
17h	Constitutional Questions to the minister/elder candidate	10	12.66%
17i	Words of greetings from guests	2	2.53%
17j	Pastoral Charge	7	8.86%
17k	Blessing/Benediction	6	7.59%
17l	No response	1	1.27%
17m	Other	0	0.00%
		N=79	100%
	Gender		
20a	Male	11	32.35%
20b	Female	22	64.71%
20c	Unspecified	1	2.94%
		N=34	100%
	Age		
21a	17-25	0	0.00%
21b	26-35	21	61.76%
21c	36-45	2	5.88%
21d	46-55	6	17.65%
21e	55-56	4	11.76%
21f	66-75	1	2.94%
21g	76+	0	0.00%

		N=34	100%
	Attendance Role in Ordination		
22a	Minister	2	4.88%
22b	Elder	6	14.63%
22c	Deacon	2	4.88%
22d	Ecumenical Guest	0	0.00%
22e	Family	5	12.20%
22f	Friend	24	58.54%
22g	Observer	0	0.00%
22h	Session Member	0	0.00%
22i	Presbytery Ordaining Commission	1	2.44%
22j	Layperson	1	2.44%
22k	No response	0	0.00%
	*some chose multiple roles	N=41	
	Race		
23a	Caucasian	28	82.35%
23b	Hispanic/Latin American	0	0.00%
23c	East Asian	1	2.94%
23d	Pacific-Islander	0	0.00%
23e	African	0	0.00%
23f	African American	0	0.00%
23g	Native American/First Nation	0	0.00%
23h	Middle Eastern	0	0.00%
23i	Jewish	1	2.94%
23j	Eurasian	1	2.94%
23k	South Asian	1	2.94%
23l	Other:	1	2.94%
23m	No response	1	2.94%
		N=34	100%

	Religious Tradition (* when more than one was chosen or when a tradition that is not listed was written in the blank space, it was counted as "Other")		
24a	None	3	8.82%
24b	Roman Catholic	2	5.88%
24c	Anglican/Episcopalian	1	2.94%
24d	Methodist	1	2.94%
24e	Congregational	0	0.00%
24f	Baptist	1	2.94%
24g	Reformed/Presbyterian	13	38.24%
24h	Lutheran	3	8.82%
24i	Pentecostal	0	0.00%
24j	Evangelical	0	0.00%
24k	Non-Denominational	1	2.94%
24l	Jewish	1	2.94%
24m	Islam	0	0.00%
24n	Buddhist	0	0.00%
24o	Other:	6	17.65%
24p	No response	2	5.88%
		N=34	100%
	Familiar with Writings/Books		
25a	*Book of Confessions of the Presbyterian Church (U.S.A.)*	14	11.76%
25b	*Book of Order of the Presbyterian Church (U.S.A.)*	15	12.61%
25c	*Book of Common Worship*	13	10.92%
25d	*Book of Occasional Services*	5	4.20%
25e	John Calvin	17	14.29%
25f	Thomas F. Torrance	1	0.84%
25g	Martin Bucer	1	0.84%
25h	Karl Barth	11	9.24%
25i	Jürgen Moltmann	6	5.04%
25j	Friedrich Schleiermacher	4	3.36%

25k	*The Church Dogmatics*	3	2.52%
25l	*Baptism, Eucharist, and Ministry*	1	0.84%
25m	*Institutes of the Christian Religion*	6	5.04%
25n	*Report of the Theological Task Force on Peace, Unity and Purity (PUP Report)*	6	5.04%
25o	*General Assembly paper, "A Proposal for Considering the Theology and Practice of Ordination in the Presbyterian Church (U.S.A.), 1992"*	2	1.68%
25p	No response	14	11.76%
	(*No response means None or no answer)	N=119	
	Theological Position		
26a	Liberal	22	64.71%
26b	Moderate	8	23.53%
26c	Conservative	0	0.00%
26d	No response	4	11.76%
26e	None of the above	0	0.00%
26f	Other: (multiple)	0	0.00%
		N=34	100%

Appendix 5

Results of Survey Questionnaire

Minister Ordination, Eastern Pennsylvania (MW)

Notes About Analysis:
Some questions offered respondents the choice to select more than one choice. Therefore, the results of some questions will show an aggregate total greater than the actual number of survey questionnaires returned, and a percentage greater than 100.

Written responses in blank spaces (such as names of Hymns/ Songs) or specific comments (such as in Q10, 18, 19) are not included in the quantitative analyses found in Appendices 2-5; those written responses will be discussed within the narrative sections of Chapter 6 under each corresponding ordination site.

N designates the number of respondents eligible to answer the question, or in some cases the cumulative number of ranked points.

Number of Survey Questionnaires Distributed: 82
Number of Survey Questionnaires Returned & Usable: 36
Return Rate: 44%

	How many ordination services have you attended, not including this one?		
1a	0-2	14	38.89%
1b	3-5	11	30.56%
1c	5-7	4	11.11%
1d	More than 7	7	19.44%
		N=36	

	Prior to attending this particular ordination service, what was your understanding of what ordination means?		
2a	God's calling upon an individual	30	19.61%
2b	Community's calling upon an individual	22	14.38%
2c	Individual responding to a call	25	16.34%
2d	Particular calling as extension of one's baptism	7	4.58%
2e	Participation in Christ's own priestly calling to serve the Church	18	11.76%
2f	Called from the baptized community to serve the baptized community	7	4.58%
2g	Equipping by the Church and the Holy Spirit for a specific ministry/service	22	14.38%
2h	Becoming an officer of the Presbyterian Church (U.S.A.) and the Church universal	13	8.50%
2i	Ordering the Church's offices	4	2.61%
2j	Other:	5	3.27%
2k	No response	0	0.00%
		N=153	100%
	During/After the particular ordination service, was your understanding of what ordination means:		
3a	Affirmed	30	65.22%
3b	Enhanced	10	21.74%
3c	Challenged	4	8.70%
3d	Changed	1	2.17%
3e	No response	1	2.17%
		N=46	100%
	What aspects of this particular ordination service affirmed, enhanced, challenged, and/or changed your understanding of what ordination means?		
4a	Written Liturgy/ Worship Order	10	5.68%
4b	Prayers (specify which prayers):	5	2.84%

4c	Scripture texts (specify which Scripture texts):	9	5.11%
4d	Sermon	22	12.50%
4e	Presentation of the Candidate for Ordination	6	3.41%
4f	Liturgical Space (specify what aspects):	2	1.14%
4g	Hymns/Songs (specify which ones):	21	11.93%
4h	Other readings used in the service (specify):	2	1.14%
4i	Constitutional Questions	20	11.36%
4j	Presentation of Gifts	2	1.14%
4k	Pastoral Charge	20	11.36%
4l	Blessing/Benediction	11	6.25%
4m	Celebration of the Eucharist/Communion (if celebrated)	1	0.57%
4n	Laying on of Hands by Presbyters	23	13.07%
4o	Invocation (invitation) of the Holy Spirit	5	2.84%
4p	Offering	8	4.55%
4q	Statement on Meaning of Ordination	5	2.84%
4r	Procession of Participants	1	0.57%
4s	Other:	2	1.14%
4t	No response	1	0.57%
		N=176	100%
	What word best describes the mood of the assembly during this particular ordination service? (some chose more than one)		
5a	Somber/Serious	4	8.70%
5b	Joyful	32	69.57%
5c	Peaceful	7	15.22%
5d	Sad	0	0.00%
5e	Other:	2	4.35%
5f	No response	1	2.17%
		N=46	100%
	What word best describes the mood of the assembly during this particular ordination service?		

5a	Somber/Serious	0	0.00%
5b	Joyful	22	84.62%
5c	Peaceful	3	11.54%
5d	Sad	0	0.00%
5e	Other:	0	0.00%
5f	No response	1	3.85%
		N=26	100%
	What do you think *ought* to be the mood of the assembly during ordination services in general? (some chose more than one)		
6a	Somber/Serious	4	8.33%
6b	Joyful	35	72.92%
6c	Peaceful	4	8.33%
6d	Sad	0	0.00%
6e	Other:	5	10.42%
6f	No response	0	0.00%
		N=48	100%
	What do you think *ought* to be the mood of the assembly during ordination services in general?		
6a	Somber/Serious	0	0.00%
6b	Joyful	25	96.15%
6c	Peaceful	0	0.00%
6d	Sad	0	0.00%
6e	Other:	1	3.85%
6f	No response	0	0.00%
		N=26	100%
	What part of the ordination service was the most important for you?		
7a	Written Liturgy/ Worship Order	1	1.49%
7b	Prayers (specify which prayers):	4	5.97%
7c	Scripture texts (specify which Scripture texts)	1	1.49%

7d	Sermon	11	16.42%
7e	Presentation of the Candidate for Ordination	4	5.97%
7f	Liturgical Space (specify what aspects):	0	0.00%
7g	Hymns/Songs (specify which ones):	7	10.45%
7h	Other readings used in the service	0	0.00%
7i	Constitutional Questions	6	8.96%
7j	Presentation of Gifts	1	1.49%
7k	Pastoral Charge	13	19.40%
7l	Blessing/Benediction	2	2.99%
7m	Celebration of the Eucharist/Communion (if celebrated)	0	0.00%
7n	Laying on of Hands by Presbyters	8	11.94%
7o	Invocation (invitation) of the Holy Spirit	3	4.48%
7p	Offering	1	1.49%
7q	Statement on Meaning of Ordination	2	2.99%
7r	Procession of Participants	1	1.49%
7s	Other:	0	0.00%
7t	No response	2	2.99%
7u	Multiple answers		
		N=67	100%
	Did you feel or sense that something special was happening at the ordination service?		
8a	Yes	32	88.89%
8b	No, not really.	0	0.00%
8c	If "No," please explain.	1	2.78%
8d	Maybe	2	5.56%
8e	No response	1	2.78%
		N=36	100%
	If yes to number 8, what do you think was happening at the ordination service that was making it special?		
9a	The minister/elder candidate was receiving an office and a big responsibility	17	10.69%

9b	The Holy Spirit was empowering the minister/elder candidate and blessing him/her	20	12.58%
9c	The Holy Spirit was blessing the community gathered together	19	11.95%
9d	The minister/elder candidate was joining the ministry of Jesus Christ and Christ's ministry through the Church	18	11.32%
9e	The community of the gathered people were representing the universal Church in blessing the minister/elder candidate into the ministry	23	14.47%
9f	Family and friends were gathering to celebrate a milestone in the service of the minister/elder candidate	25	15.72%
9g	The minister/elder candidate was joining the ranks of other Church officers – with other ministers and other elders	11	6.92%
9h	There was a connection with the apostolic faith and apostolic witness of the Church throughout the ages	17	10.69%
9i	Other:	7	4.40%
9j	No response	2	1.26%
		N=159	100%
	Did you feel that you and the rest of the gathered assembly were full participants in this particular ordination service?		
11a	Yes	31	86.11%
11b	No	0	0.00%
11c	Not sure, maybe	3	8.33%
11d	No response	2	5.56%
		N=36	100%
	If yes to number 11, what were the top three parts in the ordination service that really made you feel like the gathered assembly was fully participating and a part of this ordination service?		
	*This number designates that people answered "Yes" to Q11 AND correctly ranked Q12 with a 1-2-3 ranking order as requested in the question.	N=22	

	What do you believe was happening during the laying on of hands upon the candidate?		
13a	Holy Spirit was empowering the minister/elder candidate at that moment	13	36.11%
13b	The hands of the officers were the hands of Christ upon the candidate	10	27.77%
13c	The hands of the officers were the hands of the community	3	8.33
13d	The hands of the officers represented the universal Church in all times and in all places	7	19.44%
13e	The hands of the officers were welcoming a colleague into the ministry	3	8.33%
13f	There was a connection being made with the apostolic faith and the apostolic witness throughout the ages	5	13.88%
13g	Expression of support, blessing and love	6	16.66%
13h	Other:	1	2.77%
13i	No response	3	8.33%
		N=36	
	Was the connection and relation of ordination with Eucharist/communion and baptism made clear in this ordination service?		
14a	Yes	4	11.11%
14b	No, not really	19	52.78%
14c	Not sure	8	22.22%
14d	No response	5	13.89%
		N=36	100%
	IF YES to Q14, in what ways did you feel or experience that the connection and relation of ordination with Eucharist/communion and baptism were made clear in this ordination service?		
15a	Actual celebration of the Eucharist	0	0.00%
15b	Statement about Ordination that mentioned Eucharist and Baptism	1	11.11%

15c	The Baptismal Font was in full view	0	0.00%
15d	A call to recall our own baptisms and our baptismal calling	1	11.11%
15e	Hymns/Songs (specify which ones):	0	0.00%
15f	Prayers (specify which ones):	0	0.00%
15g	Sermon	3	33.33%
15h	Scripture texts (specify which ones):	1	11.11%
15i	Litanies	0	0.00%
15j	Pastoral Charge	2	22.22%
15k	Blessing/Benediction	1	11.11%
15l	Other:	0	0.00%
15m	No response	0	0.00%
		N=9	100%
	Was the connection of this particular ordination service with the universal Church, its officers and its ministries, made clear?		
16a	Yes	20	55.56%
16b	No, not really	5	13.89%
16c	Not sure	8	22.22%
16d	No response	3	8.33%
		N=36	100%
	If yes to number 16, in what ways did you feel or experience the connection of this particular ordination service with the universal Church made clear?		
17a	Presence of other ministers or elders from other churches	16	17.20%
17b	The laying on of hands	19	20.43%
17c	Prayers	9	9.68%
17d	Hymns/Songs	7	7.53%
17e	Sermon	11	11.83%
17f	Scripture texts (specify which ones):	2	2.15%
17g	Celebration of the Eucharist	0	0.00%

17h	Constitutional Questions to the minister/elder candidate	13	13.98%
17i	Words of greetings from guests	0	0.00%
17j	Pastoral Charge	8	8.60%
17k	Blessing/Benediction	7	7.53%
17l	No response	0	0.00%
17m	Other	1	1.08%
		N=93	100%
	Gender		
20a	Male	9	25.00%
20b	Female	24	66.67%
20c	Unspecified	3	8.33%
		N=36	100%
	Age		
21a	17-25	3	8.33%
21b	26-35	8	22.22%
21c	36-45	9	25.00%
21d	46-55	4	11.11%
21e	55-56	9	25.00%
21f	66-75	1	2.78%
21g	76+	2	5.56%
		N=36	100%
	Attendance Role in Ordination		
22a	Minister	5	8.62%
22b	Elder	10	17.24%
22c	Deacon	2	3.45%
22d	Ecumenical Guest	0	0.00%
22e	Family	1	1.72%
22f	Friend	29	50.00%
22g	Observer	1	1.72%
22h	Session Member	1	1.72%
22i	Presbytery Ordaining Commission	2	3.45%
22j	Layperson	6	10.34%
22k	No response	1	1.72%

		N=58	100%
	Race		
23a	Caucasian	21	58.33%
23b	Hispanic/Latin American	1	2.78%
23c	East Asian	2	5.56%
23d	Pacific-Islander	0	0.00%
23e	African	0	0.00%
23f	African American	6	16.67%
23g	Native American/First Nation	0	0.00%
23h	Middle Eastern	0	0.00%
23i	Jewish	0	0.00%
23j	Eurasian	0	0.00%
23k	South Asian	0	0.00%
23l	Other:	4	11.11%
23m	No response	2	5.56%
		N=36	100%
	Religious Tradition (* when more than one was chosen or when a tradition that is not listed was written in the blank space, it was counted as "Other")		
24a	None	0	0.00%
24b	Roman Catholic	2	5.56%
24c	Anglican/Episcopalian	1	2.78%
24d	Methodist	3	8.33%
24e	Congregational	0	0.00%
24f	Baptist	7	19.44%
24g	Reformed/Presbyterian	13	36.11%
24h	Lutheran	1	2.78%
24i	Pentecostal	0	0.00%
24j	Evangelical	0	0.00%
24k	Non-Denominational	2	5.56%
24l	Jewish	0	0.00%

24m	Islam	0	0.00%
24n	Buddhist	0	0.00%
24o	Other:	6	16.67%
24p	No response	1	2.78%
		N=36	100%
	Familiar with Writings/Books		
25a	*Book of Confessions of the Presbyterian Church (U.S.A.)*	18	10.59%
25b	*Book of Order of the Presbyterian Church (U.S.A.)*	21	12.35%
25c	*Book of Common Worship*	20	11.76%
25d	*Book of Occasional Services*	5	2.94%
25e	John Calvin	24	14.12%
25f	Thomas F. Torrance	4	2.35%
25g	Martin Bucer	2	1.18%
25h	Karl Barth	19	11.18%
25i	Jürgen Moltmann	8	4.71%
25j	Friedrich Schleiermacher	7	4.12%
25k	*The Church Dogmatics*	6	3.53%
25l	*Baptism, Eucharist, and Ministry*	1	0.59%
25m	*Institutes of the Christian Religion*	12	7.06%
25n	*Report of the Theological Task Force on Peace, Unity and Purity (PUP Report)*	13	7.65%
25o	*General Assembly paper, "A Proposal for Considering the Theology and Practice of Ordination in the Presbyterian Church (U.S.A.), 1992"*	2	1.18%
25p	No response	8	10.59%
	(*No response means None or no answer)	N=170	100%
	Theological Position		
26a	Liberal	5	13.89%
26b	Moderate	11	30.56%
26c	Conservative	11	30.56%
26d	No response	3	8.33%

26e	None of the above	2	5.56%
26f	Other: (multiple)	4	11.11%
		N=36	100%

Appendix 6

Graphs of Comparative Demographics of Four Field Sites

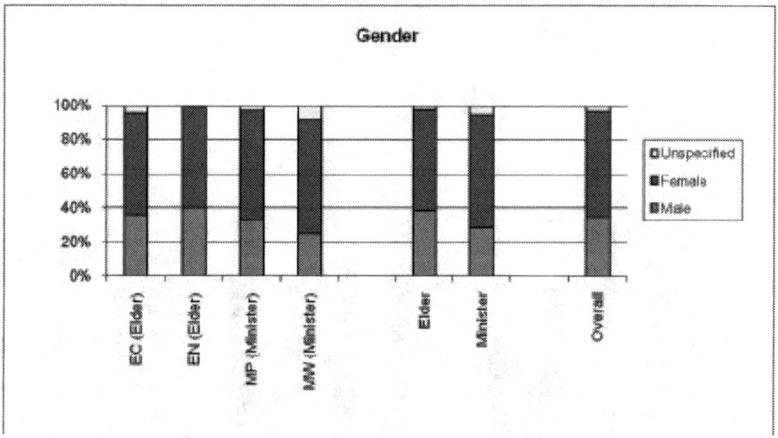

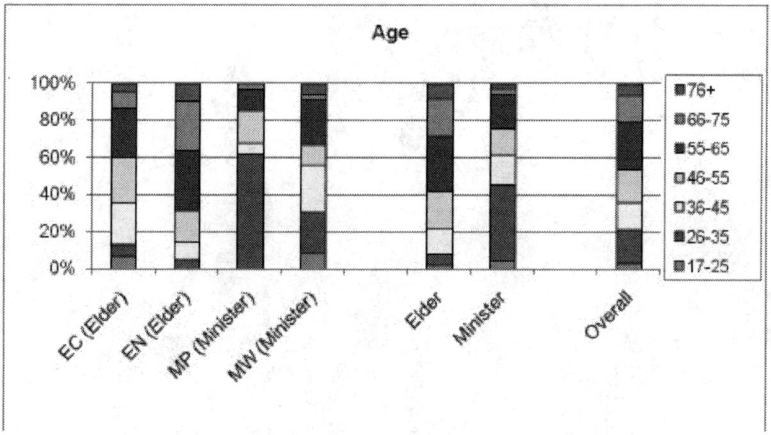

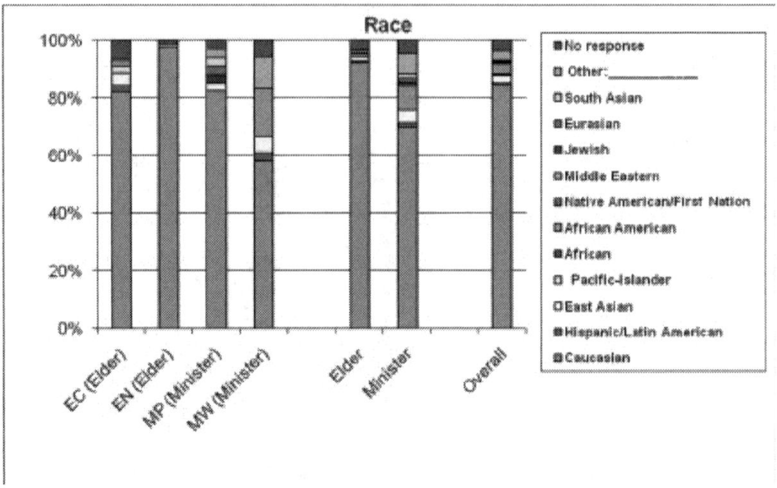

Race
100%
80%
60%
40%
20%
0%
EC (Elder)
EN (Elder)
MP (Minister)
MW (Minister)
Elder
Minister
Overall
No response
Other:___________
South Asian
Eurasian
Jewish
Middle Eastern
Native American/First Nation
African American
African
Pacific-Islander
East Asian
Hispanic/Latin American
Caucasian

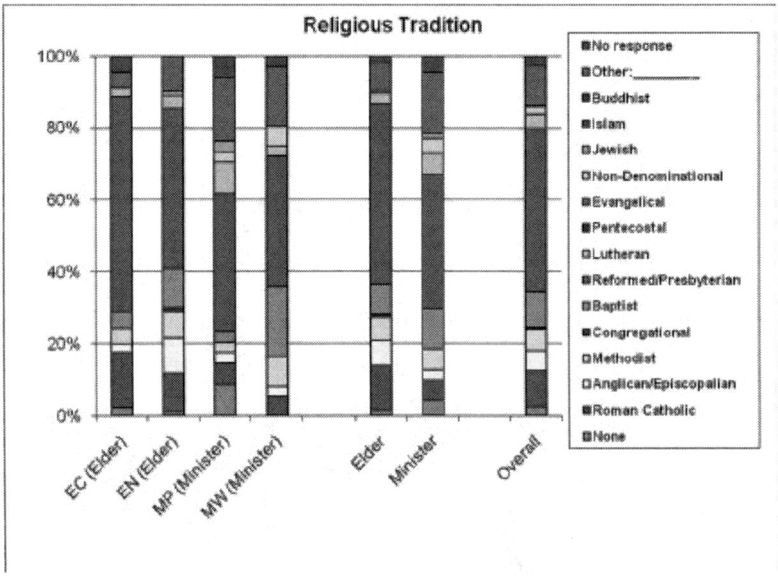

Religious Tradition
100%
80%
60%
40%
20%
0%
EC (Elder)
EN (Elder)
MP (Minister)
MW (Minister)
Elder
Minister
Overall
No response
Other:_________
Buddhist
Islam
Jewish
Non-Denominational
Evangelical
Pentecostal
Lutheran
Reformed/Presbyterian
Baptist
Congregational
Methodist
Anglican/Episcopalian
Roman Catholic
None

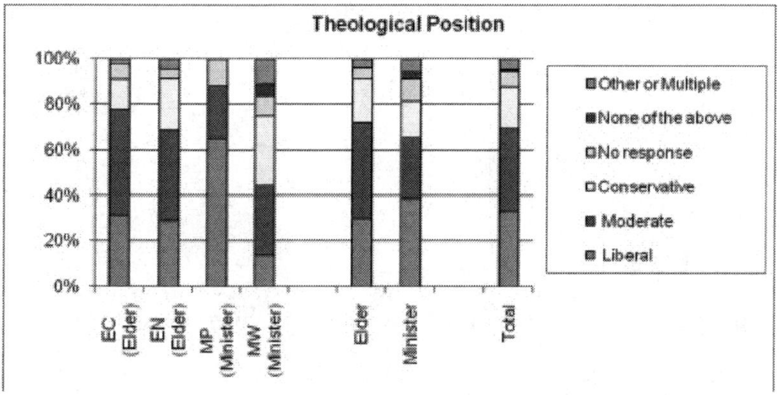
Theological Position
100%
80%
60%
40%
20%
0%
EC (Elder)
EN (Elder)
MP (Minister)
MW (Minister)
Elder
Minister
Total
Other or Multiple
None of the above
No response
Conservative
Moderate
Liberal

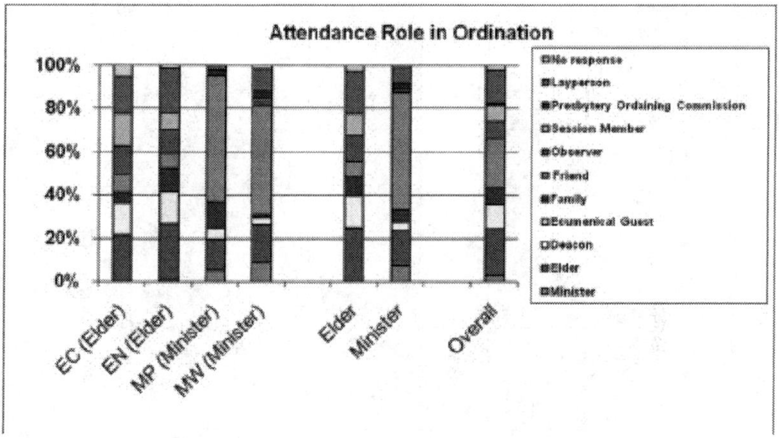
Attendance Role in Ordination
100%
80%
60%
40%
20%
0%
EC (Elder)
EN (Elder)
MP (Minister)
MW (Minister)
Elder
Minister
Overall
No response
Layperson
Presbytery Ordaining Commission
Session Member
Observer
Friend
Family
Ecumenical Guest
Deacon
Elder
Minister

Appendix 7

Comparative Familiarity to Reformed Sources

Writings/Books		EC	EN	MP	MW	Elder	Minister	Total
25a	*Book of Confessions of the Presbyterian Church (U.S.A.)*	15.22%	16.28%	11.76%	10.59%	15.96%	11.07%	13.59%
25b	*Book of Order of the Presbyterian Church (U.S.A.)*	22.83%	20.93%	12.61%	12.35%	21.50%	12.46%	17.11%
25c	*Book of Common Worship*	16.30%	12.09%	10.92%	11.76%	13.36%	11.42%	12.42%
25d	*Book of Occasional Services*	0.00%	0.93%	4.20%	2.94%	0.65%	3.46%	2.01%
25e	John Calvin	17.39%	15.81%	14.29%	14.12%	16.29%	14.19%	15.27%
25f	Thomas F. Torrance	0.00%	0.93%	0.84%	2.35%	0.65%	1.73%	1.17%
25g	Martin Bucer	3.26%	0.47%	0.84%	1.18%	1.30%	1.04%	1.17%
25h	Karl Barth	5.43%	6.98%	9.24%	11.18%	6.51%	10.38%	8.39%
25i	Jürgen Moltmann	0.00%	0.93%	5.04%	4.71%	0.65%	4.84%	2.68%

Writings/Books		EC	EN	MP	MW	Elder	Minister	Total
25j	Friedrich Schleiermacher	1.09%	0.00%	3.36%	4.12%	0.33%	3.81%	2.01%
25k	*The Church Dogmatics*	0.00%	0.47%	2.52%	3.53%	0.33%	3.11%	1.68%
25l	*Baptism, Eucharist, and Ministry*	0.00%	1.86%	0.84%	0.59%	1.30%	0.69%	1.01%
25m	*Institutes of the Christian Religion*	0.00%	1.86%	5.04%	7.06%	1.30%	6.23%	3.69%
25n	*Report of the Theological Task Force on Peace, Unity and Purity (PUP Report)*	2.17%	6.05%	5.04%	7.65%	4.89%	6.57%	5.70%
25o	*General Assembly paper, "A Proposal for Considering the Theology and Practice of Ordination in the Presbyterian Church (U.S.A.), 1992"*	0.00%	2.79%	1.68%	1.18%	1.95%	1.38%	1.68%
25p	No response	16.30%	11.63%	11.76%	4.71%	13.03%	7.61%	10.40%
	No response could mean NONE or no answer	100.00%	100.00%	100.00%	100.00%	100.00%	100.00%	100.00%

Appendix 8a

Top Three Elements/Events in Ordination Service

ELDER TO ELDER		MINISTER TO MINISTER		OVERALL ELDER	OVERALL MINISTER	OVERALL TOTAL
EC	EN	MP	MW			
30.88% Laying Hands Presbyters	29.46% Laying Hands Presbyters	26.23% Sermon	19.40% Pastoral Charge	29.95% Laying Hands Presbyters	21.09 % Sermon	22.46 % Laying on of Hands by Presbyters
13.24% Presentation of Candidate	17.05 % Sermon	11.48% Pastoral Charge	16.42% Sermon	14.21% Sermon	15.63% Pastoral Charge	16.92% Sermon
10.29% Constitutional Questions	8.53% each Hymns/ Blessing/ Statement of Meaning	9.84% Laying Hands Presbyters	11.94% Laying Hands Presbyters	9.64% Presentation of Candidate	10.94% Laying Hands Presbyters	11.38% Pastoral Charge

Appendix 8b

What Was Happening at Ordination Service

ELDER TO ELDER		MINISTER TO MINISTER		OVER-ALL ELDER	OVERALL MINISTER	OVERALL TOTAL
EC	EN	MP	MW			
15.38% Holy Spirit was empowering	16.0% Holy Spirit was blessing	21.36% gathering to celebrate a milestone	15.72% gathering to celebrate	14.8% (2 tied for 1st) Holy Spirit was empowering / blessing	17.94% celebrate a milestone	14.22% Holy Spirit was empowering
11.97% (3 tied for 2nd) Holy Spirit was blessing/ candidate was joining the rank/no response	14.55% Holy Spirit was empowering	17.48% representing the universal Church	14.47% representing the universal Church i	12.24% joining the ranks	15.65% representing the universal Church	13.46% Holy Spirit was blessing
11.11% big responsibility	12.36% (2 tied for 3rd) big responsibility/ joining the ranks	14.56% Holy Spirit was empowering	12.58% Holy Spirit was empowering	11.99% big responsibility	13.36% Holy Spirit was empowering	12.84% representing the universal Church

Appendix 9

Top Response to Interpretation of Laying on of Hands

		EC	EN	MP	MW	Elders	Minister	Total
Holy Spirit was empowering the minister/elder candidate at that moment	13a	18	26	9	13	44	22	66
The hands of the officers were the hands of Christ upon the candidate	13b	12	14	4	10	26	14	40
The hands of the officers were the hands of the community	13c	7	11	7	3	18	10	28
The hands of the officers represented the universal Church in all times and in all places	13d	4	10	7	7	14	14	28
The hands of the officers were welcoming a colleague into the ministry	13e	10	13	7	3	23	10	33
There was a connection being made with the apostolic faith and the apostolic witness throughout the ages	13f	3	20	2	5	23	7	30
Expression of support, blessing and love	13g	6	17	11	6	23	17	40
Other:	13h	1	1	1	1	2	2	4
No response or did not rank order	13i	3	5	2	3	8	5	13
	n=	45	83	34	36	128	70	198

Appendix 10

Ranked "Holy Spirit was empowering the minister/elder candidate" at the laying on of hands as number 1 who were familiar with any of the "official" sources of Reformed theology

	EC	EN	MP	MW	OVERALL		
Of those % in 6a who ranked Holy Spirit as #1 in Laying on of Hands					Elder	Minister	Total
FAMILIAR with ANY of the documents/ theologians	13	21	7	3	34	10	44
n=	18	26	9	13	44	22	66
	72.22%	80.77%	77.78%	23.08%	77.27%	45.45%	66.67%

Appendix 11

Top Two Responses as to what elements/events in the ordination service linked ordination to the Eucharist and/or Baptism

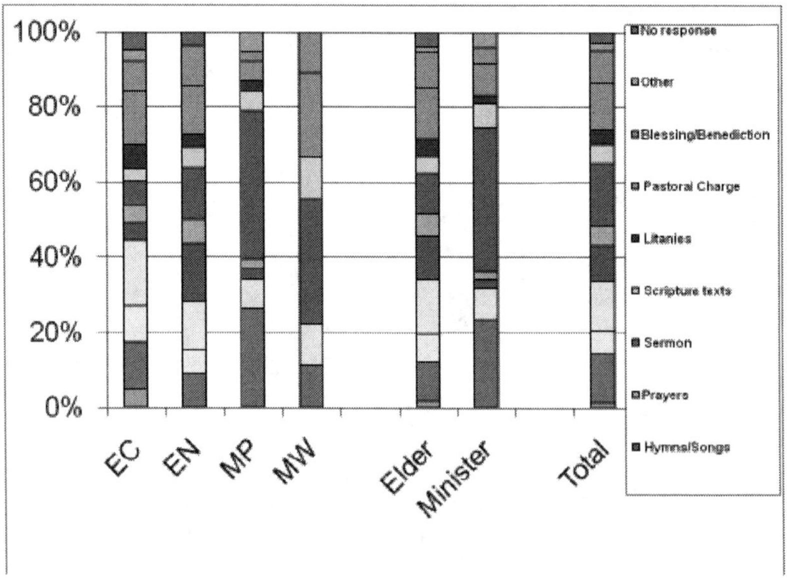

Appendix 12

Lyrics of Hymn "Here I Am, Lord"[1]

©1981 by Daniel L. Schutte

I, the Lord of sea and sky,
I have heard my people cry.
All who dwell in dark and sin
My hand will save.
I, who made the stars of night,
I will make their darkness bright.
Who will bear my light to them?
Whom shall I send?

> **Chorus**: Here I am, Lord. Is it I, Lord?
> I have heard you calling in the night.
> I will go, Lord, if you lead me.
> I will hold your people in my heart.
> I, the Lord of snow and rain,
> I have borne my people's pain.
> I have wept for love of them.
> They turn away.

I will break their hearts of stone,
Give them hearts for love alone.
I will speak my words to them.
Whom shall I send? (Chorus)
I, the Lord of wind and flame,
I will tend the poor and lame.
I will set a feast for them.
My hand will save.
Finest bread I will provide
'Til their hearts be satisfied.
I will give my life to them.
Whom shall I send? (Chorus)

1. Text and Music © 1981, OCP Published by OCP. 5536 NE Hassalo, Portland, OR 97213.

Bibliography

Ahn, Deok Weon. *Ecumenism, Inculturation and Postcolonialism in Liturgy: Based on the Responses of the Younger Churches to Baptism, Eucharist and Ministry (BEM).* Ph.D. diss., Madison, NJ: Drew University, 2004.

Ainslie, James L. *The Doctrines of Ministerial Order in the Reformed Churches of the 16th and 17th Centuries.* Edinburgh: T&T Clark, 1940.

Aune, Michael B. "Liturgy and Theology: Rethinking the Relationship." *Worship* 81, No. 1 (January 2007): 46–68.

———. "Liturgy and Theology: Rethinking the Relationship—Part II." *Worship* 81, No. 2 (March 2007): 141–169.

Baptism, Eucharist, and Ministry. Faith and Order Paper No. 111. Geneva: World Council of Churches, 1982.

Barth, Karl. *Church Dogmatics.* Translated by G.W. Bromiley. Edited by G.W. Bromiley and T.F. Torrance. Vol. IV.3.2. London: T&T Clark International,1961.

———. "Die Theologie und die Mission in der Gegenwart" (Theology and Mission in the Present Situation). Translated by Darrell Guder. *Theologische Fragen und Antworten.* Zollikon: Evangelischer Verlag, 1957.

———. *The Theology of the Reformed Confessions.* Translated by Darrell L. Guder and Judith J. Guder. Columbia Series in Reformed Theology. Louisville, KY: Westminster John Knox Press, 2002.

Barth, Markus. "Baptism and Evangelism." *Scottish Journal of Theology* 12 (1959), 40.

Bell, Catherine. *Ritual*: Perspectives and Dimensions. New York: Oxford University Press, 1997.

———. *Ritual Theory, Ritual Practice.* New York: Oxford University Press, 1991.

———. "The Authority of Ritual Experts." *Studia Liturgica* 23 (1993): 98–120.

Best, Thomas F. and Tamara Grdzelidze, eds. *BEM at 25: Critical insights into a continuing legacy* Faith and Order Paper No. 205. Geneva: WCC Publications, 2007.

Boeve, Lieven. "Theology in a Postmodern Context and the Hermeneutical Project of Louis-Marie Chauvet." *Sacraments: Revelation of the Humanity of God: Engaging the Fundamental Theology of Louis-Marie Chauvet.* Edited by Philippe Bordeyne and Bruce T. Morrill. Collegeville, MN: Liturgical Press, 2008.

Book of Common Worship. Louisville, KY: Westminster/John Knox Press, 1993.

Book of Occasional Services: A Liturgical Resource Supplementing the Book of Common Worship, 1993. Louisville, KY: Geneva Press, 1999.

Bradshaw, Paul. "Difficulties in Doing Liturgical Theology." *Pacifica* 11 (June 1998): 181–194.

———. "Preface." *The Process of Admission to Ordained Ministry: A Comparative Study* by James F. Puglisi. Translated by Mary Misrahi. Vol. II, *The First Lutheran, Reformed, Anglican, and Wesleyan Rites*. Collegeville, MN: The Liturgical Press, 1998.

———. *The Search for the Origins of Christian Worship: Sources and Methods of the Study of Early Liturgy*. 2d ed. New York: Oxford University Press, 2002.

Bruner, Jerome. *Acts of Meaning*. Cambridge, MA: Harvard University Press, 1990.

Butin, Philip W. "Christ's Ministry and Ours: A Trinitarian and Reformed Perspective on the Ministry of the Whole People of God." Unpublished paper submitted to the Ecclesiology Colloquium, May 11–13, 2009, Glen Ellyn, IL. March 28, 2009.

———. "Two Early Reformed Catechisms, The Threefold Office, and the Shape of Karl Barth's Christology." *Scottish Journal of Theology* Vol. 44 (1991): 195–214.

Byars, Ronald. "Indiscriminate Baptism and Baptismal Integrity." *Reformed Liturgy & Music* XXXI, No. 1 (1997): 36–40.

Calvin, John. *Commentaries on the Epistles of Paul the Apostle to the Philippians, Colossians, and Thessalonians*. Translated and Edited by John Pringle. Vol. XXI, *Calvin's Commentaries*. Reprint, Grand Rapids: Baker Books, 2003.

———. *Commentaries on The Epistle of Paul the Apostle to the Romans*. Translated and Edited by John Owen. Vol. XIX, *Calvin's Commentaries*. Reprint, Grand Rapids: Baker Books, 2003.

———. *Commentaries on The Epistles to Timothy, Titus, and Philemon*. Translated by William Pringle. Vol. XXI, *Calvin's Commentaries*. Reprint, Grand Rapids: Baker Books, 2003.

———. *Commentary on the Acts of the Apostles*. Edited by Henry Beveridge. Vol. XVIII, *Calvin's Commentaries*. Reprint, Grand Rapids: Baker Books, 2003.

———. *Commentary on the Epistles of Paul the Apostle to the Corinthians*. Translated by John Pringle. Vol. XX, *Calvin's Commentaries*. Reprint, Grand Rapids: Baker Books, 2003.

———. *Draft Ecclesiastical Ordinances, September and October 1541*. Vol. XXII, *Calvin: Theological Treatises*. Translated by J.K.S. Reid, The Library of Christian Classics. Philadelphia: The Westminster Press, 1954.

———. *Institutes of the Christian Religion*. Vol XXI, *Calvin: Institutes of the Christian Religion*. Edited by John T. McNeill and Translated by Ford Lewis Battles. The Library of Christian Classics. Philadelphia: The Westminster Press, 1960.

Chan, Simon. *Liturgical Theology: The Church as Worshiping Community*. Downers Grove, IL: InterVarsity Press, 2006.

Chapman, William E. "Sources of Ordination Questions." Unpublished paper. March 3, 2009.

Chase, Susan E. "Narrative Inquiry: Multiple Lenses, Approaches, Voices." *The SAGE Handbook of Qualitative Research*. Edited by Norman K. Denzin and Yvonna S. Lincoln. Thousand Oaks: Sage Publications, 2005.

Chauvet, Louis-Marie. *The Sacraments: The Word of God at the Mercy of the Body*. Collegeville, MN: The Liturgical Press, 2001.

———. *Symbol and Sacrament: A Sacramental Reinterpretation of Christian Existence*. Translated by Patrick Madigan and Madeleine Beaumont. Collegeville, MN: The Liturgical Press, 1995.

Collins, Paul M. "Cognitive and Aesthetic Approaches to Theology and *The Nature and Mission of the Church*." Paper presented at the Faith and Order Plenary

Commission of the World Council of Churches, Kolympari, Crete, October 12, 2009.

Conner, Benjamin. "The Ministry Section of BEM: A Cautious Critique." Unpublished paper. Princeton, NJ: Princeton Theological Seminary, 2005.

The Constitution of the Presbyterian Church (U.S.A.), Part I, Book of Confessions. Louisville, KY: The Office of the General Assembly 1999.

The Constitution of the Presbyterian Church (U.S.A.), Part II, Book of Order, 2011–2013. Louisville, KY: The Office of the General Assembly, 2011.

Dennison, Jr., James T., ed. *Reformed Confessions of the 16th and 17th Centuries in English Translation, Volume 1, 1523–1552.* Grand Rapids, MI: Reformation Heritage Books, 2008.

Douglass, Jane Dempsey. "What is Reformed Theology?" *The Princeton Seminary Bulletin* 11, no. 1 (1990): 4.

Driver, Tom F. *Liberating Rites: Understanding the Transformative Power of Ritual.* Boulder, CO: Westview Press, 1998.

Empereur, James. *Models of Liturgical Theology.* Alcuin/GROW Liturgical Study 4, no. 52. Bramcote: Grove Books Limited, 1987.

Fagerberg, David W. *Theologia Prima: What is Liturgical Theology?* 2d ed. Chicago: Hillenbrand Books, 2004.

Fink, Peter E. "Toward a Liturgical Theology." *Worship* 47, No. 10 (December 1973): 601–609.

The Final Report of the Theological Task Force on Peace, Unity, and Purity of the Church (PUP). Louisville, KY: Office of the General Assembly, 2006.

The French Confession of 1559. Translated by Ellen Babinsky and Joseph D. Small. Louisville, KY: Office of Theology and Worship, 1998.

Garrigan, Siobhán. *Beyond Ritual: Sacramental Theology after Habermas.* Burlington, VT: Ashgate, 2004.

Gerrish, Brian A. "An Introduction" *The French Confession of 1559.* Translated by Ellen Babinsky and Joseph D. Small. Louisville, KY: Office of Theology and Worship, 1998.

Grdzelidze, Tamara. "Ecclesiology and Shared Identity: Twenty-five years after its publication *Baptism, Eucharist and Ministry* requires a fresh reflection in the context of ecclesiology and the unity of the church" in *BEM at 25: Critical insights into a continuing legacy.* Faith and Order Paper No. 205. Edited by Thomas F. Best and Tamara Grdzelidze. Geneva: WCC Publications, 2007.

Grimes, Ronald L. *Beginnings in Ritual Studies.* Revised edition, Columbia, South Carolina: University of South Carolina, 1995.

Guder, Darrell. "The Nicene Marks in a Post-Christendom Church." *Bearing the Marks of the Church.* Re-Forming Ministry Occasional Paper Series no. 1. Louisville, KY: PC(U.S.A.) Office of Theology and Worship, 2006.

Hartwell, Herbert. "Karl Barth on Baptism." *Scottish Journal of Theology* 22 (1969):16.

Henderson, Robert W. "Concerning the Eldership, Part I." *Reformed World* 32, No. 8 (December 1973): 363–372.

———. "Concerning the Eldership, Part II." *Reformed World* 33, No. 1 (March 1974): 10–17.

———. *The Teaching Office in the Reformed Tradition: A History of the Doctoral Ministry.* Philadelphia: The Westminster Press, 1962.

Hoffman, Lawrence A. "How Ritual Means: Ritual Circumcision in Rabbinic Culture and Today." *Studia Liturgica* 23, no. 1 (1993): 78–97.

Holper, James Frederick. *Presbyteral Office and ordination in American Presbyterianism: A liturgical-historical study*. Ph.D. diss., Notre Dame, IN: University of Notre Dame, 1988.

Hooke, Ruthanna Brinton. *The Preacher's Words and God's Word: The Divine-Human Relationship in Preaching*. Ph.D. diss., New Haven, CT: Yale University, 2007.

Hoon, Paul. *The Integrity of Worship: Ecumenical and Pastoral Studies in Liturgical Theology*. Nashville: Abingdon Press, 1971.

Hughes, Graham. *Worship as Meaning: A Liturgical Theology for Late Modernity*. Cambridge: Cambridge University Press, 2003.

Hunsinger, George. "The Dimensions of Depth: T.F. Torrance on the Sacraments of Baptism and the Lord's Supper." *Scottish Journal of Theology* Vol. 54.2 (2001), 157–161.

———. *The Eucharist and Ecumenism: Let Us Keep the Feast*. New York: Cambridge University Press, 2008.

Irwin, Kevin W. *Context and Text: Method in Liturgical Theology*. Collegeville, MN: The Liturgical Press, 1994.

Johnson, William Stacy. *The Mystery of God: Karl Barth and the Postmodern Foundations of Theology*. Columbia Series in Reformed Theology. Louisville, KY: Westminster John Knox Press, 1997.

Kavanagh, Aidan. *On Liturgical Theology*. New York: Pueblo Publishing Co., 1984.

———. "Response: Primary Theology and Liturgical Act." *Worship* 57 (1983): 322.

LaCugna, Catherine Mowry. "Can Liturgy ever again become a Source for Theology?" *Studia Liturgica19* (1989): 1–13.

Lathrop, Gordon. *Holy Things: A Liturgical Theology*. Minneapolis, MN: Fortress Press, 1993.

———. "'Is that your liturgical movement?': Liturgy and Sacraments in an Ecumenical Ecclesiology." *Sacraments: Revelation of the Humanity of God: Engaging the Fundamental Theology of Louis-Marie Chauvet*. Edited by Philippe Bordeyne and Bruce T. Morrill. Collegeville, MN: Liturgical Press, 2008.

Lazareth, William F. and Nikos Nissiotis. "Preface." *Baptism, Eucharist and Ministry*. Faith and Order Paper No. 111. Geneva: World Council of Churches, 1982.

Legrand, Hervé. "Personal, Collegial and Synodal Responsibility in the Roman Catholic Church: What Convergences Are There Between Reception of Vatican II and BEM?" in *BEM at 25: Critical insights into a continuing legacy*. Faith and Order Paper No. 205. Edited by Thomas F. Best and Tamara Grdzelidze. Geneva: WCC Publications, 2007.

Lindbeck, George. *The Nature of Doctrine: Religion and Theology in a Postliberal Age*. Philadelphia: The Westminster Press, 1984.

Marshall, Paul V. "Reconsidering 'Liturgical Theology': Is there a *Lex Orandi* for all Christians?" *Studia Liturgica* 25 (1995): 129–150.

McGrath, Alister E. *The Genesis of Doctrine: A Study in the Foundation of Doctrinal Criticism*. Grand Rapids, MI: William B. Eerdmans Publishing Co.; Vancouver, British Columbia: Regent College Publishing, 1997.

McKee, Elsie. *Elders and the Plural Ministry: The Role of Exegetical History in Illuminating John Calvin's Theology*. Geneva: Librairie Droz S.A., 1988).

McNeill, John T. "The Doctrine of the Ministry in Reformed Theology." *Church History* Vol. 12, No. 2 (June 1943): 87–88.

Members of Elder Ordination Service of CH and CR (pseud.). Interview by author, 18 January 2009, upstate New York. Transcription, Action Reporting Service, Syracuse, NY.

Members of Elder Ordination Service of MK (pseud.). Interview by author, 19 October 2008, Central New Jersey. Transcription. Robert J. Cirillo, Inc, Florham Park, NJ.

Members of Minister Ordination Service of AB (pseud.). Interview by author, 20 December 2008, eastern Pennsylvania. Transcription. Dineen Communications, Ltd., Wayne, PA.

Members of Minister Ordination Service of EW (pseud.). Interview by author, 6 December 2008, Eastern Pennsylvania. Transcription. DiPiero Court Reporting, Philadelphia, PA.

Migliore, Daniel. "Reforming the Theology and Practice of Baptism: The Challenge of Karl Barth." *Toward the Future of Reformed Theology: Tasks, Topics, Traditions.* Edited by David Willis and Michael Welker. Grand Rapids, MI:Wm. Eerdmans, 1999.

"A Ministry of Service: A Guide to the Meaning of Ordination and Church Office in the Presbyterian Church (U.S.A.)." Louisville, KY: Office of Theology and Worship, 1996

Mitchell, Nathan. "Rituality and the Retrieval of Sacrament as 'Language Event.'" *Sacraments: Revelation of the Humanity of God: Engaging the Fundamental Theology of Louis-Marie Chauvet.* Edited by Philippe Bordeyne and Bruce T. Morrill. Collegeville, MN: Liturgical Press, 2008.

Moltmann, Jürgen. *The Church in the Power of the Spirit: A Contribution to Messianic Ecclesiology*. New York: Harper & Row, 1977.

Moore-Keish, Martha. *Do This In Remembrance of Me: A Ritual Approach to Reformed Eucharistic Theology.* Grand Rapids, MI: William B. Eerdmans Publishing Co, 2008.

Moore-Keish, Marth and Neal Presa. "Finding a Theology of Ordination and Vocation in Baptism." *The Presbyterian Outlook.* (Issue 188–21, June 2006).

Mugambi, Jesse N.K. "Some Problems of Authority and Credibility in the Drafting and Reception Processes of the BEM Document" in *BEM at 25: Critical insights into a continuing legacy.* Faith and Order Paper No. 205. Edited by Thomas F. Best and Tamara Grdzelidze. Geneva: WCC Publications, 2007.

The Nature and Mission of the Church: A Stage on the Way to a Common Statement. Faith and Order Paper No. 198. Geneva: World Council of Churches, 2005.

Newman, David R. "Observations on Method in Liturgical Theology." *Worship* 57 (1983): 377–384.

Old, Hughes Oliphant. *The Shaping of the Reformed Baptismal Rite in the Sixteenth Century.* Grand Rapids, MI: William B. Eerdmans Publishing Co., 1992.

Polkinghorne, Donald E. *Narrative Knowing and the Human Sciences.* Albany, NY: State University of New York Press, 1988.

A Proposal for Considering the Theology and Practice of Ordination to Office in the Presbyterian Church (U.S.A.). Louisville, KY: The Theology and Worship Unit, Presbyterian Church (U.S.A.), 1992.

Puglisi, James F. *The Process of Admission to Ordained Ministry: A Comparative Study: Volume II – The First Lutheran, Reformed, Anglican, and Wesleyan Rites*. Translated by Mary Misrahi. Collegeville, MN: The Liturgical Press, 1998.

Redeker, Martin. *Schleiermacher: Life and Thought*. Translated by John Wallhausser. Philadelphia: Fortress Press, 1973.

Rohls, Jan. *Reformed Confessions: Theology from Zurich to Barmen*. Columbia Series in Reformed Theology. Louisville, KY: Westminster John Knox Press, 1997.

Ross, Melanie. "Joseph's Britches Revisited: Reflections on Method in Liturgical Theology" *Worship* 80, No. 6 (November 2006): 528–550.

Saliers, Don E. *Worship as Theology: Foretaste of Glory Divine*. Nashville: Abingdon Press, 1994.

Samartha, Stanley J. "The Asian Context: Sources and Trends." *In Voices from the Margin: Interpreting the Bible in the Third World*, ed. R.S. Sugirtharajah. Maryknoll, NY: Orbis Books, 1991.

Savage, Carl and William Presnell. *Narrative Research in Ministry: A Postmodern Research Approach for Faith Communities*. Louisville, KY: Wayne E. Oates Institute, 2008.

Schaff, Philip, ed. *Creeds of Christendom: With a History and Critical Notes, Volume III: The Evangelical and Protestant Creeds*. New York, NY: Harper Row, 1931; reprint, Grand Rapids, MI: Baker Book House, 1990.

Schleiermacher, Friedrich. *Brief Outline of Theology as a Field of Study*. Translated by Terrence N. Tice. Volume 1, *Schleiermacher Studies and Translations*. Lewiston, New York: The Edwin Mellen Press, 1990.

———. *The Christian Faith*. Edited by H.R. Mackintosh and J.S. Stewart. Edinburgh: T&T Clark, 1928.

Schmemann, Alexander. *Introduction to Liturgical Theology*. New York: St. Vladimir's Press, 1966.

Small, Joseph D. "Authority in the Church and The Authority of the Church in the World." *Ordination and Authority*. Office of Theology and Worship Church Issues Series, No. 8. Louisville, KY: Office of Theology and Worship, 2009.

Small, Joseph D. "Ordained? To What?" *Ordination and Authority*. Office of Theology and Worship Church Issues Series, No. 8. Louisville, KY: Office of Theology and Worship, 2009.

———. "Undivided Plural Ministry: Ordered Ministry and Episcopé in the Presbyterian Tradition." *Ecumenical Trends* 31, no. 1 (January 2003): 5–11.

Souletie, Jean-Louis. "The Social Sciences and Christian Theology After Chauvet." *Sacraments: Revelation of the Humanity of God: Engaging the Fundamental Theology of Louis-Marie Chauvet*. Edited by Philippe Bordeyne and Bruce T. Morrill. Collegeville, MN: Liturgical Press, 2008.

Sprinkle, Stephen V. *Ordination: Celebrating the Gift of Ministry*. St. Louis, MO: Chalice Press, 2004.

Stephens, W.P. *The Holy Spirit in The Theology of Martin Bucer*. Cambridge: Cambridge University Press, 1970.

Stotts, Jack L. Jack L. Stotts, "Introduction: Confession After Barmen" *Reformed Confessions: Theology from Zurich to Barmen* by Jan Rohls. Columbia Series in Reformed Theology. Louisville, KY: Westminster John Knox Press, 1998.

Sweeney, Douglas A. "The Church" in *The Princeton Companion to Jonathan Edwards*. Edited by Sang Hyun Lee. Princeton: Princeton University Press, 2005.

Taylor, Barbara Brown. *Leaving Church: A Memoir of Faith*. New York: HarperCollins, 2006.

Thompson, Bard. *A Bibliography of Christian Worship*. ATLA Bibliography Series, No. 25. Metuchen, NJ: The American Theological Library Association and The Scarecrow Press, Inc., 1989.

Thurian, Max, ed. *Churches Respond to BEM: Official Responses to the "Baptism, Eucharist, and Ministry" text*. Volume 1. Faith and Order Paper No. 129. Geneva: World Council of Churches, 1986.

———, ed. *Churches Respond to BEM: Official Responses to the "Baptism, Eucharist, and Ministry" text*. Volume II. Faith and Order Paper No. 132. Geneva: World Council of Churches, 1986.

———, ed. *Churches Respond to BEM: Official Responses to the "Baptism, Eucharist, and Ministry" text*. Volume III. Faith and Order Paper No. 135. Geneva: World Council of Churches, 1987.

———, ed. *Churches Respond to BEM: Official Responses to the "Baptism, Eucharist, and Ministry" text*. Volume IV. Faith and Order Paper No. 137. Geneva: World Council of Churches, 1987.

———, ed. *Churches Respond to BEM: Official Responses to the "Baptism, Eucharist, and Ministry" text*. Volume V. Faith and Order Paper No. 143. Geneva: World Council of Churches, 1988.

———, ed. *Churches Respond to BEM: Official Responses to the "Baptism, Eucharist, and Ministry" text*. Volume VI. Faith and Order Paper No. 144. Geneva: World Council of Churches, 1988.

Tice, Terrence. "Interviews with Karl Barth and Reflections on His Interpretations of Schleiermacher." *Barth and Schleiermacher: Beyond the Impasse?* Edited by James O. Duke and Robert F. Streetman. Philadelphia: Fortress Press, 1988.

Torrance, Thomas F. "Consecration and Ordination." *Scottish Journal of Theology* 11, No. 1 (March 1958): 225–252.

———. *Royal Priesthood: A Theology of Ordained Ministry*. 2nd ed. Edinburgh: T&T Clark, 1993.

Turner, Victor. "Liminality and Communitas." *Foundations in Ritual Studies: A Reader for Students of Christian Worship*. Edited by Paul Bradshaw and John Melloh. Grand Rapids, MI: Baker Academic, 2007.

Turretin, Francis. *Institutes of Elenctic Theology*. Edited by James T. Dennison, Jr. Translated by George Musgrave Giger. Volume 3, *Eighteenth Through Twentieth Topics*. Phillipsburg, NJ: P&R Publishing, 1997.

Van de Poll, G.J. *Martin Bucer's Liturgical Ideas: The Strasburg Reformer and His Connection with the Liturgies of the Sixteenth Century*. Assen, Netherlands: Van Gorcum, 1954.

Van'T Spijker, Willem. *The Ecclesiastical Offices in the Thought of Martin Bucer*. Translated by John Vriend nd Lyle D. Bierma. Leiden: E.J. Brill, 1996.

Vischer, Lukas. "The Convergence Texts on *Baptism, Eucharist, and Ministry*: How Did They Take Shape? What Have They Achieved?" *Ecumenical Review* 54:4 (October 2002): 432.

———, ed. *Eldership in the Reformed Churches Today: Report of an International Consultation held at John Knox Centre in Geneva from August 26–31, 1990*. Geneva: World Alliance of Reformed Churches, 1990.

———, ed. *Reformed Witness Today: A Collection of Confessions and Statements of Faith Issued by Reformed Churches*. Bern, Switzerland: Evangelische Arbeitsstelle Oekumene Schweiz, 1982.

Vogel, Dwight W. "Liturgical Theology: A Conceptual Geography." *Primary Sources of Liturgical Theology: A Reader.* Edited by Dwight Vogel. Collegeville, MN: Liturgical Press, 2000.

Von Allmen, Jean-Jacques. *Le Saint Ministère selon la conviction et la volonté des Réformés du XVI siècle*. Neuchatel: Delachaux et Niestlé, 1968.

———. "Ministry and Ordination According to Reformed Theology." *Scottish Journal of Theology* 25 (1972): 75.

Wainwright, Geoffrey. *Doxology: The Praise of God in Worship, Doctrine, and Life.* New York: Oxford University Press, 1980.

Westra, Helen. *The Minister's Task and Calling in the Sermons of Jonathan Edwards.* Studies in American Religion 17. Lewiston, NY: The Edwin Mellen Press, 1986.

Whitsitt, Landon. *Open Source Church: Making Room for the Wisdom of All.* Alban Institute: 2011.

Wilton, Carlos E. *"As One Who Serves": Diakonia as a Paradigm for Ordination to Ministry of the Word and Sacrament in the Presbyterian Church (U.S.A.): A Study in the History of Doctrine.* Ph.D. diss., St. Andrews, Scotland: University of St. Andrew, 1994.

Witvliet, John. "For our own purposes: the appropriation of the social sciences in liturgical studies." *Foundations in Ritual Studies: A Reader for Students of Christian Worship*. Edited by Paul Bradshaw and John Melloh. Grand Rapids, MI: Baker Academic, 2007.

World Alliance of Reformed Churches. "Interim Report of Commission on Ordination and the Ministry." Geneva, Switzerland: World Alliance of Reformed Churches, 1954.

———. "God's reign and our unity: The Report of the Anglican-Reformed International Commission, 1981–1984." Geneva, Switzerland: World Alliance of Reformed Churches, 1984. Also available online: http://warc.jalb.de/warcajsp/news_file/3.pdf

———. "The Presence of Christ in Church and World: Final Report of the Dialogue between the World Alliance of Reformed Churches and the Secretariat for Promoting Christian Unity,1977." Geneva, Switzerland: World Alliance of Reformed Churches, 1977. Also available online:http://warc.jalb.de/warcajsp/news_file/31.pdf ; Internet.

———. "Report on the study of episcope" in *Report of the Committee on Theology to the 20th General Council (Nairobi),* by James I. McCord, chairman (Geneva, Switzerland: World Alliance of Reformed Churches, 1970); Online: http://www.warc.ch/where/ugc /report/02.html#txt3

———. "Study on Ordination and the Ministry: Summary of Comments on the Interim Report on Ordination." Geneva, Switzerland: WARC Department of Theology, 1960.

Yocum, John. *Ecclesial Mediation in Karl Barth.* Burlington, VT: Ashgate, 2004.